PAULINE AUTOBIOGRAPHY:
TOWARD A NEW UNDERSTANDING

SOCIETY
OF BIBLICAL
LITERATURE

DISSERTATION SERIES

Charles Talbert, Editor

Number 73

PAULINE AUTOBIOGRAPHY:
TOWARD A NEW UNDERSTANDING

by
George Lyons

George Lyons

PAULINE AUTOBIOGRAPHY
Toward a New Understanding

Scholars Press
Atlanta, Georgia

PAULINE AUTOBIOGRAPHY
TOWARD A NEW UNDERSTANDING

George Lyons

Ph.D., 1982
Emory University

Advisor:
Dr. Hendrikus Boers

© 1985
Society of Biblical Literature

Library of Congress Cataloging-in-Publication Data

Lyons, George.
  Pauline autobiography.

  (SBL Dissertation ; no. 73)
  Thesis (Ph.D.)—Emory University
  Bibliography: p.
  1. Bible. N.T. Epistles of Paul—Criticism,
Interpretation, etc. 2. Paul, the Apostle, Saint.
3. Christian biography—Rome—History and criticism.
I. Title. II. Series: Dissertation series (Society
of Biblical Literature) ; no. 73.
BS2650.2.L96 1985   227'.066   84-1289
ISBN 0-89130-730-3
      0-89130-765-6 (pbk)

Printed in the United States of America
on acid-free paper

Contents

Abbreviations and Translations

All abbreviations of frequently used periodicals, reference works, and serials follow the Instructions for Contributors to the *Journal of Biblical Literature* (95 [1976] 83-97). In addition to those listed there, I use *NIDNTT* to refer to the *New International Dictionary of New Testament Theology*, edited and translated by Colin Brown and others.

All translations from scripture are my own, unless otherwise indicated. These exceptions are generally from the Revised Standard Version (1973). All quotations from classical works depend on the editions and translations of the Loeb Classical Library.

Acknowledgments

Many people have contributed to the completion of this dissertation. Thanks are due first of all to my almost ever-patient wife, Terre, who across the nine years involved in my completing the Ph.D. learned when to goad and when to bite her tongue. During half those years she was the family breadwinner. During the past nearly three years our daughter, Kara, has kept her busy enough without the additional burden of "Daddy's dissertation"—quite a mouthful for a two-year-old. At every stage in the process Terre has been my able typist, from the course papers, through the *rough* drafts, to the finished copy. Without her encouragement, support, insistence, and confidence I probably would never have completed the dissertation.

I am appreciative of the assistance given by my adviser, Dr. Hendrikus Boers, who always promptly reacted to the various drafts, even while on sabbatical leave in France. The personal interest and advice of Dr. William A. Beardslee are also gratefully acknowledged.

Part of the reason for the delay in the completion of the dissertation came as a result of my appointment as Assistant Professor of Biblical Literature at Olivet Nazarene College—an assignment that has been far more fun than the hard work of writing a dissertation in my "spare time." Thanks are due to my colleagues in the Division of Religion and Philosophy, particularly Drs. J. Ottis Sayes, Forest T. Benner, and Kenneth Hendrick, who for the past five years have kindly but persistently reminded me that my dissertation had to be finished. Divisional secretary, Mrs. Marjorie Sparrow, graciously prepared the index. From outside my division I have received invaluable assistance from Drs. Stephen Taylor and Michael Vail.

Thanks are also due to many students who stimulated my thinking, showed a genuine interest in what I was doing, and helped as they were able. Particular mention should be made of Edith Vogel, James K. Bennett, John Mohler, James Philip Fuller, Patricia Berg, and Daniel McFeeley.

Others, too many to mention, have also contributed to the long-awaited completion of this project by their interest, understanding, and moral support—especially our families and many friends.

Gratitude should also be expressed for my major professor at Nazarene Theological Seminary, Dr. Willard H. Taylor, whose encouragement went well beyond that of his professional responsibilities. His untimely death in 1981 has made it impossible for me to fulfill my plan of sharing the results of my research with the professor who first excited me to the study of Paul.

Introduction

PURPOSE

Remarkably little scholarly attention has been given the literary phenomenon and function of autobiographical remarks in the letters of the apostle Paul.[1] Most existing approaches to the subject have been so dominated by historical questions, that, as Nils Alstrup Dahl observes, "the prior problem of the literary character and scope of Paul's autobiographical statements [has] often been unduly neglected."[2] Hans Dieter Betz suggests that "Paul's 'self-presentation' in his letters is a literary

---

[1]See Béda Rigaux (*The Letters of St. Paul: Modern Studies*, ed. and trans. Stephen Yonick [Chicago: Franciscan Herald, 1968] pp. 122-23), who devotes a single page to the classification of the "autobiographical passages" according to their "different forms." He recognizes the similarity between Paul's practice and "the profane letter [which] usually began with some news concerning the correspondent," noting that "his correspondence is impregnated with personalistic expressions." Rigaux proposes five kinds of autobiographical forms in Paul's letters, which offer little assistance in clarifying their functions. They include: (1) "Simple autobiography" (1 Cor 16:5-9; 2 Cor 7:5; Rom 1:11-14; Phil 1:12-26); (2) "Apostolic autobiography" (1 Thess 2:1-12, 18; 3:1-2, 6-9; 1 Cor 1:12-16; 2:1-5, 10, 11, 23; 3:9-13; 7:8; 2 Cor 1:8-6:10; Rom 15:17-21; Col 2:1-3; 3:7-9); (3) "Apologetic or polemic autobiography" (1 Cor 9:1-27; 15:9; 2 Cor 10:1-12:21; Gal 1:11-2:14); (4) "Mystical autobiography" (2 Cor 12:1-10; Eph 3:1-13); (5) Typical autobiography (Rom 7:14-25). See also the authorities cited in chapter 2 n. 1.

[2]Nils Alstrup Dahl, "Paul's Letter to the Galatians: Epistolary Genre, Content, and Structure," paper circulated among members of the SBL Paul Seminar, 1973, p. 36.

problem which needs further investigation."[3] Similarly, Abraham J. Malherbe calls for a serious exegetical investigation of "the self-descriptions" of Paul as compared with those of others in antiquity.[4]

The present dissertation has as its purpose to redress the scholarly neglect of Paul's autobiographical remarks and to rectify the general misunderstanding of them in reply to the literary question, What are the functions of such remarks? The investigation is by no means complete, since it concentrates primarily upon just two of Paul's letters, Galatians and 1 Thessalonians (see chapters 3 and 4 below). This would appear to be an appropriate place to begin since these letters are probably Paul's earliest and their authenticity and literary integrity are generally recognized by New Testament scholarship. Thus they may provide a basis for comparison with the later letters and those whose Pauline authorship and/or original unity is a matter of scholarly debate, should other scholars be stimulated to join in the investigation of this neglected area of Pauline research.

PROVENANCE

My attention was first called to the significance of Paul's autobiographical remarks in a graduate seminar on Galatians conducted by Hendrikus Boers in the Winter Quarter of 1974 at Emory University. Betz's comparison of 2 Corinthians 10-13 and the tradition of Plato's *Apology of Socrates*[5] suggested to Boers that the autobiographical sections which generally follow the thanksgiving periods in Paul's letters, or the ironic rebuke in the case of Galatians, are to be identified formally as "the apostolic apology" (cf. Rom 1:14-16a; 2 Cor 1:12-2:17; 7:5-16; 10:7-12:13; Gal 1:10-2:21; Phil 1:12-26; 3:2-14; 1 Thess 2:1-12). Here, Boers

---

[3]Hans Dieter Betz, *Plutarch's Ethical Writings and Early Christian Literature* (SCHNT 4; Leiden: Brill, 1978) p. 379 n. 43. Cf. idem, *Galatians: A Commentary on Paul's Letter to the Churches in Galatia* (Hermeneia; Philadelphia: Fortress, 1979) p. 123 n. 87, where Betz notes the need for an investigation of the Pauline ἐγώ.

[4]Abraham J. Malherbe, "'Gentle as a Nurse,' the Cynic Background to I Thess ii," *NovT* 12 (1970) 203-17.

[5]Hans Dieter Betz, *Der Apostel Paulus und die sokratische Tradition: Eine exegetische Untersuchung zu seiner "Apologie": 2 Korinther 10-13* (BHT 45; Tübingen: Mohr [Siebeck], 1972).

concluded, Paul defends and/or establishes "himself and his proclama-tion,"[6] his "apostleship,"[7] and/or his "authority in the gospel,"[8] before proceeding to his actual purpose for writing.

In the course of my investigation of "the apostolic apology," it became obvious that Boers' suggestion was in need of certain corrections. (1) These passages lack the features necessary to identify them generi-cally in terms of either form or function, despite their similar autobio-graphic content. (2) Similar autobiographical statements are found in other sections of Paul's letters. (3) Paul's autobiographical remarks are seldom ancillary to his main purpose in writing, but generally anticipate and support it. (4) The term "apostolic" suggests that Paul's autobiograph-ical concern is primarily to assert his authority, whereas it is more often to establish his ethos, his customary moral character and conduct. (5) The term "apology" conveys the mistaken impression (unintended by Boers) that Paul's personal remarks respond to the concrete accusations of actual opponents. Thus the dissertation evolved into an investigation of the function of Paul's autobiographical remarks.

PROCEDURE AND ASSUMPTIONS

In its approach to Paul's autobiographical remarks the present disserta-tion rejects two widely held assumptions of New Testament scholarship. Betz probably speaks for the critical consensus when he claims, first, that Paul is hesitant "to make long statements about himself"[9] and "only rarely talks about his past,"[10] and, second, that when he does, his autobiographi-cal statements are uniformly "apologetic in tendency."[11] Some scholars even deny that there are any truly autobiographical remarks in Paul's letters.[12]

Chapter 1, "Autobiography in Antiquity," seeks to demonstrate the

---

[6]Hendrikus Boers, "The Form Critical Study of Paul's Letters. I Thessa-lonians as a Case Study," *NTS* 22 (1976) 153. The suggestion first assumed written form in his 1974 paper, "The Structure and Purpose of Galatians."

[7]Idem, "Gen. 15:6 and the Discourse Structure of Galatians," SBL Seminar paper, 1976, p. 13.

[8]Idem, "The Structure and Meaning of Galatians," paper, 1976, p. 3.

[9]Betz, *Galatians,* p. 69 n. 126. See the introduction to chapter 2 and chapter 2 n. 1 below.

[10]Ibid., p. 67 n. 103.

[11]Ibid., p. 68 n. 113; cf. p. 222 n. 30.

[12]See chapter 1, section B, below.

mistaken character of the first assumption, which arises in part from an
inadequate awareness of and appreciation for the autobiographical phenomenon in antiquity. A survey of the variety of autobiographical expressions in the Greco-Roman Mediterranean world of the Hellenistic age
makes it clear that, although Paul's *personalia* are by no means "autobiography" in the modern sense, they are fully at home in their ancient context. Chapter 1 makes no attempt to explain how Paul learned his autobiographical techniques.

That the personal remarks in Paul's letters are parallel in many
respects to other autobiographical expressions in antiquity does not decide
in advance the nature of his relationship with the contemporary world.
The difficult question of Paul's education and background has been frequently asked but has not yet been satisfactorily answered.[13] Samuel
Sandmel properly warns of the dangers of "parallelomania"—illuminating
parallels, however impressive, do not necessarily imply identity or even
influence of thought.[14] As Leander E. Keck picturesquely puts it, "In
antiquity ideas did not flow in pipes."[15] It is probable, as E. P. Sanders
observes, that "Paul's thought was not simply taken over from any one
scheme pre-existing in the ancient world."[16] It is difficult, if not impossible, to determine both the extent to which Judaism, even Palestinian
Judaism, and Hellenism were culturally distinct during the syncretistic
first century A.D., and the nature of the influence of these on Paul. The
same data—Paul's letters and contemporary literature—have been interpreted very differently by equally competent New Testament scholars.
For example, as a result of his study of the *Form and Function of the
Pauline Thanksgiving* in comparison with Hellenistic Greek antecedents in
papyrus and official letters, Paul Schubert concluded that, although the
Apostle was a Jew, he was an "indigenous," "spontaneous Hellenist," even
"more of a Hellenist than the average 'Hellenist'."[17] James M. Robinson,

---

[13]See Edwin A. Judge, "St Paul and Classical Society," *JAC* 15 (1972)
19-36.
[14]Samuel Sandmel, "Parallelomania," *JBL* 81 (1962) 1-13; cf. Edward C.
Hobbs, "Recognition of Conceptuality as a Hermenueetical Tool," *SE* 3
(= TU 88) (1964) 464-77.
[15]Leander E. Keck, *Paul and His Letters* (Proclamation Commentaries;
Philadelphia: Fortress, 1979) p. 11.
[16]E. P. Sanders, *Paul and Palestinian Judaism: A Comparison of Patterns of Religion* (Philadelphia: Fortress, 1977) p. 12.
[17]Paul Schubert, *Form and Function of the Pauline Thanksgiving*
(BZNW 20; Berlin: Töpelmann, 1939) p. 184.

however, after comparing the same Pauline thanksgivings with the surviving literature of Palestinian Judaism, notably the Qumran thanksgiving hymns, concluded that Paul's practice was also fully at home in that milieu.[18]

Since Paul's letters addressed predominantly Greco-Roman readers, he appears to have made a concerted effort to avoid conflict with their sense of propriety, even in his approach to "autobiography." He follows, although unwittingly, the advice of Plutarch's moral essay on how to avoid the offensiveness of self-praise, which provides an apology for autobiographical remarks based on the prevailing cultural traditions.[19] But this still does not explain where a strict Jew learned all this. It is not impossible, as Andrew T. Lincoln contends, that such traditions were common knowledge in the Hellenistic world and that Paul became acquainted with them "from their employment in popular culture and conventions."[20] If Betz is correct in his analyses of Paul's supposedly apologetic letters, 2 Corinthians 10-13 and Galatians, the Apostle must have read extensively in pagan authors. Paul's Judaism does not necessarily exclude either possibility. "It is interesting and instructive," as Richard N. Longenecker observes, ". . . that the Talmud speaks of a rabbinic training in the second

---

[18]James M. Robinson, "Die Hodajot-Formel in Gebet und Hymnus des Fruhchristentums," *Apophoreta: Festschrift für Ernst Haenchen*, ed. W. Eltester and F. H. Kettler (Berlin: Töpelmann, 1964) pp. 194-235, esp. 201-2. Similarly, J. P. Audet, "Literary Forms and Contents of a Normal εὐχαριστία in the First Century," *SE* 1 (= TU 73) (1959) 643-62.

[19]See chapter 1, section F.

[20]Andrew T. Lincoln, "'Paul the Visionary': The Setting and Significance of the Rapture to Paradise in II Corinthians xii.1-10," *NTS* 25 (1979) 206. So also Judge, "St Paul and Classical Society," p. 36. Hans Dieter Betz (*Paul's Apology II Corinthians 10-13 and the Socratic Tradition*, Protocol of the 22nd Colloquy, ed. Wilhelm Wuellner [Berkeley: Center for Hermenueutical Studies in Hellenistic and Modern Culture, 1975] p. 30) does not disagree, although the extensive influence he assumes would disagree, although the extensive influence he assumes would seem to require that Paul's knowledge was far less diffuse than this means of access might be expected to permit. This would seem to require an awareness of literary as opposed to merely oral traditions. See idem, *Apostel Paulus*. Albert Henrichs' conclusion that Betz implies that Paul utilized literary traditions is responsible for his critique: "We shall never know whether Paul's pagan reading had acquainted him with the Socratic tradition . . . , and, if so, whether he was bookish enough to imitate it consciously" (review of Betz's *Apostel Paulus*, *JBL* 94 [1975] 312).

century A.D. as including the study of the 'wisdom of the Greeks' [B. Sot. 49b]."[21] Henry Fischel's evidence suggests that Greco-Roman rhetorical handbooks may well have been used in Pharisaic circles well before Paul's time.[22]

Although John Dillon and Thomas Conley concede that Paul may have known more about Greek thought than some suspect, both take exception to Betz's attempt to find Paul's autobiographical apology in 2 Corinthians 10-13 in virtual agreement with pagan Hellenistic traditions. Both consider Paul's compliance with the provisions of Plutarch and the Greco-Roman philosophical and rhetorical traditions he follows for the inoffensive utilization of autobiographical references to be incomplete, probably unconscious, and perhaps purely coincidental.[23] Edwin A. Judge is even more emphatic. Far from finding Paul in compliance with these traditions, he insists that Paul was "in violent reaction to much that was central to the classical way of life."[24] The dissertation will suggest that although Paul's autobiographical technique does not differ significantly from that of pagan authors, the ideals he pursues give expression to his distinctively Christian theological commitments.

---

[21] Richard N. Longenecker, *Paul, Apostle of Liberty* (Grand Rapids: Baker, 1976; reprint of 1964 ed.) pp. 57-58.

[22] Henry Fischel, "Story and History: Observations on Graeco-Roman Rhetoric and Pharisaism," *American Oriental Society, Middle West Branch, Semi-Centennial Volume,* ed. Denis Sinor (Asian Studies Research Institute, Oriental Series, 3; Bloomington, IN: Indiana University, 1969) pp. 78-79.

[23] In their critiques of Betz, *Paul's Apology,* pp. 17-20 and 21-23, respectively. Rudolf Bultmann (*Der Stil der paulinischen Predigt und die kynisch-stoische Diatribe* [FRLANT 13; Göttingen: Vandenhoeck & Ruprecht, 1910] p. 2) long ago expressed doubts that Paul consciously employed rhetorical style.

Although Betz's critics have appreciatively noted the remarkable parallels he has drawn between Paul's autobiographical "apologies" and those in the ancient rhetorical tradition, they almost uniformly agree that the conclusions he draws go well beyond the evidence. See Judge, pp. 34-35; Lincoln, p. 206; Hendrikus Boers, review of Betz's *Apostel Paulus, Int* 27 (1973) 488-90; Henrichs, pp. 310-14; Wayne A. Meeks, review of Betz's *Galatians, JBL* 100 (1981) 304-7; C. K. Barrett, "Galatians as an 'Apologetic Letter,'" *Int* 34 (1980) 414-17.

[24] Judge, p. 36. Cf. Dillon as reported in Betz, *Paul's Apology,* p. 17: "I find Paul insuperably alien to what I know of Greek culture, in his language and [especially] in his way of thought."

The above survey should serve to demonstrate that there is no scholarly consensus as to how Greco-Roman antiquity's approach to autobiography was mediated to Paul. Few would deny that at least superficial or coincidental resemblances exist. What continues to be debated is whether Paul was influenced more or less consciously or unconsciously, directly or indirectly, formally or informally, through oral or written traditions, and in a Jewish or Hellenistic setting. A resolution of such questions is both beyond the scope of this dissertation and inconsequential for its purposes. The emergence of individual consciousness in antiquity, which made autobiography possible, was not restricted to the Western Mediterranean environs of Greece and Rome, but extended as far east as China, India, Persia, and Palestine.[25] Similar autobiographical modes of expression may have arisen quite independently of the influence of a single tradition. Furthermore, Plutarch's prescriptions for rendering autobiographical remarks inoffensive, for the most part, merely give literary expression to what would have been obvious to anyone with a common sense understanding of human psychology and the problems of interpersonal relationships[26]—something Paul certainly had.[27]

Because of the general deterioration of classical training and the neglect of the literature of antiquity, modern readers have tended to reach anachronistically mistaken conclusions about Paul's autobiographical remarks. Even if we remain ignorant as to the precise influences, what Paul says about himself and the way in which he says it must be understood within the context of antiquity and not on the basis of modern assumptions. It is the thesis of this dissertation that Paul's autobiographical remarks are fully intelligible when set in this context, apart from the solution to such historical questions.

Chapter 2, "A Critique of Existing Approaches to Paul's Autobiographical Remarks Demonstrated in Galatians," attempts to show the extent to which most treatments of Paul's autobiographical remarks build on demonstrably perverse assumptions—the methodologically suspect interpretive technique known as "mirror reading" and the questionable utilization of extra-textual data. This has resulted in explanations of the function of Paul's autobiographical remarks that are no more secure than the

---

[25]See chapter 1, section B, below.

[26]Cf. Betz, *Plutarch's Ethical Writings*, p. 373: "The underlying problems are religious and ethical in the stricter sense, i.e., those of psychology and interpersonal relationships."

[27]Cf. George Milligan (*St Paul's Epistles to the Thessalonians* [London: Macmillan, 1908] p. lvii), who refers to Paul's "rhetoric of the heart."

speculative historical reconstructions which they presume. The chapter
calls into question these and other widely held assumptions sponsoring the
pervasive misconception that Paul's autobiographical remarks characteristically arise out of a polemical context and function apologetically. This
conception fundamentally affects the interpretation not only of the
autobiographical sections, but of the letters as a whole. Ernst Käsemann
insists that apart from the "insight" that Paul writes from an apologetic
or defensive position, "Romans cannot be interpreted correctly." He
claims further that "the problem of Paul's apostolate," i.e., his fears of
"the mistrust and suspicions of both his person and his work" and his
struggle for recognition of his apostolic legitimacy in the face of opposition, "influences almost all his epistles and is often their crucial point.
The authority which he asserts does not accord with what is conceded to
him in fact."[28] It is the thesis of this dissertation, that Paul's rhetorical
approach, not his opponents' reproaches, is responsible for the form in
which he presents his "autobiography."

Chapter 3, "The Function of Paul's Autobiographical Remarks in His
Letter to the Galatians," and chapter 4, "The Function of Paul's Autobiographical Remarks in 1 Thessalonians," attempt to demonstrate that such
remarks are fully intelligible apart from conjectural reconstructions
concerning his presumed opponents and their accusations. Chapters 3 and
4 are primarily an attempt to discover the rhetorical or argumentative
functions of Paul's autobiographical remarks and are only secondarily
concerned to interpret these remarks fully. Detailed exegesis is beyond
the purview of the present dissertation except as it serves to answer the
primary question. These chapters also studiously avoid moving from the
literary question of function to the historical question, "What really
happened?" Their concern is strictly literary. Such an approach would
appear to be the necessary prerequisite of any responsible historical
reconstruction utilizing Paul's autobiographical statements. For until the
question of function is answered, the historical value of these statements
remains in doubt. As with other autobiographers in antiquity, it appears
that Paul's concern is primarily to be persuasive and to promote virtue
and not to be merely informative. Furthermore, what he says appears to
reveal more about his personal concerns than about the deficiencies of his
converts.

---

[28]Ernst Käsemann, *Commentary on Romans,* trans. and ed. Geoffrey W. Bromiley (Grand Rapids: Eerdmans, 1980) pp. 19-20.

DEFINING AUTOBIOGRAPHICAL REMARKS

Before turning to the major chapters of the dissertation, one preliminary question needs to be considered by way of definition. How are Paul's
autobiographical references to be identified as such? Chapter 1 defines
autobiographical references as statements made by an author about
himself which could be the basis for autobiography. Although autobiography narrates its author's past life, descriptions of his present status and
future plans may also be considered to be loosely autobiographical.[29] Like
other writers in antiquity and today, Paul mentions himself in a number of
different ways—by name, by means of personal pronouns, through self-
descriptions and/or longer or shorter narratives. The following is a survey
of the various means by which "Paul" refers to himself throughout the
Pauline corpus, not only in the homologoumena. For despite the debated
authorship of 2 Thessalonians, Colossians, Ephesians, and the Pastoral
Epistles, they are clearly distinguishable from the non-Pauline New Testament literature which is mostly anonymous and contains few autobiographical notices, whether pseudonymous or genuine.

Outside the epistolary framework of prescript and postscript, references to the name "Paul" in the letters are infrequent—only twelve of the
twenty-nine occurrences.[30] More often Paul refers to himself employing
titles or other succinct self-descriptions, nearly all referring to his relation to God and/or to his churches. The most frequently employed of these
is "apostle," but also appearing more than once are "slave of Jesus Christ"
(Rom 1:1; Gal 1:10; Phil 1:1), "minister of Jesus Christ to the Gentiles"
(Rom 15:16; cf. 2 Cor 9:12; Col 1:25; Eph 3:7), helper of Christ and

---

[29]The latter category may be used only with caution, since future plans
are contingent upon their completion. Thus, e.g., many of the first person
singular references in Romans 1 and 15, in which Paul discusses his intention to visit Rome, may be characterized as "autobiographical" only with
caution, since it is likely that an executioner's blade cut short his future
plans. The claim of 1 Clement 5:7 and the Muratorian Canon 38-39 that
Paul realized his plans to evangelize in Spain does not appear to depend on
an otherwise unknown historical tradition but on a presumptuously opti-
mistic reading of these chapters (cf. Günther Bornkamm, *Paul*, [trans.
D. M. G. Stalker; New York: Harper & Row, 1971] pp. 104-6).

[30]Prescript: see the first verse of each of the letters. Postscript: 1 Cor
16:21; Col 4:18; 2 Thess 3:17; Phlm 19. Elsewhere: 1 Cor 1:12-13 (3 times);
3:4-5 (2 times), 22; 2 Cor 10:1; Gal 5:2; Eph 3:1; Col 1:23; 1 Thess 2:18;
Phlm 9.

steward of the mysteries of God (1 Cor 4:1; cf. 3:22; 4:6; Eph 3:2-3), "prisoner of Christ Jesus" (Phlm 9; Eph 3:1; cf. 4:1), ambassador for Christ (2 Cor 5:20; cf. Eph 6:20; Phlm 9), and various familial images: parent (2 Cor 12:14), father (1 Cor 4:15; 1 Thess 2:11), mother (Gal 4:19; cf. Phlm 10; 1 Thess 2:7), and brother (implicit in his frequent address of his readers as brothers and sisters, e.g., Rom 1:13; 7:1; passim). In a few instances he refers to himself obliquely by means of the third person singular or similar constructions.[31] Not surprisingly, however, the vast majority of Paul's personal references involve the use of first person pronouns and/or pronominal verb endings.

A number of complicating factors in the last means of self-reference require some additional observations. The obvious use of the first person singular pronoun "I" to refer to the author alone and the first person plural pronoun "we" to refer to the author and others is not so obvious as it may appear. In some instances Paul's "I" has been understood to be nearly equivalent to "anyone," and thus not strictly autobiographical.[32] In still other instances it appears that Paul writes autobiographically, while using the pronoun "we." Paul's first person plural is at times used so inclusively as to comprehend him, his readers, and/or an even larger circle. But it may be used so exclusively as to exclude everyone but himself. The letters only infrequently clearly specify who is included with Paul in his "we." In the majority of cases it becomes necessary to determine exegetically the precise nuance intended, since the distinction between the exclusive and inclusive "we" is seldom unambiguous and the circumference of the circle seldom clearly drawn.

The exclusive "we" normally involves the opposition "we—you," and in Paul's letters would include only those who are conceived as joining with him in sending the letter as distinct from or even in opposition to his/their

---

[31] Third person singular: the most significant: 2 Cor 12:1-5; quoting or paraphrasing what others said of him: Gal 1:23; 2 Cor 10:10. Substantive adjectival participles: "he who plants": 1 Cor 3:6-7; and perhaps "he who called": Gal 1:6; 5:8.

[32] See Rom 3:7; 1 Cor 6:12, 15; 10:29-30; 13:1-3, 11-12; 14:11, 14-15; Gal 2:18-20. The most difficult example of this anthropological "I" is found in Romans 7:7-25. Despite the fact tht it is now more than half a century old and in need of correction at numerous points, the only comprehensive investigation remains that of Werner Georg Kümmel, *Römer 7 und die Bekehrung des Paulus* (Leipzig: Hinrichs, 1929 [republished in *Römer 7 und das Bild des Menschen im neuen Testament* (München: Kaiser, 1974)]) pp. 7, 132, passim.

readers. With the exception of Romans, Ephesians, and the Pastorals, all Paul's letters mention co-senders in their opening greetings.[33] A number of the letters conclude with the names of others who join him in sending greetings,[34] and virtually all of them include some reference to named and unnamed associated individuals and/or communities.[35] Several of the letters imply that Paul made use of amanuenses.[36] Any number of these

---

[33]Sosthenes—1 Cor 1:1; Timothy—2 Cor 1:1; Phil 1:1; Col 1:1; 1 Thess 1:1; 2 Thess 1:1; and Phlm 1; Silvanus—1 Thess 1:1 and 2 Thess 1:1; and unnamed "brothers"—Gal 1:2.

[34]See Rom 16:21-23; 1 Cor 16:19-20; 2 Cor 13:13; Phil 4:21-22; Col 4:10-14; 2 Tim 4:21; Tit 3:15; Phlm 23-24.

[35]See Earle E. Ellis, "Paul and His Co-Workers," *NTS* 17 (1971) 437-52.

[36]The first person singular reference to Tertius in Rom 16:22 makes it certain that Paul at least once employed an amanuensis. The references to autographic letter closings (subscriptions) in 1 Cor 16:21; Gal 6:11; Col 4:18; 2 Thess 3:17; and Phlm 19 imply that Romans was probably not a unique exception. This is also the assumption of the colophons included in the *Textus Receptus,* and thus in the KJV.

This does not answer the question of how Paul used his secretary. It is generally assumed that he dictated his letters, although a minority of scholars have argued that, upon occasion at least, he gave the secretary only general guidelines according to which he would compose the letter following the conventional patterns. Both methods were used at the time (see Quintilian, *Institutio oratio* 10. 3. 19-21). The minority view has been defended by Otto Roller, *Das Formular der paulinischen Briefe: Ein Beitrag zur Lehre vom antiken Briefe* (BWANT 4; Stuttgart: Kohlhammer, 1933) pp. 92ff. and the accompanying endnotes; and more recently by Gordon J. Bahr, "The Subscriptions in the Pauline Letters," *JBL* 87 (1968) 27-41; and idem, "Paul and Letter Writing in the First Century," *CBQ* 28 (1966) 465-77. Both Roller and Bahr appear to take the position for apologetic reasons, i.e., by assuming that Paul allowed his amanuensis such liberty, they are able to discount the apparent differences between his generally accepted letters and those often presumed to be pseudonymous. See the critiques of Roller's views in Martin Dibelius and Hans Conzelmann, *The Pastoral Epistles: A Commentary on the Pastoral Epistles,* trans. Philip Buttolph and Adela Yarbro; ed. Helmut Koester (Hermeneia; Philadelphia: Fortress, 1972) p. 5.

Betz's call for a "fresh investigation" of how Paul composed his letters is certainly in order. Given the fact of co-senders, the strong possibility of amanuenses, and the conventions of letter writing in Paul's time, his letters assume "more and more the character of a document and less the character of a private letter." Accordingly, "the problem of authorship may be more complicated than we have previously imagined" (*Galatians,*

individuals could conceivably be included in Paul's exclusive "we."
Although this might be taken to imply some kind of joint authorship, most
scholars doubt it. Whatever role Paul's associates may or may not have
had in the composition of his letters, they probably account for his use of
"we" in few of its instances.[37]

---

p. 1). Betz nonetheless rejects the possibility of actual joint authorship.
Of the few scholars who suppose that one or more of these factors support
the assumption of co-authorship, few consider these alone to be decisive.

[37]Occasionally Paul specifies those included in his exclusive "we." For
example, in 2 Cor 1:19, besides himself, Paul's "we" includes Silvanus and
Timothy; in Gal 2:9-10 it includes also Barnabas; in 1 Cor 3:9; 4:6 and 9 it
includes Apollos and perhaps others. More often the antecedents must be
inferred from the context with a greater or lesser degree of certainty.
For example, on the assumption that the questions in Rom 3:1 and 9 are
parallel, the RSV translates the first person plural in the latter verse as
"we Jews," although the word "Jews" appears only in the former. Whether
or not this "we" is exclusive of some or all of Paul's readers depends on
one's assumptions about the ethnic composition of the Roman churches,
which is a matter of scholarly debate. (On this problem see Walter
Schmithals, *Der Römerbrief als historisches Problem* [SNT 9 Gütersloh:
Mohn, 1975] pp. 24-50.)

Even the alternation between "we" and "you" need not always imply
that the "we" is exclusive. Gal 3:21-4:7 illustrates well the difficulty of
distinguishing the inclusive and exclusive "we" and its relation with "you."
The argumentative third person form appears in 3:21-22, 28 and 4:1-2,
whereas the applications in 3:23-25; 4:3-5 and 6b employ the first person
plural, 3:26-29 and 4:6a the second person plural, and 4:7 the second
singular. It is possible, as some argue, that the "we" of 3:23-25 implies
only Paul and his fellow Jews, in contrast to the Gentile Galatians' "you"
in 3:26-27—note the reference to "those under the law" in 4:5 (so, e.g.,
Theodor von Zahn, *Introduction to the New Testament* [3 vols.; trans.
Melancthon Williams Jacobus, et al.; Edinburgh: Clark, 1909] 1:193 n. 6;
Krister Stendahl, *Paul Among Jews and Gentiles and Other Essays* [Phila-
delphia: Fortress, 1976] pp. 18, 21-23; idem, "The Apostle Paul and the
Introspective Conscience of the West," *HTR* 56 [1963] 207; and Hans
Lietzmann, *An die Galater* [3rd ed.; HNT 10; Tübingen: Mohr (Siebeck),
1932] p. 19). For the opposing view, see Ulrich Luz, *Das Geschichts-
verständnis des Paulus* (BEvT 49; München: Kaiser, 1968) pp. 152, 155-56.
Luz correctly concludes, "Dieses 'wir' keineswegs auf die Judenchristen
eingeschränkt werden kann" (p. 155). His entire discussion of Gal 3:1-4:7 is
instructive (pp. 146-56, 182-86).

Closer inspection makes such a distinction unnecessary and Paul's
alternation between persons somewhat explicable. Paul's argument in 4:3-

The inclusive "we" incorporates some or all of the readers of the letter into the circle of Paul's "we" and often includes a larger, more or less inclusive group—Christians in general, the Pauline churches, Paul's supporters, "the strong" (Rom 15:1), "the perfect" (Phil 3:15), etc.[38] Perhaps the greatest temptation for modern readers anxious to find contemporary relevance in Paul's letters is to assume mistakenly that a "we" which has a narrower and time-bound reference is an all-inclusive Christian "we." Although recognition of the distinction between the inclusive and

---

5 strongly suggests that the existence of both Jews and Gentiles before the coming of Christ (3:24 and 4:4-5, or equivalently "the faith" in 3:23 and 25) was one of slavery, distinguishable only in that Jews were enslaved under the "law" (3:23; 4:5) and Gentiles under the "elemental spirits" (4:3; on the latter, see H.-H. Esser, "στοιχεῖα," NIDNTT 2:451-53). According to 3:22, "The scripture imprisoned everything [including all humankind] under the power of sin in order that what was promised by faith in Jesus Christ might be given to those who believe [i.e., to all Christians]." (See Walter Bauer, A Greek-English Lexicon of the New Testament and Other Early Christian Literature [2nd ed.; trans and ed. William F. Arndt, F. Wilbur Gingrich, and Frederick W. Danker; Chicago: University of Chicago Press, 1979] s.vv. πᾶς, πιστεύω, συγκαλέω).

The two ἵνα, "in order that," clauses in 4:5, like those in 3:22 and 24, refer to the purpose of Christ's coming in terms of redemption and adoption as the defeat of both oppressive powers. In 4:6-7 Paul begins by addressing his readers, continues by referring to the consequences of Christ's coming shared by all Christians, Jews and Gentiles alike, and concludes with the individualized second person plural: "And because you [plural] are sons, God has sent the Spirit of his Son into our hearts, crying, 'Abba! Father!' So through God you [singular] are no longer a slave but a son, and if a son then an heir" (RSV. In an obviously secondary attempt to bring consistency to the passage, for "our hearts" some inferior manuscripts have "your hearts." On the gift of the Spirit, see 3:6-18 which equates this with God's "promise" to Abraham, which is the inheritance of all his offspring—i.e., all who believe in Christ, whether Jews or Gentiles [3:7, 14, 29], since in Christ all such distinctions are abolished [3:28]).

[38]See F. Blass and A. Debrunner, A Greek Grammar of the New Testament and Other Early Christian Literature (trans. and rev. Robert W. Funk; Chicago: University of Chicago Press, 1962) §280; A. T. Robertson, A Grammar of the Greek New Testament in the Light of Historical Research (3rd ed.; New York: Doran, 1919) p. 678; and W. F. Lofthouse, "Singular and Plural in St. Paul's Letters," ExpTim 58 (1947) 180. Other interpretations of the the reference to "the perfect" are possible, cf. the commentaries.

exclusive "we" is helpful, it by no means solves the problem of Paul's use of the first person plural.

The uneven distribution of the first person singular and plural in Paul's letters and the frequent and often inexplicable alternation between the two make it extremely improbable that the fact of co-senders significantly influences his use of "we." The statistical evidence does not support Nigel Turner's claim that "we" is more frequent in those letters in which Paul seems to be "writing on behalf of a group," as the attached note demonstrates.[39] At least it does not explain why the first person

---

[39]Nigel Turner, *Syntax,* vol. 3, *A Grammar of New Testament Greek,* by J. H. Moulton (Edinburgh: Clark, 1963) p. 28.

The following simplifies the statistics tabulated in Ernst von Dobschütz, "Wir und Ich bei Paulus," *ZST* 10 (1932) 254; and Roller, pp. 153-87 and 578-96. The ratio of instances of the first person singular as compared to the plural (including both personal pronouns and pronominal suffixes) arranged in order is as follows: Philippians—12.56, Philemon—6.75, 2 Timothy—3.87, Galatians—2.39, 1 Corinthians—2.28, 1 Timothy—1.8, Romans—1.28, Colossians—1.22, 2 Corinthians—.91, Ephesians—.64, Titus—.56, 2 Thessalonians—.07, 1 Thessalonians—.04. But this does not take into consideration the frequency of the first singular or plural in relation to the length of the letter. To provide an approximate tabulation of this, the total number of instances of singular and plural separately and combined in a letter have been divided by the approximate number of pages it occupies in the Nestle text (25th ed.). The results have been arranged by order of frequency.

Singular		*Plural*		*Singular and Plural*	
Phlm	16.8	1 Thess	13.0	Phlm	19.4
Phil	14.7	2 Thess	11.0	2 Cor	17.4
2 Tim	9.7	2 Cor	9.1	Phil	15.8
Gal	9.0	Tit	4.4	1 Thess	13.6
2 Cor	8.3	Rom	4.1	Gal	12.8
1 Cor	7.4	Gal	3.8	2 Tim	12.2
Rom	5.2	Eph	3.5	2 Thess	11.8
1 Tim	3.3	1 Cor	3.2	1 Cor	10.6
Col	2.9	Phlm	2.6	Rom	9.3
Tit	2.5	2 Tim	2.5	Tit	6.9
Eph	2.2	Col	2.3	Eph	5.7
2 Thess	.8	1 Tim	1.9	Col	5.2
1 Thess	.6	Phil	1.1	1 Tim	5.2

plural is more than twice as prominent in 1 and 2 Thessalonians and 2 Corinthians as in the other letters, including those which also mention co-senders (cf. n. 33).

It is impossible to account for every first person plural in Paul's letters by appeal to some kind of genuine plurality. The conclusion that "we," at least sometimes, means only "I" cannot be avoided.[40] This specialized use of "we" has been variously identified, according to the supposed nuance intended, as the literary plural, epistolary plural, stylistic plural, rhetorical plural, plural of authorship, editorial "we," *pluralis sociativus, pluralis auctoris, pluralis maiestiticus,* or *pluralis modestiae.* The singular and plural alternate as capriciously in other contemporary writers of Greek as they do in Paul, as numerous examples in Karl Dick's definitive 1900 study, *Der schriftstellerische Plural bei Paulus,* illustrate. Dick demonstrated persuasively that the antecedent of each occurrence of the first person plural in Paul's letters must be determined exegetically within its unique context, not by mechanically applied rules.[41] Most grammarians agree that Dick proved that the literary plural was completely "idiomatic" in Hellenistic Greek, although it was by no means "invariable"—i.e., not

---

Average
Pauline Corpus:

6.4	4.8	11.2

Homologoumena:

9.0	4.2	14.1

Deutero-Pauline:

3.4	4.2	7.8

These statistics, of course, do not take into consideration such complicating factors as the possibility of composite letters or redactional additions.

[40] Attempts to do so require psychologizing appeals to Paul's supposed subtle changes of moods or his attempts to convey some other nuance. See, e.g., W. F. Lofthouse, "Singular and Plural," pp. 179-82; idem, "'I' and 'We' in the Pauline Letters," *ExpTim* 64 (1952/53) 241-45.

[41] Karl Dick, *Der schriftstellerische Plural bei Paulus* (Halle: Niemeyer, 1900) pp. 33-83—examples from the Hellenistic period; pp. 166-69—conclusions. Dick's research has been supplemented by Milligan, p. 131; James Hope Moulton, *Prolegomena,* vol. 1, *A Grammar of New Testament Greek* (3rd ed.; Edinburgh: Clark, 1930) pp. 86, 246; and Béda Rigaux, *Saint Paul: Les Epîtres aux Thessaloniciens* (Etudes Bibliques; Paris: Lecoffre, 1956) pp. 77-80.

every instance of the first person plural may without examination be equated with a singular.[42] Whether a given "we" refers to Paul alone or represents a larger group is a matter for exegesis not grammar to decide.[43] Both Cicero and Josephus, whose autobiographical works are surveyed in chapter 1, like Paul, at times use "we" to refer exclusively to themselves.

---

[42]Moulton, 1:86-87; Turner, 3:28; C. F. D. Moule, *An Idiom Book of New Testament Greek* (2nd ed.; Cambridge: Cambridge University Press, 1959) p. 118; Robertson, pp. 406-7; Ethelbert Stauffer, "ἐγώ," *TDNT*, 2:356; BDF §280.

[43]Moulton, 1:86-87; Robertson, pp. 406-7; Moule, p. 118; and Turner, 3:28 and n. 1.

1
Autobiography in Antiquity

INTRODUCTION

This chapter surveys the phenomenon of "autobiography" in antiquity. The object of the survey is, of course, to serve as a basis for comparison with Paul's apparently "autobiographical" remarks.[1] For this reason his name occasionally obtrudes into the discussion. The survey focuses, however, on autobiography in the Greco-Roman Mediterranean world of the Hellenistic age apart from him. It attempts to answer such questions as: What was autobiography like in antiquity? How does it differ from modern autobiography? and Why? Of what historical value are ancient autobiographies? For what reasons did ancient men write autobiographically? How were their autobiographies received? What was the relationship of autobiography to the social, religious, political, and intellectual environment of antiquity?

The chapter is organized as follows: In section A it is argued that autobiography may be identified as a description of a human life by the individual who live it, i.e., by a definition in terms of content not genre. The variety of autobiographical forms which prevents a generic definition of this mode of literary expression is surveyed in section E. Sections B-D first consider the diversity that exists between ancient and modern autobiography. The two are so different, in fact, that section B must defend the right of ancient autobiography to the designation. One essential difference, arising from the influence of rhetoric, is the tendentious

---

[1] The shift from the noun "autobiography" to the adjective "autobiographical" is deliberate. The terms, though related, are distinguishable. The importance of this distinction will emerge in the course of the following discussion, see section E 1 below.

character of the ancient expression. Section C considers this influence
and its implications for discerning the functions of autobiography in
antiquity. Because autobiography was almost always written with ulterior
motives, persuasiveness being considered more important than truthfulness, section D considers the question of the veracity of ancient autobiography. The variety of autobiographical expressions is illustrated by four
different ancient lives in section E. Despite the widespread utilization of
the relatively new form of autobiography, among leading intellectual and
political figures of antiquity—or perhaps because of it, the popular sense
of propriety was offended by autobiographical production. Section F
focuses on the reasons why these figures found it useful to use autobiography and how they attempted to mitigate its inherent offensiveness.

A. THE IDENTITY OF AUTOBIOGRAPHY: DEFINITION

The term "autobiography" is of comparatively recent origin,[2] formed in
English by the combination of Greek roots. It may be tentatively defined
etymologically as a written description (γραφία) of a human life (βίος) by
the individual himself (αὐτο-).[3] The term conveys nothing regarding its
literary genre, referring only to the identity of the work's author and
contents.[4] The related term "biography" is derived from the Greek word
βιογραφία, but even it does not seem to have been used earlier than the
fifth century A.D.[5] This is not to suggest that men of antiquity never
wrote about themselves or others. The usual term designating both literary enterprises was in Greek βίος and in Latin vita, "life." Although the

---

[2] *The Supplement to the Oxford English Dictionary*, 1972 ed., s.v., gives
1797 as the earliest known use in English. The terms "self-biography" and
"selbstbiographieen" appeared a year earlier. Cf. Georg Misch, *A History
of Autobiography in Antiquity*, 2 vols., trans. author and E. W. Dickes
(Cambridge: Harvard University Press, 1951) 1:5; and Arnaldo Momigliano,
The Development of Greek Biography (Cambridge: Harvard University
Press, 1971) p. 11.

[3] Misch, 1:5; Momigliano, p. 14. For a more complete etymological definition, see James Olney, "Autos-Bios-Graphein: The Study of Autobiographical Literature," *South Atlantic Quarterly* 77 (1978) 113-23.

[4] Misch, 1:7; Momigliano, p. 11.

[5] Henry George Liddell, Robert Scott, and Henry Stuart Jones, eds. *A
Greek-English Lexicon*, new ed. (Oxford: Clarendon, 1940), s.v., notes only
one example of the term (Damascius *Vita Isidori*) dating from the late
fifth century A.D.; see Momigliano, p. 14.

designation may be modern, there are numerous ancient precedents in works of various genres whose material content, wholly or in part, can be no better characterized than as "autobiography" or "autobiographical." Nevertheless, the differences in connotations and expectations between ancient and modern autobiography are not to be ignored.[6]

Most recent studies agree that it is difficult, if not impossible, to define autobiography in terms of literary genre. Generic definitions that have been proposed tend to be either so inclusive as to be of little real formal value or so restrictive as to exclude much that is autobiographical in substance.[7] Georg Misch, whose two-volume *History of Autobiography in Antiquity*[8] has aptly been called "in the best manner of German scholarship, both exhaustive and exhausting,"[9] refers to autobiography as a "chameleon-like genre" which includes a "wealth of forms" that "defies classification" and precise definition.[10] Arnaldo Momigliano's more concise but comparably important study, *The Development of Greek Biography*,[11] likewise offers little precision in defining autobiography as a genre.[12] The examples of ancient autobiography offered by both Misch and Momigliano are not confined to any one of the three overarching ancient rhetorical genres—much less to a more narrowly defined genre, or to any one form, setting, or intention. The distinguishing feature is

---

[6]See D. A. Russell, *Plutarch* (London: Duckworth, 1973) pp. 101-2, 115. He refers specifically only to biography. Momigliano (p. 14) rejects the view of Friedrich Leo (*Die griechisch-römische Biographie nach ihrer literarischen Form* [Hildesheim: Olms, 1965 (original 1901)] Vorwort), who totally distinguishes biography and autobiography.

[7]James Olney, *Metaphors of Self: The Meaning of Autobiography* (Princeton: Princeton University Press, 1972) pp. 38-39.

[8]Misch's work was originally published in 1907 as *Geschichte der Autobiographie*; 2nd ed., 1931; 3rd ed. vol. 1, part 1, 1949, part 2, 1950. All subsequent references are to the English translation.

[9]Olney, *Metaphors*, p. ix.

[10]Quotations are from Misch, 1:7, 4, 5 respectively.

[11]Momigliano's work was originally given as the 1968 Jackson Lectures at Harvard University. See also idem, "Second Thoughts on Greek Biography," *Mededelingen der Koninklijke Nederlandse Akademie van Wetenschappen*, Afd. *Letterkunde, nieuwe reeks* 34, 7 (1971) 245-57.

[12]Hans Dieter Betz (*Galatians: A Commentary on Paul's Letter to the Churches of Galatia* [Hermeneia; Philadelphia: Fortress, 1979] p. 14) considers Momigliano's "emphasis on the interrelationships between various literary genres" to be one of his "major contributions."

content alone.[13] Thus autobiography is not a genre, but a literary attitude. J. Arthur Baird uses the term "mode" to identify "a set of characteristics that cut across various forms and genres and identify patterns of
thought or praxis that do not have the natural cohesive integrity of a form
or a genre."[14] This would seem to apply to autobiography.

Despite attempts to do so, it is doubtful that either ancient or modern
autobiography may be identified as a literary genre. Form critics generally consider similar content alone an insufficient basis for establishing
the genre of a work. Similarity or identity in the following literary features is also necessary: (1) formal structure, outline, general pattern, or
organizing principle; (2) social setting or *Sitz im Leben*; (3) general and
specific intention, purpose, motive, or function; and (4) attitude, mood, or
tone.[15] Particularly in the literature of antiquity, rhetorical units with
autobiographical content and similar formal structures often appear in
different literary settings with very different functions.[16] Autobiographi-

---

[13]Similarly, Charles H. Talbert's (*What is a Gospel? The Genre of the
Canonical Gospels* [Philadelphia: Fortress, 1977] pp. 16-17) excursus on
biography as a genre, despite its references to form and function, succeeds in demonstrating only the centrality of content as the distinctive
feature.

[14]J. Arthur Baird, "Genre Analysis as a Method of Historical Criticism," *SBL 1972 Seminar Papers*, ed. Lane C. McGaughy (Missoula, MT:
Scholars Press, 1973) 2:387.

[15]Gene M. Tucker, *Form Criticism of the Old Testament* (Guides to
Biblical Scholarship, OT Series; Philadelphia: Fortress, 1971) pp. 11-17; cf.
Talbert, pp. 6, 15, 25-131.

Baird suggests "five phenomena that must be present in order to call a
particular set of literary characteristics a genre: uniqueness, recurrence,
coherence, persistence, transference" (p. 387; cf. p. 388). He identifies
autobiography as a genre of the historical type, but distinguishes it from
eighteen other genres, including the theological-philosophical genres apology and epistle, the historical genres romance and aretalogy, and the
sayings-oriented genres diatribe, memoir, and gospel (pp. 393-94). These
distinctions are not fully appropriate in the context of antiquity and are
apparently inapplicable to mixed genres.

[16]See Henry Fischel, "Story and History: Observations on Graeco-
Roman Rhetoric and Pharisaism," *American Oriental Society, Middle West
Branch, Semi-Centennial Volume,* ed. Denis Sinor (Asian Studies Research
Institute, Oriental Series 3; Bloomington: Indiana University, 1969) pp. 59-
88; idem, "Studies in Cynicism and the Ancient Near East: The Transfor-

cal writers seem to have exploited a number of literary and rhetorical genres and methods which cannot be easily pigeonholed.[17] Before pursuing the various forms and functions of the autobiographical expressions of antiquity, it is necessary first to consider the distinctiveness of ancient as compared to modern autobiography.

B. THE DIVERSITY OF ANCIENT AND MODERN AUTOBIOGRAPHY

That autobiography may not be defined generically applies to both ancient and modern expressions. But the two are very different in a number of important respects, so different, in fact, that some scholars hold that autobiography was unknown in antiquity—a view made authoritative by Friedrich Leo and Ulrich von Wilamowitz-Moellendorff.[18] One modern authority, for example, insists that although "there are numerous autobiographical statements in classical Greek and Roman literature," these are not *genuine* autobiographies.[19] "*True* autobiography involves a distinctive mode of presentation—and . . . a distinctive psychological characteristic of European civilisation."[20] "Autobiography *proper*" involves the reconstruction and interpretation of a life along chronological and developmental lines in a coherent narrative told from a particular standpoint.[21] Such claims would be unobjectionable if the word "modern" were substituted for each of the underlined words. Modern autobiography

mation of a Chria," *Religions in Antiquity,* ed. Jacob A Neusner (Leiden: Brill, 1968) pp. 372-411; Howard Clark Kee, "Aretalogy and Gospel," *JBL* 92 (1973) 414, 416-17; and Talbert, p. 12.

[17]See V. Nutton, "Galen and Medical Autobiography," *Cambridge Philological Society, Cambridge, England, Proceedings,* 198 (1972) 50-62, for an excellent example.

[18]See Leo's Vorwort; and Ulrich von Wilamowitz-Moellendorff, "Die Autobiographie im Alterum," *Internationale Wochenschrift für Wissenschaft, Kunst und Technik* 1 (1907) 1105.

[19]Roy Pascal, *Design and Truth in Autobiography* (Cambridge: Harvard University Press, 1960) p. 21. He assumes that "autobiography is only one form among many in which a writer speaks of himself and the incidents of his personal experience." Thus it is "necessary first to discriminate between autobiography proper and other literary forms that have autobiographical content" but lack its distinctive features (pp. 2-3; cf. pp. 2-9).

[20]Ibid., p. 3 (my emphasis).

[21]Ibid., pp. 9-10 (my emphasis); Talbert, pp. 1-17.

is to be distinguished from its ancient ancestors, but it cannot disown them.

It is a widely held opinion that Augustine's *Confessions* (ca. A.D. 400) is the earliest autobiography.[22] This opinion, assumed by many biblical scholars, accounts for their view that Paul's *personalia* are not autobiographical. For example, Krister Stendahl claims, "Augustine, who has perhaps rightly been called the first truly Western man, was the first person in Antiquity or in Christianity to write something so self-centered as his own spiritual autobiography."[23] Günther Bornkamm claims that despite their frequent personal references, Paul's letters "are, of course, in no sense autobiography, but arose out of the apostle's work."[24] Werner Jaeger, however, has emphasized that in antiquity a man's work (πρᾶγμα or παιδεία) often provided the occasion for autobiographical expression.[25] The ancient "life" referred as often to the expression of a man's career as to his characteristic way of living.[26]

Although both Misch and Momigliano insist upon the distinctiveness of modern autobiography, they are equally insistent that the more ancient Greco-Roman antecedents may not be denied the name autobiography.[27] Modern autobiography was not created by Augustine *ex nihilo*. He only brings to a culmination an innovation of antiquity beginning as early as the eighth century B.C.[28] This era, called by Karl Jaspers the "axial"

---

[22]So e.g., ibid., pp. 11, 21-24.

[23]Krister Stendahl, *Paul Among Jews and Gentiles and Other Essays* (Philadelphia: Fortress, 1976) p. 16.

[24]Günther Bornkamm, *Paul*, trans. D. M. G. Stalker (New York: Harper & Row, 1971) p. xiv.

[25]Werner Jaeger, *Paideia: The Ideals of Greek Culture*, 3 vols., trans. Gilbert Highet (New York: Oxford University, 1944) 3:46-70: "The Rhetoric of Isocrates and its Cultural Ideal."

[26]Misch, 1:315. On other differences between ancient and modern biography and autobiography, see Momigliano, *Development*, p. 13; idem, "Second Thoughts"; Russell, pp. 101-2 and 115; and Duane Reed Stuart, *Epochs in Greek and Roman Biography*, Sather Classical Lecutres, 4 (Berkeley: University of California Press, 1928) p. 178. Nutton's discussion provides an illustration of the varied forms of autobiographical *personalia* which fall outside "the restricted category of βίος proper" (p. 54; see p. 60 n. 1), as applied to the life and work of Galen, the second century A.D. Greek physician and sophistic writer.

[27]Momigliano, *Development*, pp. 13 and 62.

[28]Misch (1:17) continues to assign special importance to Augustine's *Confessions* (1:17, 175; 2:372, 519, 633-69).

period, is marked by the emergence or discovery of individual consciousness. For the first time in history man came to conceive of himself as an individuated, autonomous, and responsible "I," rather than as an indistinguishable member of an anonymous community "we." Among the leaders in this, at first, minority movement on the Eurasian continent were in China—Confucius and Lao-tse; in India—Gautama Buddha; in Persia—Zoroaster; in Greece—Thales, Pythagoras, Socrates, and Plato; and in Israel—the prophetic movement, especially deutero- and trito-Isaiah and Jeremiah, Ezra and Nehemiah, and Jesus and Paul.[29] The innovation and minority status of this breakthrough in human consciousness and self-awareness may account in part for the repeatedly raised question in antiquity of the propriety of autobiography, which is discussed in section F below.

Contrary to much recent New Testament scholarship, both Misch and Momigliano recognize Paul's place in the history of the development of autobiography.[30] Edwin A. Judge goes so far as to claim, "Paul probably has no equal in laying bare his own complexities before St. Augustine."[31] The opposite extreme, represented by Stendahl's distinction between "The Apostle Paul and the Introspective Conscience of the West,"[32] serves to

[29] Karl Jaspers, *The Origin and Goal of History* (London: Routledge & Keegan Paul, 1953) pp. 1-77, as summarized by William M. Thompson, *Christ and Consciousness* (New York: Paulist, 1977) p. 20. Thompson reports (esp. pp. 20-27, 48-57) similar views advocated by John B. Cobb, *The Structure of Christian Existence* (Philadelphia: Westminster, 1967) pp. 52-59; Eric Voegelin, *Order and History*, 4 vols. (Baton Rouge: Louisiana State University Press, 1956-74), vol. 2: *The World of the Polis*, pp. 1-24; and vol. 4: *The Ecumenic Age*, pp. 1-58; and Eric Weil, "What is a Breakthrough in History?" *Daedalus* 104 (1975) 21-36. Momigliano (*Development*, pp. 17, 32, 35-38), Misch (1:177-98) and Stuart (pp. 38-39) essentially concur with this view.
[30] Misch, 1:17, 193; 2:530-33; 576, 580, 633, 660-61, 669, 671, 681; Momigliano, *Development*, pp. 13, 62. Cf. Thompson, pp. 27, 56, 62, 100-102, 117, 128.
[31] Edwin A. Judge, "St. Paul and Classical Society," *JAC* 15 (1972) 21; see pp. 19-36.
[32] Stendahl, "The Apostle Paul and the Introspective Conscience of the West," *HTR* 56 (1963) 199-215; also in idem, *Paul Among Jews and Gentiles*, pp. 78-96. See Ernst Käsemann's critique of Stendahl's thesis in "Justification and Salvation History in the Epistle to the Romans," *Perspectives on Paul*, trans. Margaret Kohl (Philadelphia: Fortress, 1971) pp. 60-78; and Stendahl's reply in *Paul Among Jews and Gentiles*, pp. 129-32.

caution against the ever-present danger of reading Paul's *personalia* with the anachronistic expectations of modern autobiography. Paul's autobiographical remarks are to be interpreted fully within the context of Greco-Roman antiquity. They are neither *sui generis* nor are they modern. The modern conception of autobiography is as inappropriate for him as for other writers of his day.

Although some ancient autobiographical works seem to have been designed merely to entertain and inform, most have professional, philosophical, political, or personal objectives. They are characteristically intended to affect the reader's behavior—to accuse or defend, to persuade or dissuade, to praise or blame. These represent the categories of rhetoric, which must be considered in any study of the literature of antiquity.[33] This is the concern of section C below.

C. THE TENDENCY[34] OF ANCIENT AUTOBIOGRAPHY: RHETORIC

The polemics of ancient philosophers notwithstanding, rhetoric's role "in shaping antiquity's own understanding of itself" must not be underestimated.[35] The running battle between the advocates of philosophical (i.e., theoretical) and of rhetorical (i.e., practical) education was a matter

---

[33]I do not pretend to be a specialist on the subject of ancient rhetoric. The essentials are discussed below only because, due to "the deterioration of classical training," they can no longer be presumed (Nils A. Dahl, "The Pauline Letters Proposal for a Study Project of an SBL Seminar on Paul," paper presented at the SBL Annual Convention, 1970, p. 42). See E. A. Judge ("Paul's Boasting in Relation to Contemporary Professional Practice," *AusBR* 16 [1968] 37-50), who emphasizes the need for a definitive handbook on NT rhetoric comparable to Walter Bauer's *Greek-English Lexicon of the New Testament and Other Early Christian Literature*, 2nd ed.; trans. and ed. William F. Arndt, F. Wilbur Gingrich, and Frederick W. Danker (Chicago: University of Chicago Press, 1979) on lexicography and F. Blass and A. Debrunner's *Greek Grammar of the New Testament and Other Early Christian Literature*, trans. and rev. Robert W. Funk (Chicago: University of Chicago Press, 1962) on grammar (Judge, ibid., pp. 45-46).

[34]The word "tendency" should be understood to convey the force of the German *Tendenz*, i.e., tendentiousness, bias, or prejudice.

[35]E. A. Judge, "Paul's Boasting," p. 42; see pp. 40-42.

of emphasis and style as well as substance.[36] Philosophers employed
rhetoric as a means of discovering truth (see Plato *Gorgias* 540d; Aristotle
Rhetoric 1.1.12); and rhetoricians claimed philosophy as the source of
their persuasive powers (see Cicero *De Oratore* 1.3.6-12, 1.20.91,
3.34.142-43; Quintilian *Institutio oratoria* 3.1.15). If philosophy and rhetoric, truth and persuasion, were not as antithetically opposed as some
claimed, their differences were not insignificant. Still, the earliest rhetorical handbook of note was written by the philosopher Aristotle.

1. The Major Features of Rhetoric

Following Aristotle, ancient theorists characteristically divided rhetorical oratory into three genres: (1) the forensic (δικανιὸν γένος, *genus
iudiciale*), (2) deliberative (συμβουλευτικόν, *deliberativum*), and (3) epideictic (ἐπιδεικτικόν, *demonstrativum*). These were distinguished
according to the *aptum*, i.e., the relationship presumed to exist between
the speaker and his speech's content, audience, setting (time and occasion), and objective (τέλος, *causa*).[37] Highly litigious Athens considered
forensic oratory the most important, and accordingly this type is given
the greatest space in the ancient rhetorical handbooks. Before Aristotle,
deliberative oratory was not regarded as a genre nor given formal expression. The broadest genre, epideictic, comprehended all that did not fit the
other two.[38]

The distinctive content and concern (τέλος *causa*) of forensic oratory
was justice, i.e., to prove the just; of deliberative, propaganda, i.e., to

---

[36] See the satirical dialogue on this struggle in (pseudo- ?) Lucian of
Samosata's *Parasite: Parasitic an Art,* trans. A. M. Harmon, *Lucian* (LCL).
[37] Aristotle *Rhetoric* 1.3; Quintilian, *Institutio oratoria* 3.4.1. See
George Kennedy, *The Art of Persuasion in Greece* (Princeton: Princeton
University Press, 1963), pp. 85-87; Heinrich Lausberg, *Handbuch der lite-
rarischen Rhetorik,* 2 vols. (München: Hueber, 1960), §§241, 258, 437;
Wilhelm Wuellner, "Paul's Rhetoric of Argumentation in Romans: An
Alternative to the Donfried-Karris Debate over Romans," *CBQ* 38 (1976)
343.
[38] Lausberg, §§61, 224-54; Kennedy, pp. 203-4; see Theodore C.
Burgess, "Epideictic Literature," *University of Chicago Studies in Classical Philology* 3 (1900) 89-261. Cf. Edwin Black (*Rhetorical Criticism: A
Study in Method* [Madison: University of Wisconsin Press, 1978] pp. 138-
77) on the exhortation intended to change belief and behavior by means of
emotion or reasoned discourse.

26   Pauline Autobiography

advise as to the expedient; and of the epideictic, education, i.e., to display the honorable. In the forensic and deliberative genres the hearer acted as a judge; in the former, of what had been done in the past, and in the latter, of what was to be done in the future. In epideictic the hearer acted as an interested spectator of presently existing conditions as if he were a judge. The native setting of the forensic genre was the courts of law, that of deliberative oratory was funeral and festival orations, and of the epideictic genre all other settings, especially the lecture hall. Each genre was divided into two species based on its objective, purpose, or goal, whether positive or negative. The goal of forensic oratory was either to accuse (κατηγορία, accusatio) or defend (ἀπολογία, defensio); of deliberative to persuade (προτροπή, suasio) or dissuade (ἀποτροπή, dissuasio); of epideictic to praise (ἔπαινος, laudare) or blame (ψόγος, vituperatio).[39]

The organization or structural arrangement (τάξις, dispositio) of a speech or written discourse was a refinement of the simple pattern of introduction, body, and conclusion.[40] The basic arrangement, applicable with minor adaptations to a speech of any of the three genres, was as follows: introduction (προοίμιον, exordium), narrative (διήγησις, narratio), proof (πίστις, probatio, argumentatio, or confirmatio), and conclusion (ἐπίλογος, peroratio or conclusio). Occasionally optional parts were introduced, before the proof, an indication of its parts (partitio, propositio); after the proof, a refutation of apparently contradictory evidence (refutatio); and/or a digression (digressio) before the conclusion.[41] The introduction and conclusion are particularly important for any determination of the genre and species of an oration, for here, if anywhere, the speaker makes his causa explicit. Here also he indicates the aptum of his speech and the decision he expects his audience to render. Since each of the genres prescribes essentially identical configurations of the basic

---

[39]Aristotle 1.3.4-6; Quintilian 3.8.1-5. See Heinrich Lausberg, Elemente der Literarischen Rhetorik, 3rd ed. (München: Hueber, 1967), §22.

[40]In Plato's dialogue Phaedrus (264C; trans. Harold North Fowler, [LCL]) Socrates observes that every discourse must be organized so as to have a beginning, middle, and end. See Kennedy, pp. 32 and 113.

[41]Kennedy, pp. 10-11, 56; idem, The Art of Rhetoric in the Roman World. 300 B.C.-A.D. 300 (Princeton: Princeton University Press, 1972), pp. 114-16, 266, 339; Lausberg, Handbuch, §§260-442; idem, Elemente, §§46-90.

divisions, the rhetorical genre of a speech may not be determined by its
τάξις, "arrangement."[42]

2. Rhetoric and Autobiography

Among the most important proofs is the argument of the speaker's
ethos (ἦθος/ἔθος), i.e., his distinguishing or customary moral character.
To be persuasive the speaker must first persuade his audience to trust
him. This favorable presentation of the speaker's ethos usually appears in
the introduction, but it may play a part in the narrative, often serves as a
secondary proof, and usually reappears in the conclusion of the speech.
Thus the entire speech may be scattered with autobiographical notices, all
serving its overarching goal.[43] A more lengthy discussion of the speaker's
ethos becomes an amplification or digression (αὔξησις, διατριβή, excur-
sio or commoratio).[44] It is only a short step from this to the speech

---

[42]This is to be emphasized against Betz's application of rhetorical
analysis to Paul's letter to the Galatians, in which the presumed structure
decisively influences his identification of the letter as an apology in letter
form (pp. 14-25). This is not to suggest that he is unaware of the crucial
role of the exordium and/or peroratio (pp. 44-46, 313), but only that he
gives the stated causa a less decisive role in determining the letter's
encompassing genre than his conjectural analysis of the structure. Even if
he is correct in his analysis, which is not without its problems, has he
established the genre? I think not. In support of my claim, see W. J.
Brandt, The Rhetoric of Argumentation (New York: Bobbs-Merrill, 1970),
pp. 14, 22; and Chaim Perelman and L. Olbrechts-Tyteca, The New
Rhetoric: A Treatise on Argumentation, trans. John Wilkinson and Purcell
Weaver (Notre Dame, IN: University of Notre Dame, 1969).

[43]Aristotle 3.16.11ff.; Quintilian 4.2.1-132; cf. Kennedy, Persuasion,
pp. 11, 88-90, 121; idem, Quintilian, (Twayne's World Authors Series, 59:
Latin Literature; New York: Twayne, 1969) pp. 63, 65, 67-68.

[44]See the discussion in George L. Kustas, Diatribe in Ancient Rhetorical Theory, Protocol of the 22nd Colloquy, ed. Wilhelm Wuellner
(Berkeley: Center for Hermeneutical Studies in Hellenistic and Modern
Culture, 1976). It is noteworthy that the diatribe in ancient rhetorical
theory was not considered a genre, an informal invective sermon or
harangue on a moral subject, employing dialogue and other characteristic
features. The name for such discourses was διαλέξεις. Cf. Burgess, p.
239; and E. A. Judge, "St. Paul and Classical Society," p. 33 n. 72. See
Barbara P. Wallach, A History of the Diatribe from the Origin up to the
First Century B.C. and a Study of the Influence of the Genre upon Lucretius III, 830-1094 (Ph.D. diss., University of Illinois, 1974; Ann Arbor, MI:
University Microfilms, 1974).

28   Pauline Autobiography

devoted entirely to autobiography. The object of such excursuses or more complete autobiographies was generally not so much to add to the hearers' information as to improve their moral behavior.[45] In antiquity, as Howard Clark Kee observes, "Rhetoric was used in the service of more than communications: the goal was to propagate virtue and to redeem society."[46]

The rhetorical genre most suited to autobiography and autobiographical digressions was the epideictic. The personal encomium (ἐγκώμιον) was devoted to the more or less extravagant praise (ἔπαινος) of the good qualities of a person, whether the speaker himself or another.[47] Polybius (The Histories 10.21) defines the encomium as a somewhat exaggerated account of a man's life and achievements. Thus, in practice the gap between the encomium of an individual and his "life" was "so narrow that neat separation is impossible."[48] The personal apology (ἀπολογία) of the forensic genre likewise is pervasively biographical or autobiographical. In defending an individual against real or imagined charges, the object is often not merely to exculpate him, but to open the possibility of praise (ἔπαινος). Whether encomiastic or apologetic, similar topics often appear when an individual is a speech's subject matter. Although the goals may differ, the topics of an author's own "life," encomium, or apology are hardly distinguishable.

Customary autobiographical topoi include: (1) a treatment of the person's immediate and remote ancestry, his native city or country (γένος), and the noteworthy facts attending his birth (γένεσις); (2) A discussion of the circumstances of his youthful upbringing (ἀνατροφή and ἀναστροφή), his education (παιδεία), and the choices revealing his character and deciding his profession (ἐπιτηδεύματα); (3) a usually topically, but sometimes chronologically, arranged presentation of the person's actions (πράξεις) intended to illustrate his customary moral character (ἦθος and ἔθος) and purpose (προαίρεσις); and (4) a comparison of the individual with other exemplary persons (σύγκρισις), often accompanied by an appeal to imitation of his virtues (μίμησις).[49] These features were by no means invariable. Although certain topics were recommended, an author's relationship to his subject matter, audience, circumstances, and intentions

---

[45]Kustas, p. 38, reporting the view of Edward C. Hobbs.
[46]Kee, p. 415.
[47]Burgess, pp. 113, 116-17.
[48]Momigliano, Development, p. 83; cf. Stuart, pp. 32, 96, 197.
[49]This summarizes the results of Burgess, pp. 117-42, where the ancient literature is cited.

appears to determine which topics assumed prominence or were omitted in actual practice.

D. THE VERACTIY OF AUTOBIOGRAPHY IN ANTIQUITY

Modern interpreters must be cautious in reaching historical conclusions based on the information provided in ancient autobiographies. The varied influences of rhetoric on the origins of autobiography serve as a reminder that truth is secondary to persuasion in its purposes. Contrary to the modern conception of biography and autobiography as subtypes of historiography, history was completely distinguished from both in antiquity in terms of origin, subject matter, and ideals. Both began and developed independently of history. They never were types of history and never applied the Thucydidean and Herodotean criteria of the historian. Furthermore, the subject matter of history was states, not individuals.[50] The not-quite-attainable ideal of impartial and objective historical interpretation, which has been applied to modern biography and autobiography, differs markedly from the political, personal, professional, philosophical, and rhetorical ideals of their ancient counterparts. It should be borne in mind, of course, that Hellenistic history also differs from its modern descendant.[51]

1. Philosophical Lives

In the ancient lives of philosophers, writers, poets, and artists the individual represented the school to which he belonged. Insofar as a biography or autobiography supported one "philosophy" as over against another, "it can be said to have pursued professional aims. Philosophers of various schools and unphilosophic critics were involved in it."[52] Whether in praise or polemics, "the virtues and vices of individual philosophers were brought into assessments of the merits of their schools."[53] There

---

[50]Momigliano, Development, pp. 2, 6-7, 12, 39, 104; idem, "Second Thoughts," pp. 245-57, esp. p. 248.

[51]See W. C. van Unnik, "Luke's Second Book and the Rules of Hellenistic Historiography," Les Actes des Apôtres, ed. J. Kremer (BETL 48; Gembloux: Duculot, 1979) pp. 37-60.

[52]Momigliano, "Second Thoughts," p. 257.

[53]Ibid., p. 256. For an amusing ancient assessment of such competition among the various schools of philosophy, see Lucian of Samosota's satires, Philosophies for Sale and The Dead Come to Life, or the Fisherman, trans. A. M. Harmon, Lucian (LCL).

was always the concern to demonstrate the consistency of theory and practice on the part of the autobiographer and the inconsistency of his rivals. Thus the "philosopher" becomes not only a representative but an embodiment of his "philosophy." And his self-praise or -defense or -recommendation becomes apparently, or in fact, praise or defense or recommendation of his "philosophy," and perhaps also blame or accusation or negative propaganda directed against competing "philosophies" and "philosophers." It is often difficult to ascertain whether this is merely a technique designed to remove the offensiveness of autobiography (see section F below) or whether the autobiography is designed to prove the practical, living truth of the "philosophy."

In any case, the rhetorical and philosophical ideals of ancient biography and autobiography joined to "put a premium, not on truth but on the fulfillment of a purpose arbitrarily preconceived, on making out a case, pro or con with literary effectiveness."[54] The philosophy supplied the purpose—the cultural ideal; rhetoric made the case—the persuasive element. The major interest of most ancient biographers and autobiographers was not historical reality but human potentiality and idealization. Thus, exaggeration and/or suppression were considered legitimate devices. Ancient biographers and autobiographers seldom began with personal experiences, but from existing ideals and literary forms, whether from consciously imitated model works, philosophical presuppositions as to the constituents of virtue, or generally followed rhetorical rules. This partnership of rhetoric and philosophy resulted in a dubious mixture of sincerity and posing, fact and fantasy, truth and fiction, actual and ideal.[55]

2. Political Lives

The situation is little different for the lives of kings, politicians, and generals. They also exploited rhetoric, but in the service of self-propaganda. In their hands autobiography was a weapon of "self-assertion and self-defense."[56] By this means they hoped to determine, to some extent, their role in the memory of future generations[57] so as to achieve

---

[54]Stuart, pp. 59-60.
[55]Ibid., pp. 60-64, 75, 78; Misch, 1:63, 175, 233, 300; Momigliano, Development, pp. 46, 57, 102-3; idem, "Second Thoughts," p. 248.
[56]Momigliano, Development, p. 103.
[57]Ibid., p. 15; Misch, 1:237-38.

"social immortality."[58] The political and personal aims they pursued show little interest in "giving an honest and unvarnished account" written "for its own sake."[59] Unlike the philosophical "lives," their distortions of the truth were less through the use of idealization and exaggeration than through strategic omissions of facts which did not suit their purposes.[60] But, even so, these autobiographers generally managed to compare favorably with existing cultural models of ideal politicians.

3. History and Autobiography

The frequent protests of adherence to historical truth in both the philosophical and political lives were more a matter of rhetorical technique than actual fact.[61] The "facts" they report or omit are influenced by aims other than interest in the truth, the whole truth, and nothing but the truth. Rhetoric was not above "enhancing" the truth in the interests of persuasion, although it was not opposed to the naked truth in the same interests. A "fact" that is completely in the interests of the autobiographer is most plausible when it is true. But whether true or false, the object is to make facts appear as plausible as possible.[62]

From the beginning historiography was something different. According to the rule established by Herodotus and Thucydides, historians were supposed to tell the truth. Although this rule was often broken, it was always recognized as valid.[63] In all types of biography and autobiography "the borderline between fiction and reality was thinner . . . than in ordinary historiography," but especially in the encomiastic lives.[64] Polybius (*The Histories* 10.21) allows for encomiastic history, providing it "distributes praise and blame impartially, demands a strictly true account and one which states the ground on which either praise or blame is based." Truth was his major concern, but he insisted that the history, like the personal encomium, also had an ethical purpose—to meet the need for the improvement of a reader, enabling him to emulate and imitate the

[58]See I. L. Horowitz, "Autobiography as the Presentation of Self for Social Immortality," *New Literary History* 9 (1977) 173-79.
[59]Misch, 1:233.
[60]Ibid., pp. 233 and 241; Momigliano, *Development*, pp. 93-100; Stuart, p. 225.
[61]Burgess, 116.
[62]Quintilian 4.2.34.
[63]Momigliano, "Second Thoughts," p. 248.
[64]See idem, *Development*, p. 56.

examples of eminent men.[65] Although biographers and autobiographers "never felt bound to tell the truth in the way Polybius told the truth, . . . even among historians Polybius was the exception."[66] Political loyalties and rivalries made it difficult to distribute praise and blame as impartially as Polybius required, and the ethical goal of history sometimes compromised its ideal of truth.

4. The Classification of Ancient Lives

Since historical veracity was not a dominant issue in ancient biographies and autobiographies, the usual categories for classifying them, advanced first by Friedrich Leo, are both inappropriate and anachronistic. He organizes them according to their historical concern for chronological arrangement and truth. From the least to the most historical they are: (1) the popular or romantic life; (2) the encomium type; (3) the Peripatetic or Plutarchean type; and (4) the Alexandrian or Suetonian variety.[67] Such a classification system involves an arbitrary judgment on the part of the interpreter and sheds little light on the problems of ancient lives.[68] So-called "peripatetic" lives were sometimes chronologically arranged, while so-called "Alexandrian" lives were sometimes systematically arranged. Despite the assumption that the "Alexandrian" lives were primarily informative, their difference from encomia is slight and they sometimes make their subjects examples to be imitated.[69]

In his study of the genre of the canonical gospels, Charles Talbert suggests an alternative method of classifying ancient lives "on the basis of the function(s) of the writings in their social-intellectual-spiritual

---

[65]Trans. W. R. Patton, *Polybius The Histories* (LCL), p. 4. These ideals are repeated by Lucian of Samosota in his *How to Write History,* trans. K. Kilburn (LCL). He describes the first vice of "shoddy historians" as their failure to recognize the essential difference between history and encomium, which is that "history cannot tell a lie, even a little one." But he, like Polybius, allowed for occasional praise and blame in history if "given at the proper time and kept within reasonable limits" (9), distributed impartially to friend and foe alike (39, 41), and "free from slander, supported by evidence, cursory, and not inopportune" (59).

[66]Momigliano, "Second Thoughts," p. 257.

[67]See Leo; Momigliano, *Development,* pp. 10, 19-20, 45-46, 76, 86-87.

[68]Talbert, pp. 92-93 and 17.

[69]Momigliano, *Development,* pp. 86-87; 18-20, 103; idem, "Second Thoughts," pp. 245-47.

milieu."[70] He mentions five functions (= aims, intentions, purposes, or motives) or functional categories into which these may be grouped. Type A lives function "to provide the readers a pattern to copy."[71] Type B lives "aim to dispel a false image of the teacher and to provide a true model to follow." The proper model emerges in the life's "'defense' of the teacher in contrast to distortions."[72] Type C lives "intend to discredit a given teacher by expose" and, therefore, often function to provoke Type B lives.[73] The purpose of Type D lives was "to indicate where the 'living voice' was to be found in the period after the founder" and was characteristically a biography followed by a "list of or narrative about his successors." Often originating in "controversy" as both defensive and offensive "weapons," "the list or narrative functioned as an instrument of a school's attempt to delimit its true tradition."[74] Type E lives "aim at validating and/or providing the hermeneutical key for the teacher's doctrine." The account of his life and character serves as an introduction and invitation to and an interpretation and legitimation of his teachings.[75]

Although a step in the right direct, Talbert does not go far enough. His categories overlap considerably and suffer from the deficiency of *ex post facto* description. As I have already suggested, the most appropriate system of classification for ancient autobiographies may be found in the genres and sub-species of rhetoric. These, like Talbert's types, identify the function and purpose of a discourse, but with certain advantages over his categories. The genres of rhetoric reflect the possibilities then available to the ancient autobiographer. Mixed genres do not require the creation of hybrid categories. Furthermore, historical conjecture as to the occasion of a given autobiography is obviated, thus making the analysis more strictly literary.

E. THE VARIETY OF AUTOBIOGRAPHICAL EXPRESSIONS IN ANTIQUITY

1. The Diversity of Forms and Functions

It was argued in section A that autobiography defies generic definition.

---

[70]Talbert, pp. 92-113.
[71]Ibid., p. 94; see p. 96 for examples.
[72]Ibid., pp. 94-95; see pp. 94 and 96 for examples.
[73]Ibid., p. 95; see pp. 95-97 for examples
[74]Ibid., pp. 95-97; see pp. 105-6 for examples.
[75]Ibid., pp. 96-97; see pp. 102-4 for examples.

It may be defined only in terms of content as a mode of literary expression in which the author and the subject matter are identical. The demonstration of this argument is forthcoming. The variety of forms employed in ancient autobiography is particularly striking. Misch suggests,

> Hardly any form is alien to it, historical record of achievements, imaginary forensic addresses or rhetorical declamation, systematic or epigrammatic description of character, lyrical poetry, prayer, soliloquy, confessions, letters, literary portraiture, family chronicle and court memoirs . . .—all these forms have been made use of by autobiographers.[76]

Misch is probably too willing to classify "any piece of poetry and prose which contained personal elements, whatever their nature and whatever their purpose" as autobiography. For this reason Momigliano considers his study a valuable history of what men of antiquity thought about themselves, but a confusing history of autobiography per se.[77]

Momigliano avoids this confusion by distinguishing between the noun "autobiography" and the adjective "autobiographical." The adjective may apply to any statement made by an author about himself. The noun should be restricted to those "works or sections of works whose explicit purpose is to give some account" of the author's past life rather than merely to express his present state of mind or his future plans.[78] Like Misch, however, Momigliano emphasizes the multiplicity of and the interrelationships between the various ancient literary genres that may be considered autobiographical.[79] In addition to works specifically designated βίος or vita, ancient autobiographical material appears in the form of letters, apologies, encomia, dialogues, memoirs, genealogies, accounts of journeys and military campaigns, etc.[80]

It is neither possible nor necessary to offer here a full history of the development of autobiography in Greco-Roman antiquity. I assume

---

[76]Misch, 1:4.

[77]Momigliano, *Development*, p. 18.

[78]Ibid., p. 23, see pp. 29, 32, 39, and 85. Hendrikus Boers makes a similar distinction between "theology" and "theological" in his *What is New Testament Theology?* (Guides to Biblical Scholarship, NT Series; Philadelphia: Fortress, 1979) p. 13.

[79]Ibid., p. 23.

[80]Momigliano, *Development*, pp. 14-15, 17, 23, 39, 57-71, and 90; idem, "Second Thoughts," pp. 245-57; Misch, vols. 1 and 2, passim.

throughout the results of those more versed than I in the discipline. Disagreements among them are the inevitable result of the loss of much of the ancient literature, which makes even the most expert reconstructions little better than well-informed guesses. Where disagreements exist I have adopted what appears to be the majority opinion. Scholars are about evenly divided on whether the earliest important example of autobiography is Isocrates' *Antidosis* or Plato's *Seventh Letter*.[81] The debate is purely academic for our purposes since both pre-date Paul by more than four centuries and certainly had earlier precedents themselves. They both illustrate something of the variety of ancient autobiographical expressions and their professional as well as personal interests.

Many ancient autobiographical works are known only by their titles preserved in other literature. That the titles of some surviving works give no clue as to their autobiographical content suggests that many more may be completely unknown. For example, neither Isocrates' *Antidosis* nor Xenophon's *Anabasis* give a hint of the nature of their accounts. Titles alone do not tell the whole story. The advisor and court historiographer of Herod the Great, Nicolaus of Damascus, designated his autobiography Περὶ τοῦ ἰδίου βίου καὶ τῆς ἑαυτοῦ ἀγωγῆς, "Concerning my own life and conduct;" the second century A.D. Roman physician Galen called his, Περὶ διαβολῆς ἐν ᾧ καὶ περὶ τοῦ ἰδίου βίου, "Concerning slander in which is contained also matters concerning my own life." Despite the similarity of the titles, the two are quite different in emphasis. Nicolaus' autobiography is a philosophical analysis of his character (ἦθος), evaluated in terms of Aristotle's *Nicomachean Ethics*. His not unexpectedly favorable self-evaluation gives the work the dominant tone of self-praise, which is made less offensive by the use of the third person rather than the first person form. Galen's autobiography, on the other hand, is a rhetorical analysis of his career (πρᾶξις) in reply to his medical adversaries. The dominant tone is that of *apologia,* self-defense. These factors, taken by themselves, however, suggest too sharp a distinction between the two works. Galen boasts of his moral as well as his medical superiority, and

---

[81]Misch (1:119-54) defends the former, Momigliano (*Development,* pp. 23-62), the latter, although both acknowledge earlier examples. See, e.g., the eleventh century B.C. "Journey of Wen-Amon to Phoenicia" (in James B. Pritchard, ed., *Ancient Near Eastern Texts Relating to the Old Testament,* 2nd ed. [Princeton: Princeton University Press, 1955] pp. 25-29) and the autobiographical memoirs in the OT book of Nehemiah.

Nicolaus evaluates his political successes, arising from his rhetorical gift, in deliberate comparison to others.[82]

In addition to works devoted entirely to autobiography, autobiographical remarks within other literature are not uncommon. This use of *personalia* fully accords with ancient rhetorical theory and practice. Aristotle and his pupils delighted in personal anecdotes, used for their own sake, to serve various argumentative functions, and most often to illustrate vices and virtues.[83] In his *Rhetoric* (3.17.10-12) Aristotle recommends autobiographical vignettes (περὶ αὐτοῦ remarks "about oneself") as a useful kind of digression (διατριβή) or amplification (αὔξησις) within a speech of any one of the three traditional rhetorical genres. He refers specifically to the example of Isocrates, whose speeches and writings frequently brought in biographical and autobiographical episodes. In addition to the illustrative and argumentative value of such remarks, they served an essential ethical function. According to Aristotle, "It is more fitting that a virtuous man should show himself good than that his speech should be painfully exact" (*Rhetoric* 3.17.12).[84] Hermogenes (Περὶ μεθόδου δεινότητος 418.3—419.15) similarly recommends the use of personal digressions for the opportunity they afford the speaker to present his character as a model for his hearers to imitate.[85] The *Rhetorica ad Herennium* (1.4.8) recommends discussing oneself (*ab nostra*) as a method of making the hearers of an oration well disposed to the speaker's argument, especially in the introduction (*exordium*) of a speech.[86]

2. Examples of Ancient Autobiography

Introduction

The following are selected examples from four ancient autobiogra-

[82]On Nicolaus, see Momigliano, *Development*, p. 14; and Misch, 1:307-15. On Galen, see Nutton, pp. 50-62.

[83]Momigliano, *Development*, pp. 68-89.

[84]Trans. John Henry Freese (LCL).

[85]See Willis Peter de Boer (*The Imitation of Paul: An Exegetical Study* [Kampen: Kok, 1962] pp. 24-50) on the notion of imitation in the Jewish and Greco-Roman world contemporary with Paul.

[86]Other digressions recommended by Aristotle include attacks on an opponent and attempts to arouse emotion (3.17.3, 10). *Rhetorica ad Herennium* 1.4.8 also mentions discussion of the person of our adversaries and that of our hearers. See similarly Cicero *De Inventione Rhetorica* 1.16.22; and Hermogenes 418.3—419.15.

phers, Isocrates, Demosthenes, Cicero, and Josephus; the first two, Greek, the third, Roman, and the fourth, a Hellenistic Jew. The first two belong to the fourth century B.C., the third, to the first century B.C., and the fourth, to the first century A.D. The first was written by an intellectual, a professor of rhetoric; the second and third were written by successful politicians; the fourth, by an unsuccessful politician who had become a historian. All four autobiographies have elements of self-praise, although the first two make concerted efforts to soften its offensiveness. The third was aware of, but flaunted, the impropriety of autobiographical encomia; the fourth shows little or no sensitivity for popular sentiments. Only the third lacks the element of real or pretended apology, although even it shares with the others polemical overtones, attacking real or potential rivals or opponents. All four were written with an explicit memorial instinct, a concern for their fate in the memories of generations to come as much as for the views of their contemporaries. All four were written with obvious ulterior motives, i.e., professional or philosophical aims, not merely to provide accurate historical information about their personal lives.

It cannot be claimed that these are representative examples. First, to the extent that any life is an *auto*biography (ἰδίου, ἐμαυτοῦ) it is unique, although this is significantly less true of ancient as opposed to modern autobiographies due to the tendency to idealization. Second, the variety and mixture of types makes it difficult to determine what a representative example might be. Finally, it is uncertain that the surviving examples accurately represent what once existed and not merely the accidents of preservation or the tastes of the later generations that preserved them. It is perhaps enough to claim that these examples are illustrative of autobiography in antiquity.

a) Isocrates

Although Isocrates frequently mentions himself in his speeches, the *Antidosis* (ca. 353 B.C.) is unquestionably his most autobiographical. Jaeger describes it as a "peculiar blend of forensic oratory, self-defense, and autobiography."[87] Misch considers it the "earliest explicit example" of "conscious and deliberate literary autobiography."[88] Isocrates claims

---

[87] Jaeger, 3:132-33.
[88] Misch, 1:155; Jaeger (3:133) agrees; Momigliano (*Development*, pp. 60-62) considers Plato's *Seventh Letter* earlier.

that his recent loss in a law suit[89] led him to believe that the populace at
large (οἱ ἰδιῶται) held mistaken ideas about him that needed correction
(4-5). It is to this task that his *Antidosis* dedicates itself.

> But when my eyes were opened . . . to the fact that a greater
> number than I supposed had mistaken ideas about me, I began
> to ponder how I could show to them and to posterity the truth
> about my character, my life, and the education to which I am
> devoted. (6)

He decided, as he says, "that the only way in which I could accomplish this
was to compose a discourse which would be, as it were, a true image
[εἰκών] of my thought and of my whole life . . . as a monument, after my
death" (7).

The form in which Isocrates chose to cast his autobiographical monument seems to have been influenced by the model of Plato's *Apology of
Socrates,* a fictitious defense pleading in court.[90] But even Plato's
pseudo-autobiographical apology seems not to have been unprecedented.
Misch observes that "in Attic literature fictitious pleadings associated
with a case that had actually been heard had long been a favorite form of
narrative."[91]

The charges Isocrates pretends to answer are the stock charges against
every professor of rhetoric: that he corrupts the youth by teaching them
to gain unjust advantage in the courts, acquiring great wealth in the
process (30-31; 56; 89-90, 96-97), and that he cleverly makes the weaker
cause appear the stronger (5, 15; 89-90; on both charges, cf. Plato *Apology* 17B; 19B; 23C-D; 32D; and Aristophanes *Clouds* 874ff.). Isocrates'
claim to be ineffective in speaking, unlike many of his rhetorical followers imitation of it, seems to have been sincere. He did not declaim in

---

[89]The ἀντίδοσις, "exchange," or "challenge," from which the oration
acquired its title. See *Antidosis* 8 and 145 and the explanation of the suit
by the translator, George Norlin, *Isocrates* (LCL, 2:181, 268-69).

[90]Misch, 1:167. Momigliano (*Development,* p. 48) notes that both
defenses are conventional forms, rhetorical exercises "never uttered
before a court of law." The same is true of Xenophon's *Apology of
Socrates* (52-53).

[91]Ibid., p. 166. For Misch's authorities see 1:344 n. 33. Momigliano
("Second Thoughts," pp. 246-47) concurs. Friedrich Leo (p. 316), however,
makes Plato's *Apology* the primary model of Greek biography and
Aristotle's *Ethics* the main criterion by which lives were judged.

court, but was satisfied to teach and write only. He claims to write his autobiography not in self-defense but in defense of the truth of his power, philosophy, and profession (50; cf. Plato *Apology* 20D, E). Furthermore, his friends' and disciples' receipt of Athens' golden crown of honor furnishes irrefutable evidence against the irresponsible charges against him (93ff., 243-48).

The fiction of an apology permitted Isocrates at the same time to distinguish himself from the less serious practitioners of rhetoric—the "sophists," and "to establish his standing in competition with the new prestige acquired by philosophy through Plato and the Academy."[92] He claims that true rhetoric is true philosophy. "What some people call philosophy is not entitled to the name" (270; cf. 266). "They characterize men who ignore our practical needs and delight in the mental juggling of the ancient sophists as 'students of philosophy,' but refuse this name to whose [*sic* = those] who pursue and practice those studies" (284-85). "Among the professors of disputation there are some who talk no less abusively of the art of speaking on general and useful themes than do the most benighted of men. . . . I could, perhaps, say much harsher things of them than they of me, but I refrain . . ." (258-59).

> I maintain also that if you compare me with those who pro-
> fess to turn men to a life of temperance and justice, you will
> find that my teaching is more true and profitable than theirs.
> For they exhort [παρακαλοῦσιν] their followers to a kind of
> virtue and wisdom which is ignored by the rest of the world
> and is disputed among themselves; I, to a kind which is recog-
> nized by all. (84)

True philosophy requires a correspondence between words and deeds. "The argument which is made by a man's life [ἐκ τοῦ βίου] is of more weight than that which is furnished by words [ὑπο τοῦ λόγου]" (278). Isocrates claims to be the embodiment of his philosophy. The truth of his words is demonstrated by his character and vice versa (see 52-54 and 86-88). Therefore he bases his defense upon the character of his life, conduct, and words (168) and so writes autobiographically.

Despite its surface form, Isocrates' real autobiographical motive seems

---

[92] Misch, 1:158; cf. 165-67, and 173; and Jaeger (3:133-51) who writes: "Every word of his polemic is aimed straight at the Socratics" (3:56). "Isocrates was always careful to make his own position clear by distinguishing himself from others" (3:143).

40   Pauline Autobiography

to have been less self-defense than self-glorification.[93] In the introduction to the *Antidosis* he admits that he adopted the fiction of a self-apology against accusations for both strategic and practical reasons (8). His real object was to reveal the truth about himself (13) in order to praise himself (ἐπαινεῖν ἐμαυτόν) inoffensively (8). Turning his opponents' accusations into accolades, he writes, "Now for this I deserved praise [ἐπαίνου] rather than prejudice [διαβολῆς]" (152). "When I was indicted . . . I reviewed my life and my actions, dwelling longest on the things for which I thought I deserved approbation [ἐπαινεῖσθαι]" (141).

Although he considered his "life worthy of praise and emulation," he was reluctant to approach his autobiography in this way (141, cf. 140-51). The insidiousness of direct encomium would not have permitted him to cover all the points he proposed to discuss without repulsing his audience (8 and 141), whereas "the pretense of self-justification" permitted him to write inoffensively in an autobiographical mode.[94] Nearly half a millennium before Plutarch's essay on how to praise oneself inoffensively, Isocrates "follows" its recommendations (see section F below).

b) Demosthenes

Demosthenes' *De corona* is a somewhat later example (ca. 330 B.C.) of a forensic autobiography like that of Isocrates. Although arising from an actual court pleading, its forensic style is purely incidental to the published work. It was conceived from the outset as a positive statement and "not merely the product of an enforced defensive."[95] Demosthenes had already been exonerated of the charges against him, his opponents subjected to the penalties required of prosecutors who failed to win one-fifth of the jury's votes, and the crown (ὁ στέφανος) of public honor, which they had sought to deny him, had been duly granted before the publication of his literary work.[96] Thus it is a matter of rhetorical posing, not

---

[93]Misch, 1:166.

[94]Jaeger, 3:133. Momigliano (*Development*, pp. 60, 82) considers Isocrates' *Antidosis* a mixture of the forensic (apologetic) and encomiastic genres of rhetoric.

[95]Misch, 1:158, and 343 n. 19. Although Momigliano (*Development*) considers Isocrates' apology the inspiration of Demosthenes' (p. 60), he recognizes the two as being "very different" (p. 58).

[96]Trans. C. A. Vince and J. H. Vince, *Demosthenes* (LCL), vol. 2, "Introduction to the *De corona*," pp. 3-17. See pp. 14-15 for a summary analysis of the entire speech.

spontaneous sincerity, that leads him in the introduction of his oration to apologize for his autobiographical remarks (τ' ἰδίου βίου, 8). He writes:

> . . . There is the natural disposition of mankind to listen readily to obloquy and invective, and to resent self-laudation. To him [his opponent, Aeschines] the agreeable duty has been assigned; the part that is almost always offensive remains for me. If, as a safeguard against such offence, I avoid the relation of my own achievements I shall seem to be unable to refute the charges alleged against me, or to establish my claim to any public distinction. Yet, if I address myself to what I have done, and to the part I have taken in politics, I shall often be obliged to speak about myself [λέγειν . . . περὶ ἐμαυτοῦ]. Well, I will endeavour to do so with all possible modesty; and let the man who has initiated this controversy bear the blame of the egoism which the conditions force upon me. (3-4)[97]

In his autobiographical apology Demosthenes is concerned to present in as favorable a light as possible his βίος, "life," and ἦθος, "character," his λόγοι, "words," and πράγματα, "deeds," both public and private (10-125, 188-251, 276-96, and esp. 8, 109, 268ff.). Although the central charge against him concerned his failed policy of resistance against the aggressions of Philip of Macedon, Demosthenes takes the opportunity to recount events even of his youth (257ff.). He is not content merely to vindicate himself; he viciously attacks both the public and private life of his antagonist (see 126-59, 252-75), accusing Aeschines of the crimes with which he was charged, adding for good measure the standard *ad hominem* charges of flattery (162), sophistry (227), and low birth (258ff., 265-66). He accepts responsibility for his rigorous pursuit of Athens' anti-Macedonian party, but assigns its failed outcome to the will of God (see e.g., 192-94, 249, 289, and 303-4). He embodies the characteristics of the well-meaning citizen of Athens and all that survives of its greatness, freedom, honor, and the tradition of democracy (321).[98] His "crime" of patriotism was in fact his "triumph." For in refusing to bow to Philip, in his person, Athens was undefeated (ὥστ' ἀήττητος ἡ πόλις τό κατ' ἐμέ, 247). Unlike his opponent, he did not prosper by Athens' defeat as if it were good news

---

[97] Note his observance of the recommendations of Plutarch (section F below) before the fact. He is frequently cited as an example of acceptable autobiographical practice.

[98] Misch, 1:158.

(εὐαγγελιζόμενον, 323). On the contrary, his oration concludes with a curse against the alien conquerors and a prayer for the speedy salvation (σωτήριον) of Athens (324).

c) Cicero

Cicero produced a number of autobiographical works of various literary genres, he says, so as "not to let slip any method of singing my own praises" (*Letters to Atticus* 1.19).[99] Partly serious and partly in jest[100] he adds:

> If there is any more fitting subject for eulogy [*laudetur*], then I am willing to be blamed [*vituperemur*] for not choosing some other subject. However, my compositions are not panegyrics [ἐγκωμιαστικά] at all but histories [ἰστορικά]." (*Letters to Atticus* 1.19)

The use of Greek terms in an otherwise Latin letter suggests that his words "encomium" and "history" were intended with *technical* significance. This is not to be confused with *modern* significance, however. "History" here should not be taken to imply entirely truthful or free from praise or blame, but refers only to the narrative form of his autobiography.[101] Plutarch writes of Cicero with greater objectivity and truth. He says that he filled his speeches and books with "praises of himself [τῶν ἐγκωμίων]," (Plutarch *Cicero* 14.2). "He praises not only his deeds and actions, but also his speeches" (Plutarch *Demosthenes and Cicero* 2.2).

Cicero's failure to utilize the approach of the philosophical lives, which characterized a man's βίος and ἦθος,[102] is consistent with his rejection

---

[99] Trans. E. O. Winstedt (LCL).

[100] Cicero was well known for his biting use of irony, sarcasm, and humor. See the excellent examples in Plutarch's life of *Cicero* 26, 38, and 40; trans. Bernadotte Perrin (LCL)

[101] Misch, 1:251. Cicero (*De oratore* 2.15.62) knows the generally accepted rules of history of his day: Tell nothing that is untrue, conceal nothing that is true, and tell it impartially. But he finds the simple unadorned truth unrhetorical and too Roman as opposed to the Attic Greek style he prefers.

[102] This is not to suggest that he rejects "philosophy," however. Cicero often claims to be a philosopher and claims never to send "a letter without a theme and a moral" (*Letters to Atticus* 1.19). Cicero "often asked his friends not to call him an orator, but a philosopher because he had

of the prevailing value placed on the imitation of stereotyped ideals, which viewed differences among individuals as blameworthy defects. He suggests that "everybody . . . must resolutely hold fast to his own peculiar gifts, in so far as they are peculiar only and not vicious" (*De officiis* 1.31.; cf. also 1.30 and 21).[103] The choice of autobiographical types was also dictated by his political career. When as a young man Cicero had inquired of the Delphic oracle "how he could become most illustrious, the Pythian priestess enjoined upon him to make his own nature [τὴν ἑαυτοῦ φύσιν], and not the opinion [δόξαν] of the multitude, his guide in life" (Plutarch *Cicero* 5.1). Nonetheless, he sought "glory" (δόξα) also (Plutarch *Moralia* 541A).

From Cicero's surviving letters we know something of his autobiographical production. The letters themselves are full of personal vignettes and dominated by repeated I's and we's, which he uses interchangeably to refer to himself. These genuinely occasional letters, written to various friends throughout the checkered course of his political career, were published posthumously without discrimination and against his intentions.[104] What is revealed of Cicero's character here is consistent with what he expresses in his strictly autobiographical works—unmitigated arrogance and egotism. In addition to his personal letters he himself published a letter addressed to Pompey "On his Deeds and the Highest Affairs of State."[105] His other forms of autobiographical expression include an epic poem (*Letters to His Friends* 1.7), a heroic poem, a Greek ὑπόμνημα and Latin *commentarium*, both "memoirs" (52 B.C.), ostensibly narrating only the achievements of his consulate (*Letters to Atticus* 1.19, 20; 2.1), and a bitter "private memoir [ἀνέκδοτα]" (*Letters to Atticus* 2.6), to which he devoted fifteen years.[106]

It is widely assumed that at least Cicero's lost memoirs are a source

---

chosen philosophy as an occupation but used oratory merely as an instrument for attaining the needful ends of a political career" (Plutarch *Cicero* 12.5).

[103] Trans. Walter Miller (LCL).

[104] In a section of a letter to Atticus in which Cicero particularly praises his achievements (1.16), he inserts the parentheses, "I don't think I am boasting unduly [*insolenter gloriai*] in saying so to you privately, especially in a letter which I would rather you didn't read to anyone." See Misch, 2:359.

[105] Misch, 1:248.

[106] Ibid., 1:249.

for Plutarch's biography of the politician.[107] Plutarch reports that Cicero's birth was attended by the conventional omens of his future greatness as Rome's greatest orator. As a child prodigy he won fame among his schoolmates for his natural talent "so that their fathers used to visit the schools in order to see Cicero with their own eyes and observe the quickness and intelligence in his studies for which he was extolled" (Plutarch *Cicero* 1.2.13). In Greece he so excelled in his advanced training in rhetorc, philosophy, and politics that one of his teachers was moved to say, "Thee, indeed O Cicero, I admire and commend; but Greece I pity for her sad fortune, since I see that even the only glories which were left to us, culture and eloquence, are through thee to belong also to the Romans" (Plutarch *Cicero* 4.5). His entire career was reportedly attended by omens such as fires, lightning, dreams, earthquakes, and specters—all common enough occurrences in the autobiographies of politicians of antiquity.[108]

The chief concern of Cicero's autobiographical endeavors, by his own claim, is to praise his consulate and in particular his resuce of Rome from the conspiracy of Catiline (Plutarch *Cicero* 11-24). As a result of this the citizens designated him "saviour and founder of his country" (22.3), and in the greatest honor ever accorded a Roman gave him the title "father of his country" (23.2).[109] Given supreme power in the state, Cicero, Plutarch writes, "made himself generally odious, not by any base action, but by continually praising and magnifying himself" (24.1).

The reason Cicero wrote autobiographically, as for all ancient politicians, arose from his concern for the judgment of history. As he wrote his friend Atticus, "That is a thing I fear much more than the petty gossip of those who are alive today" (*Letters to Atticus* 2:5). Cicero's self-praises

---

[107]Ibid., see 2:348 n. 110 for Misch's authorities.

[108]See Misch, 1:199-286: "Autobiography in Political Life."

[109]Cf. Cicero *Letters to Atticus* 1:19: "I brought Pompey, the man who had held his peace too long about my achievements, into a frame of mind for attributing to me the salvation of the empire and the world not once only, but time after time and with emphasis in the House. That was not so much for my benefit—for my achievements were neither so obscure that they required puffing up—but for the State's sake." Of Pompey he writes later: "Please don't imagine I have allied myself to him solely to save my skin. . . . He speaks, I may tell you, far more glowingly about my achievements than about his own, though many have tried to set him against me" (*Atticus* 2.1). After Cicero's assassination, Augustus, who had been a party to the plot, described Cicero as "a learned man and a lover of his country" (Plutarch *Cicero* 49.3).

ran headlong into the popular sense of propriety—expressed particularly in Plutarch's *On Praising Oneself Inoffensively,* in which he writes critically, "Cicero boasted not from necessity but for glory" (*Moralia* 541A).[110] Cicero was not unaware of the popular reticence with respect to autobiographical production. In his letter to Lucius Lucceius (56 B.C.), he impatiently urges Lucius to carry through his frequently avowed intention to eulogize him. "But if I fail to induce you to grant me this request . . . , I shall perhaps be forced to do what some have frequently found fault with [*reprehenerunt*]—write about myself [*scribam ipse de me*]; and yet I should be following the example of many distinguished men" (*Letters to His Friends* 5.12.8). He expresses the views of the Roman aristocracy when he writes, "Ambition [*studium laudis*] moves all of us, and the nobler a man is the more he is led by the idea of fame. We should not disclaim this undeniable fact but rather admit it unabashed" (*Pro Archia poeta* 11.26).[111] Quintilian, the first century A.D. Roman rhetorician, aware of the criticism surrounding Cicero's practice, defends his open boasting (*gloriari*) as "more tolerable, owing to its sheer straight-forwardness, than that perverted form of self-praise, . . . the most ostentatious kind of boasting [which] takes the form of actual self-derision" (11.1.21-22).[112]

Cicero considers the inherent disadvantage of encomiastic autobiography to be that the author is expected "to write about himself with a certain reserve, when there is anything to be praised [*laudandum*]" and assumed "to pass over what is deserving of censure [*reprehendum*]" (*Letters to His Friends* 5.12.8). Thus his composition fails to achieve its historical objective, while remaining objectionably immodest and unconvincing. This is apparently the reason why he adopted the conventional solution of rhetoric, which was to consider "memoirs" non-literary. These were "sent" to a poet or historian to be put into literary shape. In this way they were converted from autobiographies to biographies or histories.[113] That this was purely a literary fiction for Cicero, at least, is clear from

---

[110]Trans. Phillip H. DeLacy (LCL). Note the antithetical construction.

[111]Trans. N. H. Watts (LCL). See Misch, 1.187.

[112]Trans. H. E. Butler (LCL). Aristotle (*Nicomachean Ethics* 4.7.2-17), who has no use for self-depreciators, has even less for boasters. He also considers some mock-humility to be really disguised boastfulness. Cicero was capable of both boasting and mock-modesty. When an opponent accused him of bringing more men to death as a hostile witness than he saved for it as an advocate, he replied, "I admit that my credibility is greater than my eloquence" (Plutarch *Cicero* 26.4).

[113]Misch, 1:237.

his description of the time and care he had devoted to rhetorically elabo-
rating his *commentarium* and ὑπόμνημα. He claims to have exhausted "all
the scent box of Isocrates, and all the rouge-pots of his pupils, and some
of Aristotle's colours too." He so succeeded that he writes to Atticus
(2.1):

> I have flabbergasted the whole Greek nation: so I have ceased
> to be plagued by people who were always hanging around
> about asking me to give them something of mine to polish up.
> If you like the book you will see to it that Athens and other
> Greek towns have it in stock; for I think it may add some
> lustre to my achievements.

He refers to several besides Lucius who failed in their promise to produce
the biographical praises he desired including Archias (*Pro Archia poeta*
11.28), Posidonius, and others (*Letters to Atticus* 1.16, 20, 21). His friend
Atticus, however, complied, evoking Cicero's evaluation: "Yours (which I
read with pleasure) seemed to me a trifle rough and unadorned, yet its
very lack of ornament is an ornament in itself." Was he any more sincere
in this than he was in this similar "compliment" of Caesar's "memoirs" as
artfully crude? In view of Cicero's lack of affection for Caesar and his
own clear preference for ornate Attic style it is improbable that he found
his friend's biography fully satisfying, despite his admitted egotistic
pleasure in its subject matter (*Letters to Atticus* 2.1).

d) Josephus

The autobiography of Flavius Josephus is of interest more for its
authorship by a first century A.D. historian of Jewish ancestry than for its
content. Because the *Life* of Josephus (βίος) stands as an appendix to his
Antiquities, it lacks both the prefatory statement and original title given
his other literary works.[114] That he considered it his autobiography,

---

[114] Misch (1:315) considers it "the first known autobiographical work of
an author of Jewish origin, faith, and training writing for the Greco-
Roman civilized world." There are comparatively few autobiographical
notices in the works of another prominent Jewish writer of the same
period, Philo of Alexandria (but see his *Legatio ad Gaium*, trans. F. H.
Colson [LCL] and *Philo of Alexandria: The Contemplative Life, Giants and
Selections*, trans David Winson, [Classics of Western Spirituality; Ramsey,
NJ: Paulist, 1980]). Josephus' *Life* is also of interest as one of few surviv-

however, is clear from parallel notices within the two works. He closes the *Antiquities* with the announcement that it will be followed with ὑπο-μνήματα, "memoirs," of his γένος, "genealogy," and βίος, "life" (*Antiquities* 20.266).[115]

Josephus begins his autobiographical narrative with his genealogy, traced back through five generations of eminent priests on his father's side and to the Hasmonaean high-priest and King Jonathan on his mother's, thus identifying himself with the priestly ruling class of Israel (*Life* 1-6).[116] He writes, "with such a pedigree [γένος] . . . I can take leave of the would be detractors of my family" (6). He turns next to his

---

ing Hellenistic autobiographies (Misch, 1:307-26). Misch writes that "his formless work . . . does not deserve the title it bears— *Bios*—if we understand that word in its philosophical sense, referring to the characteristic way of living and not merely as the comon expression for the author's career. It is a strange mixture of the historian's military and political memoirs, moral or religious *apologia*, and self-commendation" (1:315).
See also H. Peterson, "Real and Alleged Literary Projects of Josephus," *American Journal of Philology* 79 (1958) 262 n. 11; David M. Rhoads, *Israel in Revolution: 6-74 C.E.: A Political History Based on the Writings of Josephus* (Philadelphia: Fortress, 1976), pp. 4-19: "Josephus"; David A. Barish, "The Autobiography of Josephus and the Hypothesis of a Second Edition of His Antiquities," *HTR* 71 (1978) 64 and n. 16 and 69; Shaye J. D. Cohen, *Josephus in Galilee and Rome: His Vita and Development as a Historian* (Columbia Studies in Classical Tradition, 8; Leiden: Brill, 1979), esp. pp. 101-80: "Vita: Aims and Methods"; and Sean Freyne, "The Galileans in the Light of Josephus' *Vita*," *NTS* 26 (1980) 397-413.

[115]Within the rhetorical school of Hellenistic historiography, to which Josephus belongs, the "memoirs" designated the rough drafts from which more elaborate histories were composed. See Misch, vol. 1, passim; and H. W. Attridge, *The Interpretation of Biblical History in the Antiquities of Flavius Josephus* (HDR 7; Missoula, MT: Scholars Press, 1976) pp. 29-70.

[116]The antithetical construction of the opening sentence is noteworthy: "My family is no ignoble one, but is descended back from priests." The antithetical construction is resumed in the third sentence: "Not only is my family of priestly descent, but it is also of the first of the twenty-four courses" (*Life*, 2). The translation here is mine, to emphasize the construction. I depend elsewhere on the translation of H. St. J. Thackeray [LCL]). Such constructions are as frequent throughout Josephus' writings as they are in Paul's. Josephus' tendency to alternate between the first person singular and plural, used equivalently to refer to himself alone, in his narrative, which likewise has a parallel in Paul's practice, should also be noted.

upbringing and education in Jerusalem (7-12): "I made great progress [προὔκοπτον] in my education [παιδείας], gaining a reputation for an excellent memory and understanding. While still a boy, about fourteen years old, I won universal applause for my love of letters . . ." (8-9).[117] He claims to have investigated personally the sects (αἱρέσεων) of the Sadducees, Pharisees, and Essenes and to have spent three years in the wilderness with a Jewish ascetic named Bannus, all between his sixteenth and nineteenth years (10-12). Perhaps he was precocious, but this claim is completely implausible.[118]

His autobiography concludes with the words: "Such are the events of my whole life; from them let others judge as they will my character" (430). The technical terms he uses, βίος, "life," and ἦθος, "character," are more characteristic of the Greek philosophical lives than the political memoirs which the larger part of his autobiography more closely resembles.[119] Such memoirs (ὑπομνήματα) were considered non-literary works and were dedicated for the purpose of being judged, i.e., put into literary shape by others.[120] This may account for the generally recognized crude and unliterary character of the *Life* as compared to Josephus' other works.[121]

---

[117]Misch (1:325) notes that most Hellenistic autobiographers praised their own precocity. Cf. Cicero's example cited in section E 2 c above and Paul's similar, but more modest claim in Gal 2:14a: "And I progressed in Judaism beyond many contemporaries in my race."

[118]Misch (1:325) notes that such tours of investigation through the various philosophical schools was characteristic of Hellenistic rather than Jewish education. Furthermore, everything we know about these sects, much of it from elsewhere in Josephus' other writings, makes it impossible for him to have done all he claims within the allotted time.

[119]Ibid., 1:315, 326. Josephus claims, also inappropriately, that his Jewish sect, the Pharisees, resembles that which the Greeks call the Stoic school" (*Life* 12). Similarly his discourses are described as philosophical (*Jewish War* 3.362).

[120]Ibid., 1:237, and passim. See also n. 114 above. Josephus dedicates his work to the grammarian Epaphroditus (*Life* 430). See Thackeray, *Josephus* (LCL), 1:xi.

[121]Thackeray, 1:xiv-xv. He explains its "lack of literary finish" as "due to hasty production, unaided by his former assistants" (see *Against Apion* 1.50). R. Laqueur (*Der judische Historiker Flavius Josephus: Ein biographischer Versuch auf neuer quellenkritischer Grundlage* [Giessen: Munchow, 1920 (reprinted Darmstadt: Wissenschaftliche Buchgesellschaft, 1972)] pp. 1-6) explains the defect as due to its origin as the "memoirs" of Josephus'

Despite his claim to report the events of his whole life (430), nearly ninety percent of the *Life* is devoted entirely to his conduct during the half year in which he served as governor-general of Galilee before the siege of Jotapata (28-413; i.e., 386 of the entire work's 430 paragraphs). The same events, only narrated in the third person rather than the first person and in a more elevated style, are reported in his *Jewish War* (2.566ff.) and more briefly in his *Against Apion* (1.47-56). The numerous inconsistencies and discrepancies between the accounts lend little credibility to his "autobiographical notices," betraying "either gross carelessness or actual fraud."[122] Misch describes the autobiographical section of *The Jewish War* as having "the atmosphere of a historical romance written round a hero."[123] Notwithstanding Josephus' frequently avowed adherence to the truth, his autobiographical notices reveal "a lax sense of the [modern] meaning of that word."[124]

This dubious feature of Josephus' autobiography seems to have its origin in the apparent double motive, to defend and praise himself, and his

---

conduct of his assignment in Galilee, written for submission to the Sanhedrin in Jerusalem. That is, it is a relic of his earliest work before the literary influence of Rome, not his latest work. Neither explanation takes seriously enough the fact that the bulk of the *Life* is duplicated with superior literary style and with comparable detail in his *Jewish War* (2.566-646). Perhaps he consciously imitates the crude style of the emperors' memoirs, with which he claims familiarity, in order to enhance the historical credibility of his autobiography (see *Life* 342-358; *Jewish War* 3.29; *Against Apion* 1.53-56.

[122] Trans. H. St. J. Thackeray, *Josephus The Jewish War* (LCL) 2:xxvi. His notes in *Jewish War*, 2.569-646 point out these differences.

[123] Misch, 1:317-18.

[124] Thackeray (*Josephus* [LCL] 2:xxiv), who considers the historian's narrative "as a whole" to be "trustworthy" and "veracious" (2:xxiii-xxiv). To vouchsafe the "truth" of his autobiography, Josephus more than once appeals to authorities who were not the kind of men to "keep silence had I, through ignorance or partiality, distorted or omitted any of the facts" (*Against Apion* 1.52). Yet he admits in the *Life* (338-398; see the quotation below) that he had omitted certain facts. Rhoads (pp. 13-14) observes, "As is often the case with apologists and propagandists, truth and accuracy are favorite themes with Josephus." Misch (1:324) notes, however, "It may be that Josephus is not so much to be blamed for identifying the official record of events, with the production of which he had been entrusted, with historical truth. For he actually believed that the general recognition of a certain view of history was a guarantee of its truth."

double audience, his Roman protectors and his Jewish former compatriots. His *Life* is intimately related to his work as a general and as a historian both of which have been challenged directly and indirectly. After his surrender to Vespasian, Josephus notes that "numerous accusations against me were fabricated by persons who envied my good fortune; but, by the providence of God, I came safe through all" (*Life* 425). His apologetic stance has its explanation in these accusations, as he indicates in a comment that shed considerable light also on his view of history.

> Being, therefore, now compelled to defend myself against these false allegations [ἀπολογήσασθαι] I shall allude to matters about which I have hitherto kept silence. My omission to make such a statement at an earlier date should not occasion surprise. For, while veracity is incumbent upon a historian, he is none the less at liberty to refrain from harsh scrutiny of the misdeeds of individuals, not from any partiality for the offenders, but because of his own moderation. (*Life* 338-39)

Among his Jewish detractors, the names of John of Gischala (cf. e.g., *Jewish War* 2.385-590) and Justus of Tiberias are especially maligned. Josephus digresses at length in his *Life* to refute Justus' rival account of the war as having no concern for the truth (*Life* 336-67). In his defense *Against Apion* he writes of some unnamed (τινές) Roman historians of the war, "who never visited the sites nor were anywhere near the actions described, but, having put together a few hearsay reports, have, with the gross impudence of drunken revellers, miscalled their productions by the name of history" (1.46). He, however, as an eyewitness participant asserts his "qualifications as [the] historian [τὴν ἰστορίαν] of the war. . . . Surely, then, one cannot but regard as audacious the attempt of these critics to challenge my veracity" (1.55-56). Addressing both fellow Jews of the diaspora and Greeks and Romans uninvolved in the war he writes in the preface to his *Jewish War* that his history accurately and truthfully serves to undermine the "flattering or fictitious narratives" of rival historians. Fully aware of "the rule that attack is the best defence,"[125] Josephus attacks his historian rivals for transgressions of which he himself is also guilty.

Another challenge, which Josephus dared not answer directly, came from the emperor Domitian, an "enemy of literature and the position of

---

[125]Misch, 1:323.

historians in particular."[126] Despite the loss of the imperial patronage he
enjoyed under Vespasian and Titus, Josephus claims, "The treatment which
I received from the Emperors continued unaltered," in fact, "Domitian . . .
added to my honours. He punished my Jewish accusers" (*Life* 428-29).[127]

The doubtful role Josephus claims to have played as a young man in a
mission to Rome in behalf of pious priests held there by Nero (*Life* 13-16)
provides the necessary alibi for his complicity in the Jewish revolt. He
attempts to appease both his audiences, writing that when he returned to
Palestine the revolution was already beginning and his efforts to dissuade
the mad revolutionaries went unheeded (*Life* 17-19). Josephus thus
defends not only his credentials as the historian of the war and as a
patriot, but as a true prophet. An obvious, but unemphasized, reason for
his opposition to the revolution is the threat it presented to the Roman-
protected dominance of aristocratic Jews, like himself.

Once the war began he pictures himself as a force for moderation,
consistently supplying self-serving motives for every major decision. His
few flaws are always overshadowed by his far greater virtues. He is dearly
loved by all but a few, who, whether through envy or misunderstanding,
initiate intrigues and plots against him. Repeatedly his life is threatened,
but thanks to his genius and divine intervention he is always miraculously
spared. The Romans consider the war's favorable outcome dependent in
large part on their ability to capture Josephus. Even the obvious personal
crisis that led him to his decision to surrender to the Romans rather than
die with his comrades is divinely directed.[128] Reminded of his recent
dreams (like those of his patriarchal namesake, Joseph the son of Jacob),
he prays, "Since it pleases thee, . . . who didst create the Jewish nation,
to break thy work, since fortune [τύχη] has wholly passed to the Romans,
and since thou has made choice of my spirit to announce the things that
are to come, I willingly surrender to the Romans and consent to live; but I
take thee to witness that I go, not [οὐ] as a traitor, but [ἀλλά] as thy

---

[126]Thackeray, *Josephus* (LCL) 1:xi. See Shirley Jackson Case, "Josephus' Anticipation of a Domitianic Persecution," *JBL* 44 (1925) 10-20.

[127]This suggests a date for the *Life* after the publication of the *Antiquities* (A.D. 93/4) and before the death of Domitian (A.D. 96). So Barish,
pp. 61-75. If Laqueur (pp. 1-6) were correct in his earlier date, Agrippa II
could also be seen as one to whom Josephus wished to ingratiate himself.
See Thackeray, *Josephus* (LCL) 2:xxvi-xxvii.

[128]Josephus' repeated appeals to the favor of God and fortune are
reminiscent of the political autobiography of Felix Sulla, q.v., in Misch,
1:244-48.

minister [διάκονος]" (Jewish War 3.354). Once captured, Josephus speaks the prophecy that spares his life, "You will be Caesar, Vespasian, you will be emperor, you and your son [Titus] here" (3.401-2). Josephus offers himself as the model response of Judaism to the present crisis, in which survival depends on the political realism that God's favor rests with Rome (Jewish War 6.107; Against Apion 2.277). He champions the cause of enlightened Judaism and sees as part of his historical task "making Judaism palatable to the Hellenistic world."[129]

Although Josephus frequently praises the nation Israel in his Antiquities (see also Jewish War 2.198) and defends the Jewish people against the Greeks in his Against Apion, these praises are not to be compared to his personal encomia and apologia. When he writes autobiographically, he "indulges his vanity to the full."[130] He has many rivals but no equals in all his endeavors. His autobiography is an all-too-obvious posturing, propaganda with an eye to the opinion of posterity. In an apparent attempt to enhance his own place in the continuation of the history of his people into the present, Josephus often describes himself in terms reminiscent of leading figures in Jewish antiquity. But he emphasizes his literary as opposed to his political prowess. Moses may be the Lawgiver, but Josephus wants to be remembered as the Historian. Whether he deserves the title or not is debatable. But in the case of the history of the Jewish war, so

----

[129]Rhoads, p. 13. An incident Josephus reports from the early days of the siege is of interest for the light it sheds on both his "kind of enlightened, cosmopolitan, pro-Roman Judaism" (ibid. Could this description apply equally well to Paul?) and Paul's autobiographical remarks in Galatians, where the issue is whether circumcision should be compelled of Gentiles. When two Gentile officials of Agrippa II from Trachonitis sought refuge with Josephus, he reports, "The Jews would have compelled them to be circumcised as a condition of residence among them. I, however, would not allow any compulsion to be put upon them, declaring that every one should worship God in accordance with the dictates of his own conscience and not under constraint." Although he succeeded in bringing them to his way of thinking (Life 112-13), later he writes, "The feelings of the masses were once again aroused against me by certain persons who asserted that the noble vassals of the king, who had come to me, ought not to live if they refused to conform to the customs of those with whom they had sought refuge" (Life, 149). Josephus again temporarily convinced them that the refugees "ought to be free from persecution." Eventually, however, he assisted them in making a necessary escape to another refuge (Life, 150-54).

[130]Thackeray, Josephus (LCL) 1:xiv.

intimately bound to his autobiography, there now survive no rival narratives. In this, at least, he succeeded in exerting his influence on posterity.

Conclusion

If the ancient lives surveyed here give any indication of the evolution of autobiography in the Hellenistic period, a certain development may be observed. (1) From the earlier justification of autobiography as necessary for apologetic reasons, it comes to be employed for its own sake with a view to winning the admiration of both contemporaries and posterity. This development is perhaps an aspect of the emerging sense of individual consciousness that had made autobiography possible.[131] Stereotyped, community ideals become less important than unique, individual distinctions. Freed from the necessity of satisfying cultural expectations and defending their departures from these, autobiographers were enabled to concentrate on their real interest, themselves. (2) The still questionable propriety of autobiography in antiquity[132] was probably responsible for the obvious fiction that permitted autobiography to be classified as nonliterary. Autobiographers (e.g., Cicero and Josephus) attempted to influence the presentation of themselves in the literary works of their biographers or historians. This practice also accounts for the occasional use of the third person rather than the first person by some autobiographers.[133] Praise is more persuasive and less offensive when given by another. (3) Both these developments should be distinguished from the continuing use of autobiographical statements in the service of the persuasiveness of an author's writing and/or in support of its ethical objectives.

F. THE PROPRIETY OF AUTOBIOGRAPHY IN ANTIQUITY

Each of the autobiographers selected to illustrate the phenomenon in antiquity each recognizes in his own way the popular offense caused by such expressions. Despite the prevalence of the practice—or perhaps because of it, questions were repeatedly raised in antiquity as to the propriety of autobiography. The decorum of autobiographical remarks as a rhetorical exercise was problematic on both the levels of popular morality

---

[131]See section B above.
[132]See section F below.
[133]E.g., Isocrates, Xenophon, and Nicolaus of Damascus; see section F below.

and philosophical doctrine. According to the late first century A.D. moralist, Plutarch, the self-love that motivates personal remarks (περὶ ἐαυτοῦ λέγειν) easily becomes self-flattery and vain boasting in violation of the Delphic maxim, "Know thyself [γνῶθι σαυτόν]."[134]

Hans Dieter Betz considers the ancient doctrine of "hybris-nemesis" of Greco-Roman popular religion the background assumption of all Plutarch writes. "As Plutarch presents the matter, self-praise becomes self-deification." Offensive self-praise, in addition to this religious problem, presents ethical problems for the philosophical tradition. Self-praisers are "shameless [ἀναισχύντους], since they should be embarrassed even by praise from others." Self-praise is unjust (ἀδίκους), depriving others of their right to praise. Both of the normal responses of those who hear self-praise—silent envy and insincere flattery—are wrong (539D-E). Furthermore, self-praise presents a problem for the rhetorical tradition that sponsors it. If autobiographical remarks detract from rather than enhance one's persuasiveness, the effectiveness of rhetoric is badly served.[135] It should be remembered that autobiography was an innovation which challenged the very Weltanschauung of antiquity. It asserted the role of the individual as over against the community. And it was a minority movement—few were in a position to assert themselves in this way. Accordingly, it aroused the envy more than the righteous indignation of the masses.

In his Nicomachean Ethics (4.3,8) Aristotle recommends the ideal of the magnanimous man (μεγαλόψυχος) who cultivated the habit of never discussing himself because he wants no compliments. The extremes of the boaster (ὁ ἀλαζών) and the self-depreciator (ὁ εἴρων) find their golden mean in "the straight forward [αὐθέκαστος] sort of man who is sincere both in behaviour and in speech and who admits the truth about his qualifications without either exaggeration or understatement" (4.7.2-5).[136]

---

[134]Plutarch How to Tell a Flatterer from a Friend (Moralia 48E-49A); idem, On Praising Oneself Inoffensively (Moralia 539A-547F). On the latter essay, see Hans Dieter Betz, Plutarch's Ethical Writings and Early Christian Literature (SCHNT 4; Leiden: Brill, 1978) pp. 367-93, esp. p. 374 n. 24; idem, "The Delphic Maxim in Hermetic Interpretation," HTR 63 (1970) 465-84.

[135]Betz, Plutarch's Ethical Writings, pp. 373-77, quotes from pp. 373 and 374.

[136]Trans. H. Rackham (LCL). A similar recommendation is made by Paul in Rom 12:3: "For by the grace given to me I bid every one among you not to think of himself more highly than he ought to think, to think

Thus the first century A.D. Roman historian, Tacitus, considers it not presumptuous arrogance but reasonable self-respect to narrate one's own life (*Agricola* 1).[137] Aristotle considers autobiographical remarks generally unnecessary when a man acts without ulterior motives, for "his words, actions, and conduct always represent his true character" (*Nicomachean Ethics* 4.7.5). But few philosophers and politicians acted or spoke without ulterior motives. Even such figures are recommended to "diverge from the truth, if at all, in the direction of understatement rather than exaggeration." That is because affected modesty "appears in better taste" than "boastfulness," since "all excess is offensive" (4.7.9), although boastfulness can disguise itself as mock humility (4.7.15).

If a speaker must refer to himself (περὶ αὑτοῦ λέγειν), Aristotle recommends that he use the third rather than the first person. In praising or defending our moral character "we must make another speak in our place" in order to avoid untoward reactions on the part of our hearers—envy or charges of prolixity or contradiction. He refers to the example of Isocrates, who often puts compliments on the lips of his friends (Aristotle *Rhetoric* 2.17.16). Quintilian, who prefers open boasting to mock-humility, agrees that unless compelled by necessity to do so, "Let us . . . leave it to others to praise us" (11.1.22). In compliance with such recommendations the autobiographies of Xenophon and Nicolaus of Damascus were written in the third person. Such reservations concerning the propriety of autobiography may also account for the rhetorical fiction by which "memoirs" came to be considered non-literary works.[138]

The ancient term which most closely approaches the modern "autobiography," acquired a negative connotation reflecting the prevailing cultural attitude toward the subject. As a technical term in the rhetorical schools, περιαυτολογία came to connote not merely a speech concerning oneself but self-glorification or self-praise.[139] Originally the term seems to have been coined from an expression in Demosthenes' *De corona*. In his autobiographical oration, which has the features of both apology and encomium he requests permission to speak about himself (λέγειν περὶ ἐμαυ-

---

[137]Trans. Maurice Hutton (LCL).
[138]Misch, 1:98-99, 237, 309-10. See P. Lejeune, "Autobiography in the Third Person," trans. A. Tomarken and E. Tomarken, *New Literary History* 9 (1977) 27-50.
[139]Trans. DeLacy and Einarson, *Plutarch's Moralia* (LCL) 7:110 n. a.

56 Pauline Autobiography

τοῦ; *De corona* 4, cf. 321).[140] The most extensive ancient discussion of περιαυτολογία appears in Plutarch's essay on praising oneself inoffensively.[141] Plutarch does not treat the term as simply equivalent to ἑαυτον ἐπαινεῖν, "self-praise." He seems to use it etymologically to refer to any autobiographical remark. This is suggested by his inclusion of personal calamities and tragedies under the heading of περιαυτολογία and his distinction between justified self-praise and empty boasting (539C).[142]

Although addressed to Herculanus (539A), Plutarch considers his advice particularly relevant to both politicians (see 539E, F; 541C; 545D, E) and philosophers (546D-547F). In fact, his advice is addressed to all those who, because of their profession or position in society, find autobiographical expression de rigueur. He uses the first person plural (539A-E, 546B-547F), perhaps to include himself among those needing the advice; he is, after all, a philosopher. This plural is also quite common in parenetic treatises, clearly suggesting that it was intended to give moral instruction.[143] Plutarch's essay calls attention to the tension between the theory and practice of περιαυτολογία: "It is agreed that to speak to others of one's own importance or power is offensive, but . . . not many even of those who condemn such conduct avoid the odium of it" (539A-B).

It is not περιαυτολογία as such, which is to be avoided, but κενὸς ἔπαινος, "empty praise"—needless autobiographical remarks intended only to brighten one's own glory (δόξα) or diminish another's (540A-C). Like Aristotle, Plutarch agrees that there are times when περιαυτολογία may be recommended, not in any way (οὐδεμίαν) for one's own glory or pleasure, but (ἀλλά) when the truth about oneself must be told (539E).[144] One's own good conduct and character may inspire others to similar behavior and stimulate the climate of trust and friendship conducive to further such achievements (539E-F). Plutarch goes beyond Aristotle in

---

[140]Trans. Vince and Vince. Plutarch (*Moralia* 539D, 542A, B, 543B, F) refers repeatedly to Demosthenes' *De corona*.

[141]"Πῶς ἄν τις ἑαυτὸν ἐπαινέσειεν ἀνεπιφθόνως" or *De laude ipsius* in *Moralia* 539A-547F; the term appears in *Moralia*, 539C and E, 544C, 546B, C, D, and F. See the bibliography in DeLacy and Einarson, 7:110 n. a; and Betz, *Plutarch's Ethical Writings*, p. 367 n. 1. All subsequent references to Plutarch cited in the text refer to his *Moralia*, unless otherwise identified.

[142]According to LSJ (s.v.) περιαυτολογία may mean simply speaking about oneself without the connotation of bragging.

[143]Betz, *Plutarch's Ethical Writings*, p. 367.

[144]Note the antithetical construction.

defining the extenuating circumstances which make self-praise blameless (ἀμέμπτως) (540C). But, as the examples in section E demonstrate, his advice is neither new nor original.

It is permissible to speak autobiographically for those: (1) who, on trial or in peril, are defending themselves against charges (540C-541A);[145] (2) who, despite misfortunes and adversity, courageously maintain their pride rather than stoop to self-pity and self-abasement (541A-C);[146] (3) who have been wronged and are freely speaking out (ἡ παρρησία) in behalf of justice (541C-E);[147] (4) whose "wrongs" are in fact "triumphs" (541E-F);[148] (5) whose use of antithesis (ἀντίθεσις) demonstrates that the opposite of their behavior "would have been shameful and base" (541F-542A);[149] (6) who praise their audience along with themselves (542B-C); (7) who praise "others whose aims and acts are the same as their own and whose general character is similar" (542C-D); (8) who assign part of their deeds and success to chance and to God (542E-543A).[150]

A different *aptum,* particularly as it relates to the audience's relationship to the speaker, whether hostile or friendly, requires a correspondingly different utilization of autobiographical remarks. Plutarch suggests that the foregoing techniques for avoiding the offensiveness of περιαυτολογία are best employed in adverse circumstances. More pleasant circumstances call for the use of other devices: (1) When praised for one's obvious virtues

---

[145]This was the affected position of Isocrates and Demosthenes, perhaps actual, for Josephus.

[146]This is the position Cicero claims for himself after his banishment.

[147]See Plutarch's *How to Tell a Flatterer from a Friend* (*Moralia* 59Aff.) on the subject of free speech.

[148]The example Plutarch cites is Demonsthenes' *De corona.*

[149]Again Demosthenes is Plutarch's illustration: "In general the oration *On the Crown* uses the most felicitous contrasts [ἀντιθέσεσι], as each charge is refuted, to introduce self-praise" (542A). When Plutarch compares Demosthenes with Cicero, the latter is charged with immoderate περιαυτολογία motivated by "an intemperate desire for fame" (*Demosthenes and Cicero* 2.1). Plutarch does find it a redeeming quality that Cicero was also quite free with his encomiums upon his predecessors and contemporaries" (*Cicero* 24.2), see points (6) and (7) below.

[150]Plutarch refers to the example of Sulla. In his biography of this Roman general and politician Plutarch notes his delight in assigning responsibility to τύχη or to God for his successes. Plutarch is uncertain whether it was out of sincere belief or out of boastfulness that he called himself Felix, "fortunate." Josephus also makes very similar claims for himself (see n. 128 above).

one is excused if he transfers the praise to virtues which are more worthy of praise (543A-F). (2) The tactful admission of minor failures or unenviable experiences, such as poverty or low birth, along with self-praise dilutes its offensiveness (543F-544C).[151] (3) No envy is aroused when one praises the hardship and peril which his good reputation and character cost him (544C-D). Plutarch also insists that autobiographical remarks must not only be inoffensive but "good and helpful, teaching admiration and love of the useful and profitable rather than the vain and superfluous" (546B) in order for their ethical purposes to be achieved.[152]

One ethical purpose served by autobiographical remarks is exhortation. One's example may "exhort his hearers and inspire them with emulation and ambition."

> For exhortation [ἡ προτροπή] that includes action [ἔργον] as well as argument [λόγον] and presents the speaker's own example and challenge is endued with life: it arouses and spurs the hearer, and not only awakens his ardour and fixes his purpose, but also affords him hope [ἐλπίδος] that the end can be attained and is not impossible [544C-E].[153]

Other ethical purposes calling for autobiographical remarks are correction and encouragement. Timely mention of one's past achievements may be useful at once to humble public and private enemies and to encourage friends and countrymen against despair of salvation (544F-545D). And although one normally should not "pit oneself against the praise and fame of others" (540C), it is good to contrast true self-praise of the good with praise mistakenly assigned to the deeds of evil men. "For this sort of

---

[151]Quintilian (11.1.21-22), who disapproves of this tactic, considers open-boasting "more tolerable" than this "perverted form of self-praise." As examples of such "mock-modesty" or "paradoxical encomia," Quintilian refers to the wealthy who say they are not poor, the distinguished who describe themselves as obscure, the powerful who pose as weak, and the eloquent who pretend to be unskilled and inarticulate. Isocrates similarly opposes the paradoxical encomium (*Helen* 1-13; *Panathenaicus* 36; 272).

[152]This explains Plutarch's negative evaluation of Cicero's autobiography. He boasted "not from necessity but for glory" (*Moralia* 540F-541A). Note the antithetical formulation of both remarks.

[153]Plutarch *Solon and Publicola* 1.1, 2.1. Again note the antithetical mode of expression.

praise perverts; it brings with it the imitation [τὸ μιμεῖσθαι] and emulation of what is shameful as if it were noble" (545D-546B).[154]

Plutarch's discussion concludes with advice to avoid offensive περιαυτολογία in situations where natural self-love may occasion vain self-
praise: when others are praised (546B-C), when reporting one's successful
exploits or praise received from others (546D-F), when censuring (ψόγους)
and admonishing (εἰς τὸ νουθετεῖν) others (546F-547A), when praised or
questioned by others concerning one's deeds (547A-C), and in those situations in which others have been observed falling into offensive self-praise
(547D-E).

Betz understands the intention of Plutarch's essay to be "not to recommend inoffensive self-praise, but to avoid its offensiveness." Thus Betz
concludes, "In effect this means for him the avoidance, if possible, of
open self-praise altogether."[155] Had this been Plutarch's objective, his
concentration on the many and varied situations in which autobiographical
remarks are not only ethically acceptable (καλός: 539E and 546B
ἀμέμπτως: 546C), but a necessary antidote to greater evils (544C), would
be inexplicable. The ideal is seldom possible. Although he wrote critically
of the abuse of autobiographical remarks in general, Plutarch also provided an apology for it. What he says is not new. Much of what he recommends is anticipated in the ethics of Aristotle, who probably represents
the prevailing cultural consensus and not merely the views of the Socratic
tradition. At any rate, Isocrates, no friend of the Academy, also acknowledges the impropriety of autobiography. All of the autobiographers surveyed in section E antedate Plutarch's essay, and yet they justify their
indulgence in περιαυτολογία in compliance with his recommendations.
What is new in Plutarch is his comprehensive summary of and changed
justification for the existing situation and practice. Plutarch's recommendations do not call for the removal of autobiographical remarks from
oratory but for their moral reformation.

CONCLUSION

The following is more than a conclusion to the present chapter. It
serves a twofold purpose. First, it provides a reflective summary of the
most salient features of the autobiographical phenomenon in antiquity.

---

[154]Plutarch considers Cicero's severe rebuke of Gorgias justified
because of his evil morals (*Cicero* 24.6-7).
[155]Betz, *Plutarch's Ethical Writings*, p. 377.

Second, it prepares for the application of these to the question addressed in the balance of the dissertation: What are the functions of autobiographical references in the letters of the apostle Paul? Thus to a certain extent, it introduces the remaining chapters of the dissertation. The suggested comparisons between Paul and others in antiquity do not represent the assumptions but anticipate the results of a thorough investigation of the autobiographical phenomenon throughout the Pauline corpus, even if chapters 2, 3, and 4 concentrate exclusively on the two earliest letters, Galatians and 1 Thessalonians.

"Autobiography" may be defined in terms of its content as a work or part of a work of literature whose explicit purpose is to narrate its author's past life. It lacks the distinctive features necessary for a generic definition, however, comprising a number of diverse literary forms. The adjective "autobiographical" refers more generally to any statement made by an author about himself which could be the raw material for autobiography in the more precise sense. Paul's letters contain a great deal that is clearly autobiographical, but no autobiography.

Although the word "autobiography" is of relatively recent origin, the autobiographical phenomenon originated as an expression of the emergence of individual self-consciousness in late antiquity well before the time of Paul. Though clearly related, the ancient and modern expressions of the autobiographical phenomenon are also strikingly different. (1) The influence of the ancient rhetorical tradition made moral persuasion a higher value than historical truth. Ancient autobiographies were more concerned with ethical characterization and edification than with chronology and exactitude. (2) In antiquity one's profession, philosophy, or position in life often became the occasion for autobiographical expression. The terms βίος and *vita*, both meaning "life," referred to these aspects of life as well as to a man's characteristic way of living. (3) Because of its novelty in the assertion of the individual, as over against the community, and its intrinsic boastfulness, autobiography offended the sensibilities of the ancient world. It should be noted that many of the distinctive features of the ancient phenomenon arise from the autobiographer's attempt to avoid this offensiveness. The further implications of these distinctive features and their application to ancient autobiographical writers, including Paul, are discussed in the following paragraphs.

1. The Influence of Rhetoric upon Autobiography

Rhetoric played a rather large role in shaping Greco-Roman antiquity's self-understanding and, consequently, its autobiography. Whether written only to entertain or inform the reader of previously unknown facts; to defend the author against accusations or misunderstandings; to praise him, his achievements, his profession, philosophy, etc.; or to persuade his readers to follow his example; ancient autobiographies were seldom, if ever, devoid of ulterior motives. Not uncommon in ancient autobiographies are condemnations of and accusations against the author's rivals or detractors, and/or attempts to dissuade the reader from pursuing conduct like theirs.

How an author approached his autobiography depended upon his relationship with his audience, the social setting out of which and for which he wrote, and, most importantly, his intention (τέλος/ causa) in writing. The three genres of rhetoric may define the function or motive of any discourse. Judicial oratory seeks justice either by accusation or defense; deliberative oratory offers advice either to persuade or dissuade; and an epideictic oration pursues education either by praise or blame.

When an individual wrote autobiographically in antiquity, whether in a work as a whole or as a digression within another literary work, the topics covered in his self-description included such facts as (a) the privileges that were his by birth; (b) choices revealing his character and/or deciding his profession; (c) actions illustrating his ethos and life's purpose; and (d) a comparison of the author with others and/or an appeal to imitate his virtues. The topics included or emphasized vary according to the author's intention in writing.

All of these standard topics may be found in the more lengthy autobiographical passages in Paul's letters (see e.g., Gal 1:13-2:21; 4:12-20; 1 Thess 1:4-3:10; 2 Cor 11:21b-12:13; Phil 3:2-21). What he includes, excludes, or emphasizes in an account may give some indication of his relationship to the readers and the function which the autobiographical remarks serve within a given letter. Like Plutarch, Paul appears to reject the use of autobiographical comparison as a technique of self-praise, although he does use it to heap blame upon the shameful behavior of others (Gal 6:3-4, 12-17; 2 Cor 10:7-11, 29; Phil 3:2-3, 18-19).

The influence of rhetoric upon ancient autobiography calls for caution in at least two areas: the possibility of objectivity in rhetorical analysis and the utilization of autobiographical data in historical reconstruction. The need for such cautions accounts in part for the methodology of this dissertation.

a) Rhetorical analysis

In order to determine the function of an autobiography or of autobiographical remarks within another work it is essential to know the author's relationship to his audience, the setting, and his intentions. In the absence of assured information about the historical circumstances of the work, certain questions may be answered only on the basis of surmise. By what principle of selectivity has his autobiography been shaped? What are his implicit argumentative purposes? What does he hope to achieve by his work? What does he expect his readers to do in response? But if the analysis is to be rhetorical rather than historical; the work itself must be the primary source of the answers. Otherwise the interpreter runs the risk of interpreting his theory and not the text.

The interpreter also runs the risk of being misled by the autobiographer's rhetoric. As our survey of ancient autobiographers amply illustrates, "the ostensible object of an argumentation is sometimes not the real one."[156] For example, autobiographical statements, which at a surface level appear to have an apologetic function, may only be a rhetorical device to achieve another purpose. At a deeper level an apology may be intended to malign one's opponents, to remind one's readers of the nature of true virtue, or to recommend himself as a pattern for his readers to imitate. Similarly, it is difficult to tell whether an author's attack upon his opponents is motivated by sincere ethical conviction or merely an expression of self-aggrandizing competition that seeks recognition at another's expense. If the writer hoped to achieve anything by his autobiographical remarks beyond indulging his own vanity or displaying his powers of eloquence, however, it is generally safe to assume that he has made his intentions reasonably clear at least in his introduction and/or conclusion.

Rhetorical analysis is by no means an objective enterprise. First, rhetoric was neither static nor uniform, as its long history and the disagreements among its proponents amply bear out. The threefold classification of rhetorical genres was intended to cover the existing fields of oratory, not to classify actual discourses. The three genres were only ideally distinct and mixed genres were not infrequent. That some of the ancient rhetorical handbooks question the appropriateness of mixing sections (τόποι) of one genre into speeches of another did not significantly affect the practice, as numerous examples demonstrate. Isocrates' *Panegyricus,* for one example, is a mixture of a deliberative funeral

---

[156]Wilhelm Wuellner, "Digressions in I Corinthians: The Rhetoric of Argumentation in Paul," paper presented at the SBL Paul Seminar, 1974, p. 6.

oration and an epideictic narration of the deceased person's life, into which is inserted a judicial defense of him.[157] The title suggests that his overriding concern was praise. But was it?

The ostensibly apologetic motive for Isocrates' *Antidosis* is actually a subterfuge. He adopts the fiction of answering the stock accusations raised against every professor of rhetoric in order to distinguish himself from his rivals and inoffensively to praise himself as the embodiment of the truth of his philosophy and profession, rhetoric. Because he alone is responsible for the selection of charges to which he replies, he is easily able to turn every alleged fault into a virtue to be emulated by his readers.

Demosthenes justifies his autobiographical remarks in a similar fashion. He claims to have been thrust into a no-win situation, in which to praise himself would lead to public disapproval and to fail to defend his reputation would seem to suggest that he was incapable of doing so. The "crimes" with which he has been charged had, in fact, been his "triumphs," since his policy, failure though it was, embodied the spirit of Athenian democracy. Thus his apparently apologetic autobiography functions instead as an instrument of self-praise and praise of Athenian democracy, and a weapon in his attack upon his opponents—despite the fact that he had already been exonerated before its publication.

The "no-win situation" Demosthenes claims to be in is comparable to the one Paul describes for himself in 2 Corinthians 10-13. He knows that there is nothing to be gained by boasting (12:1); that it is foolish (11:1, 16, 17, 19, 21; 12:6, 11), even insane to do so (11:23). He ought to have been commended by his converts (12:11); he ought to have been content with the Lord's commendation (10:18); he ought to have boasted of the Lord (10:17). And yet the prevailing circumstances have compelled (11:30; 12:1), even constrained (12:11), him to indulge in what might be construed as self-praise or self-defense. Still he insists that he does not praise or defend himself for selfish reasons but for the sake of his readers, whose ethical conduct he fears will not be appropriate when he visits them (12:19-21; 13:10). The "weakness" that some of the Corinthians seem to have despised in Paul was, in fact, the necessary human prerequisite for the effective operation of divine "power" in his ministry and an embodiment of the gospel of Christ crucified which he preached.[158]

---

[157]Kennedy, *Persuasion*, pp. 87, 189-90.

[158]The parallel with Demosthenes may also lend support for the essential unity of 2 Corinthians, chs. 1-9 of which presuppose a reconciliation

A second challenge to the objectivity of rhetorical analysis may be mentioned. Although it is true that some rhetoricians recommended a specific structural arrangement (τάξις) for a specific genre, this was by no means agreed upon generally nor were the existing rules pedantically followed. The recommended arrangement was not based on the analysis of actual speeches, but on an abstract conception of the ideal of speeches of a given genre. Thus, for example, the preserved speeches of Demosthenes- -supposedly a model of classical eloquence—often depart from the traditional arrangement.[159] The structural organization of a discourse is not a decisive factor in determining which rhetorical genre or subspecies is being pursued. The freedom ancient writers exercised in the mixing of genres and in the organization of a discourse complicates rhetorical analysis, making a measure of subjectivity unavoidable.[160]

The polar antitheses of vice and virtue, praise and blame, accusation and defense, persuasion and dissuasion, make antithetical constructions a common feature of ancient autobiographical statements. These parallel denials and contrasting affirmations by their fullness of expression give added force and clarity to a writer's claims, e.g., "I did not do this, but I did do thus and so." By such a claim one may infer that he did not do this as his opponents did, or that he did not do this as his opponents alleged. Or he may simply have intended the denial to strengthen his positive claim. This technique doubles the ethical value of an autobiographical remark, since both the virtue claimed and its corresponding vice may be mentioned, the former to be imitated and the latter to be avoided. The antithetical construction may be used polemically, apologetically or merely for the sake of rhetorical fullness. In the ancient autobiographical examples cited in section E, denied charges were explicitly identified as such in the work and were never inferred by reference to antithetical denials. This is seldom the case in most existing approaches to Paul's letters, where the use of the "mirror reading" assumes, with little or no textual basis, that his antithetical constructions respond to accusations made against him by his opponents.[161] Given such an approach, the

---

between Paul and Corinth, while chs. 10-13 hark back to the period of tension by means of *refutatio*.

[159]Kennedy, pp. 123, 222, 264. See Perelman and Olbrechts-Tyteca, p. 21.

[160]Black (pp. ix-xv, 27-35) notes the subjectivity of rhetorical analysis despite the ideal of objectivity.

[161]See the discussion in chapter 2 below.

correctness of one's historical reconstructions directly affect the adequacy of his rhetorical analysis.

b) Historical Reconstruction

The modern concern for the chronological development of a person's life, ideally evaluated as critically and objectively as possible, i.e., according to the standards of scientific history, is considerably different from the concern of the ancient autobiographer to characterize his life according to certain preconceived ideals. This difference is not unlike that between a motion picture and a granite monument. Accordingly, caution is in order in reaching historical conclusions on the basis of ancient autobiographical literature. Autobiography was never considered a subtype of historiography, for unlike history, it was concerned with individuals, not states, and persuasion, not truth, was its overriding concern. The emphasis upon ethical characterization and idealization permitted exaggeration and/or suppression of certain aspects of the real life as legitimate autobiographical devices. Protests of truthfulness often were made precisely at the point where truth was most seriously compromised.

One's interpretation of a document reporting presumably historical incidents is affected considerably by whether he believes that the author is trying to be informative or persuasive. An awareness of the difference provides some clue as to "how much belief to have in the veracity of detail, or even whether veracity is an appropriate issue."[162] Although the problem is more acute in ancient than modern autobiography, "every autobiography can be shown to be deficient in detailed accuracy" whether from self-deception or misrepresentation. "Autobiographical documents scarcely ever have the value of truthful records" or objective narratives. The truth of an autobiography is to be found in the consistent whole of the work, not in individual events reproduced exactly as they happened.[163]

The dubious historical value of the details of ancient autobiographies is vividly demonstrated in the work of Josephus. Despite his emphatic claim to be a historian and his professions of truthfulness, many discrepancies and improbabilities seriously call certain of his claims into question. The complicated relationship between Josephus and his audience and his intentions accounts in large part for the extent to which historical truth is compromised in his autobiography. His motivation in writing is mixed; he

---

[162]Kustas, p. 41, reporting the view of Edward C. Hobbs.
[163]The quotations are from Misch, 1:11 and 176 respectively.

seeks to defend himself against actual not merely stock charges, while at the same time praising his less than sterling performance in both his professions. His double audience introduces a further difficulty; at times he can pacify one faction only at the risk of antagonizing the other. In such dilemmas Josephus more than once introduces the alibi of divine providence; God, not he, must assume the responsibility for his conduct.

Still, it would be as misguided to reject ancient autobiographical data as of no historical value as it would to accept it uncritically as reporting only objective truths. As F. F. Bruce writes:

> Historians of Greek and Roman antiquity do not despise Plutarch's *Parallel Lives* as a source of information. They know that Plutarch was a moralist rather than a historiographer, and that the very parallelism of his biographical exercise frequently necessitated a proportion and emphasis which did not correspond entirely with historical reality. Yet, when all due allowances are made for Plutarch's perspective and purpose, his *Lives* provide the historian with some of the material for (say) a life of Caesar.[164]

The historical information provided by ancient autobiographical literature, for all its inadequacies by modern standards, is much to be preferred to no information. But because of the ulterior motives of this literature "due allowance" must be made for the authors' "perspective and purpose." It is for this reason that the function of Paul's autobiographical remarks, like those of other writers in antiquity, is an essential concern. Until the question of function is answered, their historical value remains in doubt.

The extent to which Paul was influenced by the rhetorical tradition, if at all, is a matter of debate among scholars. But it is agreed that Paul's autobiographical statements are fully at home in antiquity to the extent that they are not purely informative personal histories but serve other motives. Jack T. Sanders argues, with reference to Galatians 1-2 and 2 Corinthians 10-13, that the historicity of such autobiographical remarks, which are not simply factual but seek to establish an argumentative point, should be considered suspect.[165] He contends that if Paul can inflate his "autobiography" in his "catalogue of difficult situations" in 2 Cor 11:21b-

---

[164]F. F. Bruce, "Galatian Problems: 1. Autobiographical Data," *BJRL* 51 (1969) 294.

[165]Jack T. Sanders, "Paul's 'Autobiographical' Statements in Galatians 1-2," *JBL* 85 (1966) 335.

33 to prove his theological point, there is a good possibility that in Gal 1:13-2:10 he deflates or otherwise alters it for the same purpose.[166] He concludes that Galatians is "historically relative and therefore unreliable as a source for reconstructing either the sequence of events in Paul's life or the objective historical details related to the 'apostolic council.'"[167] Whether or not Sanders is correct cannot be decided in advance, but the question he raises of the historical credibility of Paul's autobiographical remarks is fully legitimate.

Since veracity was a subsidiary issue in ancient autobiographies, if an issue at all, the usual mode of classifying them by their adherence to or departure from the ideal of truth is obviously inappropriate. A superior approach would seem to be found in classifying both autobiography and other autobiographical statements on the basis of their rhetorical function(s). This, however, presents a different set of problems which has already been noted. It is necessary now to turn from the influences of rhetoric upon ancient autobiographies to that exercised by the cultural ideals of profession and philosophy.

2. Autobiography, Profession, and Philosophy

In many ancient lives the individual autobiographer presented himself as an ideal representative, even an embodiment, of his philosophy, profession, or the like. In this way autobiography was enlisted in the propaganda of one profession or philosophy against another. A frequent concern of ancient autobiographies was to demonstrate the consistency between one's theory and practice, often in contrast to the inconsistency of his rivals'. Those who considered themselves serious representatives of a given profession or philosophy felt compelled to distinguish themselves from less serious practitioners or to contrast themselves with their opponents in competing schools. This atmosphere of comparison and competition made it imperative that prominent men should dispel possible confusion and misunderstanding as to their true character. Thus an apologetic autobiography need not presuppose the existence of actual charges. It is no simple matter to determine in actual instances precisely what motivated an autobiographer to present himself, his profession, and his philosophy as he did.

As subsequent chapters in the dissertation demonstrate, it is obvious

---

[166]Ibid., pp. 342-43.
[167]Ibid., p. 340.

that, as in the philosophical lives, Paul's autobiographical remarks are inextricably bound to his "profession," or more accurately, his vocation as an apostle of Jesus Christ, and his "philosophy," the gospel which he proclaims and under the authority of which he himself lives. He moves easily from a presentation, whether in praise or defense, of the apostolate or the gospel to autobiographical statements and vice versa.

Cicero illustrates a significant development among autobiographical writers in his rejection of stereotyped cultural ideals, whether of philosophy or profession, as a basis for his self-description, and his recognition instead of distinctive individual characteristics not as deplorable defects but as divine endowments. Unlike some other autobiographers, Cicero is willing to admit his failure to achieve certain popular expectations. As a true aristocrat, he would prefer to say his willingness to flaunt his disdain for pedestrian values. Cicero claims to be less concerned for the opinion of his peers than for that of their progeny, i.e., the judgment of history.

A similar recognition by Paul permits him to affirm a remarkable diversity of gifts and opinions among his converts (Rom 12:6; 14:1-15:13; 1 Corinthians 12-14). Likewise, although he would prefer that they should have a favorable opinion of him (2 Cor 12:11; 13:6), he is willing to risk their rejection of him as a failure. Since it is God's opinion that really matters, it is he whom he seeks to please (see 2 Cor 13:7; 1 Thess 2:4; 1 Cor 4:1-5; Gal 1:10). Paul's eschatological perspective permits no concern for the judgment of history, but he is greatly concerned that he should win a favorable judgment from God (see e.g., 1 Cor 9:26-27; 2 Cor 10:18; Gal 6:1-5; 1 Thess 2:19-20; 3:5). Since Paul is convinced that he is an authentic apostle of Jesus Christ, he does not allow anyone but God to determine how he will execute his mission. Yet his mission is in behalf of other men whom he must be willing to accommodate in order to win as converts and to edify once they are won. Thus, although Paul expresses an almost cavalier disdain for merely human opinions (see Galatians 2), he seeks to cause no one unnecessary offense, and urges his readers to follow his example in this (see Rom 15:1ff.; 1 Cor 9:19-23; 10:31-33).

3. The Offensiveness of Autobiography

In antiquity the cultural ideal of the magnanimous man who never discussed himself came inevitably into conflict with the irrepressible impertinence of the lately self-conscious man who found it imperative to do so. Not unaware of this potential hindrance to persuasiveness, authors with an inclination to write autobiographically devised an array of techniques to remove its offensiveness or to make what had seemed a vice appear to be a virtue. It had long been recognized that trust was a necessary prerequisite for effective persuasion, especially ethical persuasion. Among the most important proofs in rhetorical discourse was that furnished by an author's distinguishing moral character, his ethos. The argument of a life was considered more persuasive than abstract theories. Thus brief autobiographical vignettes were not uncommon in various discourses of any one of the three rhetorical genres. These were intended not so much to add to the reader's information as to persuade him to accept the author's arguments, while improving his own moral behavior. Because rhetoric was used not only in the service of persuasive communication but to propagate virtue, it is difficult in a given instance to determine which motivation is stronger and leads an author to present his autobiography as he does.

Perhaps many of the "techniques" for avoiding the potential offensiveness of autobiographical remarks in the literature of antiquity should be assigned not to rhetorical artifice at all, but simply to unselfconscious common sense. Then, as now, in numerous instances where the self-assertive first person singular pronoun "I" might have been expected, the plural "we" appears instead. In this way the corporateness and mutuality rather than the uniqueness of a claim appear to be emphasized. This may account for the prominence of the first person plural in 2 Corinthians. It is often more effective for ethical purposes when the autobiographer modestly includes himself in his exhortations, "Let us do this!" rather than simply asserting, "(You) do this!" This may account for the prominence of the first person plural and the near absence of the singular in Paul's parenetic letter, 1 Thessalonians. Similarly, if praise is more persuasive and less offensive when given by another, common sense would recommend a third person narration of one's enviable experiences. For this reason, and perhaps also because autobiography was classified as non-literary, it was not uncommon for an autobiographer to narrate his own life as if it were the biography of another. The narrative of a certain man's rapture to heaven in 2 Cor 12:1-5 probably describes Paul's own experience, following this convention.

The circumstances Plutarch put forward for utilizing autobiography in the interests of truth, to inspire imitation, to encourage trust and friendship, or otherwise to help the reader achieve some worthwhile ethical purpose did little more than summarize and legitimize the existing practice. Enlisted in the cause of morality, autobiographical remarks are not only permissible but advisable, provided, of course, they are accompanied by the necessary "antidotes" for "offensiveness."

According to Plutarch, autobiographical remarks may be used in self-defense, in seeking justice, in correctly characterizing alleged wrongs as worthwhile achievements or demonstrating that the opposite behavior would have been demonstrably shameful, and in maintaining pride rather than stooping to self-pity. They are also exempt from blame when the author praises not only himself but also his audience, others whose aims and acts are similar to his own, or God as the one largely responsible for his success. Other devices removing the offensiveness of autobiographical comments are the transfer of praise from a lesser to a more worthy virtue, the admission of certain minor failures, and praise of the hardships and perils required in achieving recognition.

Though Isocrates, Demosthenes, Cicero, Josephus, and Paul antedate the advice given by Plutarch concerning the inoffensive utilization of autobiographical remarks, they all seem to be in more or less compliance with it. Betz correctly assigns the origin of this broad compliance "to the level of popular religion and morality which Greek philosophical tradition and early Christianity, together with Judaism, share." But he also assumes that Paul was a master of rhetoric and the philosophical traditions of Hellenism.[168] Nigel Turner, however, insists that Paul was "fairly innocent" of such influences.[169] The debate could be expanded considerably by reference to other issues and scholars, but to no useful purpose; the debate is purely academic. We will never know the extent to which Paul was formally or informally schooled in Hellenistic traditions. Even those who deny any direct influence admit that there are at least superficial or coincidental resemblances. But these prove nothing conclusively. The prescriptions of rhetoricians for the most part merely gave literary form to the obvious and commonsense procedures that a gifted natural orator, like Paul, would naturally have followed.[170]

Like Plutarch, Paul is sensitive to the potential offensiveness of autobiographical remarks. He excludes every human self-claim before God as

---

[168]Betz, *Plutarch's Ethical Writings*, p. 378. This assumption is the undercurrent in all of his studies of Paul. See esp. idem, *Der Apostel Paulus und die sokratische Tradition: Eine exegetische Untersuchung zu seiner "Apologie": 2 Korinther 10-13* (BHT 45; Tübingen: Mohr [Siebeck], 1972).

[169]Nigel Turner, *Style*, vol. 4, *A Grammar of New Testament Greek*, by James Hope Moulton (Edinburgh: Clark, 1976) p. 81.

[170]Cf. John Dillon's critique in Hans Dieter Betz, *Paul's Apology II Corinthians 10-13 and the Socratic Tradition*, Protocol of the 22nd Colloquy, ed. Wilhelm Wuellner (Berkeley: Center for Hermeneutical Studies in Hellenistic and Modern Culture, 1975) p. 18.

improper and inadmissible (cf. e.g., Rom 3:17; 1 Cor 1:29; 4:7; Gal 6:13-14; Phil 3:2-11). Although the two men are in this respect conceptually similar, their terminology and rationales are different, which should not be surprising in view of their different cultural backgrounds and religious commitments. Paul does not use Plutarch's expressions, περιαυτολογία or ἑαυτὸν ἐπαινεῖν, preferring instead the term καυχᾶσθαι, "to boast" or "to glory," which is not part of Plutarch's normal vocabulary.[171] Paul claims to base his practice not on the conventions enunciated later by Plutarch, but on the authority of an Old Testament dictum, Jer 9:23-24: "Let him who boasts, boast of the Lord," as cited in 1 Cor 1:31 and 2 Cor 10:15 and alluded to elsewhere (e.g., Phil 3:3-4, 10). Following Rudolf Bultmann and William Beardslee, Betz suggests that "the application of this rule is the basis for all Pauline theology, especially his doctrine of 'justification by faith.'"[172] This correctly suggests the importance of Paul's autobiographical remarks, although it probably overstates it.

Bultmann insists, and Betz agrees, that "the basic rejection of self-glorying is not contradicted by passages in which Paul boasts of his work."[173] Whenever Paul writes autobiographically in apparent self-praise, he always does so "inoffensively." He may remove the offensive edge from his self-praise by praising instead his gospel or his apostolic work and ministry (see e.g., Rom 1:16; 11:13-14; 15:15; 1 Cor 9:16-18; 2 Corinthians 3-4, 8:18; 10:13-18; Phil 1:12-18; Col 1:24-19; 1 Thess 1:5, 9; 2:1, 13). Or he may refer also to the achievements of his churches (e.g., 1 Thess 1:2-3:13; Phil 1:3-2:18), to others whose conduct is exemplary (e.g. 1 Corinthians 4; 1 Thess 2:14-16; Phil 2:19-30), and/or to the grace of God, to whom he assigns major credit for his praiseworthy behavior (e.g., Rom 1:4-5; 15:15ff.; 1 Cor 15:10; 2 Cor 1:12, 2:14-3:6; 4:1-12; 12:7-10; 13:3-4; Gal 6:14; Eph 3:7-8; Phil 1:20; 3:3-16; 1 Thess 2:1-4). He also refers exultantly to his sufferings, humiliations, deprivations, and failures (e.g., 1 Cor 1:17; 2:1-5, 2 Cor 4:7-12; 11:21-12:10; Gal 4:12-20; 6:11-17; Eph 3:7-13; 6:18-20; Phil 3:2-4:1; Col 1:24-19; 1 Thess 1:5-6; 2:1-12; 3:1-

---

[171]There is one exception, in his quotation of Pindar (*Moralia* 539C). Betz (*Plutarch's Ethical Writings,* pp. 377-93) cites a number of parallels between the views of Plutarch and early Christians toward self-praise.

[172]Betz, *Plutarch's Ethical Writings,* p. 379. On p. 379 n. 40 he cites Bultmann, "καυχάομαι, κτλ," *TDNT* 3:648-52, and William Beardslee, *Human Achievement and Divine Vocation in the Message of Paul* (SBT 31; Naperville, IL: Allenson, 1961).

[173]Bultmann, "καυχάομαι," *TDNT* 3:650; Betz, *Plutarch's Ethical Writings,* p. 379.

10) rather than to his personal strength and successes, at times in complete sincerity, at others in irony, again in unwitting compliance with Plutarch's advice.

Edwin A. Judge observes that as a consequence of the general neglect of the literature of antiquity, some modern readers of Paul mistakenly conclude from his frequent autobiographical remarks that he was both "pathologically concerned about his own status" and an inveterate hypochondriac morbidly obsessed with his petty misfortunes. The four brief surveys of others in antiquity who wrote autobiographically should serve as antidotes for this gross misconception. Paul's self-praise and self-depreciation conform to the conventions of his time, not ours, and are completely inoffensive when measured by ancient standards. In fact, 2 Corinthians 10-13 appears to be a partly serious, partly ironical, complaint that he was despised for his failure to boast in a fashion expected of one of his importance and position (see especially, 2 Cor 11:20-21).[174] He pales by comparison to the super-apostles (2 Cor 11:5; 12:11). But Paul refuses to compare himself with those who commend themselves beyond measure by such comparisons (2 Cor 10:12-13; cf. Gal 6:3-4). When he does indulge in some paradoxical boasting for the Corinthians' benefit, he apologizes, "I have become a fool. But you forced me to it, for I ought to have been commended by you" (2 Cor 12:11a-c). He insists that he writes them not to protect his image nor, at last, to secure their withheld praise, but for their edification (see 13:6-8).

Perhaps more epidemic than the popular misconception of Paul's autobiographical remarks to which Judge calls attention is the scholarly tendency to interpret them utilizing the technique of "mirror reading." The correct recognition that Paul's letters were occasioned by real life situations in his churches has been used as the basis for assumptions and conclusions about this situation which owe more to the interpreter's ingenuity than exegesis. As chapter 2 seeks to demonstrate on the basis of Paul's letter to the Galatians, the assumptions of "mirror reading" are completely implausible when consistently applied and lead to historical reconstructions which are equally unprovable apart from these assumptions.

---

[174]Judge ("Paul's Boasting," pp. 46-47) recommends (pseudo-) Dio Chrysostom (*Oration* 37) as a "quick antidote" to the assumption of ego mania, and the younger Seneca, Aelius Aristides, and Marcus Aurelius as contemporary examples of hypochondriac literature.

Although Paul may be unique within the New Testament in his extensive autobiographical statements, he is not unparalleled in antiquity. The broader attention this chapter has given the autobiographical phenomenon in antiquity confirms this. As a result of his comparison of the attitudes of Plutarch and Paul toward autobiographical self-praise, Betz suggests that "Paul's 'self-presentation' in his letters is a literary problem which needs further investigation."[175] The present dissertation, in its concentration on Galatians and 1 Thessalonians, is only a first step in the long overdue investigation of the phenomenon and function of autobiographical statements in the Pauline Corpus.

---

[175]Betz, *Plutarch's Ethical Writings*, p. 379 n. 43.

2

A Critique of Existing Approaches to Paul's Autobiographical Remarks Demonstrated in Galatians

INTRODUCTION

It has become a widely held assumption that Paul writes autobiographically only infrequently, incidentally, reluctantly, and almost always apologetically. Georg Eichholz probably represents the consensus of critical New Testament scholarship in his opinion that, because Paul's *bios* is quite unimportant to him, he characteristically makes autobiographical references only when he has been provoked by his opponents to do so.[1] As a result, the answers that are generally given to the question of the function of Paul's autobiographical remarks depend on the answers to two prior historical questions: Who are Paul's opponents? and, What are their

---

[1] Georg Eichholz, *Tradition und Interpretation: Studien zum Neuen Testament und zur Hermeneutik* (Theologische Bücherei; Neudrucke und Berichte aus dem 20. Jahrhundert, Band 29, Neues Testament; München: Kaiser, 1965) pp. 175-76. Albert Schweitzer, *The Mysticism of Paul the Apostle,* trans. William Montgomery (New York: Seabury, 1968 [German Original 1931]) pp. 325-27; Günther Bornkamm, *Paul,* trans. D. M. G. Stalker (New York: Harper & Row, 1971) p. xiv; Jost Eckert, *Die urchristliche Verkundigung im Streit zwischen Paulus und seinen Gegnern nach dem Galaterbrief* (Biblische Untersuchungen, 6; München: Pustet, 1971) p. 211; Leander E. Keck, *Paul and His Letters* (Proclamation Commentaries; Philadelphia: Fortress, 1979) p. 27. Cf. e.g., Hans Dieter Betz, *Galatians: A Commentary on Paul's Letter to the Churches in Galatia* (Hermeneia; Philadelphia: Fortress, 1979) pp. 67 n. 103, 68 n. 113, 69 n. 126, and 222 n. 30; J. Christiaan Beker, *Paul the Apostle: The Triumph of God in Life and Thought* (Philadelphia: Fortress, 1980) pp. 3-7; Ernst Käsemann, *Commentary on Romans,* trans. and ed. Geoffrey W. Bromiley (Grand Rapids: Eerdmans, 1980) p. 20.

charges against him? The adequacy of the underlying assumption, granted the status of fact, is seldom questioned.

The repeated efforts of historical-critical scholarship to find a solution to the problem of the identity of Paul's opponents and the nature of their charges are to be applauded. For such a solution would greatly enhance our ability to interpret his letters. Existing solutions have generally been arrived at on the basis of presumably relevant information found outside the letters and on the basis of assumptions about the character of Paul's argumentative approach within the letters. Thus, they are, at best, historical reconstructions having only a greater or lesser degree of certainty. But some legitimate historical questions remain unanswerable. This does not affect the need for critical exegesis of the letters, only the confidence in its results. Historical reconstruction, however intimately related to exegesis, is not to be identified with it. But when it is made the basis for exegesis, it directly affects the correctness and adequacy of the interpretation it sponsors. This chapter seeks to demonstrate that the usual approach to the presumed charges against Paul, identified on the basis of extra-textual data and the assumptions of the technique known as "mirror reading," is fundamentally mistaken. Consequently, most existing approaches to the function of Paul's autobiographical remarks are called into question.

Perhaps the one Pauline letter that has suffered most at the expense of this approach is his letter to the Galatians. In order to focus my critique on specifics as opposed to generalizations, I have chosen to concentrate on the doubtful character of most existing solutions to the literary problem of "Paul's 'self-presentation' in his letters" in this one letter. If the unsatisfactory character of "mirror reading" as a basis for determining the identity of Paul's opponents, their presumed charges, and on this basis, the function of his autobiographical remarks, can be demonstrated on the basis of Galatians, it would appear to be even less satisfactory as applied to the other letters.

A. PAUL'S GALATIANS OPPONENTS

Largely as a result of the influential legacy of Ferdinand Christian Baur and the Tübingen School,[2] the unexamined historical assumption of

---

[2]It is unnecessary to rehearse here Baur's views and the evaluations of his critics. See Werner Georg Kümmel, *The New Testament: The History of the Investigation of Its Problems,* trans. S. McLean Gilmour and

nearly all studies of Galatians, at least until recently, has been that Paul's autobiographical remarks respond apologetically to specific accusations made by invading Judaizing opponents, against which he defends the independence and/or consistency of his gospel and apostleship. Tübingen's multicolored literary hypotheses were long ago abandoned, but the uncomplicated picture Baur painted with them of early Christian history continues to have admirers. Although recent challenges to certain aspects of the widely accepted historical and methodological presuppositions[3] should have made their status as virtual postulates increasingly doubtful, these hypotheses continue to dominate the interpretation of Galatians.[4]

Howard C. Kee (Nashville: Abingdon, 1972) pp. 120-84; Stephen Neill, *The Interpretation of the New Testament, 1861-1961* (London: Oxford University Press, 1964) pp. 19-60; Johannes Munck, *Paul and the Salvation of Mankind,* trans. Frank Clarke (Richmond, VA: John Knox, 1959) pp. 69-86. The attractiveness of Baur's account of early Christianity as the struggle between its Judaizing and Hellenistic interpretations is its sheer simplicity. Simplistic solutions to complicated problems die hard. The presumption of a single and pervasive Judaizing opposition to Paul makes it possible to fill in gaps in one letter by appeal to others. Despite Walter Schmithals' (*Paul and the Gnostics,* trans. John E. Steely [Nashville: Abingdon, 1972] p. 64 n. 152) protests to the contrary, his alternative merely replaces Tübingen's pan-Judaizing with pan-Gnosticizing opponents (Robert McL. Wilson, "Gnostics—in Galatia?" *SE* 4 [Berlin: Akademie, 1968] pp. 358-64; Philipp Vielhauer, *Geschichte der urchristlichen Literatur* [Berlin: de Gruyter, 1975] pp. 120-24).

[3]Several recent studies briefly survey representative research in Galatians since the time of F. C. Baur on the question of Paul's opponents and their accusations: Schmithals, pp. 24-42: "The Heretics in Galatia"; Franz Mussner, *Der Galaterbrief* (HTKNT 9; Freiburg: Herder, 1974) pp. 11-29: "Die Gegner"; George Howard, *Paul: Crisis in Galatia. A Study in Early Christian Theology* (SNTSMS 35; Cambridge: Cambridge University Press, 1979) pp. 1-7.

These studies do not address the question of the function of Paul's autobiographical remarks, however, nor do they agree among themselves on an agenda for future research. Although they fail to propose a new and convincing alternative, they do succeed in demonstrating the inadequacy of long-secure methodological assumptions and historical conclusions. Thus, their shared dissatisfaction with the scholarly consensus helps prepare the way for a new solution.

[4]Betz's recent commentary, despite the "novelty" of its rhetorical analysis, in many ways revives the ghost of Baur. He depends on literary hypotheses reminiscent of Tübingen, e.g., in his appeals to the pseudo-

Scholarly inertia, not persuasive exegesis, appears to be responsible for the strength and longevity of the consensus.

A full investigation of the Galatian opponents is well beyond the scope of the present dissertation.[5] Until recently, virtually all exegeses of Galatians presumed that they were "Judaizers," probably intruders, from Jerusalem.[6] Now, however, a number of scholars recognize that this presupposition is more problematic than previously suspected.[7] Despite some disaffection for the old consensus, no new alternative vies to replace it. Franz Mussner doubts that full agreement will ever be reached on such issues because the words of the apostle are insufficient to categorize the opponents clearly as representatives of any known group within Judaism or early Christianity. The difficulty in identifying the opponents arises from an obvious fact, the implications of which are only infrequently acknowledged—our only source of certain information about the Galatian opponents is Paul's obviously one-sided, probably exaggerated, even distorted characterizations of them. Since they were well known to the Galatians, disinterested objectivity would have poorly served his purposes.[8]

All we know of the Galatian situation must be surmised from Paul's description, unless the evidence of Acts is permitted, in which case the opponents must certainly be identified as non-Christian Jews. Our information about the opponents can be no better than his. It may be that even

---

Clementine literature as a basis for identifying Paul's Galatian opponents (see his quotations, pp. 331-33, and index of references, pp. 344-45).

[5]This has been attempted in several recent dissertations: John J. Gunther, *St. Paul's Opponents and their Background. A Study of Apocalyptic and Jewish Sectarian Teachings* (NovTSup 35; Leiden: Brill, 1973); John Gale Hawkins, *The Opponents of Paul in Galatia* (Ph.D. dissertation, Yale University; Ann Arbor: University Microfilms, 1971); Bernard Hungerford Brinsmead, "Galatians as Dialogical Response to Opponents" (Ph.D. dissertation, Andrews University, 1979); idem, *Galatians—Dialogical Response to Opponents* (Chico, CA: Scholars Press, 1982). For additional bibliography, see Betz, p. 5 n. 22.

[6]See F. C. Baur, *Paul the Apostle of Jesus Christ, His Life and Work, His Epistles and His Doctrine*, 2 vols., trans. A. Menzies, from the 2nd ed. by Eduard Zeller, Theological Translation Fund Library (London: Williams & Norgate, 1873-75) 1:261.

[7]Robert Jewett, "The Agitators and the Galatian Congregation," *NTS* 17 (1970) 198. This is confirmed by Hawkins' dissertation (see esp. pp. 5-85).

[8]Mussner, pp. 24-27.

the designation "opponents" is inappropriate. Certainly Paul opposed some he identified as troublemakers and perverters of the gospel, but this need not imply that they had previously opposed him.[9] It is not certain whether the opposition was mutual or only from Paul's side, whether the intentions of the "opponents" were malicious or well-meaning, whether they understood Paul's position correctly or not and vice versa, whether they came from within or outside the Galatian communities, whether the traditional designation "Judaizers" is appropriate or not, and whether or not they had ties—whether official or unofficial—to Jerusalem. Any decision inevitably depends on meager and ambiguous textual evidence, utilization of data outside the letter, and/or conjectural hypotheses. Such historical reconstructions would scarcely seem to be secure bases for exegesis of the letter or for determining the function of Paul's autobiographical remarks. But it is on this basis that most existing approaches proceed.

B. THE CHARGES AGAINST PAUL
1. The Scholarly Consensus

The usual method of identifying Paul's opponents rests on the assumption that his autobiographical remarks in Galatians 1 and 2 respond apologetically to specific accusations and/or allegations against his person, office, and/or message. This widely practiced interpretive mode, which

---

[9]Munck (p. 132) proposes that it is not unreasonable to suppose that it was on the basis of their own reading of the LXX that Paul's Gentile converts in Galatia discovered the requirement of circumcision in the Law. They sought this rite not to reject Paul's teaching but to improve upon their salvation. Hendrikus Boers ("Genesis 15:6 and the Discourse Structure of Galatians," SBL Seminar paper, 1976), independently of Munck, proposes a similar explanation. If Galatians 3 rehearses Paul's earlier preaching in Galatia (so Nils Alstrup Dahl, "Paul's Letter to the Galatians: Epistolary Genre, Content, and Structure," SBL Paul Seminar paper, 1973, pp. 54, 63-64), his readers would have come to consider the status "sons of Abraham" and the inheritance of God's promise to him as "constitutive of Christian existence." Since Gen 15:6, "And [Abraham] believed the Lord; and he reckoned it to him as righteousness," is not far removed from Gen 17:10: "This is my covenant . . . between me and you and your descendants after you: Every male among you shall be circumcised" (RSV), the Galatians could easily have discovered the passage on their own, without the intervention of Judaizers (Boers, p. 22).

we call "mirror reading,"[10] may be illustrated by Joseph B. Tyson's study, "Paul's Opponents in Galatia."[11] Although his approach is representative, he makes the widely held assumptions more explicit than most. The reasoning proceeds as follows: The sharp polemic of Galatians requires the assumption that it is a defensive or apologetic letter.[12] If it is such a letter, "then a *sine qua non* for understanding its occasion is the analysis of the letter to determine Paul's specific answers to charges and to opposing teachings,"[13] which are not explicitly stated. If Paul's defenses imply specific charges, then "in most cases, the charge can be seen by taking the negative of the defense"[14] or "by reversing the defensive statements."[15]

These statements are generally found in some or all of Paul's antithetical formulations (οὐ—ἀλλά, "not--but") particularly in Gal 1:1 and 10-12, but also in the denials in 2:5, 17 and/or 21.[16] The designation "mirror

---

[10]A frequent designation, see e.g., Dahl, p. 39. Howard (p. 7) refers to it as "the charge approach."

[11]Joseph B. Tyson, "Paul's Opponents in Galatia," *NovT* 10 (1968) 243-50.

[12]Ibid., p. 243.

[13]Ibid., pp. 245-46.

[14]Ibid., p. 244; cf. pp. 249-50.

[15]Ibid., p. 249.

[16]Many interpreters simply take this for granted. Among those who explicitly defend the claim that charges by Paul's opponents are presumed by such antithetical formulation and/or denials are commentators of quite different persuasions from the nineteenth century to the present: Friedrich Sieffert, *Handbuch über den Brief an die Galater* (MeyerK, 7th ed.; Göttingen: Vandenhoeck & Ruprecht, 1886) p. 26; Theodor von Zahn, *Introduction to the New Testament*, 3 vols., trans. Melancthon Williams Jacobus, et al. (Edinburgh: Clark, 1909) 1:167; Wilhelm Lütgert, *Gesetz und Geist: Eine Untersuchung zur Vorgeschichte des Galaterbriefes* (Gütersloh: Bertelsmann, 1919) pp. 42ff.; Hans Lietzmann, *An die Galater*, 3rd ed. (HNT 10; Tübingen: Mohr [Siebeck], 1932) pp. 3, 6; George S. Duncan, *The Epistle of Paul to the Galatians* (MNTC; London: Hodder & Stoughton, 1934) p. 4; Hermann Wolfgang Beyer & Paul Althaus, "Der Brief an die Galater," *Die kleineren Briefe des Apostel Paulus* (NTD 8; 6th ed.; Göttingen: Vandenhoeck & Ruprecht, 1953) pp. 4, 8; Heinrich Schlier, *Der Brief an die Galater*, 4th ed. (MeyerK 7, 13; Göttingen: Vandenhoeck & Ruprecht, 1965) p. 27; Schmithals, pp. 19, 56; Hawkins, pp. 312, 341; Mussner, pp. 12-13, 45-46; and Bengt Holmberg, *Paul and Power* (Philadelphia: Fortress, 1980) pp. 15-16.

Few deny that these constructions require the presumption of under-reading" arises from the presumption that what Paul denies, his opponents have asserted and/or that what he asserts, they have denied. Some interpreters, most notably Walter Schmithals, go so far as to assume that the opponents affirmed for themselves what they denied for Paul and vice versa.[17]

Largely on this basis, the presumed charges against Paul are uniformly assumed to have been either or both of the following: (1) that he was dependent for his gospel and/or his apostolate on men in general and/or on the original apostles in particular—based on a "mirror reading" of 1:1 and/or 11-12;[18] or (2) that he was too independent, in that his was an

---

lying, specific charges. Betz (p. 56 n. 115) writes that "not every rhetorical denial is an accusation turned around," but he assumes that some are, esp. 2:17 (pp. 119-20). Sieffert (p. 50), whom Betz cites as supporting this view, rejects only the method's applicability to 1:10.

[17]Schmithals, pp. 19-20.

[18]Among those who claim that Paul was charged with being dependent for his gospel and/or apostolate on men or more specifically the original apostles are: Baur, 1:264, 114-15, 118-19; J. B. Lightfoot, *The Epistle of St. Paul to the Galatians* (Grand Rapids: Zondervan, 1972 [reprint of the 1865 ed.]) pp. 27, 28, 73; Heinrich August Wilhelm Meyer, *Critical and Exegetical Hand-book to the Epistle to the Galatians*, trans. G. H. Venables, ed. Henry E. Jacobs (Meyer's Critical and Exegetical Handbook; New York: Funk & Wagnalls, 1884) p. 4; Sieffert, pp. 16, 26; R. A. Lipsius, "Galaterbrief," *HKNT*, 2nd ed. rev. (Freiburg: Mohr [Siebeck], 1892) 2:8; Frederic Rendall, "The Epistle to the Galatians," *The Expositor's Greek Testament*, 5 vols., ed. W. Robertson Nicoll (London: Hodder & Stoughton, 1897-1910), 4:139-40, 149; Alfred Loisy, *L'Epître aux Galates* (Paris: Nourry, 1916) p. 31; Wilhelm Bousset, "Der Brief an die Galater," *Die Schriften des Neuen Testaments*, 3rd ed., vol. 2, ed. Johannes Weiss (Göttingen: Vandenhoeck & Ruprecht, 1917-18) 2:32; Ernest de Witt Burton, *A Critical and Exegetical Commentary on the Epistle to the Galatians* (ICC; New York: Scribners, 1920) liv; Anton Fridrichsen, "Die Apologie des Paulus Gal. 1," *Paulus und die Urgemeinde*, ed. Lyder Brun & Anton Fridrichsen; Giessen: Töpelmann, 1921) pp. 53-76; Lietzmann, p. 3; Duncan, p. 4; Herman Nicolaas Ridderbos, *The Epistle of Paul to the Churches of Galatia*, trans. Henry Zylstra (NICNT; Grand Rapids: Eerdmans, 1953) pp. 15-16; Beyer-Althaus, pp. 1, 4; C. K. Barrett, "Paul and the 'Pillar' Apostles (Galatians 1:11-2:14)," *Studia Paulina in honorem Johannis de Zwaan* (Göttingen: Vandenhoeck & Ruprecht, 1953) pp. 78-104; Erich Klostermann, "Zur Apologie des Paulus Galater 1,10-2,21," *Gottes ist der Orient. Festschrift für Otto Eissfeldt zu seinem 70. Geburtstag* (Berlin: Evangelische Verlagsanstalt, 1959) p. 84; Schlier, pp.

incomplete or otherwise deficient compromise of the true gospel—based on a "mirror reading" of 1:10.[19] As incompatible as these two charges may appear to be, they are often correlated on the assumption that it was claimed that Paul's gospel was derived from the Jerusalem leaders and that he had subsequently and wrongfully compromised this gospel, relaxing some of its rigor in order to make it more appealing to his Gentile audience,[20] and perhaps, thereby "to enhance his apostolic grandeur."[21] Every "mirror reading" reconstruction of the charges is a variation on, or combination of these. There is considerably less agreement on how these charges are to be interpreted.

2. The Inadequacies of the Consensus

If it were established that Paul's autobiographical remarks in Galatians 1 and 2 responded to one or both of the traditional charges, it could be concluded that their function was most certainly apologetic. But as

---

27, 42; Schmithals, pp. 19-20, 20 n. 21, 23-25, 29, 42, 56; idem, *Paul and James*, trans. Dorthea M. Barton (SBT 46; Naperville, IL: Allenson, 1965) pp. 38, 40-42, 63, 70; Tyson, pp. 249-50; Jewett, p. 208; Eckert, pp. 164, 181, 203-6, 208, 210, 212-14, 233; Bornkamm, pp. 18-19; Hawkins, p. 284; Mussner, pp. 45-46, 65; F. F. Bruce, "Further Thoughts on Paul's Biography," *Jesus und Paulus: Festschrift für Werner Georg Kummel zum 70. Geburtstag*, ed. E. Earle Ellis & Eric Grässer (Tübingen: Mohr [Siebeck], 1975) p. 21; Holmberg, pp. 15-16; Beker, pp. 45-46. In addition to 1:1 and 11-12, some commentators appeal to 1:20 and 2:14 in support of the charge of dependence.

[19]Among those who claim that Paul was charged with excessive independence and compromising the true gospel, whether through dishonesty or inconsistency, in order to persuade men are: Lightfoot, pp. 27-29, 79; Rendall, p. 139; Loisy, pp. 60-61; Burton, pp. liv, 31; Fridrichsen, pp. 53-76; Lietzmann, p. 6; Duncan, p. 20; François Amiot, *Saint Paul: Epître aux Galates. Epîtres aux Thessaloniciens* (VS 14; Paris: Beauchesne, 1946) p. 115; Beyer-Althaus, p. 1; Tyson, p. 249; Jewett, p. 208; Eckert, pp. 203-5, 213, 217; Bornkamm, p. 18; Dahl, p. 44; Mussner, p. 62; Traugott Holtz, "Die Bedeutung des Apostelkonzils für Paulus," *NovT* 16 (1974) 110-48, esp. 116; John Howard Schütz, *Paul and the Anatomy of Apostolic Authority* (SNTSMS 26; Cambridge: Cambridge University Press, 1975) p. 130; Betz, pp. 57, 88, 136; Beker, pp. 43-46. In addition to 1:10, some appeal also to 2:3, 17, 21; and 5:11 in support of this charge.

[20]Compare nn. 18 and 19.

[21]Beker, p. 43.

George Howard correctly objects, "A look at the context of Galatians, however, shows that the traditional understanding of Paul's purpose in this section is problematic."[22] It is problematic because (a) the usual charges are unsatisfactory for both literary and historical reasons; (b) the "mirror reading" approach itself suffers from insuperable fallacies and deficiences; (c) it misunderstands the significance of antithetical constructions; and (d) it depends on a demonstrably mistaken genre conception.

a) The Unsatisfactory Character of the Traditional Charges

(1) The Charge of Dependence

The most widely held view of the function of Paul's autobiographical remarks in Galatians 1 and 2 builds on the assumption that here Paul defends himself against the charge of dependence on men (see Gal 1:1, 11, 12). The obvious focus on his dealings with the Jerusalem church, and particularly with those who were apostles before him (see 1:17, 18, 19, 22; 2:1, 2, 6-10, 11-14), has led most interpreters to assume further that these are the men upon whom he has been accused of being dependent. Howard appears to be correct in his assessment that "although it is clear that Paul was independent of the Jerusalem apostles, his method of presenting the events of his Christian career creates doubts as to whether his purpose in recording them was actually to prove his independence."[23] Nils Alstrup Dahl argues that "the theory that Paul defends his independence may explain Gal 1:12-21, but it does not work in chapter 2," nor does it adequately "relate to the Galatian controversy and the content of the letter as a whole."[24]

Several features of 2:1-10 make it extremely unlikely that his autobiographical remarks were intended either to prove his independence from Jerusalem or his parity with the leaders there.[25] Paul's choice of words in

---

[22]Howard, p. 21.
[23]Ibid.
[24]Dahl, p. 38; cf. Boers, p. 51.
[25]Paul refers to οἱ δοκοῦντες, "the influential men" (Walter Bauer, *A Greek-English Lexicon of the New Testament and Other Early Christian Literature*, 2nd ed., trans. and ed. William F. Arndt, F. Wilbur Gingrich, and Frederick W. Danker [Chicago: University of Chicago Press, 1979], s.v. δοκέω 2b) in 2:2 and (twice) to οἱ δοκοῦντες στῦλοι εἶναι, "those who seemed to be pillars," i.e., James, Cephas, and John, in 2:9. Scholars

recounting his second visit to Jerusalem in 2:1-10 is remarkably unguarded. Despite his insistence that he went up to Jerusalem by divine appointment, i.e., "by a revelation," he admits that he went with some apprehension concerning the possible outcome (2:2).[26] "I laid before them the gospel which I preach among the Gentiles (i.e., privately before the influential men) in order that I should not be running nor had run in vain" (2:2b).

Although it may be doubted that he was actually concerned that this gospel might be invalidated—this was unassailable (see 1:8-9),[27] his words certainly admit the interpretation that it was a real, though unthinkable, possibility that these men might invalidate his "running" (cf. 4:11; Phil 2:16; 1 Thess 3:5).[28] Here, as elsewhere in his letters, Paul uses the metaphor of "running" to describe his missionary work among the Gentiles, the object of which was to establish truly Christian churches, i.e., communitites which demonstrated the truth of the gospel.[29] Had Jerusalem denied his Gentile converts fellowship and full Christian standing alongside Jewish believers, his labors would have been for nothing.[30]

---

are divided as to whether these two designations refer to the same or different people (see the bibliography in Holmberg, p. 23 n. 57), and whether Paul speaks sincerely or ironically (Holmberg, p. 25 n. 66).

[26]This is suggested by the usual meaning of μή πως (see Bauer, s.v. μή πως, who, however, offers Gal 2:2 as a singular example of a use of the expression to introduce an indirect question). Holmberg (p. 23) notes that all the other uses of μή πως in Paul's letters (1 Cor 9:27; 2 Cor 2:7; 9:4; 11:3; 12:20; Gal 4:11; 1 Thess 3:5) "refer to a real, not hypothetical possibility." See F. Blass and A. Debrunner, *A Greek Grammar of the New Testament and Other Early Christian Literature,* trans. and rev. Robert W. Funk (Chicago: University of Chicago Press, 1962) §370; and Betz, pp. 87-88 and his notes.

[27]*Contra* Schlier, pp. 67-69; and Klaus Wengst, "Der Apostel und die Tradition," *ZTK* 69 (1972) 155-56; John J. Pilch, *Paul's Usage and Understanding of Apokalypsis in Galatians 1-2: A Structural Investigation* (Ph.D. dissertation, Marquette University, 1972; Ann Arbor: University Microfilms, 1973) pp. 99-100.

[28]Holtz, p. 126; Holmberg, pp. 26-27.

[29]Victor C. Pfitzner, *Paul and the Agon Motif: Traditional Athletic Imagery in the Pauline Literature* (NovTSup 16; Leiden: Brill, 1967) pp. 99-108; Otto Bauernfeind, "τρέχω," *TDNT* 8:225-35; Holtz, pp. 122, 126; Eckert, p. 211; Schütz, p. 139.

[30]See Burton, pp. 72-73; Pierre Bonnard, *L'Epître de Saint Paul aux Galates* and Charles Masson, *L'Epître de Saint Paul aux Ephesiens* (CNT 9;

Whether in presenting his gospel to the influential men, Paul sought their approval[31] or only their opinion,[32] he made "an unnecessary concession," if he was intent on defending his independence.[33] Had this been his purpose, he might have expressed himself differently, or said nothing about his apprehension.

Is it without significance that Paul and Barnabas went to Jerusalem rather than the Jerusalem leaders to Antioch (2:1; cf. 2:11; Acts 15)? or, that it was James and Cephas and John who extended the right hand of fellowship to the two delegates and not vice versa (2:9)? or, that they recognized him and his gospel and not the reverse (2:7, 9)? Peter Stuhlmacher considers these facts to imply that Jerusalem was regarded as the mother church, whose approval Paul required.[34] J. Paul Sampley, however, suggests the possibility that whereas the Jerusalem leaders may have understood the handshake, in line with Jewish tradition, to symbolize "the superiors acknowledging the subordinates," Paul and Barnabas understood it as in Roman law to symbolize the formation of an equal partnership.[35] Both parties thereby sealed their agreement to divide their labor in the common task of preaching the one, shared gospel.[36]

The formulation of the agreement in 2:7-8 contains markedly non-Pauline langauage, suggesting, perhaps, the influence of the official "decree." In it Peter's mission to the Jews is given the explicit designation "apostolate" while Paul's mission is given no specific title.[37] This omission may be explained as an example of a quite normal ellipsis, only if it is not his objective to prove an independence and equality that was being denied

---

Neuchatel: Delachaux & Niestlé, 1953) pp. 37-38; Bornkamm, p. 37; Mussner, p. 103.

[31] Schlier, p. 66; Holtz, p. 121.

[32] See Bauer, s.v. ἀνατίθημι.

[33] Dahl, p. 46; cf. Boers, p. 51.

[34] Peter Stuhlmacher, *Das paulinische Evangelium I. Vorgeschichte* (FRLANT 95; Göttingen: Vandenhoeck & Ruprecht, 1968) pp. 87, 282; cf. Schlier, p. 68 n. 3. Dieter Georgi (*Die Geschichte der Kollekte des Paulus fur Jerusalem* [Theologische Forschung Wissenschaftliche Beitrage zur kirchliche-evangelischen Lehre, 38; Hamburg-Bergstedt: Reich, 1965] p. 17) denies that this implies any inequality.

[35] J. Paul Sampley, *Pauline Partnership in Christ* (Philadelphia: Fortress, 1980) p. 50 n. 50; see pp. 27-30. Cf. David R. Catchpole, "Paul, James and the Apostolic Decree," *NTS* 23 (1977) 428-44.

[36] Ibid., pp. 25-30.

[37] See Betz, pp. 96-98 and the accompanying notes.

him. Paul insists upon the mutuality of the two missions and assumes their equality, but makes no attempt to establish this.[38]

The logical incoherence of Gal 2:4-8 has long been recognized. It is marked by at least two anacolutha (grammatically broken constructions), in which Paul begins but fails to complete his line of thought in vv. 4 and 6. Numerous explanations have been offered,[39] but what he intended to say is far from certain.[40] He claims, on the one hand, that the influential men added nothing to him (2:6), and admits, on the other, that he willingly complied with their request to undertake a collection for the poor (2:10). Again this was an unnecessary concession, if it was Paul's object to establish his independence. Why does he mention it? Dieter Georgi suggests that, despite the Galatians' initial involvement in the collection (1 Cor 16:1-4), they subsequently withdrew, and thus they threatened to do what the pillars had not (2:2-10)—cause his missionary work to be in vain (4:11).[41]

If, as most modern commentators assume, the accounts of the apostolic council in Acts 15 and Gal 2:1-10 refer to the same event, the central issue was neither the equality and independence of Paul's (and Barnabas') apostolate, nor the collection. The controversial issue there was presumably whether Paul (and Antioch) could continue the practice of not circumcising Gentile converts. It was the possible challenge to this which he feared could have disqualified his missionary labors (2:2).[42] This, perhaps, explains Paul's reference to his Greek companion Titus not being compelled to be circumcised in 2:3. But if circumcision was the central issue at the Jerusalem conference, and since it certainly was relevant to the problem Paul confronts in Galatia (see 3:1-5; 5:2-12; 6:11-16), it is remarkable how little Paul says of his success in persuading Jerusalem to condone his practice, and how obscurely. It is strange that he fails to generalize from Titus' experience to its applicability to all Gentiles and to

---

[38]Holmberg, p. 28. Ernst Haenchen (*The Acts of the Apostles,* trans. R. McL. Wilson, et al. [Philadelphia: Westminster, 1971] pp. 465-66) argues that Paul's presentation gives the somewhat deceptive impression that his position at the council was as an equal with the pillars. See the discussion in chapter 3 section C 7 below.

[39]See Betz, pp. 89-105 and the accompanying notes.

[40]In any event, some tension would appear to exist between Paul's assertions and the apostolic decree of Acts 15:23-29. See Haenchen, pp. 468-72.

[41]Georgi, pp. 30ff.; Sampley, pp. 31ff.

[42]Betz, p. 85; Holmberg, pp. 19, 24.

note the decision of the Council to that effect. Clearly Acts' account of
the proceedings, apart from the mention of the decree, would have served
Paul's generally presumed purposes better than his account.

Morton Smith explains this anomaly as due to Paul's embarrassed
reluctance to admit that Titus was circumcised.

> His embarrassment appears in the incoherence of his clauses
> and his attempt to conceal the fact even while he concedes
> it: Titus was not compelled to be circumcised, but (he volun-
> tarily underwent the operation, in order to prevent scandal)
> because of false brethren . . . to whom we did not give way
> (in essential matters of doctrine, as opposed to concession of
> practice).[43]

Although most interpreters conclude that Titus was not circumcised,
Paul's formulation is certainly far too unguarded to assume that his denial
responds "to rumors circulating in Galatia to the effect that he had indeed
yielded in part."[44]

If the thing Paul feared (2:2b) in his visit to Jerusalem was the split of
the church into two factions, as the consensus maintains,[45] Paul's report

---

[43]Morton Smith, "Pauline Problem: Apropos of J. Munck, 'Paulus und
die Heilsgeschichte,'" HTR 50 (1957) 118. For an earlier example of this
recurrent interpretation, see Schweitzer, p. 157. Peter Richardson ("Pauline Inconsistency: 1 Corinthians 9:19-23 and Galatians 2:11-14," NTS 26
[1980] 359) considers it an open question whether Titus was circumcised.

[44]The view of Hans Conzelmann, History of Primitive Christianity,
trans. John L. Steely (Nashville: Abingdon, 1973) p. 85.

[45]The agreement has often been claimed to demonstrate the great
store Paul placed on the unity of the church (so e.g., Haenchen, p. 465;
Conzelmann, pp. 84-87; Schlier, pp. 65-66). His apprehension in 2:2 is
assumed to refer to his concern that if agreement were not reached, the
church would have been divided into Jewish and Gentile factions. But as
Betz correctly insists "a 'unity of the church' never existed before or after
the conference" (p. 99 n. 399). Even if it had, the agreement meant its
practical dissolution, for the compromise, that was achieved between the
delegates of Antioch and the leaders at Jerusalem came at the expense of
a third group Paul calls the "false brothers" (p. 82). The agreement,
authorizing or confirming a division of labor, recognizing two separate but
equal missions for Peter and Paul to the Jews and Gentiles, respectively,
offered the solution of coexistence, not integration. Whatever unity
resulted, consisted in the maintenance of the status quo and the recognition that, since God was obviously at work in both missions (2:7-9), mutual

of the Antioch incident in 2:1ff. is inexplicable. Why would he in 2:1-10 insist on the unity of the church, only to concede its practical collapse in the next pericope? The juxtaposition of Gal 2:1-10 and 2:11-21 opposes the consensus view that Paul defends his independence from the Jerusalem leaders while maintaining that they recognized his parity with them.[46] This is true whether 2:11-14 reports an incident that is chronologically subsequent to 2:1-10, as most assume,[47] or is only so aranged for rhetorical reasons.

The disagreement between Paul and Peter at Antioch on its face would appear to imply the failure and undoing of the Jerusalem agreement,[48] whatever that agreement may have involved. At the very least, it left some crucial questions still unresolved.[49] It would also seem to suggest that the unity of the church was of lesser value than the supreme value for Paul—the truth of the gospel (see 2:5, 14).[50] There appears to be no other plausible explanation of Paul's words in Gal 2:11-21 than that he "was clearly of the opinion that in denying the gospel Peter and the rest of the Jewish Christians were also denying the agreements reached in Jerusalem."[51] But more importantly, by failing to adhere to the truth of

---

toleration and cooperation were called for. Cf. Eckert, p. 221; Holmberg, p. 21; Sampley, p. 48. For a discussion of the difficulties of either a geographical or ethnic interpretation of the division of labor, see Haenchen, pp. 466-68; and Holmberg, p. 30 and nn. 94-100.

[46]Howard, p. 21.

[47]There are a few notable, but unpersuasive, exceptions. See the references in Betz, p. 105 n. 436.

[48]So e.g., Jacques Dupont, "Pierre et Paul à Antioche et à Jerusalem," RSR 45 (1957) 42-60; 225-39; Bornkamm, p. 40; Howard, p. 21; Richardson, pp. 347-62.

[49]Bornkamm, p. 40. Whether the two parties to the agreement interpreted it differently (Sampley, pp. 50 n. 50, 27-30), whether Paul "grossly over-interpreted" its implications (Holmberg, p. 21; see pp. 22, 31), whether even he and Barnabas understood it differently (Holtz, p. 114), whether he alone remained true to it (Betz, p. 82), and/or whether it was simply impracticable and finally unworkable (Stephen G. Wilson, The Gentiles and the Gentile Mission in Luke-Acts [SNTSMS 23; Cambridge: Cambridge University Press, 1973] p. 187) cannot be established.

[50]Holtz, p. 123; cf. Holmberg, p. 26.

[51]Bornkamm, p. 46. He adds, however, that "Paul's view of the matter was unwarranted" (p. 46). That Paul's judgment was hasty and that "the breach with Peter and Barnabas was not full and final" may be suggested by 1 Cor 9:6. Down to the end, Paul sought to promote the unity of the

the gospel, Cephas nullified the grace of God. This prepares for Paul's application of his autobiographical remarks to the situation in Galatia, where his readers were precipitously close to rendering his work vain (4:11) by falling away from grace (5:2-4) and by disobedience to the truth of the gospel (5:7).[52]

Why does Paul report the Antioch incident at all? Up to this point his autobiographical narrative (1:13ff.) has focused upon his activities in Jerusalem. Events elsewhere are mentioned, but only briefly, and perhaps only to indicate that they did not take place in Jerusalem. The outcome of the Antioch incident is never told. Did Paul succeed in dissuading Cephas and the other Jewish-Christians from withdrawing from table fellowship with the Gentiles?[53] Is his silence any more evidence that his position did not succeed in Antioch than his near silence with respect to the Jerusalem conference, where the evidence of Acts 15 seems to indicate that the cause of the Gentile-Christians prevailed? Or is it Paul's intention at the conclusion of his autobiographical narrative to imply that he stands alone as the only advocate of the freedom and equality of the Gentile-Christians as opposed to the other Jewish-Christians? Is this the basis for his appeal in 4:12ab, "Brothers, I beg you, become as I am, for I have become as you are"?

Obviously Paul's autobiographical remarks in Galatians 1 and 2 do not report all the events of his life up to the moment he writes the letter.[54] What is the operative principle of selectivity, and how may this explain his purpose in reporting the Antioch incident? It appears that what 1:18-24; 2:1-10; and 2:11-14 have in common is Paul's three meetings with Cephas, not his contacts with Jerusalem. The "fundamental parallelism"[55] that emerges between the two, as stated in the words of the agreement in 2:7-8, does not consist in their titles or offices but in that both had been divinely entrusted with the gospel. The preceding affirmation in 2:6, that "God shows no favoritism," indicates that what matters is not who one is

church with all his power (p. 48). This may be correct, but it does not explain why he does not mention this reconciliation of differences in Galatians.

[52]Sampley, pp. 36-37. See the discussion in chapter 3 section C below.

[53]Holmberg (p. 34 n. 117) gives a fairly complete list of interpreters who think Paul succeeded and those who think he failed. To the latter group may be added Schweitzer, p. 155; Bornkamm, p. 47; and Richardson, p. 353 n. 24.

[54]See the further discussion of this in chapter 3 below.

[55]Holmberg, p. 30; who follows Eckert, p. 190; and Mussner, p. 116.

or was,[56] but his faithfulness to the gospel (1:8-9). Paul does not insist on either independence from or equality with Cephas or the other pillars but on their mutual subordination to the gospel. Thus, it is not at all surprising that if Paul pronounces a curse on those who preach a perverted gospel (1:8-9), and if he refuses to compromise even momentarily with those who would compromise the truth of the gospel (2:5), that he should oppose Cephas publicly when his practice did not square with the truth of the gospel (2:11-14)—not because Paul wanted now to assert his superiority to Peter, but because he refused to nullify the grace of God (2:21).

Paul considered Peter's departure from Antiochene practice not only a violation of the spirit of the Jerusalem agreement, but an act of unfaithfulness to the gospel.[57] Paul's accusations are remarkably harsh. Because Cephas acted hypocritically, out of fear, and inconsistently with the truth of the gospel, through his power of influence he led others astray and himself stood condemned (2:11-14). Paul reports on the Antioch incident not to depreciate Peter, but to illustrate to his Galatian readers how easy it was to desert the grace of Christ and turn to a different gospel (see 1:6)—Peter and *even Barnabas* did.[58] Thus, although the Galatians were foolish (3:1) in doing so, they were not alone. In chapter 3 below, it is argued that Paul's concern in his autobiographical remarks is not to demonstrate his independence from Jerusalem, nor his equality with Cephas, but his faithfulness to the gospel of grace, as opposed to the Galatians' and Cephas' and even to his own earlier concern to please men. In this he does not defend himself, but establishes his ethos as one who embodies the gospel he preaches, thus demonstrating its truth in practice.

Under careful scrutiny, the theory that Paul's autobiographical account in Galatians 1 and 2 of his "conversion" and subsequent contacts with Cephas and the other "pillars" functions apologetically to establish his independence from men, particularly from Jerusalem, and his recognized equality with the original apostles meets with insuperable difficulties. The

---

[56]Munck (p. 99) suggests that ὁποῖοί ποτε ἦσαν in 2:6, whatever its interpretation, is intended by Paul to coordinate with Paul's own autobiographical description in 1:13—"formerly—now."

[57]Holmberg, pp. 28-33; cf. Richardson, pp. 347-62

[58]See Sampley, pp. 38-39. He (p. 39) notes the parallel in 1 Corinthians 4, where Paul uses "himself and Apollos as the foils by which he would point out and then mend the schismatic tendencies at work in Corinth." Note also the similar technique in 1 Corinthians 9, where Cephas and Barnabas again appear. This would suggest that, despite their disagreements, their relationship was fundamentally sound, rather than strained.

consensus view would also appear to be incompatible with the traditional identification of the opponents as Judaizers from Jerusalem. Judaizers would seem to have approved the kind of dependence the consensus view presumes Paul set out to disprove;[59] they would have found his independence, not his dependence, objectionable.[60] It is the force of this objection which leads Schmithals, who accepts the consensus view of the charge, to reject instead the traditional identification of the opponents as Judaizers.[61] Other interpreters, in order to maintain the consensus view of the charge, despite the negative textual evidence and despite its apparent incompatibility with the traditional identification of the opponents, add or substitute a second charge to/for the first. In either case its substance is essentially the same, that Paul compromised the gospel he received from Jerusalem—he was too independent.[62]

(2) The Charge of Compromise

If the textual evidence does not adequately support the presumed charge of dependence, it is considerably weaker or even lacking for that of compromise. John Gale Hawkins, whose dissertation exhaustively surveys the history of research on Paul's Galatian opponents, suspects that "it is not the data of our epistle but presuppositions about the early church derived from elsewhere which led to the assumption."[63] Whereas the former charge is presumed to be the reverse of Paul's denials in Gal 1:1, 11-12, that his apostolate or gospel are of human origin, the present

---

[59]Dahl, p. 38.

[60]Schmithals, *Gnostics*, p. 24. His reasoning is as follows: ". . . It is inconceivable that the Jerusalem apostles in Galatia accuse Paul of being dependent upon themselves or, in case they were only representatives of the Jerusalem authorities, that like themselves he is dependent upon the apostles in Jerusalem. Therewith one can indeed minimize his authority as an apostle, but certainly cannot reject his gospel. Such an assertion, however much it discredits Paul as an apostle, would rather be a commendation of his gospel" (p. 23).

[61]In order to justify dropping this identification, Schmithals must argue that Galatians 3 and 4 do not directly reflect the Galatian situation, thus compromising the working integrity of the letter in favor of his theory (ibid., pp. 41-43).

[62]Schmithals finds it incredible that "Paul would have had to bother with all the historical apparatus in chaps 1 and 2 in order to confirm this charge" (ibid., p. 25 n. 32).

[63]Hawkins, p. 284.

charge is usually considered the reverse of the implicit denials in 1:10, that he seeks human favor or tries to please men. Because of the exhaustive treatment of the charge of dependence, the charge of compromise may be considered more briefly.

Günther Bornkamm, for example, agrees with Schmithals that "Judaizing opponents would have been the last people to join battle with [Paul] on the issue of dependence on Jerusalem." But he maintains that the opponents were Judaizers and, instead, rejects the charge of dependence. Yet he does not deny that "Paul does in fact stubbornly assert his independence of all human authorities and, in consequence, the divine origin of both his gospel and his office."[64] But the only charge to which Paul responded was that of compromise. "The original apostles had set Paul right, but to his shame he had cut adrift from what he had been taught . . . arbitrarily watering it down, in order to give him an easier approach to the Gentiles (Gal. 1:10)." Paul offers his autobiographical remarks as apologetic proof, on the contrary, that God himself had vouchsafed him, his gospel, and mission and that none other than the Jerusalem apostles had confirmed the truth and legitimacy of his gospel for the Gentiles.[65]

Most interpreters accept both consensuses, that Paul's Galatian opponents were Judaizers from Jerusalem and that he was charged with dependence on Jerusalem, and explain this incongruity by appealing to the second charge: Paul had wrongfully compromised the gospel he had received to make it more palatable to his Gentile audience.[66] Schmithals insists that such explanations run aground on the fact that "not a single word" of Paul's autobiographic apology offers a defense against such an "apostasy,"[67] or "against the charge that he does not bind his communities to the law." On the contrary, one could infer from a "mirror reading" of Gal 5:11 that Paul had been charged instead with still preaching circumcision and thus law.[68] Schmithals mistakenly assumes that simply dropping the assumption of a Judaizing opposition resolves the dilemma in favor of the charge of dependence. He is correct, however, that the traditional identification of Paul's Galatian opponents as "Judaizers" from Jerusalem is not without its problems.[69]

---

[64]Bornkamm, p. 18.
[65]Ibid., p. 19.
[66]Cf. nn. 18 and 19 above.
[67]Schmithals, *Gnostics*, p. 25.
[68]Ibid., p. 42.
[69]See section A above.

Hans Dieter Betz, whose advocacy of the charge of compromise is somewhat unrepresentative of the usual approach, nonetheless provides a recent illustration of how a defense against apostasy may be surmised. He builds his case initially upon the interpretation of Gal 2:17—a notoriously enigmatic verse, as he himself acknowledges.[70] Like many other interpreters, he considers the false and apparently hypothetical argument of Gal 2:17 to contain in fact "the real argument of the opponents."[71] He considers the phrase, "Christ servant of sin," to be a quoted polemical slogan by which Paul's opponents caricatured his Christology. By preaching a gospel without law, Paul, it was said, left his converts outside the realm of salvation and did so in the name of Christ.[72] Paul's opponents criticized his gospel, which differed from theirs only in its lack of "the demand of obedience to the Torah and acceptance of circumcision."[73] Betz supports this interpretation of 2:17 on the basis of a "mirror reading" of 2:3-5, 18, 21; 5:2-12; and 6:12-13.[74]

Gal 2:17 has the form of a conditional sentence, which Betz translates, "If, however, we who are seeking to be justified in Christ are also found to be sinners, is Christ then a servant of sin? This can never be!"[75] The translation itself is not without its problems.[76] But they are complicated by the massive superstructure he builds on so narrow and insecure a foundation.

Betz considers Paul's false argument to be constructed upon two presuppositions: (1) We are seeking to be justified in Christ; and (2) We are also found to be sinners. The first he considers a continuation of the thought of v. 16 and a true condition; the second he regards as a false condition. This arises from his view that to be a "sinner" in the Jewish sense meant to live outside of "the realm of God's salvation" and that "for Paul there is no possibility of conceiving of Christians as living outside of

---

[70]Betz, p. 119 and nn. 55-58. Nearly all the commentaries on the passage, q.v., consider its interpretation the most problematic in the entire letter.

[71]Ibid., p. 113.

[72]Ibid., p. 120.

[73]Ibid., p. 7.

[74]Ibid., p. 27.

[75]Ibid., p. 113.

[76]It is more likely that the anarthrous participle ζητοῦντες should be understood adverbially than adjectivally, as Betz has taken it. Cf. the RSV: "But if, in our endeavor to be justified in Christ. . . ." See also further below.

the realm of God's grace."[77] But this argument against the truth of Paul's second condition arises from Betz's failure to take seriously enough the tense of εὑρέθημεν, which should be translated "we were found" not "we are found." The aorist indicative of the verb would appear to point to the past rather than the present. The discovery that we were "sinners" presumably took place before we were members of the "body of Christ." Thus no necessary contradiction exists and both propositions might be considered correct. Betz's view compels him to see v. 17 as a "correction" of v. 15: "If Jewish Christians are not 'sinners from the Gentiles,' which of course they are not, the same must be true of the Gentile Christians because they, in the same way, are 'seeking to be justified "in Christ." ' "[78]

It is probable that Paul's argument in 2:15-18 anticipates the conclusion he establishes exegetically in chs. 3 and 4. Betz correctly understands these chapters to suggest that the pre-Christian existence of Jews under the Torah was not fundamentally unlike that of Gentiles under the elemental spirits, since both were under sin and, therefore, outside the sphere of salvation (see especially 3:22-4:9).[79] In this light Gal 2:17 may indeed correct a misimpression of 2:15. But it is Paul's insistence that contrary to Jewish notions, Jewish-Christians were also "sinners," and like the Gentiles—outside the sphere of salvation apart from Christ (cf. Rom 3:23-24). Gal 2:21 seals Paul's argument: If the Jew could have found justification under the law, then Christ died needlessly and God's grace is nullified. Since it is Christ who establishes the need of justification for Jews (as well as Gentiles), is he, then, responsible for constituting them as sinners? Paul emphatically denies this, implicitly assigning responsibility instead to the law (see 2:19, 21), as he does explicitly in ch. 3. His concern is to make clear the inability of law either to effect or improve upon the justification Christ graciously brought (2:18-21; cf. 3:1-5, 21; 5:2ff.). Transgression comes not in turning to Christ for justification but in returning to law once it has been abandoned as a way of salvation (2:18). This interpretation of 2:15-21 is not only more apropos to the Antioch incident which incited the discourse than is that of Betz, but it also provides a smoother transition to Paul's address to the Galatians in the balance of the letter.[80] But Gal 2:17 is not really the basis for Betz's theory

---

[77]Betz, pp. 119-20 (quotation from p. 120).

[78]Ibid., p. 120.

[79]Ibid., pp. 161-219. See esp. pp. 179-80, 215-17. "Being 'under the Torah' equals being 'under the "elements of the world" ' " (p. 217).

[80]Cf. Lightfoot, pp. 116-20.

concerning the anti-Pauline opposition in Galatia and of their charges against him, but only the pretext (see section b 2 below).

I do not propose to replace Betz's problematic interpretation of Gal 2:17 with one of my own. The difficulty of the verse calls for modesty on the part of any interpreter. Whatever, it may be determined to mean, Betz is correct that it is a purely hypothetical argument, "constructed only to be criticized and refuted (vv. 18, 21)."[81] As in the diatribe style which Paul often utilizes, here he builds an argumentative barrier to prevent his readers from pursuing a path of thought he knows to be dangerously laden with land mines.[82]

Thus there is no more need to presume that a concrete accusation lies behind Gal 2:17 than behind 1:1, 10, 11, or 12, or any other denial or antithetical formulation in the letter, for that matter. The almost totally arbitrary selection of which of Paul's denials are presumed to respond to opposing accusations is largely responsible for the differences between and among the advocates of "mirror reading." Such differences are not negotiable, so long as the method itself remains unchallenged. There is no textual reason requiring the presumption of charges underlying Paul's autobiographical remarks, and certainly nothing requiring those of the consensus view. Hans von Campenhausen warns that "we should be careful to avoid the mistake of making a conjectural reconstruction of . . . [an anti-Pauline] theology by reversing his own polemical theses."[83] It is possible, as Hawkins recognizes, "to understand Paul's way of speaking simply on the basis of his desire to be emphatic."[84] The view that he responds to charges is purely conjectural, arising in large part from the (I believe, mistaken) genre conception of the letter as apologetic/polemic (see section d below).

---

[81]Betz, p. 119.

[82]This is the way in which Betz (p. 163) understands Gal 3:19-25; "It . . . prevents a wrong conclusion the readers might reach on the basis of the preceding." Cf. Rom 6:1-2. See Rudolf Bultmann, *Der Stil der paulinischen Predigt und die kynisch-stoische Diatribe* (FRLANT 13; Göttingen: Vandenhoeck & Ruprecht, 1910) esp. pp. 67-68, 103.

[83]Hans von Campenhausen, *Ecclesiastical Authority and Spiritual Power in the Church of the First Three Centuries,* trans J. A. Baker (Stanford: Stanford University Press, 1969) pp. 32-33. Even Eckert (pp. 211-12), who assumes that Paul responds to the charge of dependence, admits that our sources are inadequate to determine what the polemics of Paul's Galatian opponents may have looked like.

[84]Hawkins, p. 310.

b) The Problematic Character of "Mirror Reading"

The "mirror reading" approach to the interpretation of Galatians may be challenged on several bases. It may be shown that the methodological presuppositions on which it rests are arbitrary, inconsistently applied, and unworkable. Despite the shared methodology and widespread agreement as to the substance of the charges; as Howard amply demonstrates, "there is no consensus of opinion as to what they actually imply." This diversity in interpretation inevitably results "because the charges themselves are not clearly stated in the letter and come only as implications from some very brief and unclear statements."[85] Even if Howard's conclusion that no direct charges were made at all were mistaken, his challenge to "mirror reading" itself could be sustained. It is an inappropriate, if not entirely fallacious, method for identifying either Paul's opponents or the function of his autobiographical remarks: (1) It does not give sufficient weight to the argumentative origins of Paul's denials and antithetical formulations, while (2) it gives too much weight to extra-textual assumptions. And yet it is on this sandy foundation that most interpretations of Galatians build.

(1) The Argumentative Origins of Paul's Denials

Even those who practice "mirror reading" concede that all Paul's denials need not have had the same origin. Johannes Munck suggests that when Paul denies something he may respond to charges, but he may, instead, respond to misinformation, misunderstanding, or mistaken conclusions of

---

[85]Howard, p. 7. Mussner (pp. 11-29) likewise demonstrates that there is no real consensus among commentators. Dahl, Fridrichsen, and Betz, who are properly critical of the "consensus" understanding of Paul's autobiographical remarks in Galatians 1 and 2 (see below), by their own application of "mirror reading" perpetuate the problem. Their quite different accounts of the charges unwittingly serve to validate Howard's and Mussner's criticisms of the methodology itself.

Although I concur with Howard's rejection of the "mirror reading" approach, I am unable to endorse his alternative, which is, in fact, merely an adaptation of it. What other critics describe as specific "accusations" brought against Paul, Howard identifies as non-malicious "assertions." According to Howard, Jewish-Christian Judaizers from Jeruslalem came to Galatia, mistakenly asserting that Paul shared their views (p. 9). This adaptation involves the same problematic assumption that the position of Paul's "opponents" may be discovered in his denials, whether they are called accusations or assertions.

hypothetical arguments which he himself has constructed in order to refute them. A denial may even serve as an implicit accusation.[86] There is no way to decide conclusively which of Paul's denials respond to real charges and which are merely rhetorical.

Anton Fridrichsen, departing from his own earlier opinion, denies that the antithetical alternatives of Gal 1:1 and 11-12—not from man but from God/Christ—suggest that Paul is answering the charge that he was dependent on others for his gospel.[87] He writes, "I now think this is an unnecessary conclusion."[88] Positively Fridrichsen argues,

> It is Paul himself who formulates the alternative "of man—through Christ." We could sooner imagine that the propagandists in the churches of Galatia attacked Paul on the ground that he was not instructed and authorized by the church-leaders in Jerusalem. Paul's emphatic denial of his being dependent on man is therefore entirely rhetorical and serves only to stress the positive statement: through Christ.[89]

The intention of Paul's denial, according to Fridrichsen, is not to defend himself apologetically but to attack polemically any who would reject his gospel as rejecting "Christ's own word."[90]

Fridrichsen's passing reference to the rhetorical features of Paul's autobiographical remarks merits further attention. Isocrates' reformulation of the charges against him, so as to put himself in the best possible light, represents the standard procedure recommended in rhetorical handbooks for apologetic speeches.[91] This procedure would definitely tend either to distort or obscure actual charges, should they have ever existed. Since we have only Paul's presumed defense and not the accusation, it is necessary to exercise restraint in asserting too confidently that a specific charge existed, and if so, what it may have been. For it has yet to be proved that Galatians is, in fact, an apologetic letter.

---

[86] Munck, pp. 95, 97.

[87] Fridrichsen, pp. 53-76.

[88] Idem, *The Apostle and His Message* (UUA 3; Uppsala: Lundequistska, 1947) p. 21 n. 20.

[89] Ibid.

[90] Ibid.

[91] See chapter 2 section E 2 a above; and Hans Dieter Betz, *Der Apostel Paulus und die sokratische Tradition: Eine exegetische Untersuchung zu seiner "Apologie": 2 Korinther 10-13* (BHT 45; Tübingen: Mohr [Siebeck], 1972) esp. pp. 29-30.

(2) The Influence of Extra-Textual Factors

Implicit, if not explicit, in all historical reconstructions of the Galatian situation is the admission that the letter's text alone provides insufficient data from which the opponents may be described and their charges specified. One must resort to other Pauline letters or nearly contemporary "background" information to supply the lacunae. As necessary as this is in the process of historical reconstruction, it provides a precarious foundation upon which to construct solid exegetical conclusions. The same scholars who properly disown corpus harmonization in the reconstruction of Paul's theology, fail to see the applicability of their criticisms to such historical reconstructions used as a presupposition of exegesis. Thus, for example, if the occasional-contextual nature of Paul's theology calls for caution in Galatians to clarify a theological assertion in Romans,[92] a similar reasonable restraint should be exercised in utilizing the Corinthian correspondence in reconstructing the historical setting of Galatians. Unfortunately, it seldom is. A few examples of the consequences for the interpretation of Galatians may suffice to show the intrinsic problem of such adaptations of "mirror reading."

Schmithals and Willi Marxsen assume that Paul's knowledge of the charges was merely "hearsay."[93] Thus he was relatively uninformed or misinformed about the true nature of the Galatian situation and his opposition there. This might account for the apostle's brief, imprecise, and apparently contradictory statements which have suggested to some

---

[92]For another example, see Betz's (*Galatians,* p. 193) discussion of Paul's position in regard to slavery. "Paul's views cannot always be harmonized. Gal 3:28, 1 Cor 7:21-24, or Philemon may express different positions on the same subject."

As too often happens in historical reconstruction, a virtue is made of an unhappy necessity. John Hurd (*The Origin of 1 Corinthians* [London: SPCK, 1965] p. 15) e.g., laments, "Galatians by contrast with Paul's other letters is difficult to date by means of Acts for the very reason that the letter contains so much biographical information." But the situation is different with respect to Paul's Galatian opponents—we know very little. The absence of solid textual information allows great flexibility in constructing conjectural hypotheses. Only because we know far less about Paul's opponents' views than his, do they appear so much more consistent and predictable than he.

[93]Schmithals, *Gnostics,* pp. 18, 39, 41, 45, 50 n. 108, passim; Willi Marxsen, *Introduction to the New Testament,* trans. G. Buswell (Philadelphia: Fortress, 1974) pp. 57-58.

interpreters[94] that Paul responded to both legalistic and libertine opponents. Although Schmithals and Marxsen deny that there were two groups of opponents historically, they agree that exegetically there appears to be more than one.[95] If Paul did misunderstand his opponents and their charges, to a greater or lesser extent—which would seem to be unlikely,[96] this would seem to make the possibility of any historical deductions from the letter quite remote.[97] The assumption of misunderstanding "creates more difficulties than it solves."[98] Schmithals and Marxsen, however, cherish the farfetched notion that they are in a better position than Paul to understand his opponents, although their only certain information depends on his mistaken and/or misinformed characterizations. Actually such an assumption only succeeds in opening the door to unprovable and unfalsifiable speculations, requiring appeals to real or imagined parallels, which may or may not be relevant for understanding Paul and/or his opponents.

Although Betz cautions about the abuse of "mirror reading," he is perhaps, the best recent example of excessive dependence on presumed parallels in other Pauline letters and other extra-textual data in the interpretation of Galatians. Against those who employ "mirror reading" (differently than he), Betz objects that "not every rhetorical denial is an accusation turned around!"[99] That is,

> Not everything that Paul denies is necessarily an accusation
> by his opposition and not everything that he accuses his oppo-
> nents of doing or thinking represents their actual goals and
> intentions. Paul's references must be interpreted in terms of

---

[94]E.g., Lütgert; James Hardy Ropes, *The Singular Problem of the Epistle to the Galatians* (HTS 14; Cambridge, MA: Harvard University Press, 1929); Raymond T. Stamm, "The Epistle to the Galatians" (Introduction and Exegesis), *IB*, vol. 10 (Nashville: Abingdon, 1953) pp. 429-33.

[95]Marxsen (p. 58) specifically concludes: "As far as exegesis is concerned, therefore, there are two opponents, although historically there was only one." Schmithals (*Gnostics*, p. 41) presumes as much when he suggests that Galatians 3-4 do not address the Galatian situation. Rather Paul "succumbed to a misunderstanding of the opponent's position," taking Gnostics to be Judaizers.

[96]Argued persuasively by Mussner, pp. 231-35.

[97]So Jewett, p. 199.

[98]Dahl, p. 39.

[99]Betz, *Galatians*, p. 56 n. 115.

their rhetorical origin and function before they can be used as
the basis for conclusions about the opponents.[100]

Betz finds "this method of reconstructing the charge . . . questionable,"[101] singling out Schmithals' approach as particularly subject to
"serious methodological objections."[102] But he continues to use "mirror
reading" in his own interpretation—the only real difference being in the
denials he turns around and the accusations he considers reliable indica-
tors of the opponents "actual goals and intentions." He offers no criteria
for determining which of Paul's "rhetorical denials" are reversed accusations and which are not. He challenges "mirror reading," but fails to offer
a persuasive alternative method and continues to practice what he rejects
in principle.

Betz correctly claims that sound methodology requires that the views
of the anti-Pauline opposition in Galatia depend "primarily on the basis of
Galatians alone."[103] But, as Wayne A. Meeks objects, at times Betz

> . . . assumes remarkable clairvoyance about what the oppo-
> nents were thinking and saying about Paul. This knowledge
> does not derive so much from facts teased out of the text of
> Galatians, as from other sources that are assumed to reflect
> the coherent pattern of beliefs of a single, anti-Pauline,
> Jewish-Christian movement.[104]

The Galatian data Betz employs to reconstruct the charges and claims of
Paul's opponents are quite limited. Already noted as of greatest importance is Gal 2:17, which he regards as the "citation of an anti-Pauline
polemic."[105] This notoriously difficult verse allows him a great deal of
flexibility and room for conjecture. Among the other sources to which
Betz appeals to interpret Paul's denials are the pseudo-Clementine literature, various traditions and sources of the Hellenistic world, as well as
other Pauline letters.[106] Betz recognizes that his reconstruction of the

---

[100]Ibid., p. 6.
[101]Ibid., p. 39.
[102]Ibid., p. 6 n. 27.
[103]Ibid., p. 5.
[104]Wayne A. Meeks, review of *Galatians* by Hans Dieter Betz (see n. 1
above) in *JBL* 100 (1981) 306.
[105]Betz, *Galatians,* p. 26.
[106]See e.g., ibid., on 2:17, p. 120 nn. 64, 66.

opponents' charges and the Galatian situation depends in part on intuition[107] and other literary sources. But he argues that this is necessary for several reasons. First, rhetorical denials do not simply contradict the opposition's charges; they transform them in such a way as to "introduce the subject matter on which the defense wishes to be judged." In fact, the defense strategy may call for no mention of the actual charges at all.[108] Second, due to the "scarcity of sources"[109] and "lack of unambiguous evidence,"[110] it is necessary to appeal to supplementary documents.[111] In actual practice, more influential than either the text of Galatians or any other source are Betz's imaginative reconstruction of the Galatian "story" and his theory of 2 Cor 6:14-7:1.

This theory, advanced first in his 1973 article "2 Cor 6:14-7:1: An Anti-Pauline Fragment?" is cited no fewer than thirty times as the basis for crucial exegetical decisions in Betz's 1979 commentary on Galatians.[112] The question mark has effectively given way to an exclamation point and, as Meeks observes, the "conjecture is granted the status of fact throughout the commentary."[113] It is one thing to identify 2 Corinthians as a redactional compilation of fragments of various Pauline letters to Corinth of which 2 Cor 6:14-7:1 is one, or to assert that the passage is non-Pauline or even anti-Pauline, but Betz's claim that it represents the views of Paul's Galatian opponents is totally incredible.[114]

---

[107]See e.g., idem, "Spirit, Freedom, and Law: Paul's Message to the Galatian Churches," *SEA* 39 (1974) 145-60.

[108]Idem, "The Literary Composition and Function of Paul's Letter to the Galatians," *NTS* 21 (1975) 363; see the ancient authorities cited in his notes.

[109]Idem, *Galatians,* p. 8.

[110]Ibid., p. 7.

[111]Ibid., pp. 5-6.

[112]Idem, "2 Cor 6:14-7:1: An Anti-Pauline Fragment?" *JBL* 92 (1973) 88-108. In addition to the 14 references he lists in the index to *Galatians* (p. 343), the article is cited at least 16 additional times; see pp. 5 n. 25, 115 n. 19, 120 n. 30, 250 n. 121, 251 n. 123, 258 n. 63, 300 n. 71, 316 n. 39, 320 n. 87, and 323 n. 118.

[113]Meeks, p. 306.

[114]Meeks' criticism is telling: "The consistency and predictability attributed to the Jewish-Christians is the more remarkable in view of Betz's reluctance even to assume consistency in Paul's own beliefs between Galatians and Romans. Why were the opponents so monolithic,

Betz's interpretation of Galatians also depends heavily on his ingenious reconstruction of the historical situation to which the letter responds, i.e., the "story" which underlies Galatians. Hendrikus Boers suggests that "Betz' theory of the 'story' of Galatians . . . has become so well established in his mind that he has reached a point where, in effect, he almost no longer interprets the text of Galatians, but his theory."[115]

The "story" may be summarized as follows: As a result of Paul's missionary preaching of the gospel, his Galatian converts received the Spirit in an "ecstatic" experience.[116] Following a period of initial enthusiasm

---

while Paul is allowed the liberty to change his mind drastically from one situation to the next? Perhaps because we have so little firm evidence about these Jewish-Christians" (ibid.).

[115]Boers, p. 16. Boers argues that Betz's theory concerning the Galatians' problems with the flesh has almost no textual basis. Despite its claim to depend on the parenesis of ch. 5, this is too general for such a conclusion (p. 15).

[116]Betz, "Spirit, Freedom, and Law," p. 146. Cf. *Galatians*, pp. 5-9. Neither the evidence Betz offers nor the usual understanding of the terms compel us to assume that the Galatians' "initial experience of the Spirit was 'ecstatic' or 'enthusiastic' in nature" (*Galatians*, p. 146; cf. also p. 147). As early as the turn of the century, Ernst von Dobschütz (*Christian Life in the Primitive Church*, trans. George Bremner, ed. W. D. Morrison [New York: Putnam's Sons, 1904] pp. v-vi) warned that not everything in early Christianity may be explained by reference to ecstasy. Betz's understanding of the Galatian story at this point appears to have been influenced by a questionable view of church history going back to Rudolph Sohm's *Kirchenrecht*, I (Leipzig, 1892), which postulates a fundamental "difference between Spirit and law and the existence of a charismatic initial period of the whole of (or at least the Pauline part of) the Church." Numerous recent authorities recognize this view as "one-sided and partly erroneous" and in need of modification in light of later research (Holmberg, p. 149 n. 56).

Gal 3:26-28, according to Betz's own interpretation, "allows us to determine how the Galatians, and also Paul, interpreted the initial experience of the Spirit" ("Spirit, Freedom, and Law," p. 151). It consisted of "a new self-understanding" in which they had been changed from "ignorance" to "knowledge of God," in which they came to be children of God, and were liberated from slavery to the tyrannical rule of the astral demons, which resulted in a change of their entire way of life, religious, social and cultural (ibid.). Betz contends that the Galatians believed that transgressions/trespasses/sin were incompatible with their experience in the Spirit (ibid., p. 154). If this is correct, their "initial experience of the

the Galatians ran into problems with the flesh which caused them to change their minds about him, his message, and themselves. Their problem was the experience of sin in their daily lives, which they considered to be incompatible with their new existence in the Spirit.[117] Unable to cope with these problems "under the terms they were familiar with through Paul's teaching," they were impressed by the solution offered by other Jewish-Christian missionaries.[118] Paul's law-free gospel, by turning Christ into a "servant of sin" (2:17) commits his followers to Satan's realm and makes of them helpless transgressors (2 Cor 6:14-7:1). The solution the opponents offered was acceptance of circumcision, and conscientious observance of the Jewish Torah, apart from which there was no salvation. It was the Galatians' decision "to accept the recommendations of Paul's opponents" which led him to write his letter.[119]

The "story" in its major aspects arises naturally enough from the text itself; it is Betz's explanation of these aspects which is most suspect. And it is not what happened, but why and how, that is in dispute. Certainly Paul founded the Galatian churches, and some time after his departure at least some of his converts changed in such a way as, in his view at least, to be near deserting him, his gospel, and God. Some agitators stood behind the desertions. As to their origin and identity, what they did and why, we are uninformed. That the enticement to desert came from invading Jewish-Christian missionaries and that the opportunity came from the Galatians' problems with the flesh cannot be textually substantiated.

Betz's principle is sound, that "everything we want to know" about the story of Paul's Galatian churches must be carefully reconstructed on the basis of the letter itself, with no help from any other source.[120] In practice, however, he fundamentally and heavily depends on conjectural

---

Spirit" might be more appropriately characterized as religious, soteriological, or ethical, but need not be labeled "ecstatic" or "enthusiastic."

[117]Betz, "Spirit, Freedom, and Law," p. 154.

[118]Ibid., p. 153. Betz's account of their views is neither clear nor consistent. On the one hand, he insists that "except for the demand of obedience to the Torah and acceptance of circumcision, their 'gospel' must have been the same as Paul's" (Galatians, p. 7). On the other hand, he claims that these Jewish-Christian opponents of Paul held a theology diametrically opposed to his, which, remarkably enough has been preserved in its essence in an anti-Pauline fragment, 2 Cor 6:14-7:1 ("Spirit, Freedom, and Law," pp. 54-55).

[119]Ibid., p. 155.

[120]Ibid., p. 145.

assumptions with respect to the pseudo-Clementine literature and especially 2 Cor 6:14-7:1. Although it may be conceded that speculation and
imagination are essential parts of historical reconstruction,[121] exegesis
of the text itself remains of primary importance. That one's prior view of
the historical context in which a piece of literature emerged decisively
co-determines its interpretation is a permanent legacy of the historical-
critical method. But the highest priority of historical criticism has always
been to interpret the biblical text. It is true, as Rudolf Bultmann reminds
us, that interpretation without presuppositions is impossible. But not to be
forgotten is his further reminder, that questions put to the text which it
refuses to answer should cause us to reexamine our presuppositions. We
may be asking the wrong questions. Any and all assumptions should be recognized as such and not treated as if they are the conclusions of exegesis.
Assumptions, no matter how ingenious, which do violence to or play a
more powerful influence than the text are to be dismissed as a basis for
exegesis.[122]

Despite the precariousness of "mirror reading" in all its various forms,
it is upon the basis of its presumed ability to reconstruct the charges and
to identify the responsible opponents that most explanations of the function of Paul's autobiographical remarks begin. Hypotheses built on hypotheses are hardly the basis for persuasive exegesis. It cannot be proved that
Paul even had "opponents," properly so-called, in Galatia. Furthermore, it
is impossible to say, presuming their existence, whether or not they had
made accusations against him. Again, presuming that they had, it is
impossible to determine the extent of Paul's knowledge of them, and/or
the extent to which his letter to the Galatians refers to them. It appears
to be completely impossible to determine precisely what the content of
the presumed charges was on the basis of Galatians alone.[123] "Mirror
reading" cannot provide a satisfactory answer to the question of the function of Paul's autobiographical remarks because it assumes precisely what
needs to be established. In depending on the questionable consensus view
that he responded to specific accusations, it merely restates the presupposition that Paul apologetically responded to charges in the form of a

---

[121]Ibid.

[122]Rudolf Bultmann, "Is Exegesis Without Presuppositions Possible?"
Existence and Faith, ed. and trans. Schubert Ogden (London: SCM, 1964)
pp. 342-51.

[123]Dahl, p. 48: "The exact content of the allegations can be reconstructed only hypothetically"—which he proceeds to do, differently than
Betz. Fridrichsen (*Apostle,* p. 23 n. 17) offers still another scenario.

conclusion. "Mirror reading" is symptomatic of a more basic problem. As Nils Dahl observed a decade ago, historical questions have so dominated the discussion of Galatians 1 and 2 "that the prior problem of the literary character and scope of Paul's autobiographical statements have often been unduly neglected."[124] The present chapter seeks to substantiate Dahl's diagnosis and to prescribe a remedy for the problem. Chapters 3 and 4 below test the effectiveness of the proposed cure.

c) The Significance of Antithetical Constructions

(1) Non-Pauline Parallels

The major basis for the consensus assumption that Paul responded to charges at all stands or falls with the understanding of his use of antithetical constructions. These are generally assumed without investigation to assert what his opponents denied and/or to deny what they asserted. But that is precisely what needs to be established, not simply postulated, if "mirror reading" is to be sustained. Abraham Malherbe has shown that negative and antithetic self-characterizing formulations were employed by Cynic philosophers to distinguish themselves from charlatans even though no personal attack had been made against them.[125] Applying this to Paul's autobiographical remarks in 1 Thess 2:1-12, Malherbe concludes that "we cannot determine from his description that he is making a personal apology" in reply to specific charges.[126]

Malherbe notes that in the first century A.D. Greco-Roman, eastern Mediterranean world in which Paul moved ". . . transient public speakers were viewed with suspicion. It is understandable that the genuine philosophic missionary would want to distinguish himself from other types without his having explicitly been accused of acting like a particular type."[127] Dio Crysostom, a late contemporary of Paul and a Cynic philosopher and orator (ca. A.D. 40-120), is a good illustration of this phenomenon. In *Oration 32*, in a situation in which "there is not question of his having to defend himself . . . against specific charges that he was a

---

[124]Dahl, p. 36.
[125]Abraham J. Malherbe, "'Gentle as a Nurse', The Cynic Background to I Thess II," *NovT* 12 (1970) 214-15, 217.
[126]Ibid., p. 217; see also pp. 203-4.
[127]Ibid., pp. 204-5.

charlatan,"[128] Dio characterizes himself as "the ideal Cynic in negative and antithetic formulations designed to distinguish himself from them."[129] Although Malherbe considers Paul's autobiographical self-description in 1 Thess 2:1-12 to be "strikingly similar" to Dio's in both form and content,[130] he cautions that these similarities do "not obviate the need to give serious attention to the exegetical problems in I Thess. ii and elsewhere where the same subject is discussed." He concludes that in neither the autobiographical descriptions by Cynic philosophers nor by Paul does the use of "negative and antithetic terms" oblige one to suppose that the description is a "personal apology" or responds to specific charges.[131]

The object of Malherbe's study was to establish the existence of verbal and formal parallels between Paul's self-description—with 1 Thessalonians 2 as a test case—and "the self-descriptions of serious-minded Cynic philosophers."[132] Similar utilizations of antithetical constructions are only one formal parallel he points out. The following study responds in part to his call for serious exegetical attention to this subject in Paul, both confirming and extending his insights. Malherbe's conclusion rests solely on the basis of verbal and formal parallels in the use of "negative and antithetic" formulations by Paul and Cynic itinerant preachers. The only specific examples he cites in Paul are from 1 Thess 2:1-12, though he suggests that similar examples appear elsewhere.[133] Even these antithetically formulated constructions fail to exhaust the instances in 1 Thessalonians[134] and make no mention of Galatians. A more extensive examination of these constructions demonstrates the need for two clarifications of Malherbe's observations. These constructions are by no means strictly uniform,[135] and Cynic preachers did not have a monopoly on the construction.

---

[128]Ibid., p. 205; see 205-16.

[129]Ibid., p. 214.

[130]Ibid., p. 217. Some who share this opinion include: Henry Alford, *The Greek Testament*, 4 vols., rev. by Everett F. Harrison (Chicago: Moody, 1958) 3:50; James Moffatt, "The First and Second Epistle to the Thessalonians," *The Expositor's Greek Testament*, 5 vols., ed. W. Robertson Nicoll (London: Hodder & Stoughton, 1897-1910), 4:26; and Ernest Best, *A Commentary on the First and Second Epistles to the Thessalonians* (HNTC; New York: Harper & Row, 1972) pp. 94-99.

[131]Ibid.

[132]Ibid., p. 204.

[133]Ibid., p. 217.

[134]See also 1 Thess 2:13; 4:7-8; 5:6 and 15.

[135]See George Winer (*A Grammar of the Idiom of the New Testament*,

Existing Approaches   107

(2) Antithetical Constructions in the Pauline Letters,
with Special Attention to Galatians and 1 Thessalonians

The antithesis (ἀντίθεσις, *opposita, contraposita*) is a kind of rhetorical amplification (αὔξησις, *amplificatio*), involving pleonasm (πλεο-
νασμός) and/or correction (ἐπανόρθωσις, *correctio*),[136] by which one or
more negative clause(s) is balanced by a corresponding positive clause. In
Paul's letters, it generally involves an οὐ—ἀλλά, "not—but," contrast. It
has affinities to the antithetical variety of the Hebrew *parallelismus
membrorum*, particularly common in the Old Testament wisdom tradition
and in the teaching of Jesus recorded in the Gospels.[137] It was a characteristic feature of the so-called diatribe style of Hellenistic moral discourses in particular and of the epideictic genre of ancient rhetoric in
general.[138] Since ancient autobiographies ideally pursued a balance
between self-praise and -defense, coupled with ethical objectives, antithetical constructions are not uncommon here either, as chapter 1 above
amply illustrates. The following examples of Pauline antithetical constructions survey those found in Galatians and 1 Thessalonians, the focus
of chapters 3 and 4 below.

(a) Examples. In 1 Thess 2:1b-2a the contrast marked by the construction is only superficially antithetical. Paul calls upon the Thessalonians to
recall that his visit to them was not in vain (ὅτι οὐ κενὴ γέγονεν) but
(ἀλλά) that he was bold in God to preach the gospel. In Paul's subsequent

---

7th ed., ed. Gottlieb Lünemann, rev. and trans. J. Henry Thayer [Andover:
Draper, 1874] p. 55), who devotes a great deal of attention of the various
nuances of antithetical constructions—"rather overmuch" attention,
according to A. T. Robertson (*A Grammar of the Greek New Testament in
the Light of Historical Research,* 3rd ed. [New York: Doran, 1919] p.
1166). See also E. W. Bullinger, *Figures of Speech Used in the Bible*
(London: Eyre & Spottiswoode, 1898) pp. 715-19, 909-11.

[136]Bullinger, pp. 715-19, 909-11; see also Norbert Schneider, *Die
Eigenart der paulinischen Antithese* (Hermeneutische Untersuchungen zur
Theologie, 11; Tübingen: Mohr [Siebeck], 1970) pp. 8-15, on the role of
antitheses in ancient rhetoric.

[137]BDF, §485; cf. 491.

[138]See Bultmann, *Stil,* pp. 19, 22, 24, 29, 79-85; George L. Kustas,
Diatribe in Ancient Rhetorical Theory, ed. Wilhelm Wuellner (Protocol of
the 22nd Colloquy; Berkeley: Center for Hermeneutical Studies in Hellenistic and Modern Culture, 1976) pp. 10 n. 30, 43, 44, 46.

description of his preaching in 2:4bc the contrast is more clearly marked: "We preach, not to please men, but God . . . " (λαλοῦμεν, οὐχ ὡς ἀνθρώποις ἀρέσκοντες, ἀλλὰ θεῷ). As in the case of many other antithetical formulations this example involves an elliptical omission. Ellipsis or brachylogy "in the broad sense applies to any idea which is not fully expressed grammatically and leaves it to the hearer or reader to supply the omission because it is self-evident."[139] Thus if 1 Thess 2:4bc were fully expressed it would read: "We preach not to please men, but we preach to please God." In 2:13 Paul similarly characterizes his preaching as "not a message from men but . . . a message from God." In 4:7, Paul employs the construction in another reminder, this time of his earlier ethical instructions, "God has not called us so that we should be impure, but that we should be holy."[140] Therefore in 4:8 he warns them that whoever rejects this call rejects "not man but God."

Due to grammatical constraints imposed by the non-indicative moods of the exhortations in 1 Thess 5:6 and 15 μή—ἀλλά constructions are required, with no real difference in meaning from the οὐ—ἀλλά antithetical construction. The exhortation in 5:6, "Let us not sleep, . . . but let us watch and be sober" arises as a consequence (see οὖν) of the chiastically formulated antithetical construction in 5:5, which characterizes Christians as children of light and of the day, not of night nor of darkness. Because 5:5 places the positive half first, it does not employ the more usual οὐ—ἀλλά construction, although the force is hardly distinguishable.

---

[139]BDF, §479. BDF distinguishes this from "ellipses proper" (§480).

[140]οὐ . . . ἐπὶ ἀκαθαρσίᾳ ἀλλ᾽ ἐν ἁγιασμῷ. The lack of strict identity between ἐπί and ἐν is typical of such parallelism. Bauer (s.v. ἐπί, II. 1. B) understands the ἐπί clause to indicate the negative purpose or goal of the divine call, "not so that we should be impure." Accordingly, it is not very likely that ἐν ἁγιασμῷ should be understood periphrastically as an adverb modifying ἐκάλεσεν as it is rendered in the RSV: "For God has not called us for uncleanness, but in holiness." Rather ἐν is used for stylistic reasons as a synonym for ἐπί, to indicate the positive purpose or goal of God's call (see BDF, 235.5; Bauer, s.v. εἰς 4). A similar variation between εἰς and ἐπί appears in Gal 5:13. The prepositional phrases ἐν ἁγιωσύνῃ in 1 Thess 3:13 and ἐν ἁγιασμῷ in 4:4 and 7 appear to be fixed, formulaic expressions related to Paul's concern that the Thessalonians should demonstrate their sanctification by not fornicating (4:3; cf. 5:23). See Gordon P. Wiles, *Paul's Intercessory Prayers: The Significance of the Intercessory Prayer Passages in the Letters of St. Paul* (SNTSMS 24; Cambridge: Cambridge University Press, 1974) pp. 63-71.

In 5:15 the exhortation warns, "See that no one returns evil for evil to anyone, but always do good to one another and to all men." A similar exhortation appears in Gal 5:13. Two possible paths, that of flesh and that of spirit, lie open as a consequence of the indicative of salvation—"You were called to freedom" (5:13a; cf. 5:1). The imperative contrasts the improper and proper exercise of this freedom. God's call was "for freedom" (ἐπ᾽ ἐλευθερίᾳ, equivalently τῇ ἐλευθερίᾳ in 5:1),[141] not (μόνον μή) "to give the flesh an opportunity" (εἰς ἀφορμὴ τῇ σαρκή)[142] but (ἀλλά) "through love to serve one another."

Basically similar antithetical constructions appear in 1 Thess 2:3-4a, 5-7; and Gal 1:1, 11-12, 16c-17; 4:14; 5:6; 6:15. They are similar in that the positive ἀλλά clause is preceded by more than one negative clause. Thus it is also an example of παραδιστολή, a form of anaphora, the use of repetition for rhetorical effect.[143] Gal 1:1, 16c-17; and 4:14 employ οὐ—οὐδέ—ἀλλά constructions. 1 Thess 2:3-4a has an additional οὐδέ clause.[144] The third negative clause in Gal 1:11-12 has οὔτε rather than οὐδέ in the best manuscripts.[145] 1 Thess 2:5-7 contrasts five οὔτε clauses with the following ἀλλά clause; Gal 5:6 and 6:15 have only two οὔτε clauses followed by the ἀλλά clause. But these variations do not exhaust the differences between the constructions.

The negative side of the contrast in 1 Thess 2:3-4a, "Our exhortation is not from error nor from uncleanness nor from deceit" has only an implicit counterpart in the following ἀλλά clause—it comes from God. The contrast is quite explicit in Gal 1:1, in which Paul characterizes his apostleship as "not [οὐκ] from men nor [οὐδέ] through a man but [ἀλλά] through Jesus Christ and God the Father." This and the similar, though more complicated, construction in Gal 1:11-12[146] are reminiscent of 1 Thess 2:4 and 12 in which Paul similarly characterizes his preaching as divine rather than human. The nearly identical constructions in Gal 5:6 and 6:15— "Neither circumcision nor uncircumcision avails/is anything, but faith working through love/a new creation"—are verbally quite similar to 1 Cor

---

[141]See Betz, *Galatians*, p. 255.

[142]Bauer, s.v. ἀφορμή.

[143]Bullinger, pp. 238-43. Winer (p. 487) refers to these as "adjunctive negatives which divide a single negation into parts."

[144]Some MSS have οὔτε for the second οὐδέ.

[145]Others have οὐδέ. See Winer, p. 492, on this apparent grammatical anomaly of οὐδέ followed by οὔτε.

[146]Detailed discussion of these verses is reserved for the positive chapters 3 and 4 below.

7:19, although they are somewhat formally distinct—"Circumcision is nothing, and uncircumcision is nothing, but keeping the commandments of God [is something]." All three relativize both circumcision and uncircumcision as compared to a higher value which really matters.

A related, but not really antithetical, οὐ μόνον—ἀλλά construction appears in 1 Thess 1:5, 8; 2:8. In 1:5 it characterizes Paul's gospel as coming to the Thessalonians "not only in word, but also in power, in the Holy Spirit, and in great assurance." In 1:8 it refers to the sounding forth of the word of the Lord from the Thessalonians' faith "not only in Macedonia and Achaia, but everywhere." In 2:8 Paul describes his disposition to share with the Thessalonians "not only the gospel of God, but also our own selves." Because the positive half is stated first, the conjunction is καί rather than ἀλλά in Gal 4:18, which is otherwise quite similar: "For a good purpose it is always good to be made much of, and not only when I am present with you."

(b) *Implications*. These examples from 1 Thessalonians and Galatians, which could be supplemented with similar constructions elsewhere in the Pauline corpus,[147] are enough to suggest that such negative and antithetical formulations both inside and outside autobiographical settings are often, if not always, examples of pleonastic tautology used in the interest of clarity which need not be assumed to reply to charges. Although it is conceivable that some rhetorical denials might also respond to actual charges, there are at least two sound reasons this cannot be taken for granted as has usually been the case.

First, some such denials cannot be intelligibly understood to reply to accusations. Although I am convinced this is true in many of the examples cited in Galatians and 1 Thessalonians, examples may be cited from other

---

[147]Further examples of the οὐ—ἀλλά construction include: Rom 9:12, 16; 14:17; 4:10, 19-20 (μή); 1 Cor 6:5-6; 7:35; 9:26-27; 10:13, 33; 14:22 (twice); Phil 2:6-7; 3:9 (μή); 4:17; Col 3:22 (μή) 2 Thess 3:9; etc. Additional examples of the οὐ—οὐδέ—ἀλλά construction include: Rom 2:28-29; 6:12-13 (μή—μηδέ); 9:6b-7, 16; 1 Cor 2:6-7; 5:8 (μή—μηδέ); 2 Cor 4:2 (μή—μηδέ); 7:12; Phil 2:16-17; 2 Thess 3:7b-8; 1 Tim 2:12; 6:17 (μή—μηδέ); cf. Eph 5:3-4. Another example of the οὔτε—ἀλλά constructions appears in 1 Cor 3:7. The οὐ μόνον—ἀλλά construction appears also in Phil 1:29; cf. also μηκέτι—ἀλλά, 1 Tim 5:23. Similar constructions are very infrequent in the NT outside the Pauline corpus, see Matt 5:14b-15; 24:36; Mark 4:22; 13:32; Luke 11:33; 12:24; 18:13; John 1:13; 5:22; 8:43; 16:3-4; Acts 4:32; 7:5.

letters first to avoid prejudicing the case. Is it conceivable that it had been charged, e.g., that Abraham wavered in unbelief (Rom 4:20), or that God allows one to be tempted beyond his strength (1 Cor 10:13); or that Christ deemed equality with God something to be grasped (Phil 2:6-7)? Or should 1 Cor 3:7 be taken to suggest that it had been charged that God mattered little by comparison to his servants? Or does 1 Cor 1:17 require the presumption that Paul had been charged with having been called only to baptize, and not to preach. Far from replying to a specific charge, some denials (e.g., Rom 2:18-19 and 9:6b-7) appear in diatribe style to preclude possible misunderstandings of Paul's arguments. This is most certainly the case with the non-autobiographical examples of the construction in 1 Thess 2:4; 5:5, 6; Gal 5:13, 6; 6:15.

At the very least, it may be concluded that the presumption of charges underlying the denials and antithetical constructions in the autobiographical chapter is unnecessary. Paul's denial in 2:21a may be taken as an illustration. "I do not nullify the grace of God" need not imply "—as I am accused of doing."[148] Equally, if not more, plausible contextual implications might be,"—as I once did" (see 1:10; 2:18-20; 5:11), or "—as Cephus did" (see 2:11-16), or "—as the troublemakers do" (see 1:6-7; 5:7; 6:12-13), or "—as you Galatians are doing" (see 1:6-7; 3:1-5; 5:2-4).

Second, if it is inconceivable that all the numerous examples of denials respond to actual charges—at least no responsible scholar makes this assumption, then on what basis does one determine which ones do? In practice commentators too often have either uncritically endorsed the speculations of earlier scholarship or indulged in some innovative speculations of their own. Speculations are not all bad. But too often they have so prejudiced interpreters that the result has been the ignoring of the text itself. It would seem preferable to begin with the reasonable assumption that the frequent Pauline antithetical formulations reflect his own argumentative style, are his own rhetorical constructions, and not merely adaptations of opposing formulations. Only if they can be shown to be unintelligible on this basis need conjecture take over.

Rhetorical amplification in antithetical constructions is not only pleonastic or tautological but it clarifies by means of self-correction. John Dewar Denniston notes that the most frequent use of ἀλλά as an adversative connecting particle is the "eliminative," in which the true is substituted for the false. "Here usually, in the nature of things, either (a) the ἀλλά clause (or sentence), or (b) the clause to which it is opposed, is

---

[148]As Boers (p. 67) and Betz (*Galatians*, pp. 126-27) assume.

negative."[149] In the various antithetical constructions the negative half usually negates the antithesis of what the positive half affirms, thus making the two halves semantically equivalent although antithetically formulated. The οὐ μόνον—ἀλλά, "not only—but," construction is a fuller equivalent of a simple καί—καί "both—and," construction in which the second half is especially emphasized. The purpose of the rhetorical construction is not really to deny the first statement "but in order to direct undivided attention to the second, so that the first may comparatively disappear."[150]

If antithetical constructions serve the rhetorical function of amplification and correction, their ultimate object is positive rather than negative. That is, they are designed primarily to affirm and only secondarily to deny something. What appears to be denied, however, is not necessarily a specific actual charge but most often a potential or real misunderstanding, which Paul conceives as the antithesis of his affirmation. That is, the denials are epexegetical not polemical in purpose. In other instances the negative may deny positive claims, as opposed to charges, made by real or imagined "opponents," while the positive half affirms the Pauline position. Note that actual charges against Paul need not be at issue in either case. It is Paul who is the rhetorical opponent of the false or mistaken claims. He asserts the correct view as over against the false one. The denied negative and affirmed positive construction by its fullness of expression corrects, clarifies, and confirms its point. If it cannot be proved conclusively that Paul's negative and antithetic formulations do not deny specific charges, it definitely cannot be assumed any longer that they must do so. Barring this assumption, the possibility of confidently identifying the substance of presumed charges would appear to be extremely remote.

d) The Genre of Galatians

Scholars have almost uniformly assimilated Galatians, or at least the autobiographical chs. 1 and 2, to the forensic rhetorical genre, identifying it as apologetic and/or polemic. The assumption that Paul's antithetical formulations and denials defend himself against the accusations of opponents and/or accuse them is a correlate, if not a consequence, of this generic assumption.[151] If this assumption may be shown to be mistaken,

---

[149]J. D. Denniston, *The Greek Particles,* 2nd ed. (Oxford: Clarendon, 1959) pp. ix-xiii.
[150]Winer, p. 497. Cf. Fridrichsen, *Apostle,* p. 21 n. 20.

the entire search for charges can be abandoned. Any identification of Paul's opponents and conclusions with respect to their presumed charges against him depend upon the prior determination that Paul is writing apologetically or polemically.[152] Betz represents a more sophisticated presentation of the scholarly consensus when he claims that "Paul's letter to the Galatians is an example of the 'apologetic letter' genre."[153] John Howard Schütz, on the other hand, doubts that there is "a single sustained apology in the whole of the letter."[154] Is this difference of opinion negotiable or is the determination of genre purely a matter of speculative personal judgment?

Let us examine Betz's evidence. Beyond the consensus assumptions already dismissed as unpersuasive evidence that Paul writes apologetically, Betz's "thesis" rests almost exclusively upon his rhetorical analysis of the letter's structure,[155] a brief summary of which follows:[156]

---

[151]See under the references to the charges in the sources cited in nn. 18 and 19 above.

[152]The difference between apologetics and polemics in the context of early Christianity is minimal so far as Betz is concerned. See his "In Defense of the Spirit: Paul's Letter to the Galatians as a Document of Early Christian Apologetics," *Aspects of Religious Propaganda in Judaism and Early Christianity*, ed. Elisabeth Schüssler Fiorenza (Notre Dame, IN: University of Notre Dame Press, 1976) pp. 99-114; cf. *Galatians*, pp. 222 n. 30 and 68 n. 113.

[153]Idem, *Galatians*, p. 14. Betz refers to both the letter as a whole and the autobiographical (*narratio*) section (1:12-2:14) as Paul's apologetic "self-defense" (*Galatians*, pp. 68 n. 113; 81, 83, 85, 88, 101, 103, 110, 132, 135, 163; idem, *Plutarch's Ethical Writings and Early Christian Literature* [SCHNT 4; Leiden: Brill, 1978] p. 391).

[154]Schütz, p. 127. Albert-Marie Denis ("L'Investiture de la Fonction Apostolique par 'apocalypse,' Etude thématique de Gal., 1,16," *RB* 16 [1957] 335-62; 492-515) argues similarly that Paul does not attempt to make a self-defense in Galatians 1 and 2 but rather to describe his function as an apostle.

[155]Meeks objects: "Betz does not inspire much confidence in his thesis . . . by referring almost exclusively to rhetorical and epistolary theory rather than to specific examples of real apologies and real letters from antiquity. He does not offer us a single instance of the apologetic letter with which we can compare Galatians. We are therefore asked to interpret Galatians as an example of a genre for which no other example can apparently be cited" (p. 306). This is not quite correct. Betz (*Galatians*, p. 15 and the accompanying notes) does refer to Plato's *Seventh Letter* and the so-called "Cynic Epistles" as offering parallels—which upon inspection

Betz claims that his "formal analysis of the letter . . . permits us to arrive at some conclusions with regard to its [generic] function."[157] Certainly ancient rhetorical theory provides the impressive array of Latin nomenclature designating the various sections of the letter and specifies the appropriate tactics and intentions within these sections. But theory cannot determine in practice where the boundaries between these sections are to be drawn. It cannot determine, for example, that 1:10-11 belongs to the *exordium* as opposed to the *narratio*;[158] or that the supposed *propositio*, 2:15-21, is not a continuation of Paul's speech to Cephas begun in 2:14 and, thus, a part of the *narratio*; or that 3:1-5 is not the *propositio*; or that the letter does not lack this optional division;[159] or that the *exhortatio* does not begin in 4:31 or 5:13 rather than 5:1.[160]

---

prove to be more remote than real. He refers also to Isocrates' *Antidosis* and Demosthenes' *De corona*, which, despite their autobiographical content, offer few parallels to Galatians—unless we are to imagine that it is an apology with an encomiastic agenda (see chapter 1 above and 3 below).

[156]See Betz's detailed analysis in "Literary," pp. 353-79 (see n. 108 above); idem, *Galatians*, pp. 14-25; and the analyses at the beginning of each of the seven major divisions.

[157]Idem, *Galatians*, p. 23.

[158]As a transition (*transitus*) between the two sections, it should be considered a part of both. Betz himself considers 1:10-11 an introduction to the *narratio* ("Literary," pp. 364, 366), and can refer to 1:11ff. as the *narratio* (ibid., pp. 363, 366).

[159]Despite Betz's (*Galatians*, pp. 113-14) claim to the contrary. The *propositio* was an optional section according to most ancient handbooks; see chapter 1 section C 1 above.

Betz admits that as a *narratio* 1:12-2:14 lacks the recommended quality of *brevitas*, "brevity." It is not as clear as he would lead us to believe that the nature of the accusations against Paul "requires a long statement of facts . . . to cover his entire history from his birth on."[161] He offers no satisfactory explanation why such expansive autobiographical remarks are required to substantiate Paul's presumed denials of rhetorical sophistication in 1:11-12.

Gal 3:1-4:31 resists rhetorical analysis as the crucial *probatio*, "proof," section. Not at all dissuaded from his thesis by this difficulty, Betz argues, "Paul has been very successful—as a skilled rhetorician would be expected to be—in disguising his argumentative strategy." "The apparent confusion" is designed to conform to "the requirements of Hellenistic rhetoric."[162] Betz himself is such a skillful rhetorician in his analysis of 5:1-6:10, at the same time admitting and dismissing the fact that parenesis has no place in an apologetic letter. He concedes the "rather puzzling" contradictory evidence that "*paraenesis* plays only a marginal role in the ancient rhetorical handbooks." If it played a role in rhetoric at all, it was as the positive species of deliberative oratory or a hybrid of deliberative and epideictic oratory (see the conclusion of chapter 4 below). Betz obscures this anomaly with the inappropriate observation that "philosophical letters . . . very often have at the end a paraenetical section."[163] But do apologetic letters? One wonders what evidence Betz would require as sufficient proof against his theory that Galatians is an apologetic letter.

Betz arrives at his rhetorical outline of Galatians by a mixture of form and content analysis that is no more or less objective than any other similar scholarly attempt to determine the structure of a Pauline letter—only more sophisticated and esoteric. Rhetoric does not provide an objective,

---

[160]Betz (*Galatians*, p. 252) notes that 4:31 points "forward to the beginning of the new section of the exhortation." Despite his dismissal of Otto Merk's ("Der Beginn der Paränese im Galaterbrief," *ZNW* 60 [1969] 83-104) conclusions with respect to the beginning of the parenetic section as "not convincing" (*Galatians*, p. 253 n. 5)—it was persuasive enough to cause Werner Georg Kümmel (*Introduction to the New Testament*, rev. ed., trans. Howard Clark Kee [Nashville: Abingdon, 1975] p. 295) to revise his analysis of the letter—Betz's own analysis is not less problematic, as the following discussion seeks to demonstrate.

[161]Identical arguments in idem, "Literary," pp. 365-66; and idem, *Galatians*, pp. 60-61.

[162]Idem, "Literary," pp. 365-66; and idem, *Galatians*, p. 129.

[163]Idem, "Literary," pp. 375-76; and idem, *Galatians*, p. 254.

external standard by which to analyze structure. A perusal of Betz's authorities, which include Greek and Roman rhetoricians of various historical periods such as Aristotle, Demosthenes, Cicero, Hermogenes, Quintilian, and Plutarch, makes it obvious that rhetoric was neither static nor uniform. If one may judge by the frequency of citation, Quintilian appears to be his major ancient authority. Yet even Betz acknowledges that he often disagreed with one or even a majority of the other authorities.[164]

Given the indisputable existence of different rhetorical schools[165] and Betz's admission that Paul at times complies with Quintilian's recommendations,[166] and at other times departs from them[167] and agrees instead with those of other rhetoricians[168] or appears to mix types or genres,[169] it is obvious that Betz's "apologetic letter" pattern is an eclectic product of his own creation. Not infrequently Betz cites the generalizations of modern rhetorical handbooks rather than, in addition to, or over against certain ancient discussions.[170] He laments the fact that earlier introductions, commentaries, and other studies give little or no consideration to the criteria employed in their outline of Galatians,[171] but is his any less arbitrary? By the circular procedure which Betz employs, it might be possible to demonstrate any number of things, none of which need be either true of or particularly relevant to Galatians. Boers accurately observes that

> In Betz' investigation the model of the apologetic letter is too determinative, so that one cannot escape the impression that frequently it is primarily this model, rather than the text of Galatians itself, that reveals what Paul is supposed to have been about at a particular point.[172]

---

[164]See e.g., idem, *Galatians,* p. 59: "Contrary to others, Quintilian . . ."; p. 61: "Quintilian disagrees . . ."; p. 62: "Quintilian again goes against the practice of the majority of rhetoricians"; p. 44: "There is also disagreement . . . ." Cf. also p. 114.

[165]Idem, "Literary," p. 363.

[166]Idem, *Galatians,* pp. 59, 61.

[167]Ibid., pp. 46, 62, 239-40.

[168]Ibid., pp. 44-45, 62, 240.

[169]Ibid., p. 45.

[170]Ibid., in the notes attached to the analyses sections at the beginning of each of the seven major divisions.

[171]Ibid., p. xiv.

[172]Boers, p. 16.

Even if the rhetorical arrangement of an apologetic letter were wholly distinct from, say, that of a deliberative letter of advice—which it is not, it has already been argued that structural arrangement (*dispositio*) is less decisive than purpose (*causa*) in the determination of rhetorical genre. Essentially identical arrangements were applicable to any of the three rhetorical genres.[173] Thus Wilhelm Wuellner recommends that the best way to determine the genre is to consider the sort of judgment to which Paul's argument is ultimately directed. That is, what decision does he intend his readers to make?[174] Even if Paul's autobiographical remarks or the letter of Galatians as a whole were to be identified as Paul's apology, this need say nothing about function or purpose. Frederick Veltman's extensive study of defense speeches in antiquity demonstrates that "ἀπο-λογία had many functions in ancient times."[175]

It is finally Betz's thesis, not his reasoned conclusion, that is responsible for his understanding of Galatians as an apologetic letter. Thus although his is probably the best recent commentary available on the letter,[176] what he said of Heinrich Schlier's monumental commentary is probably also true of his own: "During the investigation of the letter, . . . it became clear that Schlier had completely, though ingeniously, misinterpreted the letter to the Galatians."[177] E. D. Hisch argues that since "an interpreter's preliminary generic conception of a text is constitutive of everything that he subsequently understands," a mistaken generic concep-

---

[173]See chapter 1 section C 1 above (and chapter 1 n. 42) and the conclusion of chapter 3 below.

[174]Wilhelm Wuellner, "Digressions in I Corinthians: The Rhetoric of Argumentation in Paul," SBL Paul Seminar paper, 1974; idem, "Paul's Rhetoric of Argumentation in Romans: An Alternative to the Donfried-Karras Debate over Romans," *CBQ* 38 (1976) 330-51. Wuellner follows W. J. Brandt, *The Rhetoric of Argumentation* (New York: Bobbs-Merrill, 1970).

[175]Frederick Veltman, *The Defense Speeches of Paul in Acts: Gattungsforschung and its Limitations* (Th.D. diss., Graduate Theological Union, 1975; Ann Arbor: Xerox University Microfilms, 1975) pp. 64, passim.

[176]See the reviews by Meeks, pp. 304-7; and C. K. Barrett, "Galatians as an 'Apologetic Letter,'" *Int* 34 (1980) 414-17. Meeks refers to "the appearance of Betz's commentary on Galatians [as] a major event" (p. 304). Barrett refers to it as "an outstanding achievement in biblical scholarship" (p. 415).

[177]Betz, *Galatians*, p. xiii.

tion inevitably results in misunderstanding.[178] For understanding occurs only as the interpreter correctly grasps the author's controlling generic conception, i.e., the purpose he hoped to achieve in writing.[179] This Betz has not done.

If the consensus assumption that Paul's object in Galatians is that of forensic oratory, to defend himself and/or to accuse his opponents, is mistaken, then the remaining possibilities are either epideictic, to praise or blame, or deliberative, to persuade or dissuade. Schütz argues that Paul does not seek to defend himself against allegations but to compare and contrast himself with his opponents.[180] "Paul appeals to himself and his own circumstances . . . in order to illustrate what he calls the truth of the gospel, not to defend the legitimacy of his apostolic claims."[181] Paul argues from his example to the gospel "to confirm the truth of the gospel."[182] Although Schütz does not employ the terminology of ancient rhetoric, it would appear that he conceives the genre of the letter, or at least the autobiographical section of it, as epideictic, i.e., intended to educate the Galatians as to the truth of the gospel.

Betz recognizes that the *exordium* of Galatians (1:6-11) "expresses his disappointment and disapproval of the Galatians for changing over to the side of the opposition."[183] Thus, Paul's statement of the letter's *causa* is in terms of the "sources of epideictic *exordia* ἔπαινος ἢ ψόγος," praise or blame.[184] Autobiographical references are characteristically epideictic in genre.[185] Even Betz refers to chs. 1 and 2 as justifiable "self-praise."[186] The contrast between freedom and slavery, a common theme of epideictic oratory,[187] obviously plays a significant place in Galatians

---

[178]E. D. Hirsch, *Validity in Interpretation* (New Haven: Yale University Press, 1967) p. 74; see pp. 88-89. "To misconstrue the purposes and emphases of a text is to misunderstand it" (p. 117).

[179]Ibid., pp. 79-81, 99-101. Hirsch insists that only as the author and interpreter share the same "intrinsic genre" (p. 86) or "overarching notion" of the whole (p. 78) may the parts be properly understood.

[180]Schütz, p. 131 n. 1.

[181]Ibid., p. 178.

[182]Ibid., p. 183.

[183]Betz, *Galatians*, p. 45.

[184]Ibid., n. 16.

[185]See chapter 1 section C 2 above.

[186]Betz, *Plutarch's Ethical Writings*, p. 386.

[187]Theodore C. Burgess, "Epideictic Literature," *University of Chicago Studies in Classical Philology* 3 (1900) 157.

(see 2:4; 3:28; 4:1, 3, 7, 8, 9, 22, 23, 24, 25, 26, 30, 31; 5:1, 13). In this case Paul's autobiographical remarks (chs. 1 and 2) and scriptural exposi- tions (chs. 3 and 4) may both be understood as in praise of Christian free- dom, in marked contrast to the slavery advocated by the troublemakers. This provides the basis for the parenesis, "For freedom Christ has set us free; stand fast therefore, and do not submit again to a yoke of slavery" (5:1 RSV). Parenesis, despite its deliberative character, is fully at home in epideictic as the moral or application of the praise or blame.[188] Despite the element of "self-praise," Paul removes its offensiveness (1) by insist- ing that he does not boast in himself but in the cross of Christ (6:14), who is the only source of authentic freedom (1 4; 2:4; 3:10-14, 23-29; 4:4-5; 5:1-13; 6:14-15), and (2) by contrasting this with praise mistakenly assigned to those who subvert freedom (1:6-9; 2:4-5, 11-14; 4:29-30; 5:7- 12; 6:12-13), and are thus deserving of blame.

Whether the autobiographical remarks in chs. 1 and 2 are understood as apologetic or epideictic, the call to imitation in 4:12-20 and the parenesis in 5:1ff. give the letter a decidedly deliberative character. Dahl, who cor- rectly recognizes Galatians as a letter of mixed genre,[189] notes that "it is generally accepted that the symbouletic [= deliberative] genre . . . com- bined two elements, counsels about what to do and . . . not to do. . . . The letter to the Galatians contains both these elements." A major, if not the exclusive "purpose of the whole of the letter is to make these churches dissociate themselves from the intruders and again follow the apostle and his gospel."[190] Despite Betz's generic identification, he also recognizes Paul's ultimate goal in writing the letter to be "to change the Galatians' mind and to reverse their present plans."[191] A choice between these generic possibilities must await the more positive examination of Gala- tians in chapter 3 below.

CONCLUSION

The assumption of a consensus of New Testament scholarship that Paul's autobiographical remarks are almost uniformly apologetic has been challenged in this chapter. It is for others to decide whether the challenge was successful or not. A sustained attack was aimed at the widely prac- ticed art of "mirror reading," although an assault was also launched

---

[188]Ibid., pp. 228-32.
[189]Dahl, p. 35.
[190]Ibid., p. 93.
[191]Betz, *Galatians*, p. 213.

against the underlying generic assumption largely responsible for the consensus, both as applied to a single battlefield, Paul's letter to the churches of Galatia.

It now appears that we know less about the historical situation to which Paul's letter responds than "clairvoyant" scholars would lead us to believe. We do not know precisely how Paul's Galatian opponents are to be identified, or whether "opponents" in the usual sense of the term is even an appropriate designation as applied to the troublemakers there. Perhaps the Galatians innocently inquired of Paul whether the command of the Law concerning circumcision for the sons of Abraham applied to them as his spiritual descendants. Paul's approach to the issue need not have been apologetic. The question, "Should one be circumcised?" might be a topic suitable to epideictic oratory; "Should the Galatians be circumcised?" is a deliberative question.[192] If they simultaneously inquired of the Jerusalem apostles,[193] an explanation might be had for the focus of Paul's autobiographical remarks on his dealings with Jerusalem. But such speculations again move beyond the only certain information we have about the Galatian situation—that supplied by Paul's letter.

What little we do know of this situation does not cohere well with the consensus view of the presumed charges against Paul derived by the various applications of "mirror reading" to the letter. In fact, a careful study of the antithetic formulations and denials utilized to reconstruct these charges, suggests that Paul's "rhetoric" rather than his "opponents" may be responsible for them. The view that he responds to charges is as conjectural as the views concerning his "opponents." The lack of sufficient data about the Galatian situation has encouraged (and permitted) scholars to add to our knowledge with presumed parallels in the other Pauline letters and other extra-textual data, along with heavy doses of speculative historical reconstructions. It is by no means certain that these attempts do not do more to supplant the text of Galatians than supplement our knowledge of it. But it is now time to beat our swords into plowshares, to turn from critique of existing approaches to offer a constructive alternative.

That we know less about the historical situation of Galatians than we have for too long imagined should be a source of relief rather than regret.

---

[192]Cf. F. Forrester Church, "Rhetorical Structure and Design in Paul's Letter to Philemon," *HTR* 71 (1978) 18 and n. 8.

[193]Cf. Wuellner's ("Digressions," pp. 11-12) suggestion of a similar situation as applied to 1 Corinthians.

For if Paul did not respond apologetically to the charges of opponents, the assumption that he did so must bear the blame for encouraging New Testament scholarship in the fruitless cultivation of an unsown field. Now that the weeds have been properly disposed of, perhaps the time is ripe for a fresh crop of investigations. Chapters 3 and 4 below attempt to break new ground in addressing in a constructive way the question that motivates this dissertation—What are the functions of Paul's autobiographical remarks? Although the investigation of Galatians and 1 Thessalonians is an appropriate place to begin, it is hoped that the fruitfulness of the approach will encourage others to put their hands to the plow and not look back.

3

The Function of Paul's Autobiographical Remarks in His Letter to the Galatians

INTRODUCTION

Chapter 3 is a continuation of chapter 2 in its concentration on Paul's letter to the Galatians. But whereas the earlier chapter was largely negative in its purpose, the present chapter is largely positive. Galatians is a particularly appropriate place to begin our constructive investigation of the function of autobiographical remarks in Paul's letters for two very good reasons. First, it is generally recognized that "autobiography" plays a prominent role in the letter. Second, the Pauline authorship and integrity of Galatians have gone essentially unchallenged, apart from a few radical nineteenth-century critics and a rare modern-day disciple.[1] Considerably less agreement exists on the questions of the letter's date and the precise geographical location of the Galatian churches.[2] For despite its extensive autobiographical statements, specific explicit information in answer to

---

[1]See Hans Dieter Betz, *Galatians: A Commentary on Paul's Letter to the Churches in Galatia* (Hermeneia; Philadelphia: Fortress, 1979) p. 1 n. 1. J. C. O'Neill's (*The Recovery of Paul's Letter to the Galatians* [London: SPCK, 1972]) recent attempt to prove that "Paul's original letter has been both glossed and interpolated" (p. 7) is a lone and unpersuasive recent revival of the earlier unsuccessful proposals of Marcion, Baruch de Spinoza, John Locke, Bruno Bauer, and Christian Hermann Weisse (see pp. 7-11). O'Neill arbitrarily rejects numerous short phrases (pp. 73, 85-86) and longer sections throughout the letter: 1:13-14, 22-24; 2:17; 3:23-25, 28; 4:1-3 (and perhaps 4-5), 8-10; and 5:13-6:10 as glosses (pp. 23-71).

[2]See Werner Georg Kümmel, *Introduction to the New Testament* (rev. ed., trans. Howard Clark Kee; Nashville: Abingdon, 1975) pp. 295-304 and the literature cited there.

these questions is lacking, making any conclusion mostly speculative.[3]

The present chapter does not presume solutions to such historical questions, since its concern is primarily literary. Speculative assumptions about the situation which led Paul to write to Galatia have for too long been inordinately decisive in determining the function of Paul's autobiographical remarks. Presuppositions have often simply reemerged as conclusions on the slenderest of textual evidence. Most problematic, as chapter 2 above attempts to demonstrate, has been the assumption that Paul wrote apologetically in response to specific charges by Judaizing opponents from outside the Galatian churches.

The consensus of New Testament scholarship, in presuming the approach of "mirror reading," implies that Paul writes autobiographically because he needs to "correct" apologetically or polemically his opponents' version of his "biography," which directly or indirectly attacks his person, office, and/or message. But it is possible that the "relevance" of Paul's *bios* to the Galatian situation was in his mind only and not inherent in the problem he addresses there. That is, it is he, not the "opponents," who introduces his past life into the discussion, without provocation, but not without ulterior motives. The object of this chapter is to determine, insofar as it is possible on the basis of the textual evidence, what those motives may have been, i.e., how Paul's autobiographical remarks function within the letter to the Galatians.

A. THE TROUBLE IN GALATIA

1. Paul's Divine Apostolate

The epistolary prescript of Galatians (1:1-5) opens, as in all the letters of the Pauline corpus, with the name Παῦλος, "Paul," and, as in all except Philippians and 1 and 2 Thessalonians, is followed by the self-designation ἀπόστολος, "an apostle." Galatians is unique, however, in its negative and antithetic elaboration upon this designation.[4]

---

[3]Betz, pp. 3-5, 9-12. On the whole Betz's cautious and only approximate solutions have much to recommend them.

[4]This unique feature has been responsible in part for the consensus assumption that Paul defends the legitimacy of his apostleship, which, however, is assumed to be normal, not exceptional. This antithetic elaboration is imitated in the pseudo-Pauline Epistle to the Laodiceans. See Edgar Hennecke and Wilhelm Schneemelcher, eds., *New Testament Apocrypha* (2 vols., trans. and ed. Robert McL. Wilson; Philadelphia: Westminster, 1963-65) 2:128-32.

Paul, an apostle—
  not from men
  nor through a man,
  but through Jesus Christ
  and God the Father,
    who raised him from the dead [1:1].[5]

In thus characterizing his apostleship, Paul insists upon its divine origin negatively, by denying a merely human source or mediation, and positively, by affirming it as from Jesus Christ and God the Father. The characterization is too thoroughly Pauline to require the assumption that he responds to the counter-claims or charges of his opponents.[6] It is instead "a carefully composed definition of the concept of apostle"[7] as it applied to him, which anticipates and closely corresponds to the equally carefully composed and considerably more complex definition of the gospel as preached by him in 1:11-12.[8] Furthermore, the underlying "man—God" contrast is a significant antithesis throughout the letter, not only in the autobiographical section.

2. The Troublemakers' Human "Gospel"

Following the prescript in Gal 1:6-9 the letter is introduced (*exordium*) with Paul's ironic expression of astonished disappointment[9] that the

---

[5]The nearly perfect chiastic parallelism between the negative and positive halves is flawed (1) in that ἀπό, "from," does not precede "God the Father" as it does "men," and (2) by the addition of the final descriptive adjectival participle phrase.

[6]Paul frequently insists upon the non-human or divine character of his apostolate and message, cf. Rom 15:15-19; 1 Cor 2:4, 13; 1 Thess 1:5; 2:4, 13. The "man—God" antithesis, so prominent throughout Galatians (see below) appears in other clearly non-apologetic/polemic settings, cf. Rom 2:29; 3:4; 14:18; 1 Cor 1:25; 3:5; 3:1-3; 14:2; 15:47; 2 Cor 4:2; 5:11, 13; 8:21; Phil 2:5-7; 3:3; Col 2:8, 22; 3:23; 1 Thess 2:15; 4:8.

[7]Betz, p. 38.

[8]The correspondence appears to be deliberate and significant, so e.g., Anton Fridrichsen, *The Apostle and His Message* (UAA 3; (Uppsala: Lundequistska, 1947) pp. 21 n. 20, 23 n. 27; John J. Pilch, *Paul's Usage and Understanding of Apokalypsis in Galatians 1-2: A Structural Investigation* (Ph.D. diss., Marquette University, 1972; Ann Arbor: University Microfilms, 1973) pp. 75-76.

Galatians are so quickly deserting "the one who called" them in the grace of Christ and turning to "another gospel" (1:6). This states the source of the problem which determines his purpose in writing (*causa*).[10] At issue is the Galatians' relationship to Paul and the gospel he preached to them (see 1:8-9; 3:1-5; 4:11-20; 5:7-12), but more fundamentally their relationship to God, which he sees as potentially threatened by the existing situation (see 3:4; 4:11, 19; 5:2-4).

It is probable that as usual in Paul's letters the expression "the one who called"—whom the Galatians are now deserting (1:6), refers to God,[11] although it may refer indirectly to Paul as the preacher through whom God's call was mediated (see Gal 4:14).[12] The identical phrase in 5:8 explicitly contrasts the Galatian troublemakers and "the one who called" (see 5:7-12). This same contrast is implicit in Paul's self-correction in 1:7; the desertion, initially described as from a person, whether God or Paul, to a message,[13] is actually to other persons. The Galatians are not really turning to "another gospel," but to some people who are troubling them and wish to pervert the gospel of Christ. They are turning from God to men.[14]

As the letter only gradually makes clear, the desertion amounts to the Galatians' receiving circumcision (see 2:3, 7, 8, 9, 12; 5:2, 3, 6, 11; 6:12, 13, 15). The present tense of the verbs in 1:6-7; 3:3; 4:16-18, 21; 6:12-13 suggests that the desertion is still in progress and that the final step has

---

[9]Nils Alstrup Dahl ("Paul's Letter to the Galatians: Epistolary Genre, Content, and Structure," paper circulated among members of the SBL Paul Seminar, 1973, pp. 14-18, 31) surveys the use of θαυμάζω, the word which introduces the ironic rebuke in 1:6, in ancient epistolary literature. There it mildly reproves negligence, lack of understanding, or some inappropriate or foolish action by the addressees, which is out of character in their essentially good relationship with the addressant.

[10]Betz, pp. 16, 44-45.

[11]Cf. e.g., Rom 8:30; 1 Cor 1:9; Gal 1:15; 1 Thess 2:12; 4:7; 5:24; 2 Thess 2:14.

[12]Somewhat similarly Dahl, pp. 47-48. "In actuality it was of course Paul who did the calling" (p. 48).

[13]Pilch approaches this contrast between person and message from the perspective of 2 Cor 11:4, which refers to "another Jesus." If "the gospel" refers to Jesus Christ, the change is from one person to a different kind of person who does not exist (p. 185).

[14]This is formulated in an οὐκ—εἰ μή construction, which appears to be a variation of the οὐ—ἀλλά construction, see chapter 2 n. 147.

not yet been taken,[15] except by a few troublemakers. But all the Galatians are apparently considering circumcision,[16] and presumably await only Paul's approval. That the desertion is not yet complete is suggested by Paul's uncertainty as to the outcome of the situation expressed in 3:3-5 and 4:8-11, the conditional nature of his blessing in 6:16 and curse in 1:8-9, and his hopeful expectation that, as a result of the letter, the troublemakers will be excommunicated (1:8-9; 4:30; 5:10, 12)[17] and the unity of

---

[15]So e.g., Ernest de Witt Burton, *A Critical and Exegetical Commentary on the Epistle to the Galatians* (ICC; New York: Scribners, 1920) pp. 18-19; Robert Jewett, "The Agitators and the Galatian Congregation," *NTS* 17 (1970) 209; Betz, pp. 45 (and n. 19) and 47.

[16]Jewett (p. 209) points out that 1:6; 3:1-5; and 5:7 imply that the problem was all-pervasive.

[17]Unfortunately, Betz's suggestion (p. 54) that "the whole act of the curse has strong legal overtones and amounts to a ban or excommunication" is not pursued further. He does note that 4:30 implies that Paul excludes from salvation altogether Gentile-Christians who convert to Judaism (p. 251) because this "sets in motion the curse of excommunication issued in 1:8-9" (p. 261, commenting on 5:4). Gustav Stählin ("κοπε-τός, κτλ" *TDNT* 3:854) considers the cruel joke in 5:12 to be a suggestion that the troublemakers should both emasculate and excommunicate themselves (denied by Betz, p. 270 n. 171).

On the whole problem of excommunication in the early church see Rudolf Bohren, *Das Problem der Kirchenzucht im Neuen Testament* (Zurich: Evangelischer Verlag, 1952); Goran Forkman, *The Limits of Religious Community: Expulsion from the Religious Community within the Qumran Sect, within Rabbinic Judaism, and within Primitive Christianity* (trans. Pearl Sjölander; ConBNT 5; Lund: Gleerup, 1972); Walter Doskocil, *Der Bann in der Urkirche* (Münchener Theologische Studien; München: Kommissionsverlag Karl Zink, 1958); and the references cited there.

A comparison of Gal 4:30 and its context with 1 Corinthians 5, which certainly recommends excommunication of the immoral man (see Rudolf Bultmann, *Theology of the New Testament* [2 vols.; trans. Kendrick Grobel; New York: Scribner's Sons, 1951-55] 2:232-35), lends further support to the argument that Paul calls for this drastic measure. In both contexts (1) Paul gives legal sanction to the excommunication by reference to the Old Testament law (Gal 4:30—Gen 21:10-12; 1 Cor 5:13—Deut 17:7); (2) refers to his personal presence and absence (Gal 4:18, 20; 1 Cor 5:3-4); and (3) quotes the proverbial saying about the pervasive influence of leaven (Gal 5:9; 1 Cor 5:6). That excommunication is required suggests that the troublemakers are Christians and probably members of Galatian churches.

Gen 17:4 requires that any uncircumcised male son of Abraham should

the Pauline understanding of Christianity restored (4:19-20, 30; 5:1, 10, 12; 6:1).

It appears that Paul is less concerned to deny the possibility of another gospel than to characterize those who preach it as troublemakers, agitators, and perverters and, as such, subject to the curse repeated in 1:8 and 9, and thus liable to excommunication. If he were concerned to deny that any other "gospel" might exist, he would not have conceded the possibility of a gospel contrary to the one he had preached and the Galatians had received in both 1:8 and 9. Nor would he have referred to man's gospel as opposed to the gospel revealed by Jesus Christ in 1:11-12, nor, to "the true gospel" versus the false in 2:4-5 and 14,[18] nor to his "gospel of the uncircumcision" as compared to Peter's "gospel of the circumcision" in 2:7.[19] These instances, which exhaust the uses of the term εὐαγγελίον, "gospel," in the letter, suggest that Paul recognized the existence of alternate interpretations of the gospel, although he rejected them for the Galatians.[20]

---

be cut off from his people. In Gal 5:12 Paul reverses the logic, expressing the wish that the circumcisers should themselves be cut off. Although this may once have referred to execution, it came to involve only excommunication.

[18]The phrase ἡ ἀλήθεια τοῦ εὐαγγελίου, literally "the truth of the gospel," is interpreted as "the true gospel" by J. B. Lightfoot, The Epistle of St. Paul to the Galatians (Grand Rapids: Zondervan, 1972 [reprint of the 1865 ed.]), p. 107; Burton, p. 86; Betz, p. 92; and others. Paul makes no explicit reference to a "false gospel," but to "false brothers" in 2:4 (cf. 2 Cor 11:26). In 1 Cor 15:15 he refers to the gospel as a "false witness," if Christ has not been resurrected. Ψεῦδος, "falsehood," and ἀλήθεια, "truth," are contrasted in Rom 1:25 and 2 Thess 2:11-12.

[19]Commentators disagree as to the meaning and origin of this twofold distinction. See the discussion in Betz, pp. 96-97.

[20]In Gal 1:8 and 9, Paul does not simply reject the preaching of any gospel, but the preaching of it "to you" (but note the textual variants). This is consistent with 2 Cor 11:4-5, in which Paul notes his fear that the super-apostles' message of "another Jesus," "a different spirit," or "a different gospel" may lead the Corinthians astray. It is not that the super-apostles preach about a different person than Paul does, but that their understanding of him is different. James M. Robinson ("Kerygma and History in the New Testament," Trajectories through Early Christianity, by James M. Robinson and Helmut Koester [Philadelphia: Fortress, 1971] p. 30) suggests that "Paul's Corinthian opponents seem to have accepted Paul's kerygma but promptly departed from Paul's understanding of it." It is my contention that the same is true of the Galatian troublemakers, although the ways in which they perverted his gospel differ.

Paul is not opposed to circumcision as such, it is in fact a matter of indifference (5:6; 6:15). But he is opposed to what its adoption by Gentile-Christians implies—the inadequacy of the death of Christ as the sole means of salvation (2:21; 5:2-4), requiring the "perfecting" of the work of God by the works of man (3:1-5). Paul does not deny that one who is already a Jew may turn to faith in Christ without abandoning his Judaism,[21] for in this case the inadequacy of Judaism to provide salvation is properly recognized (2:15-16; 3:21-22). But he regards a Gentile-Christian's turning to Judaism by receiving circumcision as a supplement to his faith in Christ an act of apostasy, for thereby he deserts the only hope of salvation. Thus, Paul vigorously opposes those, who for whatever motives—he can conceive of only malevolent or unworthy ones (4:17; 6:12-13)—are pressing circumcision upon his converts, as troublemakers, confusers, and perverters of the gospel.

The troublemakers appear to be distinguished from Paul's readers, with the possible exception of 4:21: "Tell me, you who desire to be under the law, do you not hear the law?" (RSV). Normally the readers are addressed in the second person, and the troublemakers mentioned only in the third person. They remain anonymous, identified only as "some people who trouble you and want to pervert the gospel" in 1:7, "anyone preaching a contrary gospel to you" in 1:9, "he who troubles you" in 5:10, "those who unsettle you" in 5:12, "those who wish to look good in the flesh" in 6:12, and "those being circumcised" in 6:13. Certainly Paul's descriptions of the troublemakers are not objective nor need they characterize them or their intentions either as they saw themselves or as the readers saw them. The anonymity is not due to Paul's lack of awareness of their identity. Rather

---

[21]Paul's statements on this in his various letters are not wholly clear and consistent. In Phil 3:2-11, he includes his circumcision as among the bases for fleshly confidence which for the sake of Christ he considered to be "loss," even "refuse" by comparison. But this strong rejection must be balanced against the insistence in Gal 5:6; 6:15; and 1 Cor 7:19 that both circumcision and uncircumcision are matters of indifference. Far from a radical rejection of circumcision, 1 Cor 7:17-24 calls for the status quo: "Everyone should remain in the state in which he was called" (1 Cor 7:20 RSV). Rom 2:25-29, following earlier OT precedents, spiritualizes both circumcision and uncircumcision with adherence to the requirements of the law decisive; while 4:11-12 has faith as the decisive factor. Calling attention to these passages merely points out the problem; a solution remains to be found.

it allows him to be both as inclusive as possible and to place them in the worst possible light.[22] By distancing himself and his readers as far as possible from these troublemakers, he treats the excommunication he recommends for them as if it were already an accomplished fact.

B. THE FORM AND STRUCTURE OF PAUL'S AUTOBIOGRAPHICAL NARRATIVE

Paul's autobiographical "I" appears for the first time in 1:10 and continues to dominate the narrative through 2:21. On any understanding of the letter's structure, the vocative address in 3:1, "O foolish Galatians!" and the subsequent domination of the second person mark the next major transition in the letter. The first person plural in 2:4-5 and 9-10 is clearly exclusive of the readers and has Paul and Barnabas, and perhaps also Titus (see 2:1ff.), as its antecedents. Thus even these verses are autobiographical, though not exclusively so.

A problem is presented when 2:15-17, in which the first person plural is used exclusively of Jewish-Christians, is followed by a resumed first person singular in 2:18-21. Whether the "I" in 2:18-21 refers to Paul alone or is used stylistically of the Christian in general is irrelevant. In the former case, others are not excluded (see 4:12), and in the latter case, Paul is not excluded. In either case, the events described in these verses are of a different order than the events described in 1:10-2:14a, although they are just as obviously to be understood as intimately related to the preceding narrative. Whether or not 2:15-21 was intended by Paul to be understood as a continuation of his speech to Cephas at Antioch in 2:14 cannot be determined with certainty,[23] nor is it crucial to this chapter. In any event, 2:14b and 15-21 share the character of argumentative discourse as opposed to historical narrative.[24]

Paul's autobiographical remarks in Galatians properly begin with 1:13 in which he refers to his "former conduct in Judaism" (τὴν ἐμὴν ἀναστροφήν

---

[22]See Betz, pp. 44-45 and 49 n. 65 on the common practice of avoiding free publicity for one's opponents.

[23]Despite Betz's (pp. 113-14) confident assumption to the contrary.

[24]Hendrikus Boers ("Gen. 15:6 and the Discourse Structure of Galatians," paper presented at the SBL Seminar, 1976, p. 52) observes: "The section 2:15-21 distinguishes itself from those preceding itself by its discursive character. . . . Its connection, on the other hand, is given by the fact that it almost appears to be a continuation of what he said to Peter," i.e., of 2:14b.

ποτε ἐν τῷ 'Ιουδαϊσμῷ, although the essential introduction (*prooemium*) to this narrative (*narratio*) begins in the transitional verses, 1:10-12. Gal 1:10 also concludes and explains the harsh tone of the rebuke-curse in 1:6-9, while in 1:11-12, a disclosure formula (γνωρίζω γὰρ ὑμῖν, ἀδελφοί, "For I make known to you, brothers") introduces Paul's antithetically formulated description of his gospel as divine in nature and origin.[25]

---

[25]In this analysis I depart somewhat from Betz, who refers to 1:13 as the beginning of the *narratio* section proper, which extends through 2:14 (p. 66). He considers 1:10-11 the *transitus*, "transition," which concludes the *exordium*; and 1:12 the thesis which introduces the *narratio* (pp. 16, 46, 59-62). Betz himself recognizes that the conclusion of the *exordium* is apparently reached in 1:9 (p. 46). I prefer to identify 1:10-12 as the *transitus*, which both concludes the *exordium* and introduces the *narratio*. On the significance of the disclosure, see n. 112 below.

The point at which the autobiographical narrative begins is a matter of debate among scholars. Those who identify the beginning as 1:10 include: Frederic Rendall, "The Epistle to the Galatians," *The Expositor's Greek Testament* (5 vols.; ed. W. Robertson Nicoll; London: Hodder & Stoughton, 1897-1910) 4:141; A. Lukyn Williams, *The Epistle of Paul the Apostle to the Galatians* (Cambridge Bible; Cambridge: Cambridge University, 1921) p. xlvii; M.-J. Lagrange, *Saint Paul. Epître aux Galates* (2d ed.; EBib; Paris: Lecoffre, 1926) lx; Hans Lietzmann, *An die Galater* (3d ed.; HNT 10; Tübingen: Mohr [Siebeck], 1932) p. 1; Herman Nicolaas Ridderbos, *The Epistle of Paul to the Churches of Galatia* (trans. Henry Zylastra; NICNT; Grand Rapids: Eerdmans, 1953) p. 19; Erich Klostermann, "Zur Apologie des Paulus Galater 1, 10-2,21," *Gottes ist der Orient, Festschrift für Otto Eissfeldt zu seinem 70. Geburtstag* (Berlin: Evangelische Verlagsanstalt, 1959) p. 84; Alfred Wikenhauser, *New Testament Introduction* (trans. Joseph Cunningham; New York: Herder & Herder, 1963) p. 376; Willi Marxsen, *Introduction to the New Testament* (trans. G. Buswell; Philadelphia: Fortress, 1974) p. 47; Norman Perrin, *The New Testament: An Introduction: Proclamation and Parenesis, Myth and History* (New York: Harcourt Brace Jovanovich, 1974) p. 99; Hendrikus Boers, "The Form Critical Study of Paul's Letters. I Thessalonians as a Case Study," *NTS* 22 (1975) 153.

Those who identify 1:11 as the beginning of the autobiographical narrative include: Lightfoot, pp. 65-66; Friedrich Sieffert, *Handbuch über den Brief an die Galater* (MeyerK; 7th ed.; Göttingen: Vandenhoeck & Ruprecht, 1886) p. 44; Theodor von Zahn, *Introduction to the New Testament* (3 vols.; trans. Melancthon Williams Jacobus, et al.; Edinburgh: Clark, 1909) 1:168; Burton, p. lxxii; A. W. F. Blunt, *The Epistle of Paul to the Galatians* (Clarendon Bible; Oxford: Clarendon, 1925) pp. 34, 38; George S. Duncan, *The Epistle of Paul to the Galatians* (MNTC; London:

The term ἀναστροφή, "way of life, conduct, behavior"[26] which identifies a normal topic (*topos*) in ancient autobiographies,[27] is used only in
Gal 1:13 in the generally accepted letters of Paul.[28] The related verb
ἀναστρεφεῖν, to "act, behave, conduct oneself, or live,"[29] is also used
autobiographically in 2 Cor 1:12. A synonymn, περιπατεῖν, "to walk," also
referring to a deliberately chosen "way of life" or "lifestyle," which goes
beyond mere outward behavior and conduct to express the moral quality
of one's life, is more common in Paul.[30] The emphasis of both terms is
less upon one's *bios* than upon his *ethos*, less upon the particular events of
his life than on the characteristic, customary, even habitual conduct of it.

All this suggests that the following autobiographical remarks should be
understood as in the philosophical lives to be more interested in ethics

---

Hodder & Stoughton, 1934) p. 22 (Duncan, however, treats 1:10 as transi-
tional, belonging neither to 1:6-9 nor 1:11ff.); Lagrange, pp. 4, 9; François
Amiot, *Saint Paul: Epître aux Galates. Epîtres aux Thessaloniciens* (VS 14;
Paris: Beauchesne, 1946) p. 116; Pierre Bonnard, *L'Epître de Saint Paul
aux Galates*; and Charles Masson, *L'Epître de Saint Paul aux Ephesiens*
(CNT 9; Neuchatel: Delachaux & Niestlé, 1953) p. 15; Heinrich Schlier,
Der Brief an die Galater (4th ed.; MeyerK 7, 13; Göttingen: Vandenhoeck
& Ruprecht, 1965) p. 43; Donald Guthrie, *New Testament Introduction* (3d
ed.; Downers Grove: InterVarsity, 1971) p. 469; Dahl, pp. 80-81; Kümmel,
pp. 294-95; Frederick Fyvie Bruce, "Further Thoughts on Paul's Autobiography (Galatians 1:11—2:14)," *Jesus und Paulus: Festschrift für Werner
Georg Kümmel zum 70. Geburtstag* (ed. E. Earle Ellis and Erich Grasser;
Göttingen: Vandenhoeck & Ruprecht, 1975) pp. 21-29; Boers, "Gen. 15:6,"
p. 3.

Other proposals include for 1:12: Albrecht Oepke, *Der Brief des Paulus
an die Galater* (3d ed.; rev. J. Rohde; THNT 9; Berlin: Evangelische
Verlagsanstalt, 1973) p. 28; and Betz, pp. 16-18; and for 1:13: Franz
Mussner, *Der Galaterbrief* (HTKNT 9; Freiburg: Herder, 1974) p. 77.

[26]Walter Bauer, *A Greek-English Lexicon of the New Testament and
Other Early Christian Literature* (2d ed.; trans. and ed. William F. Arndt,
F. Wilbur Gingrich, and Frederick W. Danker; Chicago: University of Chi-
cago Press, 1979) s.v. ἀναστροφή.

[27]See chapter 1 section C 2 above.

[28]Cf. Eph 4:22; 1 Tim 4:12; Heb 13:7; Jas 3:13; 1 Pet 1:15, 18; 2:12;
3:1, 2, 16; 2 Pet 2:7; 3:11. Heb 13:7 recognizes that one's ἀναστροφή may
be imitated.

[29]Bauer, s.v. ἀναστρέφω 2b. See Georg Bertram, "ἀναστρέφω, κτλ,"
TDNT 7:715-17.

[30]See e.g., 2 Cor 4:2; 5:7; 10:2-3; 12:18; Phil 3:17, 18; 1 Thess 2:12; 4:1;
cf. Eph 2:2-3; 4:17, 22.

than history. On the subject of appropriate ethical behavior, Hellenistic moralists, Jewish rabbis (*halakah* refers to "the way to walk"), and Christian preachers were in fundamental agreement.[31] Paul is establishing his divinely determined ethos, not defending his personal or official credentials. Unlike most ancient lives Paul's account of his ἀναστροφή does not include a description of his personal choices deciding his character and profession (ἐπιτηδεύματα).[32] Instead he claims that a revelation of the will of God determined his vocation as a preacher to the Gentiles (1:15-17). The emphasis is clearly on his positive claim—"from God," not its negative counterpart.

The caesura between Paul's brief description of his pre-Christian character and conduct in 1:13-14 and his "conversion"[33] in 1:15-17 is marked by the temporal particle ὅτε, "when," and the following particle δέ, which here has the contrastive force, "but." The juxtaposition of these two sections of his narrative emphasizes the contrast between Paul's former life (ποτε) as a persecutor of the church, motivated by his own zeal, and his present life as a preacher, determined by the good pleasure of God. In 1:15, as has often been suggested,[34] Paul describes his vocation in terms reminiscent of the call narratives of Jeremiah (Jer 1:5) and deutero-Isaiah (Isa 42:6; 49:1-6), implying that in the mind of God, at

---

[31]See chapter 1 section C 2 above. See the discussion in Daniel Patte, *Paul's Faith and the Power of the Gospel: A Structural Introduction to the Pauline Letters* (Philadelphia: Fortress, 1983) chap 2: "Galatians: For Freedom Christ Has Set us Free," pp. 31-86, esp. pp. 67-76.

[32]See chapter 1 section C 2 above.

[33]Betz (p. 69) correctly calls attention to the difficulty of the term "conversion" as applied to Paul. Paul himself prefers to speak of his "vocation" to the apostolate. Since Christianity and Judaism were not at the time distinct religions, Paul's change was from the Jewish sect of the Pharisees to that of the Christians. Krister Stendahl ("The Apostle Paul and the Introspective Conscience of the West," *HTR* 56 [1963] 199-215) emphasizes the psychological differences between Paul's experience and that normally called "conversion." But William Wrede (*Paul* [trans. Edward Lummis; Boston: American Unitarian Association, 1908] p. 6) is also correct that the cataclysmic transition that cut Paul's life "clean in two" and made him thenceforward conscious that he was "another man" is not inappropriately called conversion. Still it is probably best to enclose the term in quotation marks to indicate its special use.

[34]See the references in Betz, p. 69 n. 129.

least, his commission predated his birth.[35] This overlapping of periods
points to a close relationship between 1:13-14 and 15-17, which contrasts
Paul's pre-Christian and Christian ethos. Significantly the contrast is not
between the ethos he claims and the counter-claims or charges of his
"opponents." He is a paradigm of the gospel he proclaims—"By the grace
of God, I am what I am" (1 Cor 15:10a).

The next division of the narrative includes three sections, each introduced by the temporal adverb ἔπειτα, "then," and a verb indicating
movement. Paul's first visit to Jerusalem is recounted in 1:18-20; his
moves to Syria and Cilicia, in 1:21-24; and his second visit to Jerusalem,
in 2:1-10. These sections approximate the πράξεις, topoi of the ancient
lives, describing "actions" which illustrate one's customary character and
purpose, often in three parts.[36] What Paul says and leaves unsaid appears
to be directed toward the comparison that emerges in the final division
between himself and Cephas. But there is no need to assume that he
responds to opposing claims in order to reestablish his authority at Jerusalem's expense.

The final division, 2:11-21, begins like 1:15 with ὅτε δέ, "but when."
Here, however, the opening verse summarizes the entire division which
has at least three distinct stages: first, Cephas' visit to Antioch and his
conduct before (πρό) the men from James came (2:11-12a); second, his
contrasting behavior after they came (ὅτε δὲ ἦλθον) and its consequences
(2:12b-13); and third, Paul's confrontation with and discourse to Cephas
(ἀλλ' ὅτε εἶδον, 2:14, and perhaps also 2:15-21). The emphasis in this
division is on the behavior particularly of Cephas, but also of other Jewish
Christians in contrast to that of Paul. Whereas Paul remains consistently
true to the gospel, they waiver and require his remonstration.

Thus 2:11-21 functions much like the customary autobiographical
σύγκρισις topoi, which compare and contrast the ethos of the autobiographer with that of other exemplary individuals.[37] Paul finds it necessary
to refer to the negative examples of Cephas and Barnabas, not because he
is at pains to undermine their reputations in the estimate of the Galatians, but because they are Christian leaders who are otherwise comparable to himself in stature and in ethos. The consensus view mistakenly

---

[35] Mention of the γένεσις, "birth," normally precedes the ἀναστροφή in
ancient lives, see chapter 1 section C 2 above.

[36] See Theodore C. Burgess, "Epideictic Literature," *University of
Chicago Studies in Classical Philology* 3 (1900) 120.

[37] See chapter 1 section C 2 above.

implies that Paul is totally inconsistent with the principles he lays down in
Gal 6:1-5, which reject boasting by comparison to others and recommend,
instead, gentle restoration of one overtaken in a trespass. In fact, the
Antioch incident and the following discourse illustrate what such an
edifying confrontation is like. Theodore C. Burgess notes that

> The rhetoricians indicate two distinct kinds of comparison.
> There is the minor or incidental σύγκρισις, . . . where some
> one phase of a subject or a single quality is likened to some
> other, and the final or general σύγκρισις, . . . where a more
> comprehensive comparison is made.[38]

The former may be identified in the Antioch incident in 2:11-14; and the
latter, in Paul's discourse in 2:15-21.

The final verse of this discourse, Gal 2:21, also serves as a particularly
appropriate conclusion (conclusio, ἐπίλογος) to the entire narrative, 1·10
2 21, and counterpart to the introduction in 1:10.[39] The appeal for imitation (μίμησις) of his virtues, which customarily comes at this point in the
autobiographies of antiquity,[40] is reserved for sound argumentative
reasons until 4:12-20 (see section D 1 below).

The following analysis of the formal structure of Paul's autobiographical narrative in Galatians 1 and 2 summarizes the foregoing discussion:

  I. προοίμιον 1:10 12—Paul's divine gospel
 II. ἀναστροφή 1·13-17—Paul's ethos
      A. 1:13-14 –As a persecutor of the church
      B. 1:15-17—As a preacher of the gospel
III. πράξεις 1:18-2:10—Paul's conduct
      A. 1:18-20—In Jerusalem
      B. 1:21-24—In Syria and Cilicia
      C. 2:1-10—In Jerusalem
 IV. σύγκρισις 2:11-21—Cephas and Paul
      A. 2:11-14—Incidental: In Antioch
      B. 2:15-21—General: Paul and Jewish Christians
  V. ἐπίλογος 2:21—Paul does not nullify divine grace

Most crucial for understanding the function of these autobiographical
remarks are the introductory verses in 1:10-12, which are treated in
considerable detail in section C below.

---

[38]Ibid., p. 125.
[39]Suggested by Boers, "Gen. 15:6," p. 67.
[40]See chapter 1 section C 2 above.

C. THE FUNCTION OF
PAUL'S AUTOBIOGRAPHICAL NARRATIVE

Introduction

In considering the function of Paul's autobiographical narrative, two major questions need to be addressed. First, what is the role of the narrative in the letter as a whole? or, What function(s) does it serve? Second, what is the unifying concern that holds these remarks together? or, What is the principle of selectivity that determines what aul includes and excludes in his narrative?

A number of small but functionally significant words in 1:10-11 require detailed consideration. They include the conjunction γάρ, which appears as the second word in 1:10, 11, and 12, as well as 13 (section 1); the particle ἤ, which appears twice in 1:10 (section 2); and the adverbs ἄρτι and ἔτι (section 4). It is also necessary to give special attention to Paul's use of the crucial verbs in 1:10, πείθειν and ἀρέσκειν (section 3). These considerations strongly suggest that a major organizing principle of the autobiographical narrative, and the letter as a whole, is the "formerly—now" contrast (section 5). Coordinated with this antithesis is another, which has already been noted, the "man—God" contrast (section 6). Other comparisons, including that between Paul and the Galatians and Peter, only support these contrasts (section 7). The turning point of the letter and the major *raison d'être* of the autobiographical narrative is to be found in Gal 4:12-20, where Paul calls for the Galatians to imitate him (section D 1). This, with the exordium (1:6-9) and the parenesis (5:1-6:10), leads to the conclusion that the overarching genre of the letter is deliberative. Paul's autobiographical narrative serves as the paradigm of the behavior he persuades his readers to imitate.

1. The Force of γάρ in Galatians 1:10-13

Boers considers the force of γάρ "the most difficult problem for understanding" Gal 1:6-2:21, but particularly 1:10.[41] Its probable etymology from γέ and ἄρα seems to suggest an inferential or conclusive (assertive or illative) force.[42] But most authorities concede that these and other

---

[41]Boers, "Gen. 15:6," p. 47. Burton (p. 31) notes that the precise "force of γάρ is difficult to determine."

[42]J. D. Denniston, *The Greek Particles* (2d ed.; Oxford: Clarendon, 1959) p. 56; so also Burton, p. 31.

senses of γάρ, e.g., the explanatory, anticipatory, confirmatory, and assentient, are "nothing more than particular aspects of the causal."[43] Nonetheless, the particular context is decisive to any determination of the precise nuance of the γάρ clause. It appears that the γάρ in each of its four instances in 1:10-13 conveys a different nuance.

In questions, as in Gal 1:10, the English idiom requires that γάρ be left untranslated, although its functional force remains.[44] A forward reference is not impossible, i.e., the anticipatory γάρ,[45] but it is more probable that, as usual, the γάρ refers back, in this case to Paul's words in 1:6-9.[46] The connection of the questions introduced by γάρ in 1:10 is not precise, explaining the tone rather than the content of 1:6-9.[47] This understanding is strengthened by the coordination of ἄρτι in both 1:9 and 10.[48]

But what is the force of γάρ in 1:11, 12, and 13? A "succession of γάρ's have the same reference" only when the clauses they introduce are parallel,[49] which is not the case here. It is possible that each γάρ provides successive substantiation for the preceding γάρ sentence. This would suggest an intimate connection between 1:6-2:21. And indeed, Paul's denial in 2:21a, "I do not set aside the grace of God," stands in apparent contrast to the Galatians' desertion of the one who called them "in the grace of Christ" in 1:6. But the γάρ sentences in these verses do not seem to be so uniform.

The variant reading, γνωρίζω δέ, for γνωρίζω γάρ in several good manuscripts of 1:11 reflects the long-standing difficulty the γάρ in this verse has presented interpreters. Although it is certainly secondary, it

---

[43]Ibid., p. 57; see Denniston's lengthy discussion, pp. 56-89; similarly Burton, p. 31; F. Blass and A. Debrunner, *A Greek Grammar of the New Testament and Other Early Christian Literature* (trans. and rev. Robert W. Funk; Chicago: University of Chicago, 1962) § 452; A. T. Robertson, *A Grammar of the Greek New Testament in the Light of Historical Research* (3d ed.; New York: Doran, 1919) pp. 1190-91.

[44]Bauer, s.v. γάρ 1 f and 4; BDF, § 452.

[45]On this infrequent usage see Denniston, p. 68.

[46]In a departure from his normal understanding (pp. 66 n. 101, 144 n. 58, 185, 186, 200, and 243), Betz thinks that the γάρ in 1:10 is "not so much connected with the preceding, but introduces another matter" (p. 54 n. 100).

[47]See Denniston, p. 62.

[48]See section C 4 below.

[49]Denniston, p. 64.

might correctly interpret the force of the γάρ as a simple connective.[50] It is more likely, however, that the disclosure, which the γάρ introduces, supports the unstated conclusion of 1:10. The γάρ in 1:12, however, appears to introduce a parenthetical explanation (12ab) of 1:11.[51] The γάρ in 1:13 introduces the autobiographical substantiation of the preceding claims, particularly those in 1:11-12, which are in turn connected with 1:10 and through it to 1:6-9.

2. The Force of ἤ in Galatians 1:10

Alternative constructions with ἤ, "or," may be divided into two basic types, the disjunctive and the copulative.[52] The difference between the two may be well illustrated by Matt 17:25, where Jesus poses three questions to Peter: "What do you think, Simon? From whom do kings of the earth take toll or tribute? From their sons or from others?" (RSV). The first pair of alternatives, "toll or tribute," is synonymous, and the force of ἤ, copulative. It could be replaced with καί with scarcely any change in meaning. The second pair of alternatives, "their sons or others," is antonymous, and the force of ἤ disjunctive, presenting a genuine alternative. Another example of the disjunctive ἤ, in which the two halves are antithetical, appears in Jesus' question to the chief priests and elders in Matt 21:25: "The baptism of John, whence was it? From heaven or from men?" (RSV).[53] If the word "heaven" were replaced with the word "God," for which it is a circumlocution here, it would present an even more obvious parallel to the question in Gal 1:10a: "Am I now seeking the favor of men, or of God?" (RSV).

Paul's normal use of ἤ in interrogative sentences is disjunctive (see e.g., Rom 4:10; 6:16). In no instance does he join antonyms with ἤ other than disjunctively. Gal 1:10a would be the only exception, were the interpretations of Walter Schmithals[54] and Betz[55] correct. The Pauline evidence of both form and content would seem to outweigh Betz's opposing

---

[50]See the text critical discussions in Mussner, p. 65 n. 110.

[51]Defended further below. Burton (p. 35), who considers 1:10 "almost parenthetical," understands 1:11 to justify 1:6-9.

[52]BDF, § 446; Bauer, s.v.

[53]Cf. also Matt 22:17; 23:17, 19; 27:17; Luke 6:9; 22:27.

[54]Walter Schmithals, *Paul and the Gnostics* (trans. John E. Steely; Nashville: Abingdon, 1972) pp. 56-58.

[55]Betz, pp. 54-56. He recognizes the disjunctive force of ἤ in the formally parallel constructions in 3:2 and 5 (pp. 132-33, 135-36).

rhetorical parallels, notably parallels in content only.[56] Frederic Rendall appears to be correct in his claim that in Gal 1:10a, as in 3:2 and 5, the ἤ is used disjunctively and is essentially equivalent to μᾶλλον ἤ, "rather than."[57] The ἤ connecting the nearly synonymous questions in 1:10a and b, however, is copulative in force, as the following section attempts to demonstrate.

3. The Force of πείθειν and ἀρέσκειν in Galatians 1:10

In Gal 1:10 ἀνθρώπους πείθειν, "to persuade men," and ἀνθρώποις ἀρέσκειν, "to please men," both seem to have a negative connotation, although elsewhere Paul can employ both expressions favorably. For example, he approves of "persuading men" in 2 Cor 5:11. The difference does not arise from Pauline inconsistency[58] but from what appears to be a coherently conceived rationale. Section a) below surveys Paul's statements on this subject outside Galatians in an attempt to understand this Pauline motif and thereby more adequately interpret Gal 1:10, which is treated in section b).

a) Outside Galatians

In Rom 15:1 Paul says that we who are strong ought not to please (ἀρέσκειν) ourselves but instead we should (βαστάζειν) sustain the weak. The positive parallel to this is the exhortation in v. 2, "Let each of us please [ἀρεσκέτω] his neighbor." This has the specific objective of benefiting him that he might grow (15:2; see 14:19; and the similar discussion in 1 Cor 8:1). That we ought to please our neighbor in this context is a reminder of the debt to love one another which cannot be repaid (13:8).[59] The appeal to please our neighbor is buttressed by the example of Christ, who did not please himself (οὐκ ἑαυτῷ ἤρεσεν) but (ἀλλά) accepted the reproaches directed against God (15:3) after the fashion of the Suffering Servant.

The continued appeal in Rom 15:7 takes up again the Christological

---

[56]Ibid., p. 54 n. 103. He can offer no Pauline parallels.

[57]Rendall, p. 153.

[58]Contra Peter Richardson, "Pauline Inconsistency: I Corinthians 9:19-23 and Galatians 2:11-14," *NTS* 26 (1980) 347-62.

[59]Cf. Gal 5:6; and 5:13: ". . . Through love be slaves of one another."

140   Pauline Autobiography

model of v. 3 and the central motif of Rom 14:1-15:6, the call for mutual acceptance. "Therefore, accept one another, as Christ accepted you to the glory of God" (15:7). The fact that Christ accepts us was demonstrated in the earthly work of Jesus as a διάκονος, "slave," of the Jewish people (15:8). By accepting one another, we serve Christ (δουλεύων τῷ Χριστῷ), are well-pleasing to God (εὐάρεστος τῷ θεῷ), and approved by men. Pleasing one's neighbor for his good properly gives the glory to God and not inappropriately to oneself. Otto Michel observes that "to please oneself" (ἑαυτοῖς ἀρέσκειν) "denotes the inversion of human existence and evasion of God."[60]

Ernst Käsemann considers "the dialectic" (pleasing oneself vs. pleasing others vs. pleasing God) evidence that a "carefully considered" and "fundamental motif of Paul's is handled here."[61] "Pleasing God is incompatible with ignoring one's neighbor." Yet "God's good pleasure" must not be "lost for the sake of human sympathy" by "mere conformism or accommodation." "Renewed reason has to find out whom to please and in what way."[62]

When Paul writes in 1 Corinthians on a similar subject, he appeals to his own example rather than that of Christ, "Be imitators of me, as I am of Christ" (1 Cor 11:1). Although what is modeled is similar the models are different in the two passages. The difference is probably due to the addresses in Romans being mostly strangers to Paul, whereas in Corinthians he addresses his own congregation.[63] Paul expresses his exemplary behavior antithetically: "I seek to please (ἀρέσκω) all men in everything. I do not seek (μὴ ζητῶν) my own advantage but (ἀλλά) that of the many, that they may be saved" (10:33). "Let no one seek his own benefit, but the benefit of his neighbor" (10:24; cf. v. 23). Earlier Paul suggests that not seeking one's own advantage for him entails the voluntary surrender of his apostolic prerogatives (see 9:1, 4, 12, 15). "For the sake of the gospel" (9:23), "though I am free of all men, I have enslaved myself to all" (9:19). "I have become all things to all men, that I might by all means save some"

---

[60]So translated in Hans Bietenhard, "Please," *NIDNTT*, 2:815; cited from Otto Michel, *Der Brief an die Römer* (MeyerK 4, 13; Göttingen: Vandenhoeck & Ruprecht, 1966) p. 354 n. 4.
[61]Ernst Käsemann, *Commentary on Romans* (trans. and ed. Geoffrey W. Bromiley; Grand Rapids: Eerdmans, 1980) p. 381. See his entire discussion of 14:1-15:13, pp. 364-87.
[62]Ibid.
[63]See C. H. Dodd, *The Epistle of Paul to the Romans* (MNTC; New York: Harper, 1932) p. 107.

(9:22b). In a similar context in 2 Cor 5:11, ἀνθρώπους πείθειν appears to have the favorable connotation of winning converts (see section b below). The contrast between pleasing/serving self and one's neighbor is maintained alongside the contrast between being "slaves of Christ" and "slaves of men" in 1 Cor 7:22-23.

A very similar discussion in terms of both form and content appears in 1 Thessalonians 2 where Paul contrasts antithetically pleasing God and men in v. 4. But the "man pleasing" he rejects is not a denial of his self-less, love-motivated concern for the salvation and edification of his converts, which he expresses in different words in vv. 6-8. What he renounces is the self-seeking flattery of the religious charlatan (2:3-5; cf. 2 Cor 2:17; and 4:1). Since divine approval (2:4c) takes precedence over praise from men (2:6), pleasing men cannot displace pleasing God. But neither does love permit selfish pursuits to displace gentle service to men (2:7-8).

b) In Galatians

The verb πείθω in Gal 1:10a may mean either "I persuade" or "appeal to" in a good or bad sense, or "I win over" or "strive to please."[64] In the only other Pauline passage in which the active voice of the verb appears, 2 Cor 5:11, its significance is also uncertain.[65] Rudolf Bultmann takes the expression ἀνθρώπους πείθειν in both passages as parallel to Acts 18:4; 19:8; and 28:23, where it has the technical sense "to seek to win men," i.e., to secure converts. He considers the force of the ἤ in Gal 1:10a to be disjunctive. On this view, the question in this verse "demands the answer 'Men,' and it is directed against the charge that Paul is seeking to persuade God (by his preaching of freedom from the Law)." The question in 1:10b, however, "answers the different objection that, Paul seeks to please men; hence ἀνθρώποις ἀρέσκειν is materially identical with τὸν θεὸν (πείθειν)."[66] The unnecessary assumption of underlying charges aside, there is no persuasive reason why ἀνθρώπους πείθειν in Gal 1:10a should be taken in the same sense as in 2 Cor 5:11.

Betz understands both ἀνθρώπους πείθειν in 1:10a and ζήτειν ἀνθρώποις ἀρέσκειν in 1:10b to refer to the rhetorical strategy of manipulative

---

[64]Bauer, s.v. 1b and c.
[65]Rudolf Bultmann, "πείθω, κτλ.," TDNT 6:2.
[66]Ibid.

flattery.[67] Similarly, τὸν θεὸν (πείθειν) refers to the use of deception, magic, or sorcery as persuasive techniques. Thus, he considers the expected answer to 1:10a and b to be an emphatic denial. If Paul understands τὸν θεὸν πείθειν or θεῷ ἀρέσκειν to have a negative connotation here, as Betz suggests, it is unique in the Pauline corpus. He frequently uses the related adjective εὐάρεστος of man's behavior that is acceptable or well-pleasing to God.[68]

Most interpreters recognize ἀνθρώπους πείθειν and ζητεῖν ἀνθρώποις ἀρέσκειν as synonymous. Thus since the question in 1:10b "demands No as its answer, the answer required by the first disjunctive question [i.e., 1:10a] is 'God.'" Accordingly, in 1:10ab Paul says "no more than that he wants to please God rather than men."[69] Although this understanding seems to be more natural than that proposed by either Bultmann or Betz, it does not yet explain the relationship of 10a and b to 10c. Only when it is recognized that both ἀνθρώπους πείθειν and ἀνθρώποις ἀρέσκειν here have the connotation "to be subservient to men,"[70] does it become clear why "pleasing men" is incompatible with "being a slave of Christ," as 10c claims.

When Paul in Gal 1:10c insists that he is "a slave of Christ," he is not merely using "a concept describing Christian existence,"[71] but a designation which is essentially equivalent to, or at least descriptive of, the title "apostle."[72] His antithetical self-description as an apostle in Gal 1:1 contrasts a commission from man/men as opposed to one from Jesus Christ/God. It is probable that a similar contrast is intended in 1:10. Paul does not deny a concern to please/serve anyone—whether men or God—

---

[67]Betz, pp. 54-55, 56 n. 120, 46.

[68]Bauer, s.v. 2; see Rom 12:1, 2; 14:18; 2 Cor 5:9; Eph 5:10; Phil 4:18; Col 3:20.

[69]Admitted as a possible interpretation by Bultmann, "πείθω," 6:2.

[70]See Bauer, s.vv. πείθω 3 b and ἀρέσκω 1; Bultmann, "πείθω," 6:2; Werner Foerster, "αρέσκω, κτλ.," TDNT 1:455; James Hope Moulton and George Milligan, The Vocabulary of the Greek Testament: Illustrated from the Papyri and Other Non-Literary Sources (Grand Rapids: Eerdmans, 1972 [reprint of the 1930 ed.]), s.vv.

[71]Contra Betz, p. 56.

[72]As in Rom 1:1; Phil 1:1; Tit 1:1; see the related term διάκονος in 2 Cor 3:6; 6:4; 11:15, 23; Eph 3:7; 6:21; Col 1:7, 23, 25; 4:7. See Karl Heinrich Rengstorf, "δοῦλος, κτλ," TDNT 2:261-80; and Herman W. Beyer, "διακονέω, κτλ," TDNT 2:81-93.

but only men.[73] Extra-textual assumptions, e.g., that Paul responds to accusations to the contrary (Schmithals) or excessive dependence on rhetorical parallels (Betz), alone support the contrary view, that Paul disclaims "persuasion" per se. The first half of the disjunctive question in 10a and the question in 10b are nearly synonymous. The parallel to the second half of 10a, elliptically implied by the conditional sentence in 10c, would be, "Or am I still seeking to please/serve Christ?" This lends additional support to the conclusion that the two parts of 10a are disjunctive.

The form of Gal 1:10c is an example of a "remarkably scarce" period in Paul, an unreal (contrary-to-fact) conditional sentence, in which neither the protasis (conditional clause) nor the apodosis (conclusion clause) is true.[74] Here the protasis is introduced by εἰ and employs the temporally ambiguous ἤρεσκον, which links it with the complementary infinitive ἀρέσκειν in 10b. It is ἄν in the apodosis which clearly identifies the sentence as unreal. The force of 10c is thus, "If I were still pleasing men—and I am not, I would not be a slave of Christ—which I am." This presumes an answer "No!" to the question in 10b and "God" to the question in 10a. The semantic force of 10c is to deny that Paul still tries to please men and to affirm that he is a slave of Christ. Although the grammatical forms of 10a and 10bc are different, the disjunctive force is similar. In both he reiterates the affirmation of 1:1 that his apostolic commission derives from Jesus Christ/God the Father and not from men, and anticipates the affirmation of 1:11-12, that accordingly, his message is of divine and not human origin or character.

Paul's frequent treatment of the *topos* concerning whom to please suggests that it is a carefully considered motif in his personal thought. This makes it improbable that the antithesis of pleasing God versus pleasing men in Galatians arose only in response to the charges of opponents. The contrast has its origin not in Pauline polemics but in the Pauline ethos—he is a slave of Christ, an embodiment of his divinely revealed gospel, and thus beholden to no man. As chapter II above attempts to demonstrate, nothing in Galatians suggests that Paul is hard pressed to authenticate his apostolate in the face of denials. He is concerned, however, to explicate what this vocation as a slave of Christ entails, in order to present himself as a model of one whose ethos is determined by unswerving allegiance to the truth of the gospel (see 4:12-20). In appealing

---

[73]Contra Schmithals, pp. 56-58; and Betz, pp. 44, 54, 56.

[74]BDF, § 360, finds the only other Pauline examples in 1 Cor 2:8; 11:31; 12:19; Gal 3:21; and 4:15.

to the Galatians to imitate his model, he does seek to please/persuade men but "for a good purpose" (4:18)—in their best interests and in behalf of Christ, not for selfish purposes.

Paul had once persuaded the Galatians in the sense of winning them as converts to the gospel of Christ (see Gal 1:6; 3:1-5; 4:13-16). He hopes again (πάλιν) to see Christ formed in them (4:19), not simply to recapture their allegiance at the expense of the truth (4:16). He is concerned for their good, not merely with winning their favor (4:17-20). The trouble-makers, who are courting their favor, do so for selfish reasons (4:17; cf. 6:12-13) and only hinder them (5:7). Of course, Paul also wants to be in their good graces but not at the expense of their loss of the grace of Christ (4:20; 5:4). He includes himself among those upon whom the curse for preaching to the Galatians a contrary gospel might fall (1:8). He continues to be a slave of Christ and subject to the gospel he proclaims. Whereas the troublemakers boast in the flesh—the works of man, Paul boasts only in the cross of Christ—the achievement of God (6:13-14; cf. 1 Cor 1:18-25). He insists on the true gospel so as not to nullify the grace of God (2:21).

In Gal 5:7 Paul uses the present middle or passive infinitive of πείθειν. "Who hindered you from obeying (μὴ πείθεσθαι) the truth?" (RSV). Through his rhetorical question in Gal 5:8, Paul denies that God has been responsible, "This persuasion (ἡ πεισμονή) is not from the one who called you." The verb πείθειν, "to persuade" and the noun πεισμονή, "persuasion" belong to the same word family.[75] In 5:10 the perfect active of πείθειν, ἐγὼ πέποιθα, "I trust," expresses Paul's confidence that his Galatian readers will be persuaded by his view of the situation, excommunicate the troublemakers, and once again stand squarely with him on the side of God rather than men.

4. The Force of ἄρτι and ἔτι in Galatians 1:10

The adverbs ἄρτι, "now," and ἔτι, "still," in Gal 1:10a and c respectively help confirm the conclusion that the two halves of 10a are to be understood disjunctively, as defended in section C 2 and 3 above. Translating and filling out the ellipses on the basis of these conclusions, the structure of Gal 1:10 appears to be as follows:

---

[75]See BDF, §§ 488 (1) and 109 (6).

Am I now obeying men?
    or (am I obeying) God?
Am I trying to serve men?
    (or am I trying to serve God?)
If I were still trying to serve men,
    I would not be a slave of Christ.

In the Pauline corpus the adverb ἄρτι is customarily used to indicate a temporal contrast between "now, the present," and some time in the past or future.[76] Since ἄρτι is virtually synonymous with νῦν in every other Pauline occurrence,[77] it is hardly probable that the force should differ in Gal 1:9 and 10.[78]

In 1:9 καὶ ἄρτι πάλιν λέγω, "and now I say again," stands in contrast to the preceding compound verb, προειρήκαμεν, "we [= I] said previously." Paul repeats a curse he had issued previously—whether on his earlier visit, in an earlier letter,[79] or as recently as the writing of the similar but more hypothetical curse in 1:8.[80]

The repetition of ἄρτι in 1:10 draws it into a close relationship with 1:8-9, suggesting that the two questions in v. 10ab in some way hark back to the double curse in vv. 8 and 9. The opening words of v. 10, ἄρτι γάρ, appear to call special attention to the harshness of Paul's present words, while explaining and justifying them.[81] Paul's questions ask in effect, "Does one who issues such a curse appear to be concerned with winning

---

[76]See 1 Cor 4:8-13; 8:7; 13:12-13; 2 Thess 2:7.

[77]Bauer, s.v. ἄρτι 3.

[78]Oepke, p. 26. Some other interpreters (e.g., Duncan, p. 22; and Betz, p. 54 n. 100) assign ἄρτι an emphatic or logical as opposed to a temporal force in both Galatian examples.

[79]Bauer, s.v. προεῖπον 2 a; Schlier, p. 40; Betz, p. 53.

[80]Hans von Campenhausen, *Ecclesiastical Authority and Spiritual Power in the Church of the First Three Centuries* (trans. J. A. Baker; Stanford: Stanford University, 1969) p. 37.

[81]So e.g., Heinrich August Wilhelm Meyer, *Critical and Exegetical Hand-book to the Epistle to the Galatians* (trans. G. H. Venables; ed. Henry E. Jacobs; Meyer's Critical and Exegetical Hand-book; New York: Funk & Wagnalls, 1884) p. 20; Burton, p. 31; Williams, p. 9; Duncan, pp. 20-22; Amiot, p. 115; Oepke, p. 26; Herman Wolfgang Beyer and Paul Althaus, "Der Briefe an die Galater," *Die kleineren Briefe des Apostel Paulus* (NTD 8; 6th ed.; Göttingen: Vandenhoeck & Ruprecht, 1953) p. 8; Mussner, p. 63. Among the few important commentators who reject this view are Lightfoot, pp. 78-79; and Betz, p. 54.

man's favor or God's?" Although this suggestion may be taken as only tentative, it coheres well with the other aspects of the interpretation.

Walter Bauer considers the adverb ἔτι in Gal 1:10 and 5:11a an example of the present temporal sense denoting "that a given situation is continuing still, yet," in contrast to a past that is no longer.[82] The unavoidable implication of 1:10 seems to be that "Paul is conscious of having pleased men in some fashion or other in the past," but has since "changed his behavior in some way."[83] Similarly, 5:11a suggests that he once urged circumcision, whether only during his pre-Christian days or, perhaps also, in his earlier days as a Jewish-Christian.[84] Paul cites as evidence that he no longer preaches circumcision, the fact of his continuing experience of persecution.

5. The "Formerly—Now" Contrast

The stark contrast between Paul the persecutor and Paul the persecuted preacher, between his "formerly" and "now," is well attested throughout the Pauline corpus. Martin Dibelius and Hans Conzelmann call attention to 1 Tim 1:12-13 as an example of a development of this pattern.[85] In Ephesians and Colossians, as in the Pastorals, the "conversion" of Paul is "paradigmatic for all Christians."[86] The pattern also frequently appears in Acts.[87] In the generally accepted genuine letters the pattern is similar, e.g., in Phil 3:6 and 1 Cor 15:9. "Gal 1:23 indicates furthermore that Paul as the persecutor of the church became in his own time an

---

[82]Bauer, s.v. 1 a α. Duncan (p. 22) insists that the force of ἔτι in 1:10 is "the strictly logical one." This is how Bauer (s.v. 2c) understands it in 5:11b.

[83]The view is widely held; the words are quoted from Richardson, p. 359. See also Schlier, p. 42; Mussner, p. 64; Boers, "Gen 15:6," p. 4; Betz, p. 56.

[84]On this see Betz, pp. 268-69 and the authorities he cites. To those supporting the latter view may be added Richardson, p. 359.

[85]Martin Dibelius and Hans Conzelmann, *The Pastoral Epistles: A Commentary on the Pastoral Epistles* (trans. Philip Buttolph and Adela Yarbro; ed. Helmut Koester; Hermeneia; Philadelphia: Fortress, 1972) p. 28.

[86]Martinus C. de Boer, "Images of Paul in the Post-Apostolic Period," *CBQ* 42 (1980) 374; see also p. 374 n. 58; and p. 375.

[87]Ibid., pp. 375-76.

object of wonder and legend."[88] As Paul quotes the churches of Judea,
" 'He who once [ποτε] persecuted us now [νῦν] preaches the faith he once
[ποτε] tried to destroy.' " Or as Paul tells his own story in Gal 1:13, "You
have heard of my conduct formerly [ποτε] in Judaism, how I violently
persecuted the church of God and tried to destroy it." Dahl observes that

> Read in conjunction the opening and closing sections of the
> apology (Gal. 1:13-16a + 2:19-21) conforms to the pattern of
> the autobiography in Phil 3:4-22 that begins with Paul's
> recollection of his Jewish past and ends with his renunciation
> of all privileges for the sake of Christ.[89]

It appears that a significant organizing principle in more than one of
Paul's presentations of his "autobiography" is the "formerly—now" contrast.

The whole of Paul's autobiographical narrative in Gal 1:10-2:21 appears
to be framed by this temporal contrast, "formerly—now." At its beginning
ἔτι and ἄρτι in 1:10, imply that Paul once was a manpleaser, but as
Christ's slave, is no longer. Similarly, the οὐκέτι, "no longer," of Gal 2:20
at its close contrasts Paul's former egocentric existence under law and his
present Christocentric life of faith—"I died to law" (2:19); "I no longer
live" (2:20), but "Christ lives in me . . . I live by faith" (2:20). A crucial
aspect of the temporal contrast is emphasis upon the "formerly" as an
existence in dependence upon man/men, whereas the "now" is an existence
through Jesus Christ/God. These contrasts prepare for the crucial antitheses which dominate the balance of the letter: flesh—Spirit, law—grace,
slavery—freedom.

Precisely what Paul's former practice of "man pleasing" may have
involved is uncertain. The formulation of 1:10 implies that his pre-
Christian existence was characterized by an overweening concern to win
human approval at the expense of God's. If 1:13-14 are any indication, he
may refer to his former complicity in the Jewish persecution of Christians
(1:13, 23),[90] which though done out of zeal for the law, served also to
advance his reputation in Judaism (1:14; cf. Phil 3:6), and as he came to
realize subsequently, was not pleasing to God (1 Cor 15:8-10; 1 Thess

---

[88]Ibid., p. 370.

[89]Dahl, p. 41. Betz (pp. 68 n. 113, 222 n. 30) makes a somewhat similar
connection.

[90]Williams, p. 9; Boers, "Gen. 15:6," p. 50; see further references in
Betz, p. 67 n. 110.

2:14-16). Boers suggests that Paul's description of the conduct of Peter
and the other Jewish Christians at Antioch (2:11-14) may indicate what he
had in mind by his abandoned conduct in 1:10—behavior motivated by fear
of what other people might think or do.[91] Paul seems to indicate in Gal
5:11 that abandoning all former behavior unbefitting "a slave of Christ"
(1:10), entailed at least discontinuing his earlier preaching of circumcision.

Whatever pleasing men may include, it should be recognized that Paul
evaluates his earlier, probably pre-Christian, conduct from his present
Christian perspective. Paul's own testimony (see e.g., Gal 1:14; Phil 3:6)
does not suggest that he ever consciously or deliberately put the favor of
men before that of God. It is only in retrospect that he sees his outstanding success as compared to his Jewish contemporaries and his zeal for his
ancestral traditions as worthless and misguided (Gal 1:13-14; cf. Phil 3:4-
11). In Rom 9:30-10:4 he describes such contradictory behavior as typical
of non-Christian Jewish existence: "I bear them witness that they have a
zeal for God, but it is not enlightened" (Rom 10:3 RSV).

The formulation of Paul's rhetorical question in 5:11, "But I, brothers,
if I still preach circumcision, why then am I still being persecuted?"
presumes not only that his experiences of persecution are a result of his
changed practice but that they are known to his readers. He implies that
his Galatian readers are also now (νῦν) experiencing persecution as their
allegorical prototype Isaac did formerly (πότε) (4:29). He accuses the
troublemakers of compelling them to be circumcised in order that these
troublemakers might escape persecution. (6:12).

The source of the persecution, its motivation, and what it involved
remain an enigma. Was it persecution of Christians by Jews[92] or by
troublemakers?[93] Why should Jews persecute Gentile-Christians? Gentile
"God-fearers" whose conversions to Judaism lacked the final step of

---

[91]Boers, "Gen. 15:6," pp. 4 and 52. More interesting than convincing is
the proposal of Richardson (pp. 347-62, esp. 359) that Paul here repudiates
the principle of missionary accommodation put forward in 1 Cor 9:19-23
and 10:33.

[92]The allegory implies that the persecutors are the children of Hagar,
which correspond to the present Jerusalem (4:25, 29). Furthermore, 6:12
refers to persecution "for the cross of Christ." On the difficult interpretation of the allegory, see Lloyd Gaston, "Israel's Enemies in Pauline Theology," NTS 28 (1982) 400-423; and n. 128 below.

[93]Betz (p. 250 n. 117) notes advocates of both views, adopting the former himself.

circumcision were not persecuted.[94] Furthermore, persecution would seem to be a counterproductive tactic for troublemakers interested in securing the allegiance of those they were "persecuting." But perhaps Paul has in mind a more subtle form of "persecution," which he refers to elsewhere in the letter as troubling, hindering, harassing, excluding, unsettling, and compelling circumcision by means of insincere, manipulative, self-seeking flattery (see 1:7; 4:17; 5:17, 10, 12, 15; 6:12).

But Paul's persecution, at least, seems to involve physical, as opposed to merely psychological, consequences. Two cryptic references to these consequences appear in the letter. In 6:17 Paul claims to bear in his body "the marks of Jesus." A similar remark in 2 Cor 4:10 suggests that he refers to his "sufferings with Christ," experienced as a result of the fulfillment of his mission.[95] If the term τὰ στίγματα also refers to "the marks" of ownership of a slave,[96] Paul's closing words to the Galatians once again emphasize the importance of and validate his claim to be Christ's slave, first noted in 1:10. Paul's experience is contrasted with that of the troublemakers who evade persecution by their advocacy of a perverted "gospel" that removes "the stumbling-block [τὸ σκάνδαλον] of the cross" (5:11; 6:14).[97]

The second cryptic reference to persecution appears in 4:13, where Paul says it was δι' ἀσθένειαν τῆς σαρκός that he first preached to the Galatians. Although most recent interpreters presume that Paul refers to some kind of physical ailment,[98] Hermann Binder defends the older view that Paul had in mind the hardships and persecutions accompanying his mission.[99] This interpretation is strengthened by Paul's reference in 4:14 to his initial reception in Galatia "as Christ Jesus," which like 6:17 alludes to his imitation of Christ's sufferings.

Paul's experiences of persecution came in the fulfilment of his vocation

---

[94]Karl Georg Kuhn, "προσήλυτος," TDNT 6:730-36; esp. 731. See more recently, Neil J. McEleney, "Conversion, Circumcision and the Law," NTS 20 (1974) 319-41.

[95]See the discussion in Erhard Güttgemanns, Der leidende Apostel und sein Herr: Studien zur paulinischen Christologie (FRLANT 90; Göttingen: Vandenhoeck & Ruprecht, 1966) pp. 126-35.

[96]So e.g., Lightfoot, p. 225.

[97]Dahl, p. 98.

[98]See Güttgemanns, pp. 170ff.

[99]Hermann Binder, "Die angebliche Krankheit des Paulus," TZ 32 (1976) 1-13; cf. Michael L. Barré, "Qumran and the Weakness of Paul," CBQ 42 (1980) 216-27.

as "a slave of Christ" (1:10), preaching the gospel to the Gentiles (1:11,
16, 23). His autobiographical remarks in Gal 1:10-2:21 are shaped throughout by the contrast between his past and present. His past, identified with
the particle ποτε, "then, once, or formerly" in 1:13-14 is sharply marked
off from his present by ὅτε δέ, "but when," which introduces the balance
of the narrative in 1:15. The decisive event dividing Paul's "formerly" and
"now" is God's revelation to him of Jesus Christ and his call to preach him
among the Gentiles (1:12, 15-16). It was not through Paul's personal
choice, nor in order to please any man but only by the intervention of God
that Paul became an apostle (1:1, 10-12, 15-16). As a slave of Christ he
became a participant in his sufferings, and in this also an embodiment of
the gospel of Christ crucified (1:4; 2:19-21; 3:1, 13-14, 5:11, 24; 6:12-14).
It is for this reason that he opposes the tactics of the troublemakers, who
by practicing circumcision secure a persecution-free existence at the
expense of removing "the stumbling-block of the cross" (5:11). Their
theologia gloriae amounts to a return to the former existence under the
law, which nullifies the grace of God.

The formulation of Paul's autobiographical remarks in terms of "formerly—now" and "man—God" (see section C 6 below) serves a paradigmatic function, to contrast Paul's conversion from Judaism to Christianity
with the Galatians' inverted conversion.[100] This seems to account well
enough for the ἀναστροφή division (1:13-17) of his autobiographical
remarks, which contrasts his pre-Christian existence, and his "conversion"
and early years as a Christian before visiting Jerusalem. The contrast
between his human achievements, the divine revelation, and the "flesh and
blood," with whom he did not confer after his "conversion," demonstrate
the influence of the "man—God" contrast. The middle section of the
πράξεις division (1:21-24), particularly its mention of the report about
Paul circulating among Judean Christians also coheres with these patterns.

The "formerly—now" design is perhaps present, though definitely
parenthetical in the third section of the πράξεις division (2:1-10). In 2:6
Paul begins to refer to those who are reputed to be something but is
apparently sidetracked by his parenthetical evaluation of them. "What
they once [ποτε] were makes no difference to me," since it does not to
God. Betz observes that "the discrepancy between the tenses is grammatically awkward and makes one suspect that Paul created it intentionally,

---

[100]Even the verb μετατίθημι which describes their desertion of Paul
and his gospel in 1:6 has the connotation of a reverse conversion, apostasy, treachery, desertion; see Bauer, s.v. 2 b.

because he wanted to distinguish between the past and the present."[101] Johannes Munck proposes that Paul's intention seems to have been to coordinate the biographies of the influential men in Jerusalem with his autobiography in terms of a "formerly—now" arrangement.[102] The contrast between their human reputation and God's impartiality also reflects the "man—God" contrast. The same contrast is probably also implicit in Paul's mention of the motivation for his visit, "by a revelation" (2:2), and the recognition of both his mission and Peter's as marked by divine activity (2:8, 9).

A temporal contrast emerges even in Paul's two scriptural expositions in Galatians. In the first in 3:6ff., he argues that if God's earlier[103] promise to Abraham were nullified by the later coming of the law, it would no longer (οὐκέτι) be a promise (3:17). Rather the law was only a temporary, stop-gap measure, significantly introduced through the mediation of angels, not directly by God, until (ἄχρις) the coming of Christ (4:16, 19). In the second scriptural exposition in 4:21ff., a similar "formerly—now" (τότε—νῦν) contrast appears in the application of the allegory to the Galatian situation (4:29).

The paradigmatic significance of the temporal contrast throughout the letter is suggested by similar descriptions applied to both Jewish- and Gentile-Christians. Jewish-Christians are no longer (οὐκέτι) under the law as they were before (πρό) the coming of faith (3:23-25). Gentile-Christians, who were once enslaved under the elemental spirits, were also set free by the redemption in Christ (note the double use of ὅτε in 4:3-5). The decisive transition for both came by divine intervention—"We were kept under the law . . . until the faith was revealed" (3:24), ". . . until the date set by the father" (4:2). "But when the time had fully come, God sent forth his Son . . . (4:4 RSV). "So through God you are no longer a slave but a son . . ." (4:7 RSV).

The pervasiveness of the temporal contrast throughout the letter makes it implausible that the accusations of Paul's "opponents" are responsible for its presence in the autobiographical narrative. What we

---

[101]Betz, p. 93. See pp. 93-95 and the accompanying notes for a discussion of the various hypotheses as to Paul's meaning. See David M. Hay, "Paul's Indifference to Authority," *JBL* 88 (1969) 36-44.

[102]Johannes Munck, *Paul and the Salvation of Mankind* (trans. Frank Clarke; Richmond, VA: John Knox, 1959) p. 99.

[103]Note the προ-prefixes in προϊδοῦσα, "foreseeing," and προευηγγελίσατο, "preached the gospel beforehand," in 3:8 and προεκυρωμένη, "which has been previously ratified," in 3:17.

have instead is the "formerly—now" contrast of redemptive history personalized in Paul's self-description and made paradigmatic for the experience of every Christian. The contrast is specifically applied to the Galatians in 4:8-11. Here it is a contrast between the formerly (τότε), when the Galatians did not know God, but were enslaved to idols, and the now (νῦν), since they have come to know God, or rather to be known by him (vv. 8-9). It is this which makes it incomprehensible to Paul, why they should reverse the process and return (ἐπιστρέφετε πάλιν) to an existence of slavery, only now under the law (vv. 9-11, 21). Such a move would render Paul's labor in their behalf in vain (v. 11), because what they experienced as a result of his preaching would have been in vain (3:4).

The temporal contrast for the Galatians is twofold, between the slavery of their past before Christ and the freedom of their present since Christ, and between this present and the future they seem bent on pursuing, which is really a return to slavery. Thus Paul appeals in 5:1, Christ has freed us, do not be enslaved again (πάλιν), and warns in 5:2, If you receive circumcision, Christ will be of no advantage to you. Paul's autobiographical narrative anticipates and gives paradigmatic emphasis to the argument of the entire letter, as he contrasts the past, the present, and the two possible futures. The future he attempts to persuade them to pursue requires that they stand fast in the freedom that is already theirs in Christ and refuse the yoke of slavery offered by the troublemakers (5:1). This entails their continued imitation of Paul (4:12-20) and the excommunication of the troublemakers (see 4:30). For the other future, circumcision, binds them to observe the whole law and involves separation from Christ and his grace (5:2-4). Betz describes the choice as "between Paul and Judaism,"[104] but more fundamentally the choice of futures amounts to a repetition of their initial encounter with the gospel, i.e., a choice between man and God.

6. The "Man—God" Contrast

Galatians 1:11-12 obviously continues and reinforces the man/men—Christ/God contrast introduced in Paul's self-description in 1:1 and implicit in 1:10, but just as obviously marks a new stage in his argument. The conjunction γάρ provides the connection; the disclosure formula introduces the issue which the apostle's following autobiographical

---

[104]Betz, p. 251.

remarks substantiate.[105] What Paul says in the ensuing autobiographical remarks is dictated, at least in part, by the demands of the present trouble in Galatia.[106] There he and his divinely revealed gospel are being deserted in favor of troublemakers and their perverted human "gospel"— which he considers to be nothing other than a revival of the Judaism he had rejected and not really "good news" at all, but an abandonment of God for man. It is Paul, not the troublemakers, who determines the terms of the formulation of his autobiographical narrative.

Betz notes that the extremely concise formulation of Gal 1:11-12 presents the exegetical problem of "how to decode the abbreviations." His assumption, "that the abbreviations point back to a fuller account of Paul's conversion and commission,"[107] however, can be neither proved nor disproved, since we do not have this account. Parallel accounts, such as 1 Cor 15:8-11; 2 Cor 11:22-28; and Phil 3:4-11 in Paul and the accounts in Acts 9, 22, and 26, demonstrate the importance of the events but not the existence of an underlying account which Paul abbreviates.[108] Perhaps the underlying unity of the accounts arises instead from Paul's repeated utilization of the *heilsgeschichtliche* structure, "formerly—now," expanded in various ways by information he considered salient to the situations which called them forth. Even if a fuller account did exist, there is no certainty that it could be reconstructed (i.e., "decoded") by appeal to the pseudo-Clementines as Betz assumes.[109] The same reasons that require restraint in similarly drawing upon the Acts of the Apostles apply equally to this secondary source. For there is no reason to think that an "enemy" of Paul would present a more objective picture of him than a "friend."[110]

---

[105]See the discussion in sections B and C 1 above.

[106]See section A above.

[107]Betz, pp. 56 and 62 (quotations from p. 62).

[108]See Betz's (ibid., pp. 63-66) excursus on Paul's "conversion" and the extensive bibliographical references in his notes. See also J. W. Doeve, "Paulus der Pharisäer und Galater i.13-15," *NovT* 6 (1963) 170-81.

[109]See ibid., p. 62, where Betz recommends the pseudo-Clementine Homilies 17. 13-19 as a guide for filling in between the lines.

[110]Günther Bornkamm (*Paul* [trans. D. M. G. Stalker; New York: Harper & Row, 1971] p. xxi) cautions: "We may not uncritically fill in gaps in the letters from the copious material in Acts. In other words, when the one source is silent, it will not do uncritically to listen to the other. . . . Combining and harmonizing have been disastrous." Substitute "Pseudo-Clementines" for "Acts" and the caution is equally timely.

Betz's correct observation, that "in v 12, the simple denial of v 11 is made more explicit . . . negatively . . . and positively," requires a more detailed analysis than he provides, as does his claim that 1:11 announces "the argument Paul is going to prove in the 'statement of facts' and in the rest of the letter." According to Betz, they provide "the whole basis upon which Paul's gospel, as well as his own mission, and indeed his defense in the letter, rest."[111] Apart from the need to substitute the word "persuasion" for "defense," his claim is essentially correct, as we have already argued, and as a fuller analysis of 1:11-12 helps confirm.

Gal 1:11-12 is introduced by the disclosure, γνωρίζω γὰρ ὑμῖν, ἀδελφοί, "For I make known to you, brothers," concerning the nature and origin of Paul's gospel preaching—"the gospel preached by me" (1:11a). Such disclosure formulas, not at all uncommon in his letters,[112] do not seem to introduce controversial themes or respond to charges to the contrary. The disclosure merely provides a convenient means for moving to the crucial issue at hand, perhaps in response to questions posed by the readers.[113] Here it lends support for the unstated conclusion of 1:10, that Paul stands on the side of God rather than men.

The Pauline parallels seem to suggest that the introductory words of Gal 1:11 do not announce facts with which the Galatians were not already acquainted to a greater or lesser extent.[114] It is unlikely that the autobiographical information was provided for its own sake. "He includes it because of its relevance to his main theme."[115] Although the contents of Paul's remarks were not news, γνωρίζω is nevertheless correctly used because of the "relevance" of his autobiography, i.e., its rhetorical function within his argument. This evidently does introduce something new.[116] What that "relevance" was and how the autobiographical remarks served it are the central issues of this chapter.

---

[111]Betz, p. 59.

[112]Cf. 1 Cor 12:3; 15:1; 2 Cor 8:1; and the essentially synonymous negative formulation, οὐ θέλω ὑμᾶς ἀγνοεῖν, in Rom 1:13; 1 Cor 10:1; 12:1; and οὐ θέλομεν δὲ ὑμᾶς ἀγνοεῖν in 1 Thess 4:13. See Terrence Y. Mullins, "Disclosure, a Literary Form in the New Testament," NovT 7 (1964) 44-50.

[113]Dahl, p. 40.

[114]E.g., Bruce, p. 22; cf. Betz, pp. 56, 59-60.

[115]Ibid.

[116]See Bauer (s.v. γνωρίζω, 1.) on the term in 1 Cor 15:1. Betz's (p. 56) suggestion, that "Paul pretends to introduce new information," is unwarranted.

Characteristic of his antithetical formulations, Paul's first disclosure concerning his gospel in Gal 1:11b is a denial, and thus stated negatively: "It is not a human invention" (i.e., human in character or nature; κατὰ ἄνθρωπον; cf. Gal 3:15; Rom 3:5; 1 Cor 3:3; 9:8; 15:32). The positive half in 1:12c affirms that instead, it is by divine revelation, i.e., "by a revelation [δι' ἀποκαλύψεως] of Jesus Christ" (cf. 1:15; 2:2). Between the two halves in 1:12ab appear two additional negatively formulated clauses connected to the original denial with the conjunction γάρ. It has already been argued that it is doubtful that the succession of four γάρ's in vv. 10, 11, 12, and 13 all have the same reference. Instead the two intervening denials in v. 12 appear to serve parenthetically to substantiate and elaborate upon the simple denial of v. 11.[117]

For I make known to you, brothers, the gospel preached by
  me.
It is not a human invention
  (for neither did I receive it from man,
  nor was I taught it),
but it came through a revelation of Jesus Christ.

The autobiographical narrative in 1:13-2:21 supports this disclosure.

The construction of Gal 1:11-12 suggested above is supported by 1 Thess 2:3-4, which is similar except for the presence of γάρ in the former and its absence in the latter passage. In the Thessalonians passage Paul states negatively that his appeal originated not (οὐκ) out of error, but (ἀλλά) positively was spoken with divine approval. The original denial is expanded and reinforced by two essentially synonymous denials: "neither [οὐδέ] out of impure motives nor [οὐδέ] deceitfully." This complicated antithetical formulation is immediately succeeded by a second, simpler one, in which Paul claims, we speak "not to please men, but to please God who tests/approves our motives." These claims are supported by the autobiographical remarks in 1 Thess 2:5-3:13. The first, complicated antithetical formulation corresponds closely to Gal 1:11-12; the second, simpler one corresponds to Gal 1:10; and the narrative to Gal 1:13-2:21.

Paul's major concern in Gal 1:11-12 is to insist upon the divine origin of his gospel. He accomplishes this by first excluding any possible human source through a doubly reinforced denial. The parenthetical sentences

---

[117]See the discussion in section C 1 above.

introduced by οὐδέ and οὔτε make the denial more radical. To deny so emphatically that his gospel was κατὰ ἄνθρωπον, "according to man," clearly implies its more than human, therefore, supernatural, source and character. This becomes explicit in the positive affirmation of its revelatory character and in the subsequent autobiographical remarks. The appeals to ἀποκάλυψις, "revelation," in 1:12 and 2:2 emphasize Paul's understanding of both his "conversion" and his subsequent conduct, specifically at the Jerusalem conference, as manifestations of the will of God.

J. B. Lightfoot calls attention to Paul's remarkable accumulation of words in 1:15 which also emphasizes "the sole agency of God as distinct from his own efforts."[118] This supports the impression that his autobiographical remarks are significantly shaped by a concern to demonstrate that his gospel and apostleship are of divine and not human origin. It is upon the substantiation of this claim that Paul's attempt to dissuade the Galatians from following the troublemakers rests. It is his concern for their perversion of the gospel of Christ in Galatia, expressed in the harsh rebuke in 1:6-9, which occasions his rhetorical questions in 1:10 and his insistence upon the revealed nature of his gospel preaching in 1:11-12. When Paul asserts in 1:11 that his gospel is not κατὰ ἄνθρωπον but δι᾽ ἀποκαλύψεως 'Ιησοῦ χριστοῦ, he appeals to both his divine authorization to preach and to the divine content of his message. The contrast between two kinds of gospels begins with Paul's pronouncement of a curse on anyone preaching a gospel contrary to the one he had preached and the Galatians received, i.e., contrary to the gospel of Christ (1:6-9). In Paul's view, any "gospel" that did not come through a revelation of Jesus Christ was obviously of human origin and character, thus κατὰ ἄνθρωπον.

7. Other Comparisons and Contrasts

Some interpreters have claimed to discern in the opening words of Gal 1:12, οὐδε γὰρ ἐγώ . . . , "For I neither . . . ," a further, implicit contrast or comparison beyond the explicit "man—God" contrast. Although such a possibility cannot be dismissed, it would seem to be impossible to validate, unless clairvoyance is among the interpreter's gifts. How would anyone, apart from Paul and his intended original readers, know whether he denies the charges of troublemakers to the contrary, thus implying, "I did not receive my gospel from man as they charge"? Nothing in the antithetical formulation requires such an assumption, as chapter 2 above

---

[118]Lightfoot, p. 82.

argues at length. How would anyone removed by nearly twenty centuries from the occasion of the letter determine that Paul's claim to preach a divinely revealed gospel was intended to challenge a similar claim made by the troublemakers—"I did not receive my gospel from man as they also—but falsely—claim."[119] Certainly, Paul implies in 1:6-9 that the perverted "gospel" of the troublemakers is not of divine origin, but this tells us nothing of their claims.

Some propose that Paul places his claim to an unmediated gospel alongside that of the original apostles—"I no more than they received my gospel from man."[120] It is true that these apostles play a role subsequently in the narrative (1:17ff.). But is it possible that anyone who did not mull over the letter at a scholar's desk—something the original hearers are unlikely to have done—would have caught such an implication, had it been intended?

Still others find a contrast between Paul's unmediated reception of the gospel by a revelation and his converts' reception of the gospel through his preaching. And it is true that he refers in 1:9 to the gospel which the Galatians received (ὃ παραλάβετε) from him, and in 1:12 to the gospel that he did not receive (οὐδέ . . . παρέλαβον) from man. But is it likely that he would so depreciate his preaching to elevate his message? All such assumptions introduce a great deal more into the context than is there, and much of it does not seem to cohere well with the simple point of Paul's disclosure: My gospel is not from man but from God.[121]

The preceding paragraphs should not be taken as a denial of the existence in the letter of other implicit and explicit comparisons; this aspect of Paul's autobiographical remarks has already been suggested in the analysis of its form and structure in section B above. It is merely to insist that the major and controlling contrasts are the two discussed in section C 5 and 6—the "formerly—now" and the "man—God" contrasts. By comparison, others play a definitely subsidiary role. These antitheses clearly serve the positive function of explicating the character of the true gospel and Paul's embodiment of it, rather than the negative function of defending himself against the insinuations of the troublemakers. It is he who sets the terms of the discussion, not the "opponents." On this basis, Paul

---

[119]This is the controlling assumption of Walter Schmithals, *The Office of the Apostle in the Early Church* (trans. John E. Steely; New York: Abingdon, 1969).

[120]E.g., Burton, p. 39.

[121]See Lightfoot, p. 80.

contrasts himself, on the one hand, and the Galatians (section a below) and Peter (section b below), on the other.

a) The "Galatians—Paul" Contrast

Paul's "autobiography" at several points seems to be contrasted both implicitly and explicitly with the "biography" of the Galatians. But it is the paradigmatic "formerly—now" and "man—God" contrasts which determine what is contrasted. The Galatians, by foolishly seeking to improve on their salavation (3:1, 3) by supplementing it with law, circumcision, calendar observance, etc., are nullifying the grace of God and placing their salvation in jeopardy (3:2, 5; 4:10, 21; 5:2-4). By thus Judaizing (cf. 2:14), they are substituting human activity (σαρχί, "by the flesh") for divine activity (πνεύματι, "by the Spirit," 3:3; see vv. 2 and 5). By way of contrast, Paul abandoned the law in order to gain salvation by grace (2:19-20). That Christ's death is the saving event demonstrates for Paul the ineffectiveness of law as a means of salvation (see 3:21). But if the Galatians continue their pursuit of salvation by law, they will be estranged from Christ (5:4). His death will be in vain (δωρεάν, 2:21; εἰχῇ, 3:4), no longer of any benefit to them (5:2), and Paul's preaching to them will also be in vain (εἰχῇ, 4:11).[122]

Although little of autobiographical consequence appears in Gal 3:1-4:10, perhaps 3:1-5 is a subtle reminder to the Galatians that it was Paul who first preached the gospel of Jesus Christ the crucified among them and who portrayed him in his person (see 2:20). It was through him that they came to be Christians. The irrefutable evidence of the divine character of his law-free mission was validated by their own biographies.

b) The "Peter—Paul" Contrast

The first section of the πράξεις division (1:18-20) does not easily conform to either the "formerly—now" or "man—God" patterns. Its report of Paul's first visit to Jerusalem and brief encounter with Cephas may serve only to prepare for their subsequent encounters in Jerusalem and Antioch, and especially the comparison and contrast of the σύγχρισις division (2:11-21). But if the role of 1:18-20 is so insignificant, why the

---

[122]Compare: the death of Christ (cf. 2:20-21 and 3:1); salvation by faith vs. law (cf. 2:16, 19 and 3:2, 5), and the contrast between Paul and the Galatians (cf. 2:21, 2 and 3:3-4).

oath in 1:20—"In what I am writing to you, before God, I do not lie!"? Are there other issues at stake?

Unquestionably Paul's autobiographical narrative is selective in the events it reports. In view of Paul's mention of persecution in 5:11 (cf. 6:12, 17), surely some of the many hardships he reports in 2 Cor 11:21-29 occurred before the writing of Galatians. In all probability his basket escape from Damascus reported in 2 Cor 11:32-33 belongs to the same time frame as the reference to Damascus in Gal 1:17 (see Acts 9:23-25). But there is no mention of it here. Why? Paul's narrative seems to be chronologically ordered, but is by no means complete. Upon what basis does he decide what to omit and what to include? Why does Jerusalem play so prominent a role? Does this concentration on Jerusalem suggest that he reports all his visits there? To admit that the autobiographical narrative in Galatians 1 and 2 may not provide the necessary framework for reconstructing the Apostle's career is not to impugn Paul's veracity, but to recognize that his objectives are not historical but rhetorical.

The prominence of Jerusalem and the earlier apostles there emerges for the first time in the second section of the ἀναστροφή division (1:15-17) in the fact that Paul considers it important enough to mention that, immediately following his conversion, he did not go there or meet them. These denials serve in part to substantiate the claim of 1:10-12 that his gospel was of divine rather than human origin. The older notion that Paul's failure to confer immediately with human beings (1:16) implies that his stay in Arabia (1:17) was for the purpose of reflection and divine meditation,[123] however, over-interprets his claim. Betz seems to be correct that "although Paul does not say why he went to Arabia, we can assume that he did so for the purpose of mission."[124] Withdrawal for meditation can scarcely account for the hostility of the Nabatean ethnarch Paul mentions in 2 Cor 11:32-33. That he does not mention the incident here reinforces the impression that his narrative is determined by purposes other than historical. And if his participation in the sufferings of Christ validates his apostolate, his omission would also seem to suggest that this purpose is not apologetic.

There is no reason to see his claim to an unmediated gospel in Gal 1:12 as a contradiction of 1 Cor 15:1-3. In the latter passage he refers to the formulation of the gospel he received by tradition (see τίνι λόγῳ in 1 Cor 15:2). That he was once a persecutor of Christians implies a measure of

---

[123]E.g., Lightfoot, pp. 87-90.
[124]Betz, p. 74.

natural acquaintance with the facts of the gospel as a reason for his radical rejection of it (see 2 Cor 5:16). But facts and formulations are to be distinguished from the gospel, which Paul received through God's gracious revelation of his Son, which was at the same time Paul's vocation to preach the gospel to the Gentiles (Gal 1:16). This unmediated revelation of Christ validates the claim that his gospel is not human in origin or character (1:11, 15-16). After his "conversion," he did not go to Jerusalem, because, after all, he had been called to preach to the Gentiles, not to the Jews, and this he presumably did in Arabia.

According to the first section of the πράξεις division, when Paul did go to Jerusalem some three years later, he went neither to confer, nor to preach (1:16), but to visit Cephas (1:18).[125] Paul's oath in 1:20, presumably attests to the veracity of his purpose in visiting Cephas alone among the apostles and the brevity of his stay in Jerusalem.[126] But it is not clear why such an oath is called for, here or elsewhere, where it appears in the Pauline corpus (cf. Rom 9:1; 2 Cor 11:31; 1 Thess 2:5; 1 Tim 2:7).

The third section of the πράξεις division is also set in Jerusalem. Again, he is not there to preach, but this time because of a revelation, i.e., in obedience to God. He does put forward the gospel he preaches to the Gentiles for the private consideration of the influential men there. Cephas again figures prominently in the narrative. Paul's concern in this section does not seem to be to prove his independence (see chapter 2), but to emphasize instead the God-given character of both his gospel for the uncircumcision and Peter's for the circumcision. The agreement reached in Jerusalem recognized the existing division of labor between these two divinely ordained missions.[127]

The difficulties of interpretation aside,[128] it is not possible to explain

---

[125]See Bengt Holmberg's (*Paul and Power* [Philadelphia: Fortress, 1980], p. 17) discussion of Paul's "anything but unintentional" choice of terms.

[126]See J. Paul Sampley, "'Before God, I do not lie' (Gal 1. 20): Paul's Self-defence in Light of Roman Legal Praxis," *NTS* 23 (1977) 477-82. Sampley's explanation of the oath demonstrates that a conflicting version of the report need not have been at issue.

[127]See Betz, p. 72 n. 159.

[128]The recent attempts to interpret the allegory reach very different conclusions, demonstrating the extent to which historical presuppositions influence the results; see M. C. Callaway, "The Mistress and the Maid: Midrashic Traditions Behind Galatians 4:21-31," *Radical Religion* 2 (1975) 94-101; Betz, pp. 238-52; Andrew T. Lincoln, *Paradise Now and Not Yet*

the emphasis upon Jerusalem in Paul's autobiographical narrative by appeal to his allegory of Abraham's wives and sons in Gal 4:21-31, where he contrasts Hagar, "the present Jerusalem" and Sarah, "the Jerusalem above," i.e., the heavenly, divine "Jerusalem." The latter, he also says, "is free" and "is our mother"; whereas the former "is in slavery with her children" (vv. 25-26). Accordingly, "we are not children of the slave woman but of the free" (v. 31). This implicitly denies the divine character of non-Christian Judaism, something Paul explicitly claims for Jewish-Christianity in 2:7-8. All Paul's dealings with Jerusalem as reported in his autobiographical narrative involve Jewish-Christians, with the possible exception of the "false brothers" who are mentioned only in the third section of the πράξεις division (2:1-10, v. 4). Is it not significant that those men who were the catalysts in Cephas' withdrawal from table fellowship with the Gentiles in Antioch are not described as from Jerusalem but from James (2:11-21, v. 12), and that Paul condemns not their actions but Cephas'? It appears that as in the other place designations in the narrative—Arabia, Damascus, Syria and Cilicia, Judea, and Antioch—Jerusalem has a purely geographical significance. The only viable explanation for the prominence of Jerusalem is to be found in the fact that Cephas is there. Otherwise there is no explanation for the narration of the Antioch incident (2:11-21).

A reasonable question must be raised at this point. If it is the concern of Paul's autobiographical remarks to substantiate the revealed character of his gospel for the Gentiles as illustrated by his own paradigmatic embodiment of that gospel (1:10-12), why does he do so at the Jerusalem church's, particularly Peter's, expense? If he does not intend to suggest that Jewish-Christianity is somehow inferior to Pauline-Christianity, why does Peter come off so badly in the comparison of the two apostles? And why is there no comparable depreciation of the other influential Jewish-Christians of Jerusalem? James, whom, like Peter, Paul meets during both visits to Jerusalem (1:19; 2:9, 12), is given an obviously less prominent role than he. John, though mentioned (2:9), plays no individual role. Barnabas plays a supporting role alongside Paul in one instance (2:1, 9) and over against Paul in the other (2:13). Only Peter occupies a role that compares with Paul's in prominence.

As already discussed in chapter 2 above, the repeated prominence of Cephas-Peter in Paul's narrative (1:18; 2:7, 8, 9, 11-14) emerges in the

---

(SNTSMS 43; Cambridge: Cambridge University Press, 1981), pp. 9-32: "Galatians and the Heavenly Jerusalem"; Gaston, pp. 400-423.

contrasting parallelism between the two, especially emphasized in the
σύγκρισις division (2:11-21). Although Peter had been divinely entrusted
with the gospel to the circumcised, Paul charges that while Peter was in
Antioch he lived like a Gentile and not like a Jew (2:14), presumably
referring to his failure to observe the dietary laws in his meals with the
Gentiles (2:12). Paul does not identify this as the reason Cephas stood
self-condemned, however (2:11).[129] Peter condemned himself when, after
the "men from James" arrived on the scene, he gradually (the force of the
imperfect tense) withdrew and separated himself from table fellowship
with the Gentiles, in Paul's estimate, contrary to his true convictions, out
of fear of the circumcision (2:13). The third person plural in 2:14 appears
to imply that Paul considered not only Cephas but those other Jewish-
Christians who followed his insincere example, including even Barnabas,
by doing so, to be deserters of the true gospel. Yet, it is only Cephas
whom Paul confronted (2:11, 14) with the charge of compelling the Gentiles to Judaize.

It is a gratuitous assumption that Cephas' shift of positions in Antioch
"must have become one of the preconditions for the Galatians' own plans
to shift (cf. 1:6-7)."[130] It is unnecessary to assume with Betz and many
others that the Galatian agitators are Jewish-Christian missionaries from
Jerusalem who oppose Paul. Notice that Paul has no rebuke for the "men
from James," and they criticize not him but Peter (see 2:11-14).[131] This
challenges the widely held assumption that the present "troublemakers" in
Galatia, the "false brothers" in Jerusalem and "the men from James," all

---

[129] In Gal 2:18 Paul seems to argue that one who abandons Judaism only
to return to it subsequently, demonstrates that he is a transgressor. This
transgression may be in one's bad-faith abandonment of Judaism. Rom
14:23 is perhaps relevant here: "He who has doubts is condemned, if he
eats, because he does not act from faith; for whatever does not proceed
from faith is sin" (RSV). But Paul does not think this applies to Peter who
acted insincerely not in abandoning Judaism but in returning to it (2:12-
13). Peter's transgression was demonstrated perhaps in his bad-faith
return to Judaism once abandoned, but more seriously in "compelling"
Gentiles to do so. Cf. chapter 1 note 129 above.

[130] Ibid., p. 107; cf. p. 112.

[131] The simplest explanation of this and the one freest of extra-textual
assumptions belongs to Betz. In challenging Peter's conduct in Antioch,
"the 'men from James' simply insisted on the terms of the Jerusalem
agreement. Their criticism must have been that Cephas had violated those
terms" (p. 108).

represent the same position in Paul's estimate.[132] It is upon this questionable assumption that another, equally suspect, assumption depends—that
whatever Paul says about his "opponents" in one setting applies also to his
present "opponents" in Galatia.[133] Such assumptions, and not the textual
evidence, provide the rationale for the conclusion that these opponents
are invading Jewish-Christian missionaries who derived their authority
from Jerusalem.[134]

Is Peter's prominence in Paul's autobiographical narrative purely an
accident of history or has Paul deliberately selected these incidents to
serve his rhetorical purposes? The points of similarity and difference
between the two apostles, described in terms of the "formerly—now" and
"man—God" contrasts, suggest the latter. Paul dismisses certain aspects
of their respective "autobiographies" as of no importance—it does not
matter who one was (2:6). But the very fact that it is Peter and not some
obscure personality that he selects as the subject of his σύγκρισις suggests that they are in most respects alike. The similarity he chooses to
highlight is that both have been divinely entrusted with the gospel, Peter
to the circumcised and Paul to the uncircumcised (2:7-8, 15-16). Since it
is one's faithfulness to the gospel that matters (2:6; 1:8-9; cf. 1:13-15),
the difference between them consists in that, whereas Paul in Jerusalem
refused to yield to pressure from false brothers in order to preserve the
truth of the gospel (2:5), Peter in Antioch did not adhere to the truth of
the gospel (2:14). Despite his revelation, Peter stood not on the side of
God, but of men (cf. Matt 16:13-23). Paul reports the incident, not to
depreciate Peter, but to illustrate for his readers how easy it was to set
aside the grace of God and pervert the gospel—even Barnabas did.[135]
Paul's narrative makes the Antioch incident a literary precedent of the
recent events in Galatia, but there is no reason to conclude that it historically precipitated the later events, or that the same participants were
involved. Paul's autobiographical narrative functions rhetorically to
illustrate, demonstrate, and substantiate Gal 2:10-12, not to explain
historically how the Galatians had come to be in danger of deserting God

---

[132]So e.g., Betz, pp. 7, 92, 104. Betz even assumes that the Galatians
know "who the 'men from James' were and what had caused them to travel
to Antioch" (p. 107).

[133]So e.g., ibid., p. 90, cf. p. 92.

[134]So e.g., ibid., pp. 7, 90 n. 302, 92, 101: The "false brothers" are "of
coursee, behind Paul's present opponents" (pp. 104, 111).

[135]See J. Paul Sampley, *Pauline Partnership in Christ* (Philadelphia:
Fortress, 1980) pp. 38-39.

and returning to their former existence. The letter offers no etiology of the crisis in Galatia.

D. OTHER AUTOBIOGRAPHICAL REMARKS IN GALATIANS

It appears that another repeated contrast running throughout the letter, in addition to the "formerly—now" and "man—God" contrasts, is that between the circumcised and the uncircumcised. These threads are tied together in the unique circumstances of Paul, who, although he was once an adherent to Judaism—and as such, of course, a circumcised Jewish-Christian (see Phil 3:5), had been divinely called to preach the gospel of Jesus Christ to the uncircumcised, and thus lived like a Gentile (ἐθνικῶς, see 2:14). This provides the necessary link for understanding Paul's impassioned appeal in 4:12, "I beg you, brothers, become as I am, because I also have become like you are." Already in 2:18-21 Paul's use of the first person singular pronoun, ἐγώ, "I," is not so much personal as paradigmatic. Paul presents "himself as the protypical example of what applies to all Pauline Christians."[136]

Gal 4:11 provides a transition to a more strictly autobiographical section in 4:12-20. As in 1:6 it expresses Paul's frustrated disappointment over the turn of events in Galatia since his departure,[137] and as in 2:2 the unthinkable possibility that the worst may come of it: "I fear for you that my labor may prove to be in vain."[138] In this way he recalls his readers' attention to his earlier autobiographical remarks in preparation for the appeal that is immediately to follow.

1. The Imitation of Paul in Galatians 4:12-20

Both structurally and argumentatively Gal 4:12-20 occupies a central position in Paul's letter. Dahl considers 4:12 the letter's "decisive turning point."[139] Gal 4:12-20 contains repeated autobiographical and biographi-

---

[136]Betz, p. 121; cf. pp. 122-23. This dissertation is in part a response to Betz's call for an investigation of Paul's ἐγώ (p. 123 n. 87).

[137]Dahl (p. 95) considers 4:12 parallel to 1:6-9.

[138]See BDF, § 476 (3).

[139]Dahl, p. 95. William A. Smalley ("Some Interactional and Textual Interrelations in the Structure of Galatians," paper, 1976, pp. 49-52) follows John Bligh (*Galatians in Greek: A Structural Analysis of St. Paul's Epistle to the Galatians with Notes on the Greek* [Detroit: University of

cal notices from Paul's initial meeting with the Galatians (4:13) and concludes with the wish once again to be present with them (παρεῖναι, 4:20). Although his concern is obvious, Paul does not directly appeal to them to be reconciled to him. What he does request[140] is that they should become or remain like him because he has become and remains like them (ὡς ἐγώ . . . ὡς ὑμεῖς, 4:12). He does not explicitly indicate how he became like them, nor how they are to become like him. His enigmatic appeal would be scarcely intelligible apart from the autobiographical narrative in Galatians 1 and 2 which precedes it.[141]

According to Dahl, Paul's appeal to imitate him in 4:12 should be seen, against this background, as an appeal for the Galatians, like Paul, to uphold the freedom given in Christ (1:6; 3:27-28; 5:1, 5-6, 27; 6:14-15).[142] Although the expression μιμηταί μου γίνεσθε, "become imitators of me," does not explicitly appear, Gal 4:12 as certainly as 1 Thess 2:14; 1 Cor 4:16; 11:1; and Phil 3:17 calls for imitatio Pauli.[143] Most recent commentators agree that Paul's point is that the Galatians should become/remain as Gentile-Christians free from the law as a means of salvation—what he became in order to preach to them.[144] This allegiance

---

Detroit, 1966]) in describing Gal 4:19-20 as "the interactional center of the book" (p. 51).

[140]See Carl J. Bjerkelund (Parakalō: Form, Funktion und Sinn der parakalō-Sätze im den paulinischen Briefen [Bibliotheca Theologica Norvegica 1; Oslo: Universitetsforlaget, 1967] pp. 177-78), who discusses Gal 4:12 as an atypical παρακάλω sentence; and Willis Peter de Boer (The Imitation of Paul: An Exegetical Study [Kampen: Kok, 1962] pp. 188-96), who recognizes Gal 4:12-20 as a distinctively different but actual call to imitation, despite the objections of some interpreters, e.g., Oepke, p. 104.

[141]Sieffert, p. 263. Sieffert suggests that in view of 4:13-20, 4:12 could be taken to be merely an appeal for the Galatians to love Paul as he loves them, i.e., for renewed favorable relations. But γίνεσθε, "become," is hardly an appropriate expression for love. That Paul's readers should become something for love's sake is not the same as an appeal to love.

[142]Dahl, pp. 86-87, cf. 95.

[143]So e.g., Anselm Schulz, Nachfolgen und Nachahmen: Studien über das Verhältnis der neutestamentlichen Jüngerschaft zur urchristlichen Vorbildethik (SANT 6; München: Kösel, 1962) p. 323. See also note 140 above.

[144]E.g., Meyer, pp. 181-82; Sieffert, pp. 263-64; Lietzmann, pp. 26-17; Burton, p. 236; Williams, p. 73; Ragnar Bring, Commentary on Galatians (trans. Eric Wahlstrom; Philadelphia: Muhlenberg, 1961) pp. 208-9; Blunt, p. 113; Lagrange, pp. 110-11; Bonnard, pp. 91-92; Amiot, pp. 194-95;

to Christian freedom would effect a reconciliation of relations between Paul and his deserting converts,[145] but it would also place them, like Paul, on the side of God rather than men, and require the rejection of the troublemakers and the return to their former slavery, which these represent (4:30-5:1).

Paul reminds the Galatians of the circumstances of his earlier encounter with them. "I preached the gospel to you intially δι' ἀσθένειαν τῆς σαρκός" (4:13). The untranslated phrase is usually rendered "because of a physical ailment."[146] But as noted earlier, the precise meaning of ἀσθένεια is in doubt and may indicate persecution rather than illness as the reason. In 4:24 the term πειρασμός, "trial," as descriptive of the effect this had on the Galatians supports this possibility.[147] Even if the textual variant of the possessive pronoun describing πειρασμός is decided in favor of the less likely and easier reading μου rather than ὑμῶν, i.e., "my trial" rather than "your trial,"[148] the verse would remain difficult to translate.[149]

Part of the difficulty arises from Paul's employment of an antithetical construction in 4:14. Despite the way in which they might have been expected to receive him, they received him not as a trial to be avoided, but favorably, as if he were an angel, even Christ himself. Betz correctly observes that Paul's intention here is not to exalt his own importance but to praise the Galatians for their demonstration of true friendship.[150]

A contrast between the relationship of Paul and the Galatians "formerly" and "now" is implicit in the two rhetorical questions in 4:15a and 16 and the metaphorical reference to their earlier favorable reception of him in 15b. Things have certainly changed since the time when they would

---

Duncan, pp. 138-39; Schlier, p. 209; Beyer-Althaus, p. 36; Mussner, pp. 305-6; Betz, pp. 222-23; Schulz, pp. 322-23.

[145]See Schlier, pp. 207-9. This is Paul's major concern in the view of some interpreters, e.g., Oepke, pp. 104-5; Rendall, p. 177.

[146]So Bauer, s.v. διά, B II 1; s.v. ἀσθένεια, 1 a: "because of a bodily ailment."

[147]The parallels to 1 Thessalonians are also supportive. There the reference is clearly to persecution (cf. 1 Thess 1:6; 3:3, 4, 7; also 2:2, 14-16; 3:5). See n. 99 above.

[148]Cf. Bruce M. Metzger, *A Textual Commentary on the Greek New Testament* (London: United Bible Societies, 1971) p. 596.

[149]Bauer, s.v. πειρασμός, 1 and 2 offers two possibilities; cf. Betz, pp. 224-25.

[150]Betz, p. 226.

have sacrificed anything for Paul (4:15b). Whereas Paul was once their friend (φίλος),[151] and whereas they once had received him warmly (4:14, 15b), their present desertion of him (1:6) suggests that he has now become their enemy (ἐχθρός, 4:16). It is they, and not Paul, who have changed.[152] The implicit contrast between Paul and the troublemakers in 4:17 and 18 highlights the incongruity of their shift of attitudes. "Have I become your enemy while maintaining the truth for you" (4:16; see 2:5); and the troublemakers have become your "friends" while only flattering you (4:17-18).[153]

A similar incongruous shift of attitudes appears to be presumed in 4:15a: "Where then is your blessing?" The subjective genitive interpretation of "your blessing" might refer to the Galatians' blessing of themselves or to their blessing of Paul, i.e., their favorable reception of him.[154] The translation of the NEB attempts to combine these two possibilities, "Have you forgotten how happy you thought yourselves in having me with you?" Less likely, since the reference is to their change of attitudes not his, is the objective genitive, which would refer to Paul's former blessing of them, which has now become a curse (1:8-9).

In contrast to the concern of 4:12-16 with the former and present relations between Paul and the Galatians, vv. 17-18 address the Galatians' relations with those he considers the source of their changed attitudes. As elsewhere in Galatians, Paul denounces the troublemakers' motives as selfish because of the disastrous consequences their success would bring the Galatians, not because of firsthand psychological information he has about them. Paul's description may be paraphrased: "They seek to win your favor for a sinister purpose. Insisting on your exclusive attentions, they want to exclude you from the grace of Christ [cf. 5:2-4]. I, too, seek your favor but for a sincere purpose, and always, not only when I am present with you." The implicit contrast between παρουσία, "presence,"

---

[151] The term is not used but the concept is clearly assumed. Betz (pp. 220-37) amply illustrates the allusions to the theme of friendship (περὶ φιλίας) throughout the passage.

[152] The connection with Paul's references earlier to his efforts to preserve ἡ ἀλήθεια τοῦ εὐαγγελίου (2:5, 14) in order that the Galatians might obey the truth (3:1; 5:7) precludes the possibility of his changing.

[153] Here the presumed antonym of ἀληθεύω, "I tell the truth," is not ψεύδομαι, "I lie," but κολακεύω, "I flatter"—in 4:17 ζηλάω in a bad sense. Cf. Betz, pp. 229-30.

[154] Contra Lightfoot (p. 176) who specifically rejects this, "because" he says, "the word μακαρισμός would ill express their *welcoming* of him."

and ἀπουσία, "absence," (παρεῖναι in 4:18 and 20) leads Paul to voice his wish to be present with the Galatians once again. (4:20).

In 4:19 Paul addresses his alienated friends as his children for whom he once again experiences birth pangs until they are fully Christian. He is perplexed about their changed attitudes (4:20b) and would like to visit them in person, if his circumstances permitted.[155] The perplexity Paul expresses is reminiscent of his expression of amazed disappointment in 1:6. A somewhat ambiguous infinitive phrase, ἀλλάξαι τὴν φωνήν μου, expresses the purpose his presently impossible wish should serve. Perhaps Betz is correct that Paul merely indicates his frustration with the limitations of epistolary address and his preference for oral communication a personal visit would allow, "'to exchange my voice.'"[156] But to be preferred is Dahl's interpretation, that the subsequent appeal introduced by the allegory of Abraham's two wives and two sons expresses what Paul would say if he were present with them.[157] He prefers to change from his harsh tone of rebuke (1:6-9; 3:1-5) to a warm appeal in order once again to win their favor (ζηλοῦσθαι, 4:18).

2. Boasting in the Cross in Galatians 6:11-17

The remainder of the letter, other than the autographic conclusion in 6:11-17, lacks autobiographical features. This autographic conclusion is both autobiographic[158] and paradigmatic,[159] and recapitulates to a great extent Paul's argument throughout the letter.[160] Thus Betz argues that "it contains the interpretive clues to the understanding of Paul's major

---

[155]BDF, § 359, refers to this as "a wish impossible of fulfilment."

[156]So Betz, p. 236.

[157]Dahl, p. 86.

[158]See the examples of the first person singular in vv. 11 (twice), 14 (three times), and 17 (four times).

[159]In Gal 6:14 Betz (p. 318 n. 66) refers to an "exemplaric 'I' which stands for every Christian" as in 2:19-21. There he identifies it as a "paradigmatic 'I'" (p. 122) in which Paul is the "protypical example of what applies to all Pauline Christians" (p. 121).

[160]This is recognized widely by commentators, see e.g., ibid., p. 23. Betz identifies 6:12-17 as a *recapitulatio*, "recapitulation." Gordon J. Bahr ("The Subscriptions in the Pauline Letters," *JBL* 87 [1968] 27-41) considers this the major function of the conclusions ("subscriptions") of Hellenistic letters.

concerns in the letter as a whole and should be employed as the hermeneutical key to the intentions of the Apostle."[161]

What Paul says about himself (and all those who share his view of
circumcision, cf. 6:15-16; 5:10) and the troublemakers, in the context of
the letter as a whole, is set in stark contrast. Whereas Paul no longer
preaches circumcision (5:11), they compel the Galatians to be circumcised
(6:12). Their values are grossly distorted. In Paul's estimate neither circumcision nor uncircumcision is decisive. What matters is the "new creation" (6:15), or "faith working through love" (5:6). One who has faith in
Jesus Christ alone for salvation, who belongs to Jesus Christ is Abraham's
child whether he is a Jew or Gentile, slave or free, male or female (3:27-
29), and so belongs to the Israel of God (6:16). One who belongs to Christ
has "crucified the flesh with its passions and lusts" (5:24), knows that the
Son of God died on the cross because he loved him and gave himself up for
him (2:20) and is enabled by the Spirit of his Son (4:6) to love others and
thus fulfill the law (5:13-14, 22-23).[162] Although Paul solemnly testifies
that every man who receives circumcision is obliged to do the whole law
(5:3), those who are being circumcised and are compelling others to be
circumcised, do not themselves keep the law (6:13; cf. 6:2).

Whereas Paul's preaching of the cross of Christ without requiring his
Gentile converts to be circumcised results in his persecution (5:11), his
opponents compel circumcision, first, in order to avoid persecution for the
cross of Christ (6:12). Paul's final personal reference in the letter, his
claim to bear in his body the στίγματα of Jesus (6:17), strongly emphasizes the priority of the *theologia crucis* to the *theologia gloriae*.[163] The
cross is the only basis on which the resurrection can be understood correctly. Paul's suffering is a participation in that of the crucified Christ
(2:19-20; cf. Col 1:24), whose slave (1:10) and authorized representative
(1:1) he is. This is reminiscent of a major concern in his earlier autobiographic remarks in Galatians 1 and 2, where "formerly—now" contrasts
Paul the persecutor and Paul the preacher.[164]

A second reason the opponents want the Galatians to be circumcised is
that they may boast in their flesh (6:13). Such boasting is not only "incompatible with the Christian faith"[165] but clearly in contrast with Paul's

---

[161]Ibid., p. 313.

[162]Cf. ibid., pp. 263-64.

[163]Cf. the discussion in section C 5 above.

[164]Dahl, p. 98.

[165]Betz, p. 317. Betz refers (p. 317 nn. 52, 53) to Rom 2:17, 23; 5:3, 11;
1 Cor 1:29-31; 4:7; 2 Cor 10:17; 11:18; Phil 3:2ff.; etc.

"boasting." The quotation marks are appropriate because Paul does not really boast at all, but gives praise to God (ἐμοὶ δὲ μὴ γένοιτο καυχᾶσθαι, "But may I never boast at all," 6:14). If he "boasts" it is of the cross of the Lord Jesus Christ (6:14). That is, he modestly assigns his "achievement" to the grace of God (cf. 1 Cor 15:10-11; 1:28-31; 2 Cor 12:9-10). This is reminiscent of the earlier "man—God" contrast of chs. 1 and 2.

Unlike the troublemakers and those Galatians they are leading astray, Paul does not nullify the grace of God, thereby rendering Christ's death purposeless (cf. 2:21; 5:2-4), once again returning to the former existence before Christ. He does not remove the stumbling block of the cross (5:11). He does not stymie the will of God that by the death of Christ sins should be forgiven (cf. 1:3-5). He has been crucified with Christ (2:20), and by the cross of Christ the world has been crucified to him and he to the world (6:14; cf. 5:24)—the human has given way to the divine. Paul implies that the troublemakers, however, either did not preach the cross of Christ, or by advocating circumcision emptied it of its saving significance, substituting human achievement for that of God in Christ (6:11; 5:11).

Gal 6:16 is a conditional blessing on those Galatians who do not receive circumcision (cf. 6:15), in contrast to the curse Paul pronounced at the outset of the letter on those who pervert the gospel (1:8-9).[166] It is by now quite clear that this perversion amounts to the requirement of circumcision as an improvement on simple faith (cf. 3:1-5; 5:1-12). Paul is hopeful that those who thus trouble the Galatians (1:7; 5:10) will bear their judgment (5:10), that they will be excommunicated (1:8-9; 4:30; 6:17).

CONCLUSION

Several features of Paul's autobiographical statements in Galatians resemble the practice of autobiography in antiquity. Paul's presentation of himself as an ideal representative of the gospel is comparable to the philosopher's claim to be an embodiment of his philosophy. As section C above argues, the conventional *topoi* of the ancient lives are paralleled by the various parts of Paul's narrative. Paul removes the offensiveness of his apparent "self-praise" by means of antidotes comparable to those

---

[166]Betz, pp. 320-21.

recommended by Plutarch.[167] But the question which motivates the chapter requires a concise answer: What is the function of Paul's autobiographical remarks in his letter to the Galatians? The answer which has already been implied needs to be made more explicit. Various strands of evidence come together to support the conclusion that Paul presents his "autobiography" as a paradigm of the gospel of Christian freedom which he seeks to persuade his readers to reaffirm in the face of the threat presented by the troublemakers.

That Paul offers his autobiographical narrative in 1:13-2:21 as substantiation of his claim in 1:11-12 concerning the nature and origin of his gospel suggests that he considers himself in some sense a representative or even an embodiment of that gospel. As in the ancient philosophical lives, the consistency between his ἀναστροφή, "conduct," and πράφεις, "deeds," and his λόγοι, "words," demonstrates the truth of his philosophy, the gospel of Jesus Christ. He is a paradigm of the gospel he preaches among the Gentiles. The formulation of Paul's autobiographical remarks in terms of "formerly—now" and "man—God" serves the paradigmatic function of contrasting Paul's conversion from Judaism to Christianity with the Galatians' inverted conversion, which is really nothing other than a desertion of "the one who called [them] in the grace of Christ" (1:6) and a surrender of Christian freedom for the slavery of the law (see 2:4; 3:28; 4:1-9, 22-31; 5:1, 13).

Despite the close identification between Paul and his message, he remains subject to the gospel. The curse he pronounces on perverters of the gospel would apply equally to himself or the troublemakers (1:8). He can say, "Christ lives in me" (2:20), "You received me as Christ Jesus" (4:14); and "I bear in my body the marks of Jesus" (6:17). Yet he is not a "reincarnation" of Christ, but his "slave" (1:10). "I live by faith in the Son of God, who loved me and gave himself for me" (2:20). By including himself among those for whom Christ died, Paul tries to identify himself with his converts as a redeemed sinner, a recipient of grace (1:3-4, 13-17; 2:15-21; 4:4-5). It was the gracious event of the revelation of Christ, which determined his vocation, and divided his life in two—his "former" life as a zealous persecutor of the Church and his "now" as a preacher of the faith he once tried to destroy (1:13-17, 23), his past as a man-pleaser and his

---

[167]See chapter 1 section F above. In his review of Betz's commentary, Wayne A. Meeks (*JBL* 100 [1981] 306) asks rhetorically, "Will anyone who has actually read the *Zauberpapyri* to which Betz refers and then reads Galatians, really imagine that he is reading the same kind of literature?"

present as one who is concerned to please God. As John Howard Schütz observes, "Both the message and the messenger proclaim grace and both embody grace, grace as event."[168]

But past events and experiences may be in vain; freedom must be preserved (2:5; 3:4; 4:11; 5:1-7). Throughout the letter Paul emphasizes the futurity of justification (2:16, 17; 3:8, 24; and especially 5:4). He, as much as his converts, lives with the tension of the "already-but-not-yet." He too must contend for freedom against those who would impose the bondage of the law (2:4-5). It would have been possible even for him "to build up again those things which [he] tore down," to return to law as a means of salvation. But to no advantage; it would only prove him once again a sinner (2:17-18). It would be to turn foolishly from the Spirit to the flesh, from God to man (3:1-5; cf. 2:15-17). "For if a law had been given which was able to give life, then indeed justification would have been by law—but this is not the case" (3:21). Thus, Paul insists, "I do not set aside the grace of God, for if justification were through law, then Christ died in vain" (2:21).

The conditional curse on those who preach a different gospel than his at the letter's beginning (1:8-9) and the corresponding conditional blessing on those who remain loyal to him at the end (6:16) lead Betz to assume that Galatians functions in part as a "magical letter."[169] But in this Galatians is far more like Demosthenes' *De corona* (323-24) than the magical papyri.[170] A more satisfactory explanation of this correlation of blessing and curse is to be found in Betz's obervation that Paul's expression of "disappointment and disapproval of the Galatians" in 1:6-9 closely resembles the negative kind of epideictic oratory, ψόγος, "blame," which has ἔπαινος, "praise," as its positive counterpart.[171] In Gal 4:14-15 Paul's words "amount to a praise of the Galatians" for their expression of true friendship to him during his earlier visit.[172] And certainly the conditional blessing in 6:16 amounts to praise of those who remain his loyal friends.

This in turn may provide an explanation for the puzzling absence in Galatians of the characteristic thanksgiving period which usually follows the prescript in Paul's letters. In its place stands an indignant rebuke of the apostatizing Galatians and an even more intense attack on those who

---

[168]John Howard Schütz, *Paul and the Anatomy of Apostolic Authority* (SNTSMS 26; Cambridge: Cambridge University, 1975) p. 134.

[169]Betz, p. 25.

[170]See chapter 1 section E 2 b above.

[171]Betz, p. 45 and n. 16.

[172]Ibid., p. 226.

have misled them. In contrast to those on whom he heaps blame for turning from Christ to Judaism, Paul praises his own conduct of turning from reliance on Judaism to Christ (1:13-2:21).[173] But Paul removes the potential offensiveness of self-praise by means of a number of conventional antidotes, discussed below. Although this would seem to suggest that the genre of the letter is epideictic, there are stronger reasons for determining that epideictic is only a prominent feature and not its overarching genre.

But the forensic genre of apology generally applied to Galatians also explains only an aspect of it. The antithetical formulation of Paul's autobiographical statements is designed not to respond to the accusations of opponents, but to serve the moral purpose of demonstrating the shameful character of behavior opposite his. He establishes his ethos as a means of promoting confidence in himself and the gospel he represents to dispose his readers favorably toward his argumentation, and to present himself as a model for them to imitate. These features serve also as antidotes against the offensiveness of his apparent self-praise, means of dispelling actual or potential misunderstanding of his record, and an indirect means of attacking his "opponents." But as chapter 2 above attempts to demonstrate, the apologetic genre inadequately accounts for many of the most crucial features of Galatians.

The Galatians' alliance with the troublemakers is more than a personal affront to Paul. For by turning to circumcision, they are turning from Christ (5:2); by turning to law, they are turning from grace (1:6; 4:11; 5:2-4); by turning to the flesh, they are turning from the Spirit (3:2-5; 4:29; 5:13-25); by turning to slavery, they are turning from freedom (2:4; 5:1, 13). This calls not for apology and polemics or for self-praise and blame of the troublemakers and those who are deserting Paul because of their persuasion. It calls for counter-persuasion and dissuasion. On the effectiveness of his argument and their decision hang their Christian existences and the fruits of missionary labors (3:4; 4:11). Yet Paul's confidence is not in his rhetoric, but "in the Lord" that they will be of the same mind as he —that they will take the side of God not man (5:10).

The *causa* of the letter is not the personal threat to his apostolic authority that Paul experiences as a result of the possible desertion of his converts. On the contrary, it is they who are threatened (see 1:6-9; 3:1-5; 5:1-12). It is they who in trying to please men have risked the good

---

[173]Idem, *Plutarch's Ethical Writings and Early Christian Literature* (SCHNT 4; Leiden: Brill, 1978) p. 386.

pleasure of God (1:10; see 4:17-20). It is they who are in danger of nullifying the grace of God and rendering Christ's death ineffective (2:21; cf.
5:2-4). This is not to suggest that Paul is personally unconcerned; his
letter witnesses to the contrary. He does not want to see his labor go for
naught (4:11; cf. 2:2), for after all, his labor is an expression of the effective operation of the grace of God (1 Cor 15:10), which is not to be
accepted in vain (2 Cor 6:1).

The only remaining rhetorical genre to be considered is the deliberative. Its applicability to Galatians may be confirmed from various perspectives. F. Forrester Church observes that success in achieving the
objectives of deliberative rhetoric consists in "establishing two primary
motives for action, honor (honestas) and advantage (utilitas)."[174] The
former motive may account for the elements of praise in the letter. Paul's
warning to those Galatians who are considering circumcision demonstrates
the latter. "Christ will be of no advantage to you. . . . You are cut off
from Christ, . . . you are fallen from grace" (5:2-4). The warning in 5:2
and 3 of the negative consequences of Gentile-Christians receiving circumcision and the connection between 1:10 and 5:11 suggest that the
question Paul addresses in the letter is, Should the Galatians receive
circumcision?—clearly a deliberative question.

In his account of the Antioch incident, Paul holds up Peter and Barnabas as illustrations of the possibility of falling out of step with the truth
of the gospel and how he deals with such lapses. Like the Galatians, they
were running well, but were hindered from obeying the truth (2:11-14; cf.
5:7). Unlike Paul, who refused to surrender "the freedom we have in
Christ" for even a moment in the preservation of the truth of the gospel,
they yielded to the fear of men (2:4-5, 12-13). In reminding both them and
the Galatians of the truth, he was acting not as an enemy but as their true
friend, and following his own advice (6:1-5). The troublemakers, who were
urging the Galatians to be circumcised, were false-friends and flatterers,
who had only their selfish interests in mind (4:12-20; 6:12-13). The disastrous results of heeding their advice would be the loss of salvation altogether. "They want to shut you out" (4:17), Paul warns, "Instead, cast
them out!" (4:30).

Although the antithesis of "slavery" and "freedom," a characteristic

---

[174]F. Forrester Church, "Rhetorical Structure and Design in Paul's
Letter to Philemon," HTR 71 (1978) 19; see 19 n. 12 for the ancient
authorities.

feature of epideictic oratory,[175] is obviously prominent in Galatians, it is hardly treated academically. As the theme of the parenetic section, freedom is not merely praised or explained. There is an obvious urgency in Paul's twofold appeal to stand fast in Christian freedom and to resist the fleshly forces that would enslave, whether legalism or antinomianism (5:1ff.). The obvious genre of this parenesis is deliberative, persuasion and dissuasion.[176] In fact, this concern emerges earlier as Paul urges his wayward converts to become like him (4:12-20). Paul's perplexity over the Galatians' desertion of him, his gospel, and God, his curse of preachers of a contrary gospel (1:6-9), and the ironic questions which begin the argumentative part of the letter (3:1-5), all suggest that his overarching concern was not praise or blame but persuasion. The persuasion was specifically directed toward securing the Galatians' excommunication of the troublemakers, rejection of their perverted "gospel," and renewed allegiance to the gospel of freedom, that they like Paul might abandon Judaism for Christ, that they might turn once again from man to God.[177]

The temporal contrast, "formerly—now," as applied to the Galatians, requires them to choose between two possible futures. The one Paul recommends is a reaffirmation of the freedom that is already theirs in Christ; the other future is only a return to the slavery of their pre-Christian days. His warning is emphatic, "Now I, Paul, say to you that if you receive circumcision, Christ will be of no advantage to you" (5:2 RSV). It should be recalled that in deliberative oratory, the hearers act as judges of what is to be done in the future.[178] The *narratio* is often missing in speeches of this genre, as Aristotle says, "because no one can narrate things to come; but if there is a narrative, it will be of things past, in order that, being reminded of them, the hearers may take better counsel about the future."[179] This is clearly the case with Galatians. This fact would also seem to bring about the collapse of whatever evidence there might remain to support Betz's analysis of Galatians as an apologetic letter by appeal to the characteristic structural feature, the *narratio*.[180]

That Paul has preserved the gospel of freedom in the face of opposition

---

[175]Burgess, p. 157.

[176]See the discussion of the genre of parenesis in the conclusion of chapter 4 below.

[177]See chapter 2 section B 2 d above.

[178]See chapter 1 section C 1 above.

[179]Aristotle *Rhetoric* 3.16.11, trans. John Henry Freese (LCL).

[180]See chapter 1 section C 1 above.

serves also to extend to his readers the hope that they too will prevail. "Let us not grow weary in well-doing, for in due season we shall reap, if we do not lose heart" (6:9 RSV). "For through the Spirit, by faith, we wait for the hope of righteousness" (5:5 RSV). "I have confidence in the Lord that you will take no other view than mine; and he who is troubling you will bear his judgment, whoever he is" (5:10 RSV). The survival of the letter implies that his confidence was not misplaced.

4

The Function of Paul's Autobiographical Remarks in 1 Thessalonians

INTRODUCTION

The autobiographical remarks which appear in 1 Thessalonians 1-3 are very different from those in Galatians 1 and 2. They have, however, a striking similarity to Gal 4:12-20 in that both passages share a number of philophronetic *topoi*. The differences are to be assigned not only to the different kinds of facts they report, but more basically to the very marked difference in the relationship (*aptum*) between Paul and the Thessalonians, on the one hand, and Paul and the Galatians, on the other. Whereas Paul's dissatisfaction with the Galatians leads him to omit the thanksgiving period entirely, to replace it with an ironic rebuke, his satisfaction with the Thessalonians is so complete that the first three chapters of the letter assume the form of thanksgiving. It is in this context that his autobiographical remarks are found, framed by "biographical" praise of the Thessalonians as his imitators. The parenetic remarks that occupy the last two chapters of the letter do not suggest that Paul's praise is a subtle means of approaching a serious problem in Thessalonica needing correction. He does concede that they are not perfect (3:10), but on the whole his advice is simply, "As you are doing, do so more and more" (see 4:1, 10; 5:11).

The Pauline authorship and integrity of 1 Thessalonians, as with Galatians, are today taken for granted, despite a number of unique features of the letter.[1] The earlier challenges to Pauline authorship by Ferdinand

---

[1] In addition to those unique features noted in the next few paragraphs, other notable differences include 1 Thessalonians' uncharacteristically un-Pauline soteriological vocabulary. Instead of referring to justification by faith or the cross, Paul describes the "conversions" of the Thessalonians

Christian Baur and the Tübingen school have been totally dismissed. Recent attempts to prove the letter a compilation have met with little success,[2] although the suggestion that 1 Thess 2:13-16 as a whole or in part may be a deutero-Pauline interpolation has found more support.[3] But as the excursus on this passage below attempts to demonstrate, there are more satisfactory explanations for its origin and position in the letter on the assumption of its originality than on the assumption that it is an interpolation.

By comparison with the other letters of the Pauline corpus, 1 Thessalonians opens with an unusually brief prescript (1:1). Paul's name, joined with those of two co-addressants, Silvanus and Timothy, is not further specified by reference to either official or unofficial designations. Although only the prescripts of Romans, Colossians, and the Pastoral Epistles mention no co-senders, all except those of 1 and 2 Thessalonians identify Paul as an "apostle" or "slave" or Christ. The naming of the addressees and the salutation are similarly concise. This unadorned prescript is followed by an unusually expansive thanksgiving period, whether its limits are defined as 1:2-10 or 1:2-3:13.[4] The thanksgiving, however,

---

using traditional mission terminology—"You turned to God from idols, to serve a living and true God, and to wait for his Son from heaven . . . " (1:9-10); see Leon Morris, *The Epistles of Paul to the Thessalonians* (TNTC; Grand Rapids: Eerdmans, 1957) p. 39; D. E. H. Whiteley, *Thessalonians in the Revised Standard Version* (New Clarendon Bible; London: Oxford University Press, 1969) p. 39; and Ernest Best, *A Commentary on the First and Second Epistles to the Thessalonians* (HNTC; New York: Harper & Row, 1972) p. 81; see pp. 82-87 for further references. In 1 Thessalonians Paul uses only one δικ- word, and that in a sense that departs from its frequent and characteristic use in the other letters of the homologoumena (see 3:6). In another apparent departure from his usual practice, he uses the verb εὐαγγελίζεσθε, "to preach the gospel," only once, and in an unusual, almost secular sense (see 3:6); see Gerhard Friedrich, "εὐαγγελίζω, κτλ," *TDNT* 2:707-17 and 720.

[2]See Werner Georg Kümmel, *Introduction to the New Testament* (rev. ed.; trans. Howard Clark Kee; Nashville: Abingdon, 1975) pp. 260-62; and in greater detail idem, "Das literarische und geschichtliche Problem des ersten Thessalonicher-briefes," *Neotestamentica et Patristica. Eine Freundsgabe. Herrn Professor Dr. Oscar Cullmann zu seinem 60. Geburtstag Überreicht* (NovTSup 6; ed. W. C. van Unnik; Leiden: Brill, 1962) pp. 213-27.

[3]See the discussion in the excursus on 2:13-16 in section B 3 below.

[4]Cf. e.g., the thanksgivings in 1 Cor 1:4-9; 2 Cor 1:3-7; Phil 1:3-11;

gives no clear indication of a specific problem which determines Paul's purpose in writing (*causa*), unless it is simply the involuntary separation of friends which necessitates epistolary, as opposed to oral, communication (2:17-18), and a sense of gratitude that this has not affected their friendship.[5]

These unusual features are accompanied by another throughout the letter, the dominance of the first person plural and the virtual absence of the first person singular, which appears only four times in all of 1 Thessalonians (2:18; 3:5—twice; 5:27). Taking into consideration the lengths of the various letters, the plural is about three times more frequent, and the singular about ten times less frequent in 1 and 2 Thessalonians than in the other letters.[6] In some instances the "we" may include Paul's co-worker Silvanus, perhaps Timothy (see 1:1; 3:2, 6), other unidentified apostles (see 2:7), and/or other Jewish-Christians (see 2:15-16), or a more inclusive group, comprising also the Thessalonians and/or all Christians (see 1:3, 10; 2:19; 3:13; 4:14; 5:5, 6, 8-10, 23, 28). There are sound reasons for concluding, however, that in most instances the primary, if not the exclusive reference, of the first person plural is to Paul alone as the actual author of the letter.[7] Thus, in those instances in which "we" is the subject, the

---

Phlm 4-7. Thanksgiving is fairly lengthy in Romans (1:8-15) and entirely absent in Galatians, where it is replaced by an ironic rebuke (1:6-9). On the termination of the thanksgiving in 1 Thessalonians, see the discussion in section A 4 below.

[5]See nn. 13-14 and 122-39 below.

[6]This is a feature it shares with 2 Thessalonians. Only 2 Corinthians approaches this frequency. See the discussion in the introductory chapter above. Since these letters are hardly unique in the mention of co-senders, their involvement cannot provide an adequate explanation of the phenomenon.

[7]On the literary plural in general, see the introduction to this dissertation; with specific application to 1 Thessalonians, see e.g., Ernst von Dobschütz, *Die Thessalonicher-Briefe* (MeyerK; 7th ed.; Göttingen: Vandenhoeck & Ruprecht, 1909) p. 68: "Mann wird also dem Gefühl, das Paulus dies 'Wir' in die Feder diktierte, am ehesten gerecht werden, wenn man zunächst immer nur an ihn selber denkt, daneben bald an diese, bald an jene Kategorie, mit der er sich solarisch fühlt. Die 'Mitverfasser' kommen dabei höchstens mit in Betracht, haben aber gar keine Prärogative." James Everett Frame (*A Critical and Exegetical Commentary on the Epistles of St. Paul to the Thessalonians* [ICC; Edinburgh: Clark, 1912] p. 90) agrees that Paul is "speaking mainly for himself." Similarly Walter Schmithals (*Paul and the Gnostics* [trans. John E. Steely; Nashville: Abing-

references may be appropriately labeled "autobiographical."[8]

A dominant feature of the first three chapters of the letter is Paul's discussion of "his past, present and future relations with the Thessalonians."[9] This autobiographical section may be divided into two major divisions. The concern of the first, 1:2-2:16, is the relationship of friendship established between Paul and the Thessalonians during the time of his founding visit (εἴσοδος, 1:9; 2:1), whereas the second, 2:17-3:13, concerns this relationship since Paul's departure (ἔξοδος) from Thessalonica and their separation (ἀπορφανισθέντες, 2:17). In the latter section Paul emphasizes his repeated attempts to visit them again (2:17-18), twice describes the mission of Timothy to Thessalonica as his representative (3:1-5), their mutual longing to see one another (3:6), and closes with the prayer that God would direct his way (ὁδός) to them (3:10-13). They are true friends; for though they are separated in person, they are not in heart (2:17; 3:10).

Hans Dieter Betz's survey of the concept of friendship in antiquity in his interpretation of Gal 4:12-20 is applicable also to the autobiographical section of 1 Thessalonians. True friendship is possible only on the basis of equality, unanimity, likeness, reciprocity, frankness, and constancy[10]—all qualities explicitly mentioned as characterizing the relationship between Paul and his Thessalonian converts. "To be sure, true friendship does not change even when the friends are separated."[11] The letter itself serves as a stop-gap measure to overcome the severest test of friendship—physical and temporal separation.[12]

The transition from 1 Thess 3:13 to 4:1 is almost uniformly recognized

---

don, 1972] pp. 135-55) regards all the first person remarks as specifically relevant to Paul alone.

[8]See e.g., Abraham J. Malherbe (*Social Aspects of Early Christianity* [Baton Rouge: Louisiana State University, 1977] p. 23) and Béda Rigaux (*The Letters of St. Paul: Modern Studies* [ed. and trans. Stephen Yonick; Chicago: Franciscan Herald, 1968] p. 122) who explicitly identify much of the first three chapters of 1 Thessalonians as "autobiographical."

[9]Best, p. 27. It is this conclusion which leads most commentators to identify 1:2-3:13 as autobiographical.

[10]Hans Dieter Betz, *Galatians: A Commentary on Paul's Letter to the Churches in Galatia* (Hermeneia; Philadelphia: Fortress, 1979) pp. 220-37. These characteristics of true friendship are those suggested by the writers of antiquity, most notably Cicero and Plutarch.

[11]Ibid., p. 232. This paraphrases Plutarch's *How to Tell a Flatterer from a Friend* in *Moralia* 97B.

[12]See the discussion of 2:17-3:13 in section C below.

as the major break in the logical structure of the letter. Both sections, 1:2-3:13 and 4:1-5:24, conclude with intercessory prayers which are very similar in both form and content, 3:10-13 and 5:23-24.[13] A consensus of scholars agrees that the first section is essentially autobiographical and the second parenetic.[14] Differences arise in their answers to the follow-

---

[13]Gordon P. Wiles, *Paul's Intercessory Prayers: The Significance of the Intercessory Prayer Passages in the Letters of St Paul* (SNTSMS 24; Cambridge: Cambridge University, 1974) pp. 63-71.

[14]Abraham J. Malherbe, "I Thessalonians as a Paraenetic Letter," paper presented at the SBL annual meeting, 1972, pp. 1-15. For the agreed identification of 1:2-3:13 as the first major unit of 1 Thessalonians during the past century, see e.g., Charles August Auberlen and C. J. Riggenbach, "The First Epistle of Paul to the Thessalonians" (trans. John Lillie; *Commentary on the Holy Scriptures*, 12 vols.; ed. John Peter Lange and Philip Schaff; Grand Rapids: Zondervan, 1960 [reprint of the 1860ff. ed.]), 11:13; Gottlieb Lünemann, "Critical and Exegetical Hand-book to the Epistles to the Thessalonians" (trans. Paton J. Gloag; Meyer's Critical and Exegetical Handbook 8; New York: Funk & Wagnalls, 1889) p. 436; A. J. Mason, "The First Epistle of Paul the Apostle to the Thessalonians," *The Epistles to the Colossians, Thessalonians, and Timothy* (ed. Charles John Ellicott; London; Cassell, 1889) p. 81; J. B. Lightfoot, *Notes on Epistles of St. Paul* (ed. J. R. Harmer; Grand Rapids: Baker, 1980 [reprint of the 1895 ed.]) pp. 3 and 8; George Milligan, *St. Paul's Epistles to the Thessalonians* (London: Macmillan, 1908) pp. 2 and 5; Dobschütz, pp. 27-28, 62-63; Frame, pp. 17 and 72; Alfred Plummer, *A Commentary on St. Paul's First Epistle to the Thessalonians* (London: Scott, 1918) pp. xix and 5; John W. Bailey, "The First and Second Epistles to the Thessalonians," *IB* (12 vols; New York: Abingdon, 1951ff.) 11:256; Béda Rigaux, *Saint Paul: Les Epîtres aux Thessaloniciens* (EBib; Paris: Lecoffre, 1956) pp. 37 and 356; Henry Alford, *The Greek Testament* (4 vols.; rev. Everett F. Harrison; Chicago: Moody, 1958) 3:249; Kümmel, "Problem," p. 219; Albrecht Oepke, "Die Briefe an die Thessaloniker," *NTD* vol. 8, 9th ed. (Göttingen: Vandenhoeck & Ruprecht, 1962) p. 160; K. Theime, "Die Struktur des erst Thessalonicherbriefes," *Abraham Unser Vater. Juden and Christen im Gespräch über die Bibel. Festschrift für Otto Michel zum 60. Geburtstag* (ed. O. Betz, M. Hengel, and P. Schmidt; Leiden: Brill, 1963) pp. 450-58; Best, pp. 64-65; Ronald A. Ward, *Commentary on 1 and 2 Thessalonians* (Waco: Word, 1973) p. 191; and similarly: Martin Dibelius, *An die Thessalonicher I II. An die Philipper* (HNT 11; 3rd ed.; Tübingen: Mohr [Siebeck], 1937) p. 1; and A. L. Moore, *1 and 2 Thessalonians* (NCB; Greenwood, SC: Attic, 1969) p. 20.

In support of the general acceptance of 1 Thessalonians 4-5 as parenesis, see Otto Merk, *Handeln aus Glauben. Die Motivierungen der paulinischen Ethik* (Marburg: Elwert, 1968) pp. 45-58.

ing questions: (1) What is the function of the autobiographical section? (2) Is Paul's main objective in writing the letter fulfilled in the autobiographical or parenetic section? (3) Does the parenesis reflect the situation in Thessalonica?[15] (4) What is the terminal limit of the thanksgiving period which begins with 1:2?

A. AUTOBIOGRAPHICAL OR PARENETIC

1. Autobiographical Apology?

The major issue at stake in the first question is whether the autobiographical section, as a whole or in part, is an apology directed in response to concrete accusations in Thessalonica against which Paul defends himself. A number of commentators have seen in 1:2-2:16 an *apologia pro vita et labore suo* and in 2:17-3:13 an *apologia pro absentia sua*, or similarly identified the whole of the first three chapters as an apologetic response to charges and insinuations against Paul's character or apostolic office.[16] Others limit the *apologia* to 2:1-12.[17] In either case these scholars generally agree that the major thrust of the letter is to be found in the apologetic autobiography of the first three chapters, as opposed to those who emphasize the parenetic chapters.[18]

---

[15]Malherbe, "I Thessalonians," p. 10.

[16]So e.g., James Moffatt, "The First and Second Epistles to the Thessalonians," *The Expositor's Greek Testament* (5 vols.; ed. W. Robertson Nicoll; London: Hodder & Stoughton, 1897-1910) 4:26 and 29; Frame, pp. 14, 17, 140 passim; Theodor von Zahn, *Introduction to the New Testament* (3 vols.; trans. Melancthon Williams Jacobus et al.; Edinburgh: Clark, 1909) 1:215-16; Morris, pp. 18 and 42; Bailey, p. 251.

[17]In response to charges: Auberlen-Riggenbach, p. 28; Milligan, p. xlix; cf. pp. xxxi-xxxii, xliii, lxiv, and 16; Paul M. Schubert, *Form and Function of the Pauline Thanksgiving* (BZNW 20; Berlin: Töpelmann, 1939) p. 7; Whiteley, pp. 29 and 40; D. Edmond Hiebert, *The Thessalonian Epistles: A Call to Readiness* (Chicago: Moody, 1971) pp. 76-77; Schmithals, pp. 125 and passim; Kümmel, *INT*, pp. 255 and 258.

Some consider the designation apology appropriate even if it is not in response to actual charges: Best, pp. 16-18 and 55; Hendrikus Boers, "The Form Critical Study of Paul's Letters. I Thessalonians as a Case Study," *NTS* 22 (1975) pp. 150 and 152.

[18]Early advocates of the latter view include John Calvin, *The Epistles of Paul the Apostle to the Romans and to the Thessalonians* (trans. Ross

The widely held opinion that Paul apologetically responds to concrete accusations[19] has not resulted in any clear agreement as to the identity of his presumed opponents or on the specific nature of their charges.[20] The existence of opponents and charges is simply postulated and has not been demonstrated. As with the similar situation with respect to Galatians, this fundamental methodological problem is compounded by another—the overpowering influence of non-textual data. Due to the lack of concreteness in Paul's "apology" in 1 Thessalonians, the opponents are generally identified by appeals to presumed parallels in other Pauline letters, especially in Galatians and the Corinthian correspondence, Acts, and/or other nearly contemporary literature.[21] But the absence of a "clear consensus of opinion as to the identity of Paul's opponents" elsewhere in his letters is hardly a secure basis for conclusions here.[22]

As has been the case with the letter to the Galatians, the opponents' charges in 1 Thessalonians are characteristically reconstructed by appeal

---

Mackenzie; ed. David W. Torrance and Thomas F. Torrance; Grand Rapids: Eerdmans, 1960) p. 332; Ferdinand Christian Baur, *Paul the Apostle of Jesus Christ, His Life and Work, His Epistles and His Doctrine* (2 vols.; trans. A. Menzies from the 2nd ed. by Eduard Zeller; Theological Translation Fund Library; London: Williams & Norgate, 1873-75) 2:85; W. Bornemann, *Die Thessalonicherbriefe* (vol. 10; MeyerK; 6th ed.; Göttingen: Vandenhoeck & Ruprecht, 1894) pp. 265ff.; Dobschütz, pp. 106-7; see Aberlen-Riggenbach, pp. 27-28 for references to earlier proponents; more recent advocates include Rigaux, *Thessaloniciens*, p. 356; 51-62; 397-98; Dibelius, pp. 10-11; Charles Masson, *Les deux Epîtres de Saint Paul aux Thessaloniciens* (CNT 11; Neuchâtel: Delachaux & Niestlé, 1957) pp. 8 and 32; Günther Bornkamm, *Paul* (trans. D. M. G. Stalker; New York: Harper & Row, 1971) pp. 61-64.

[19]Schmithals claims that "on this point the exegetes from the time of the Fathers down to the last century have never been in doubt" (p. 151; cf. 137 n. 36).

[20]See the survey in Best, pp. 17-22.

[21]See e.g., Schmithals (pp. 123-24), who admits, "I Thess. undoubtedly reveals its concrete occasion to the ordinary reader less than any of the author's other letters" (p. 124), before claiming, nevertheless, "the corresponding passages in the epistles to Corinth and Galatia leave no doubt that the charges appearing there were raised against Paul in the communities (p. 125).

The only vaguely apologetic tone, lack of concrete epistolary situation, and parallels with other letters in 1 Thessalonians were F. C. Baur's major arguments against its authenticity (2:316-22).

[22]Best, p. 16.

to a "mirror reading" of selected antithetical formulations.[23] It is claimed
that "we may infer from some of Paul's strongest affirmations, and most
emphatic denials when in controversy with opponents, that the opposite of
what Paul is saying had been argued by these opponents."[24] But interpreters differ among themselves as to which affirmations or denials are emphatic enough to require the presumption that Paul responds to opponents.
Thus, despite the agreed methodology, the permutations of opponents and
charges are limited only to the ingenuity of the interpreter.

The same reasons that make "mirror reading" and its concomitant
methods inappropriate as applied to Galatians pertain in 1 Thessalonians.
It should be noted that the entire letter, not simply the so-called "apology," is marked by antithetical constructions, not all of which can be
reversed to find opposing charges.[25] It is simply impossible to imagine
that opponents claimed the reverse of the denials in 5:9—that God has
destined us to wrath, not for salvation; or in 5:15—that one should always
repay evil for evil and not do good to one another. Simply because a
statement may be intelligibly reversed is not evidence that this must have
taken place. Antithetical constructions require a literary and rhetorical
rather than a historical explanation. They were far too common in the
normal synagogue preaching of Hellenistic Judaism and the moral discourses of itinerant Cynic and Stoic philosophers in clearly non-polemical
settings to assume, as the consensus of New Testament scholarship has
done, that Paul's antithetical constructions uniformly respond to opposing
charges.[26]

---

[23]See esp., Auberlen-Riggenbach, p. 18; Bailey, p. 256; Schmithals, p.
137; Robert Jewett, "Enthusiastic Radicalism and the Thessalonian Correspondence," paper presented at the SBL Paul Seminar, 1972, pp. 20, 23,
and the following note.

[24]C. L. Mearns, "Early Eschatological Development in Paul: The Evidence of I and II Thessalonians," NTS 27 (1981) 145.

[25]Within 2:1-12 the antithetical construction occurs in 2:1-2, 3-4b, 5-7,
and 8; outside this unit it appears in 1:5, 8; 2:13, 17; 4:7, 8; 5:6, 9, and 15.

[26]See chapter 2 above. It has long been recognized that the formulation of Paul's "apology" in 1 Thessalonians is similar to those of certain
Cynic Philosophers, which arose not in response to contrary charges but
from the need to distinguish themselves from charlatans; see Frame, p.
10; Dibelius, pp. 7-11. Malherbe's comparison of the Cynic parallels and
1 Thess 2:1-12 demonstrates the impossibility of reconstructing charges
on the basis of antithetical formulations (" 'Gentle as a Nurse,' The Cynic
Background to I Thess ii," NovT 12 [1970] 203-17; cf. idem, "I Thessalonians"). The parallels in non-Cynic autobiographers noted in chapter 1
above illustrate that the Cynics did not have a corner on the form.

2. Autobiographical Parenesis?

Perhaps the second question, whether the letter's objective is primarily autobiographical or parenetic, presents a false alternative. Perhaps they are complementary. Hendrikus Boers, who denies the necessity of the presumption of charges underlying Paul's "apology," argues instead that it functions to reestablish or reaffirm his apostolic authority and proclamation with his readers, in order to dispose them to comply with the following parenesis. Thus he refers to 1 Thess 2:1-12 and similar autobiographical sections in the letters as "apostolic apology."[27] But Paul mentions his apostleship only once in the letter—in 2:6, and there only to de-emphasize his authority. It appears that what he reestablishes is not his authority but his ethos, and not for the purpose of defense but for parenesis. To this extent the autobiographical section distinguishes itself from Plato's *Apology of Socrates,* to which tradition Boers considers it to belong.[28]

Malherbe demonstrates that the distinctive features of the autobiographical section in 1 Thessalonians are just as characteristic of a parenetic letter as the generally recognized parenetic section. "The descriptions of the readers as μιμηταί, the theme of remembrance of what is already known, expressed by οἴδατε and μνημονεύετε, the description of Paul in antithethic manner, the theme of *philophronesis,* all contribute to this conclusion."[29] But to describe the letter as primarily parenetic as opposed to autobiographical has not yet addressed the question of its rhetorical genre. Nor has it answered the question motivating this study— What are the specific functions of Paul's autobiographical remarks in the letter? Answers to these questions are necessarily deferred until the conclusion of this chapter.

3. Traditional Parenesis?

At issue in the third question is whether the parenesis in chs. 4 and 5 is merely traditional ethical advice of a general character or directly addresses the Thessalonian situation. Largely through the influence of

---

[27]Boers, pp. 153 and 158; cf. idem, "Gen. 15:6 and the Discourse Structure of Galatians," seminar paper presented at SBL meeting, 1976) p. 12.

[28]Idem, "Form Critical."

[29]Malherbe, "I Thessalonians," pp. 16-17.

Martin Dibelius,[30] the specifically ethical discourses which characteristically conclude Paul's letters have been called "parenesis" (παραίνεσις, "exhortation").[31] He defines parenesis as a series of unconnected exhortations or "admonitions of general ethical content" which "ordinarily address themselves to a specific . . . audience." They are generally "very diverse in content, lacking any particular order, and containing no emphasis upon a special thought of pressing importance for a particular situation."[32] They are almost completely traditional in character and as such have little or nothing to do with the actual situation to which they are presumably addressed. He classifies 1 Thess 4:1-12 and 5:1-22 as conforming to the parenentic genre.[33] Dibelius would leave only 4:13-18 of chs. 4 and 5 as directly addressed to the situation in Thessalonica.

The clear connections between the autobiographical and parenetic sections suggest that Dibelius' theory is in need of some modification. In all probability Paul, like Seneca, has a high regard for traditional advice, but has nevertheless accepted the necessary task of selecting, adapting, and applying it to the specific situation in Thessalonica.[34] Seneca writes metaphorically:

> Assume that prescriptions have been handed down to us for the healing of the eyes; there is no need of my searching for others in addition; but for all that, these prescriptions must be adapted to the particular disease and to the particular stage of the disease.[35]

---

[30]Cf. Martin Dibelius, "Zur Formgeschichte des Neuen Testaments (ausserhald der Evangelien)," *TRu*, n.F. 3 (1931) 212-19; idem, *From Tradition to Gospel* (trans. Bertram Lee Woolf; New York: Scribner's Sons, 1935) pp. 238ff.; idem, *James: A Commentary on the Epistle of James* (rev. by Heinrich Greevan, trans. Michael A. Williams, ed. Helmut Koester, Hermeneia; Philadelphia: Fortress, 1976).

[31]Henry George Liddell, Robert Scott, and Henry Stuart Jones, *A Greek-English Lexicon* (new ed.; Oxford: Clarendon, 1940) s.v. See the discussion and further references in Betz, pp. 253-54.

[32]Dibelius, *James,* p. 3.

[33]Ibid., pp. 2-3.

[34]Malherbe ("I Thessalonians," pp. 2 and 19 n. 6) cites Ilsetraut Hadot, *Seneca und die griechisch-römische Tradition der Seelenleitung* (Berlin: de Gruyter, 1969) pp. 179-90.

[35]Seneca *Ad Lucilium epistulae morales* 64.8, trans. Richard M. Gummere (LCL).

It is not improbable that "certain new and unique situations" might have called forth exhortations composed "on an *ad hoc* basis, using no, or only very few, traditional paraenetic elements."[36] The interconnectedness of the autobiographical and parenetic sections suggests that the advice may be less general in application than Dibelius and his followers allow. He does seem to be correct, however, that the moralist's advice tells us more about his ethical concerns than about his audience's ethical deficiencies.

4. Autobiographical Thanksgiving?

The autobiographical section is formally a part of the letter's unusually lengthy thanksgiving period, which begins in 1:2 and probably extends through 3:13. This terminal limit is a matter of considerable scholarly debate,[37] although the repeated references to thanksgiving in 2:13 and 3:9 suggest that this is at least a major theme throughout the section. Although such repeated or prolonged emphasis on thanksgiving is formally unparalleled in Paul's letters,[38] Theodore C. Burgess describes the letter

---

[36]Karl Paul Donfried, *The Setting of Second Clement in Early Christianity* (NovTSup 38; Leiden: Brill, 1974) p. 111; cf. idem, "False Presuppositions in the Study of Romans," *CBQ* 36 (1974) 341.

[37]See the discussion in Boers, "Form Critical," pp. 149-52. The "unusually long thanksgiving section" is one of the reasons motivating Boers' elimination of 2:13-16 as an interpolation, to bring about "a virtual metamorphosis of I Thessalonians" (p. 152). The "metamorphosis" is not to be denied; the question remains whether the surgery eradicates a foreign growth or emasculates an integral part of the original letter.

[38]Schubert, whose 1939 study provided the early impetus for recent form critical studies of Paul's letters, identifies the thanksgiving period as "an indivisible entity" comprising 1:2-3:13 (pp. 17-27, 21, 62, quotation from p. 20). Three apparently separate thanksgiving sections, 1:2-5; 2:13-14; and 3:9-13 are interrupted by "digressions," which "from the point of view of form, function and content are . . . fully legitimate and indeed constitutive elements of the general Pauline thanksgiving pattern" (p. 17). Schubert, nonetheless, found 2:13-16 "very peculiar as to both form and content" (p. 23). He notes, however, that the strikingly frequent use of γίνομαι in 1:2-2:12, even when another verb might be expected, continues in 2:13-16 (pp. 19-20).

Jack T. Sanders ("The Transition from Opening Epistolary Thanksgiving to Body in the Letters of the Pauline Corpus," *JBL* 81 [1962] 348-62) identifies two thanksgiving periods, 1:2-10 and 2:13-3:13, interrupted by the body of the letter, 2:1-12 (p. 356; see pp. 348-56).

of thanksgiving (ἀπευχαριστικός) as among the more common types of
epideictic letters in antiquity.[39] The possibility of describing 1 Thessalonians as a letter of thanksgiving was first suggested by Ernst von
Dobschütz and accepted by Paul Schubert in his important study, *Form
and Function of the Pauline Thanksgiving.*[40] But whether "thanksgiving"
describes the letter as a whole or only the autobiographical section of it,
here, as in all Paul's letters, the important epistolary function of the
thanksgiving is "explicitly or implicitly paraenetic."[41] The thanksgiving,
which is a regular part of Paul's letters—absent only in Galatians—was
not a rigid convention in contemporary letters and is longer in its briefest
form in Paul than its parallels elsewhere.[42] The formal objection to the
appropriateness of this prolonged thanksgiving is not a serious problem.
Boers properly cautions,

> One should be careful not to assume that Paul's letters had to
> conform to a particular pattern. Paul was undoubtedly, con-
> sciously and subconsciously influenced by the conventions of
> Hellenistic letters, but it would be a mistake to assume that
> his letters had to follow a given pattern.[43]

Other form critical studies have identified 1 Thess 1:2-10 alone as the
thanksgiving; see Robert Funk, *Language, Hermeneutic, and Word of God*
(New York: Harper & Row, 1966) p. 269; idem, "The Apostolic Parousia:
Form and Significance," *Christian History and Interpretation: Studies Pre-
sented to John Knox* (ed. by W. R. Farmer, C. F. C. Moule, and R. R.
Niebuhr; Cambridge: Cambridge University, 1967) p. 254; John Lee White,
*The Form and Function of the Body of the Greek Letter: A Study of the
Letter-Body in the Non-Literary Papyri and in Paul the Apostle* (SBLDS 2;
Missoula, MT: SBL, 1972) pp. 114-18; Boers, "Form Critical," p. 153.

[39]Theodore C. Burgess, "Epideictic Literature," *University of Chicago
Studies in Classical Philology* 3 (1900) 186-87.

[40]Schubert, pp. 7 and 26. In this he follows Dobschütz, p. 62.

[41]Schubert, ibid., pp. 89 and 26. So also more recently Peter Thomas
O'Brien, *Introductory Thanksgivings in the Letters of Paul* (NovTSup 49;
Leiden: Brill, 1977) pp. 141-44, 165, 262-63.

[42]In addition to the studies mentioned in the above notes, see the survey in William G. Doty, *Letters in Primitive Christianity* (Guides to Biblical Scholarship, NT Series; Philadelphia: Fortress, 1973).

[43]Boers, "Form Critical," p. 142. F. Forrester Church ("Rhetorical
Structure and Design in Paul's Letter to Philemon," *HTR* 71 [1978] 28)
warns against the "tendency to identify 'sections' that do not exist in
order that the specific text may be made to accord with the generic
form."

Close inspection of the three references to thanksgiving in 1:2; 2:13; and 3:9, reveals striking similarities alongside significant differences. In all three the personal object of the thanksgiving is the same, "you," the Thessalonians; "God" is one to whom thanks is given; and thanks is said to be unending ("unceasingly" in 1:2 and 2:13; "night and day" in 3:10). Nevertheless, that for which Paul gives thanks in each particular case is different. The differences suggest a logical progression. In the first, Paul's expression of thanks to God is based on his knowledge of their divine election—"God has chosen you" (1:4). In the second, the basis for thanks is identified as their response to the word of God—"You accepted it not as the word of men, but as it truly is, the word of God" (2:13). The third gives voice to Paul's relief and gratitude at the good news brought by Timothy of their perseverance in the faith despite their afflictions—"You stand firm in the Lord" (3:8). The progression (cf. 1:3) confirms that the extended thanksgiving is, as Paul's adverbs—"unceasingly" and "night and day"—suggest, continual not simply repeated.

B. Autobiographical Reminiscences:
1 Thessalonians 1:2-2:16

Paul first voices his continual thanksgiving to God for the Thessalonians in 1:2-4. He recalls their tangible expressions of the familiar triad of Christian virtues, faith, hope, and love (1:3; see also 5:8) which demonstrate their divine election (1:4). In 1:5-10, Paul offers two further proofs of the divine election of his converts: first, the character of his proclamation of the gospel (1:5), and second, the character of their response to the gospel (1:6-10). In 2:1-16, he expands on these proofs in the same order, this time giving more lengthy attention to his character (2:1-12), and referring more briefly to theirs (2:13-16).

1 Thess 1:5 is the first strictly autobiographical reference in the letter, as Paul explains the circumstances of the Thessalonians' election in terms of his participation in it, juxtaposing a description of his gospel and himself. "Our gospel did not come [ἐγενήθη] with words only, but also with power and with the Holy Spirit and with full conviction. You know what kind of men we were [ἐγενήθητε] among you on your behalf" (1:5). His parallel description of the divine power accompanying his visit among the Thessalonians (1:9; 2:1, 13) clearly emphasizes the unity existing between the proclaimer and the proclamation. This unity is accompanied by another, that between Paul and his converts. It is Paul's rhetorical and argumentative goal, not his "opponents," which determines that he shall

present his ethos as an embodiment of his gospel and his converts' ethos as
an imitation of his.

1. The Thessalonians: Imitators
and Examples

Although Paul appeals for imitation in other letters (1 Cor 4:16; 11:1;
Gal 4:12; Phil 3:17; 2 Thess 3:7, 9), he nowhere else explicitly affirms that
they have become imitators as he does both here and in 2:13.[44] Nor does
he elsewhere claim that his readers were themselves an example (τύπος)
for imitation by other believers (1:7). But here Paul says that the Thessalonians, like him, spread "the word of the Lord" by their conduct, speaking
more eloquently on the subject of perseverance in the face of persecution
than mere precepts (cf. 1:8 and 5 and 2 Cor 8:1-12).[45] These distinctive
features arise from the function their imitation serves in the logic of the
letter as confirmation of their divine election.

Paul embodies the gospel he preaches. In 2:13 he emphasizes that the
word (λόγος) of God which he preached and which they accepted is "at
work in you who believe." They are also representatives of the gospel.
Both Paul's ethos and theirs demonstrate the truth of the divine *logos*. The
unity between Paul and his converts, explained in 1:6 as due to their
imitation of him and of the Lord, in 2:14 is due to their imitation of the
churches of Judea. Although the models differ, the imitated ethos is
identical—perseverance in the face of opposition (see 1:6; 2:1-2; 2:14-16).
The two "biographical" sections also differ in that the first emphasizes
that the Thessalonians' imitation of Paul made them an example to
believers in Macedonia and Achaia, and the second emphasizes that their

---

[44]See Willis Peter de Boer, *The Imitation of Paul: An Exegetical Study*
(Kampen: Kok, 1962) p. 123; and Hans Dieter Betz, *Nachfolge und Nachahmung Jesu Christi im Neuen Testament* (Tübingen: Mohr [Siebeck],
1967) pp. 143-44. Wilhelm Michaelis ("μιμέομαι, κτλ," *TDNT* 4:659-74) is
mistaken in his claim that their imitation refers only to the fact of their
conversion in 1:6 and of their experience of suffering in 2:14. This is pre-
cluded in that they became imitators not only of Paul but of the Lord (see
1:6 and 2:15), and in that their imitation made them a model to believers,
not to potential believers (Dobschütz, p. 73): "die Gläubigen (nicht
Glaubigwerdenen)."

[45]Seneca similarly finds *exempla* more helpful and easier to follow
than *praecepta* (*Ad Lucilium epistulae morales* 6.5f.; 75.1ff.; 40.1; cited
in Malherbe, "I Thessalonians," p. 7).

imitation made them participants in suffering, like the churches of Judea, the prophets, Paul, and the Lord Jesus. Both 1:5-10 and 2:13-16 contain the same "sequence of thoughts: the word coming from Paul, the divine working, the imitation."[46] It is the same activity of God which is responsible for the exemplary ethos of both the Thessalonians and of Paul. The two "biographical" sections, 1:5-10 and 2:13-16, which focus more directly on Paul's Thessalonian μιμηταί, "imitators," than on him are nearly identical in length to the autobiographical description of the τύπος, "model," of Paul in 2:1-12. All this is supportive of Paul's emphasis throughout the letter on the equality, mutuality, and reciprocity of the relationship between him and his converts.

2. Paul's Exemplary Ethos

The first of the two proofs Paul offers as confirmation of the divine election of the Thessalonians (1:4), his ethos as a preacher of the gospel (1:5), is expanded upon at length in 2:1-12, before the second, their perseverance in persecution, already the subject of 1:6-10, is reiterated in 2:13-16.[47] The connection between 1:2-10 and 2:1-12 is provided by the conjunction[48] γάρ and numerous terminological features: their mutual knowledge and memory[49] of each other's behavior and Christian labors[50]

---

[46]De Boer, p. 113. Nearly all commentators agree that the virtue remains the same although the model changes. See e.g., Frame, pp. 82-83; Rigaux, *Thessaloniciens*, pp. 380-81, 441; Lünemann, p. 453; Milligan, p. 10; Best, p. 77; Victor Paul Furnish, *Theology and Ethics in Paul* (Nashville: Abingdon, 1968) p. 221; D. M. Stanley, " 'Become Imitators of Me': The Pauline Conception of Apostolic Tradition," *Biblica* 40 (1959) 865 and 868.
It is of interest that the two "biographies" and the "autobiography" each occupy 30 lines of the Nestle text. In this balance Paul's autobiographical remarks, incidently, if not intentionally, conform to the advice of Plutarch to praise one's audience and others whose aims and actions are similar to one's own.

[47]This analysis is shared by numerous commentators; see e.g., Lightfoot, p. 18; and Best, p. 88.

[48]See e.g., Best, p. 89.

[49]Cf. εἰδότες, "We know," in 1:4 and οἴδατε, "you know," in 1:5; 2:1, 2, 5, and 11. Cf. μνημονεύοντες, "we remember," in 1:3 and μνημονεύετε γάρ, "you remember," in 2:9.

[50]Cf. ἔργον and κόπος, "work," of the Thessalonians in 1:5 and of Paul in 2:9 (κόπος, μόχον, and ἐργαζόμενοι).

as a result of Paul's missionary visit.[51] He begins the strictly autobiographical section in 2:1-12 by referring to his example of suffering (v. 2).
The underlying relationship between Paul's description of the Thessalonians' ethos and his ethos is the correlation of imitators—model.

a) Boldness Inspired by God

Paul's description of his founding visit in 1 Thess 2:1-2 assumes the
form of an antithetical construction, parenthetically expanded in the
positive half. The force of Paul's denial that his visit to Thessalonica had
not proven to be κενός, "empty," is ambiguous apart from the following
affirmation.[52] The word κενός might have the force "empty of truth,
false," and thus anticipate the point of 2:3-8.[53] But there he refers to his
παράκλησις, "appeal" (2:3), whereas here he refers to his εἴσοδος, "visit"
(2:1), for which "false" hardly seems appropriate.[54] Perhaps Paul implied
that his visit was not empty of results, fruitless, thus emphasizing again
the conversion and perseverance of the Thessalonians.[55] But the response
of his converts to his preaching does not seem to be the concern of 2:1-12,
as it is in 1:6-10 and 2:13-16. Here, his attention is directed to the influence of his character on the character of his converts.[56]

The force of κενός which best matches the positive half of the antith-

---

[51]Cf. the reference to Paul's εἴσοδος, "visit," from the perspective of
the Madeconians and Achaians in 1:9 and of Paul and the Thessalonians in
2:1; see 1:5.

[52]Albert-Marie Denis ("L' Apôtre Paul, Prophète 'Messianique' des Gentils: Etude Thématique de 1 Thess., II 1-6," *ETL* 33 [1957] 245-318) correctly recognizes that the autobiographical section is neither apologetic
nor polemic (p. 245), but exploits the ambiguity of the passage grossly to
overinterpret the evidence. He sees in Paul's use of κενός a reference to
Isa 49:4, in which the Servant's work is described as fruitless. Although
Paul insists that his work was not fruitless, Denis concludes that the
vocabulary of 1 Thess 2:1-6 implies that he considered himself a messianic
prophet to the Gentiles in the tradition of the Suffering Servant of
Yahweh.

[53]So e.g., Whiteley, p. 40; see Walter Bauer, *A Greek-English Lexicon
of the New Testament and Other Early Christian Literature* (2nd ed.;
trans. and ed. William F. Arndt, F. Wilbur Gingrich, and Frederick W.
Danker; Chicago: University of Chicago Press, 1979) s.v. 2 a α.

[54]Best, p. 89.

[55]So e.g., Bauer, s.v. κενός 2 A b; Best, pp. 89-90.

[56]So e.g., Lightfoot, p. 18.

esis is empty of power, powerless, thus repeating the point of 1:5 and anticipating the point of 2:13.[57] He implies, "Our visit to you was not without the power of God," contrasting the divine activity in his mission and the powerlessness of the false gods of idolatry from which his converts had turned (1:8-10). Such dumb idols were unable to inspire the boldness that enabled him to proclaim the gospel in the face of opposition (2:1-2).[58] It was Paul's perseverance despite suffering and insult (2:2) that provided the pattern for the Thessalonians' Spirit-inspired joy under similar circumstances (1:6). That Paul contrasts a powerless versus a God-inspired mission also best accounts for the continuation of his autobiographical remarks in 2:3-12. The recognition of God as the source of his gospel and his bold preaching of it and the antithetical formulation of this claim serve, too, as "antidotes" against the potential offensiveness of his apparent self-praise. The antithetical formulation has an ethical rather than a polemical origin and object, since it is unthinkable that anyone should have accused Paul of deriving his boldness from idols.

b) Responsible to God

1 Thess 2:1-2 is joined to the following verses by means of the explanatory conjunction γάρ. Had his message been merely a human word and his visit devoid of divine power, Paul would never have come to Thessalonica or, once there, would have succumbed in the struggle. This is evidence enough that he has been entrusted with his message by God to whom alone he is responsible (2:3-12).

The first section of 1 Thess 2:3-12, vv. 3-4, contains two complicated antithetical constructions.[59] The subject of the first, Paul's παράκλησις, refers to his activity of preaching in its intention to win acceptance of the message rather than on its content.[60] Paul describes his characteris-

---

[57]So e.g., Frame, p. 91.

[58]In Jewish thought an idol (εἴδωλον) was "a vain thing" (κενός, see Jer 18:15). Compare the claim in Jer 10:14-15, that these "non-entities" are ψευδός, "false," and lack πνεῦμα, "spirit," and ἰσχύς, "strength" with Paul's opposite claim in 1:5.

[59]See the discussion in chapter 3 section C 3 b above.

[60]As in the related verb παρακάλειν in 2 Cor 5:20-6:1. In 1 Thess 2:11; 3:2; 4:1, 10; and 5:14 the verb appears to have the more restricted sense of ethical exhortation. See Carl J. Bjekelund, *Parakalō: Form, Funktion und Sinn der parakalō-Sätze in den paulinischen Briefen* (Bibliotheca Theologica Norwegica 1; Oslo: Universitetsforlaget, 1967) pp. 125-40; Frame, p. 94; Best, p. 93.

194   Pauline Autobiography

tic preaching first negatively as not ἐκ πλάνης, "from error" but ἐκ τοῦ
θεοῦ, "from God" (implicit in 2:3-4; cf. 1:5; 2:2). In the context of Paul's
description of the Thessalonians' conversions to the living and true God in
1:9 (cf. 2 Thess 2:11-12), πλάνη would seem to refer to "a false concept of
God, the idolatry of the heathen," from which they had been delivered (cf.
Rom 1:27).[61] Paul's gospel obviously does not have its origin in such
"error" or "delusion."[62]

The sense of πλάνη as "deceit" or "deception"[63] is conveyed by the
second of the two οὐδέ clauses by which this basic denial is parenthetically expanded. Here Paul denies that he employs "deception" (ἐν δόλῳ)[64]
as a means of persuasion (παράκλησις)—again, unlike the practices of
pagan idolatry (cf. Rom 1:29).[65]

The first parenthetical οὐδέ clause denies that Paul's preaching is ἐκ
ἀκαθαρσίας (2:3). Although the term may refer to "immorality" of any
kind, in Paul's letters it characteristically has reference to sexual sins.[66]
In its only other appearance in 1 Thessalonians, ἀκαθαρσία is associated
with the behavior of "pagans who do not know God" (4:5 and 7; cf. Gal 4:8-
9; Rom 1:21), and contrasted with the example and instruction of Paul

---

[61]Bauer, s.v. Chs. 11-15 of Wisdom of Solomon contain one of the OT's
most severe indictments of idolatry as a "delusion," see 11:15; 12:24;
14:22. The latter passage is also of interest for its antithetical formulation and Paul's allusion to it later in 1 Thessalonians: "Afterward it is not
enough for them to err [τὸ πλανᾶσθαι] about the knowledge of God, but
they . . . call such great evils peace" (Wis 14:22 RSV; cf. 1 Thess 5:3).
[62]See Herbert Braun, "πλανάω," TDNT 6:230-51; contra Schmithals, pp.
143-44.
[63]Bauer, s.v.
[64]Bauer, s.v. δόλος.
[65]Idolatry and deception are treated as synonymous in Wis 14:20. In Wis
14:22-26 as in 1 Thess 2:3, δόλος appears in a vice list alongside πλάνη and
ἀκαθαρσία.
The word πλάνη appears only three times in the Pauline corpus, Rom
1:29; 1 Thess 2:3; and 2 Cor 12:16. In the latter passage it probably refers
to financial fraud. The related verbal form in 2 Cor 4:1-2 appears in an
antithetical formulation which is conceptually similar to 1 Thess 2:1-2. On
the use of δόλος as a technical term for fraud, see J. Paul Sampley,
Pauline Partnership in Christ (Philadelphia: Fortress, 1980) pp. 93-94 and
the accompanying notes.
[66]See Bauer, s.v. 2; and Friedrich Hauck, "ἀκάθαρτος, ἀκαθαρσία,"
TDNT 3:427-29. Had Paul intended to limit his reference only to sexual
immorality, he could have chosen the term πορνεία. See Best, p. 94.

(4:1). He apparently shares the view of Hellenistic Judaism that describes
ἀκαθαρσία as the consequence of idolatry (cf. Rom 1:24 ff.).[67] Paul's
parenensis in 4:1-8 repeats his earlier παράκλησις concerning the sexual
morality incumbent upon Christians. The central exhortation, that they
should abstain from πορνεία, (v. 3) is repeatedly given divine sanction as
what is pleasing to God (v. 1), the will of God (v. 3), and the object of
God's call to sanctification (v. 7; cf. v. 3 and 5:23-24). The seriousness of
the appeal is doubly reinforced by the solemn warnings, "The Lord is an
avenger in all these things" (v. 6b RSV); and, "Therefore whoever disregards this, disregards not man but God, who gives his Holy Spirit to you"
(v. 8 RSV). All these features suggest an intentional correlation between
the autobiographic and parenetic sections, in which Paul's ethos provides
the implicit model for the continued imitation of his converts.[68]

Those who argue that this sense of ἀκαθαρσία does not fit the context
of Paul's autobiographical statements in 1 Thess 2:1-12 do so on the basis
of the "mirror reading" assumption that his denials reply to actual accusations. And as Walter Schmithals correctly observes, "That anyone ever
should have seriously charged Paul with sexual license is . . . incredible."[69] Thus he and others who follow this line of reasoning[70] fail to see
that Paul is not denying charges, but clarifying his ethos and the character of the gospel of the living and true God in contrast to the character of
paganism from which the Thessalonians had only recently been

---

[67]See Ernst Käsemann, *Commentary on Romans* (trans. and ed.
Geoffrey W. Bromiley; Grand Rapids: Eerdmans, 1980) pp. 36-52. Several
traditional vice lists in the Pauline corpus (Gal 5:19-21; Col 3:5; Eph 5:3-
6) associate ἀκαθαρσία and εἰδωλολατρία with πορνεία, "illicit sexual
activities." This association appears in Wisdom of Solomon 14: "For the
making of idols was the beginning of fornication" (v. 12). "They [the
pagans] no longer keep their lives or their marriages pure [καθαρούς], but
they . . . grieve one another by adultery. . . . For the worship of idols . . .
is the beginning and cause and end of every evil" (vv. 24 and 27 RSV).

[68]Compare e.g., the references to (1) the Spirit's activity in Paul's gospel (1:5) and the Thessalonians' joyful endurance of affliction (1:6) with
4:8; (2) the "man—God" contrast (cf. 2:1-2, 4, 13, and 4:8 and 5:19; cf.
also 2 Thess 2:13-15); (3) Paul's example of avoiding ἀκαθαρσία (cf. 2:3
and 4:1, 7); (4) Paul's παράκλησις, "appeal"; (5) the Thessalonians' call (cf.
1:4; 2:12, and 4:7).

[69]Schmithals, p. 145; cf. idem, *Gnosticism in Corinth* (trans. John E.
Steely; Nashville: Abingdon, 1971) pp. 164-66.

[70]See ibid., *Gnostics*, p. 145 n. 67 for further references.

converted.[71] This contrast also may help account for Paul's uncharacteristic soteriological language.[72]

The positive half of the first antithetical construction in 1 Thess 2:3-4 is complicated by a comparatively rare correlative (καθώς—οὕτως) construction. Paul's point is clear enough despite its difficult formulation. "Our work is not self-appointed but a sacred trust or commission; for which we are responsible to Him."[73] What I preach are not my words but God's. I preach not for my own advantage nor of my own volition (cf. 1 Cor 9:15-18). The thrust of the first antithetical construction is simply, "My appeal is not like that of paganism but originates with God" (2:3-41). This is complemented by the second antithesis, "I preach not to please men but to please God" (2:4b).

The terminology and the antithetical parallelism by which Hellenistic Judaism expressed its abhorrence of Gentile idolatry in Wisdom of Solomon 11-15 was probably a more immediate influence on Paul's formulation of 1 Thess 2:1-4 than the uniformly Cynic background Malherbe proposes.[74] The negative description of Paul's character in vv. 5-8, however, does seem to be at home in the Hellenistic world of political rhetoric and demagoguery.[75] But both are fully intelligible on the assumption that Paul wishes to speak emphatically and with clarity for parenetic purposes, making suspect, or at least superfluous, the assumption that he responds to charges.

c) Gentleness Inspired by Love

Paul's antithetical self-description in 2:5-8 is also quite complicated. The γάρ in v. 5 and the use of οὔτε in each of the three denials in vv. 5-6 suggest that vv. 5-8 specifically apply Paul's general description of the character of his preaching set forth in vv. 3-4. The temporal particle ποτέ (v. 5), the shift from the customary present tense of vv. 3-4 to the past tenses of vv. 5-8, Paul's appeal to the Thessalonians' knowledge (v. 5), and mention of his presence with them (v. 7), all imply that he refers to his behavior during the time of his visit. The twice repeated verb, ἐγενήθη-μεν, "we were," (vv. 5 and 7; cf. 1:5; 2:10) suggests that the focus has

---

[71]See Lightfoot, pp. 20-21; and Frame, pp. 95-96.
[72]See note 1 above.
[73]Moffatt, p. 26.
[74]See Malherbe, "Gentle as a Nurse," pp. 206, 214-16.
[75]So e.g., Denis, pp. 287ff.

subtly shifted from the character of his appeal (2:2-4) to the appeal of his character (2:5-8). 1 Thess 1:5 has already suggested how intimately Paul conceives his person and message to be united. A similar claim is made in 2:8b, "We were pleased to share with you not only the gospel of God but also our very selves." As a good philosopher, Paul's word and deed fully correspond, a fact which validates the truth of his philosophy. Itinerant street philosophers and preachers in the Hellenistic world of Paul's day were viewed with suspicion. By his denials Paul distinguishes himself from the typical selfishly-motivated charlatan not for his own defense, but for the edification and education of his readers.[76]

The complicated antithetical formulations in 2:5-8 in general contrast what Paul was not, viz., selfish, and what he was, selfless. The language he uses suggests that implicit in his self-description is a rejection of the practices of many contemporary preachers, perhaps not all of them pagans (see 2 Cor 2:17). But the emphasis is on the positive side of the contrast as Paul reaffirms his deep affection and self-effacing love for his converts (see ἀγαπητοὶ ἡμῖν ἐγενήθητε in 2:8). Paul's concern in 2:5-8 is to maintain on the one hand that he pleases God not men (see 2:4), and yet that he is a true friend to the Thessalonians. Although he does not allow pleasing men to compromise his higher priority of pleasing God, neither does he permit selfish concerns to deter him from properly serving his converts.[77] And although he preached the gospel with boldness (ἐπαρρη-σιασάμεθα, 2:2), he was at the same time gentle (2:7).

Many itinerant preachers of Paul's day made their living by means of "flattery." Plutarch's moral essay, *How to Tell a Flatterer from a Friend,* describes παρρησία, "boldness" or "freedom of speech," as the opposite of flattery and the language of true friendship.[78] Other philosophical preachers, especially the Cynics, overreacting to the ploys of the flat-terer, were noted not so much for their boldness or frankness as for their excess of it. They confused the necessary bold confrontation of their audiences' shortcomings with reviling, berating, and insolence. In response to such abuses, serious preachers emphasized their understanding, gentle-ness, and authentic friendship[79] as Paul does here—not to combat oppo-nents but to distinguish themselves from their unworthy counterparts. Let

---

[76]Dibelius, "Thessalonicher," pp. 7-10.

[77]See the discussion of the dialectic of pleasing God vs. pleasing men vs. pleasing self in chapter 3 section C 3 a above.

[78]Plutarch *Moralia* 48E-74E.

[79]Malherbe, "Gentle as a Nurse," pp. 208-11; and Stanley B. Marrow, "Parrhesia and the New Testament," *CBQ* 44 (1982) 435-36.

us move from the general thrust of Paul's antithesis in 2:5-8 to its specific content.

The negative half of the antithesis, 2:5-6, extends and explains (γάρ) the dialectic of pleasing God versus pleasing men noted in 2:4b with a threefold denial. The first denial in v. 5a asserts, "We never resorted to flattering speech"—the insincere, manipulative, exploitive, self-serving words of an orator bent on favorably impressing and persuading his audience at any cost.[80] The second denial in v. 5b calls upon God to witness to the true character of his motivation—he never disregarded the rights of others in his efforts to win converts.[81] Paul appeals to God, not because his motives had been challenged, but because, although the Thessalonians could vouch for his behavior, only God could know his motives. In the third denial Paul claims, "Nor did we ever seek glory from men" (2:6a).[82] As with the first and second denials, this also elaborates on Paul's rejection of man-pleasing (2:4b). Not only did he not usurp the rights of others in self-aggrandizement, he relinquished his apostolic right to respect, authority, and support (2:6b).

The positive half of the antithesis continues Paul's emphasis upon the mutuality and equality of his relationship with the Thessalonians (see ἐν μέσῳ ὑμῶν in 2:7a).[83] His claim is simply, "But we were gentle among you" (2:7b). The predicate adjective "gentle" is filled with content by the qualifying correlative (ὡς—οὕτως) sentences,[84] which compare Paul's self-

---

[80]See Johannes Schneider, "κολακεύω," TDNT 3:817-18; and the literature cited in H. D. Betz, Galatians, p. 55 nn. 105-17, which is more relevant here than Betz's application of it to Gal 1:10.

[81]The denied behavior, πλεονεξία, has a broader connotation than avarice, covetousness, or greediness, and as J. B. Lightfoot suggests, in his comment on Col 3:5, refers to the "'entire disregard for the rights of others'" (Paul's Epistles to the Colossians and to Philemon [Grand Rapids: Zondervan, 1959 (reprint of the 1879 ed.)] p. 212).

[82]Perhaps implicit in the denial of seeking glory from men is Paul's hope of sharing instead the glory of God (see 2:12 and 20). That the reference to "men" is emphatic is borne out by its elaboration in 2:6b—"neither from you nor from other men."

[83]Lightfoot, Notes, p. 25. This is true whether the original reading in 2:7 is νήπιοι, "babies," or ἤπιοι, "gentle." The weight of external evidence favoring the former is balanced by the internal evidence favoring the latter reading, which is to be preferred in my judgment. See Bruce M. Metzger, A Textual Commentary on the Greek New Testament (London: United Bible Societies, 1971) pp. 629-30.

[84]Compare the similar construction in 1 Thess 5:2.

giving ministry among the Thessalonians (2:8) to the loving care of a nursing mother for her own children. The metaphor, used also in Cynic self-descriptions,[85] emphasizes Paul's longing affection for his converts. Because of his authentic friendship with the Thessalonians, Paul considered it a pleasure to share with them not only the gospel of God but himself as well. His gentleness was inspired by his love for his converts— "because you became beloved [ἀγαπητοί] to us" (2:8). He reminds them of his model of self-giving love in the prayer closing the autobiographical section of the letter, "And may the Lord make you increase and abound in love to one another and to all men, as we do to you" (3:12 RSV). In the parenetic section Paul expresses his satisfaction with their behavior in this area and yet encourages continued progress (4:9-10).

d) Worthy of God

Once again γάρ[86] provides the connection between the preceding autobiographical remarks and its continuation in 2:9-12, which validates and illustrates Paul's claim of unselfish love for the Thessalonians in 2:5-8. The focus is still on the sort of man Paul was among them (see ἐγενή-θημεν in 2:10 as in 5 and 7), but the emphasis is less on his character than on his moral purpose and motives. The first validation of Paul's claim in vv. 5-8 was his "labor of love" among the Thessalonians,[87] expressed in three different words referring to work in v. 9. In v. 6 Paul claims not to have placed any "demands" or "burdens" (βάρος) on them, as he might have as an apostle. In v. 9 he explains the motives underlying his behavior: "For you remember, brothers, our labor and toil. We preached to you the gospel of God while we worked night and day so as not to be a burden [ἐπιβαρῆ-σαι] on anyone of you."

It appears that in both Corinth and Thessalonica, Paul waived his apostolic right to financial support and preached the gospel free of charge, plying a trade instead to earn his livelihood (see 1 Cor 9:1-18; 2 Thess 3:6-12; Phil 4:16; 2 Cor 11:8-10; 12:13-14).[88] If the "burden" he refused to place on them was financial in nature, "labor" does not refer

---

[85] Malherbe, "Gentle as a Nurse," p. 211.

[86] The connective word is γάρ in 2:1, 3, 5, and 9.

[87] Frame, p. 102.

[88] See David L. Dungan, *The Sayings of Jesus in the Churches of Paul: The Use of the Synoptic Tradition in the Regulation of Early Church Life* (Philadelphia: Fortress, 1971); and Sampley, pp. 81-87 on "Paul's personal and Public Finances."

merely to his preaching activity.[89] Rather Paul's manual labor serves as
the model for his explicit parenesis on work in 4:11. In both 2:6-9 and
4:11-12 not being a burden on others is a tangible expression of brotherly
love (cf. 2:8 and 4:9; 2:9 and 4:12),[90] for which Paul also provides the
model (see 2:5-8, 17-18; 3:6, 10, and 12).

The second validation of Paul's claim in 5-8 to gentle concern for his
converts is his irreproachable moral conduct and the motives for it in
2:10-12. "You are witnesses, and God is also, that our behavior toward you
believers was holy and righteous and blameless" (2:10).[91] In the following
verses, Paul turns from his model to his fatherly advice,[92] ". . . We ex-
horted . . . and encouraged . . . and charged you to lead a life [περιπα-
τεῖν] worthy of God . . ." (2:11-12). His example and his advice were
motivated (εἰς τό plus the infinitive) by a concern that the Thessalonians
should conduct themselves in a manner worthy of the God who called
them to be Christians and to live holy lives (see 4:7; 5:23-24).

Paul's prayers at the close of the autobiographic and parenetic sections
again express the concern that the Thessalonians' moral behavior might,
like his, be blameless and pleasing to God (see 3:11-13 and 5:23-24).
Between these prayers, he exhorts them to the moral conduct he

---

[89]Best, p. 103. See John G. Strelen's survey of the βάρος word group in
Pauline usage in "Burden-bearing and the Law of Christ: A Reexamination
of Galatians 6:2," *JBL* 94 (1975) 266-76. The financial connotation which
appears to be present here is debatable in the passage to which he wishes
to apply it, Gal 6:2, however; see Betz, *Galatians*, pp. 298-99. Rigaux
(*Thessaloniciens*, p. 417) understands the connotation to be that of the
moral weight of apostolic authority in both 2:7 and 9.

[90]Ronald Hock, *The Social Context of Paul's Ministry: Tentmaking and
Apostleship* (Philadelphia: Fortress, 1980) pp. 48 and 91-92 nn. 199-203.
See the other works by Hock listed in the bibliography below.

[91]"There is no implicit contrast here between those who believe and
those who do not, as if Paul's conduct varied towards different groups; he
is merely directing attention to his behaviour as they knew it as members
of the Christian community." Best, p. 105. Cf. Gal 6:10.

[92]The metaphor of a father instructing his children in 2:11-12 is a
familiar one in parenetic literature. In 1 Cor 4:14-16 it provides the rationale for Paul's appeal, "Be imitators of me" (4:6). The advice given by a
father to his son may have been the original *Sitz im Leben* of parenesis
(Malherbe, "I Thessalonians," p. 4). In the OT book of Proverbs (see e.g.,
Prov 6:20; 13:1) as in numerous examples of Hellenistic moral literature
(see Malherbe, ibid., pp. 4-5 and 21 n. 20; and idem, *Social Aspects*, p. 28),
the sage exhorts his disciples as a father addressing nis children.

consistently exemplified and taught while he was with them.[93] His call to remember his model and his fatherly instruction in 2:9-12 appears to be an implicit call for them to continue to imitate[94] his example of brotherly love, hard work, morally acceptable behavior, and mutual encouragement.[95] In a letter in which hope is a major concern and the imminent parousia a reminder of the need for ethical seriousness (see 1:10; 2:12, 19-20; 3:12-13; 4:13-18; 5:5-11, 23-24), Paul's exemplary behavior also gives his readers hope that the moral end to which God has called them can be achieved; their hardships need not deter them just as his had not deterred him. The extent to which his autobiographical remarks have a decidedly parenentic function challenges the assumption that they arise out of a polemical situation in which he must deny accusations.

---

[93]See 4:1: ". . . As you learned from us how you ought to lead your lives [περιπατεῖν] and to please God, so live [περιπατεῖτε], in order that you may do so even more." Περιπατεῖν, "to walk," in Paul's letters generally refers to moral behavior (see chapter 3 section B and the accompanying notes above). Note also Paul's exhortation in 4:11-12 that they should conduct themselves respectably (εὐσχημόνως) toward outsiders, live quietly, and mind their own business (see Käsemann's discussion on a similar parenesis in Rom 13:11-14 [p. 363]). In 1 Thessalonians ἀρέσκειν, "to please," appears exclusively in contexts referring to Paul's exemplary behavior (see 2:4, 15; and 4:1). In 2:15-16 Paul's Jewish opponents do not please God because they prevent Paul from doing what pleases God and what he has been called to do—preach the gospel to the Gentiles that they may be saved.

[94]Malherbe, "I Thessalonians," p. 4. Seneca suggests that the best models are men "who teach us by their lives, men who tell us what we ought to do . . . and then prove it by their practice" (*Ad Lucilium epistulae Morales* 52:8; cited in ibid., p. 6). Earlier Xenophon wrote of Socrates, "The very recollection of him in absence brought no small good to his constant companions and followers" (*Memorabilia* 4. 1. 1; trans. E. C. Marchant [LCL]). Pliny emphasizes the reciprocal value of referring to one's own example: "I mention this, not only to enforce my advice by example . . . , but also that this letter may be a sort of pledge binding me to persevere in the same abstinence in the future" (*Ad Lucilium epistulae morales* 7. 6). Reminders of the example of one's parents in parenetic settings serve as imlicit calls "to conduct oneself as a μιμητής of the model" (ibid., pp. 4 and 14; Malherbe cites several apropos ancient examples).

[95]We have already referred to the parenetic employment of the first three models. The fourth may be seen in the verbal connections between such passages as 2:11; 3:2, 7; 4:1 and 10 of Paul; and 4:18; 5:11 and 14 of the Thessalonians. Note esp. 5:11: "Exhort one another and edify one another, as indeed you are doing."

3. Excursus: The Problem of
1 Thessalonians 2:13-16

Scholars nave repeatedly found 1 Thess 2:13-16 problematic for several reasons: (a) literary, (b) historical, (c) grammatical, and (d) theological. In an attempt to resolve these problems, some have proposed to treat the unit, in whole or in part, as a non-Pauline interpolation, and/or to treat the letter as a redactional compilation. Not only are the explanations of the present state of the text on the assumption of redactional interference unsatisfactory, the presumed problems are not compelling enough to require such drastic solutions.[96] Although this excursus by no means solves all the problems of 1 Thess 2:13-16, it does offer a plausible rationale for treating it as an integral and original part of Paul's letter to the Thessalonians.

---

[96]For references to nineteenth-century advocates of various interpolation theories, see Kümmel ("Problem," pp. 220-21), who rejects this solution, and Moffatt (p. 29), who considers only 2:16c an interpolation. More recent advocates include K. G. Eckart ("Der zweite echte Brief des Apostels Paulus an die Thessalonichers," *ZTK* 58 [1961] 30-44), who excludes not only 2:13-16, but also 3:5; 4:1-8, 10b-12; 5:12-22, and 17; and considers the remainder a conflation of two genuine letters; Walter Schmithals (*Gnostics,* p. 180 n. 212, 180-181. and 213; and idem, "Die Thessalonicher als Briefkomposition," *Zeit und Geschichte: Dankesgabe an Rudolf Bultmann zum 80. Geburtstag* [ed. Erich Dinkler; Tübingen: Mohr (Siebeck), 1964] pp. 295-315), who perhaps excises 2:15-16, and considers the canonical letters a compilation of four partially fragmentary letters; Birger A. Pearson ("I Thessalonians 2:13-16: A Deutero-Pauline Interpolation," *HTR* 64 [1971] 79-94); Boers ("Form Critical," *NTS* 22 [1976] 151-52), who follows Pearson; and Daryl Schmidt ("1 Thess 2:13-16: Linguistic Evidence for an Interpolation," *JBL* 102 [1983] 269-79).

For arguments opposing such views see in addition to Kümmel (above): B. W. Bacon, "Wrath 'unto the Uttermost,'" *Expositor,* ser. 8, 24 (1922) 356-76; J. Coppens, "Miscellanees bibliques. LXXX. Une diatribe antijuive dans I Thess., II, 13-16," *ETL* 51 (1975) 90-95; Klaus Haacker, "Paulus und das Judentum," *Judaica* 33 (1977) 161-77; R. F. Collins, "The Theology of Paul's First Letter to the Thessalonians," *Louvain Studies* 6 (1977) 315-37; idem, "Apropos the Integrity of I Thess," *ETL* 55 (1979) 67-106.

a) Literary Problems

From Paul's almost doxological[97] reference to God as the one who calls the Thessalonians to his kingdom and glory in 2:12, the transition to a thanksgiving to God for them in v. 13 is not all that abrupt, nor, in view of the concern announced in 1:4, is it unexpected. With 1 Thess 2:13 Paul resumes his concern announced in 1:4 for the evidence of the Thessalonians' divine election, which is also the subject of 1:6-10. Mentioned more than twenty times in Paul's autobiographical remarks in 1 Thess 2:1-12, Paul's readers come again to occupy his attention. In 1 Thess 2:13-16 the focus turns directly to the readers, not as independent of Paul but in their role as imitators of him (see vv. 15 and 16) and fellow sufferers with him (see 1:6). Since he has already contrasted his behavior with that of others in 2:1-8, it is not at all surprising that he refers to those responsible for both their suffering and his (2:14-16). The first "biography" digresses in 1:8-10 into a discussion of the influence of their example among the believers in Macedonia and Achaia. It concludes with a reference to Jesus, "who delivers us from the wrath to come" (v. 10c). The second "biography" digresses in 2:15-16 into a polemical discussion of Paul's Jewish opponents. It concludes with a reference to the wrath which has come upon them (v. 16c).

b) Historical Problems

The most persuasive argument against the genuineness of these verses has been that they are an "anti-Jewish polemic" reflecting the situation after A.D. 70.[98] But "it is quite arbitrary to single out the destruction of Jerusalem as the reference in mind, instead of occurrences recent to a writer of 50 A.D."[99] A number of possible events, not all of which are equally plausible, have been suggested.[100] Still, in view of our limited knowledge of this historical period, it is not impossible that Paul has in mind "some event unknown to us" but "well-known to his readers."[101] The passage is fully in line with other examples of inter-Jewish polemic in the forties of the first century A.D. And as in all such polemics, the tendency

---

[97]Sanders (p. 356, see also p. 360) suggests that 2:12 is "reminiscent of a doxology."

[98]See esp. Pearson, pp. 81-87.

[99]Bacon, p. 364.

[100]See ibid., pp. 356-76, for a fairly representative list.

[101]Best, p. 120.

to rhetorical exaggeration has so distorted the facts that historical identification is extremely complicated if not impossible.[102]

c) Grammatical Problems

Commentators have repeatedly experienced difficulty in explaining the
logic of the phrase at the beginning of 1 Thess 2:13a, καὶ διὰ τοῦτο καὶ
ἡμεῖς εὐχαριστοῦμεν τῷ θεῷ ἀδιαλείπτως.[103] To what does the δια
τοῦτο refer? If it refers back to what Paul has said previously it should be
translated "therefore."[104] It may, however, refer forward to the causally
understood ὅτι clause in 13b, in which case it may be translated, "For this
reason . . . (because) . . . ."[105]

What is the force of the emphatic καὶ ἡμεῖς, especially in view of the
initial καί? Some presume that Paul refers to a letter from the Thessalonians in which they also gave thanks.[106] Others suggest that the καί
may simply have a weakened sense emphasizing ἡμεῖς, "we for our part"
(cf. Eph 1:15; Col 1:9).[107] But it is more likely that the second καί should
be taken with the following verb εὐχαριστοῦμεν (cf. 3:5).[108] The initial
καί is then simply a copulative particle meaning "and,"[109] which connects
the second thanksgiving with the first in 1:2, thus, "We also/again give
thanks."

---

[102]Haacker, pp. 168-69. It was not uncommon in ancient
autobiographies to attack one's opponents; see chapter 1 above.

[103]See Schmithals, Gnostics, pp. 133-34; idem, "Briefkomposition," pp.
304-5.

[104]So e.g., Frame, pp. 106-7.

[105]So e.g., Best, pp. 109-10.

[106]So e.g., Frame, Thessalonians, pp. 105-6; cf. others noted in Leon
Morris, The First and Second Epistles to the Thessalonians (NICNT; Grand
Rapids: Eerdmans, 1959) p. 86 n. 38.

[107]So e.g., Lightfoot, Notes, p. 30; Best, p. 110.

[108]So F. Blass and A. Debrunner, A Greek Grammar of the New Testament and Other Early Christian Literature (trans. and rev. Robert W.
Funk; Chicago: University of Chicago Press, 1962) § 442 (12).

[109]So Boers, "Form Critical," p. 151. If an explanation is needed for
the "editorial" character of this usage another is possible besides the presumption of an interpolation (Boers) or the joining of two letters at this
point (Schmithals). Paul could have paused after dictating the letter
through 2:12 and continued only after the scribe had read back what he
had recorded. With the thanksgiving in 1:2 fresh in his mind, he resumed,
"And we also give thanks to God constantly, because . . . ." This is no
better or worse a conjecture than the others, but it is only that.

The repetition in 2:13 of the rare ἀδιαλείπτως,[110] "constantly," from 1:6 reinforces the third interpretation. Its use subsequently in 5:17, "pray constantly," between the exhortation in 5:16, "Always rejoice" and 5:18a, "give thanks in all circumstances," may even suggest that Paul's repeated references to his constant prayers of thanksgiving (1:2; 2:13; 3:9) are another aspect of his model for their imitation. His joy even in persecution appears to be an aspect of his model (cf. 1:6)—it is joy which twice characterizes his constant ("night and day") prayer of thanksgiving in 3:9-10 (περὶ ὑμῶν ἐπὶ πάσῃ τῇ χαρᾷ ᾗ χαίρομεν δι' ὑμᾶς). Furthermore, like his model of avoiding "uncleanness" (2:3; cf. 4:1-8, esp. 3 and 7), his model of rejoicing, praying, and giving thanks constantly (5:16-18a) is described as "the will of God" (see 5:18b).

d) Theological Problems

The widely held theological assumptions that "the 'anti-Semitism' of this passage contradicts all that Paul says elsewhere about his attitude to the nation of his fathers"[111] is an exaggeration that fails to take seriously the polemical nature of Paul's remarks. Paul's remarks about the Law are no more contradictory (cf. e.g., Rom 2:13 and 3:20; 7:12; 8:3-4 and Gal 3:17-26). It should be noted that 1 Thess 2:14 speaks favorably of the Christian churches in Judea, the members of which were most certainly Jews (cf. Gal 1:22)—it even places their model alongside that of Paul. The polemic is not anti-Semitic but "anti-persecutor."[112] It is remarkable that scholars who deplore corpus harmonization elsewhere on the grounds that Paul had no fully developed theology, should insist that his attitude toward Israel must be thoroughly consistent.[113]

----

[110]In the NT only in Rom 1:9; 1 Thess 1:3; 2:13; and 5:17, all in connection with prayers of thanksgiving.
[111]Schmithals, *Gnostics*, p. 180 n. 212.
[112]This is correctly recognized by Daniel Patte (*Paul's Faith and the Power of the Gospel: A Structural Introduction to the Pauline Letters* [Philadelphia: Fortress, 1983], ch. 4: "First Thessalonians: Beloved and Chosen by God"). See Jerry L. Daniel, "Anti-Semitism in the Hellenistic-Roman Period," *JBL* 98 (1979) 45-65; and the references in Betz, p. 268 n. 148.
[113]G. E. Okeke ("I Thess. ii. 13-16: The Fate of the Unbelieving Jews," *NTS* 27 [1980] 127-36) provides arguments against the presumption that Paul's theological reflection on Israel was thoroughly consistent and unchanging and speculates as to the reasons for his apparently changed attitude (so also Patte, ch. 4). For attempts to make Paul thoroughly con-

For Paul's favorable attitude toward the Jews, scholars generally point to Romans, particularly chs. 9-11. Admittedly he does say, "And so all Israel will be saved" (11:26a). But this is not before his stinging polemic against the Jews and Jewish tradition in Rom 2:1-3:20, which is a subsection of 1:18-3:20, the thematic statement of which is, "The wrath of God is presently being revealed from heaven against all ungodliness and unrighteousness of men . . ." (1:18). The rhetorical question in Rom 2:3 clearly implies that Jewish wrongdoers will not escape God's judgment. "By your hardness and impenitent heart you are storing up for yourself wrath in the day of wrath and revelation of God's righteous judgment" (2:5). For the disobedient there is threatened divine wrath, fury, affliction, and anguish, directed first toward the Jew (2:8-9). Among crimes of the Jews, Paul cites Isa 52:5: "'God's name is blasphemed by the Gentiles because of you,'" reversing the text's original meaning. "What causes the Gentiles to blaspheme is no longer the suffering of Israel but the behavior which denies its mission."[114] In 1 Thess 2:14-16 Paul refers to their behavior which frustrates his mission to the Gentiles in behalf of the true and living God of Israel.

Even in Romans 9-11 Paul speaks of God's judgment on his disobedient people. In 9:3 he describes them as under a curse (cf. 9:18ff.) and implies that they are "vessels of wrath fitted for destruction" (9:22). In 11:3 he recites Elijah's charge against Israel that "they killed the prophets" (1 Kgs 19:14; cf. 1 Thess 2:15). Although only apparently rejected (cf. 11:15), they are presently "enemies" of God.[115] What is truly remarkable is Paul's ability to maintain in dialectic these harsh criticisms of Jewish unbelief alongside Rom 11:26a, "And so all Israel will be saved."[116] It is by no

---

sistent, cf. e.g., Clark M. Williamson, *Has God Forsaken His People? Anti-Judaism in the Christian Church* (Nashville: Abingdon, 1982); and Lloyd Gaston, "Israel's Enemies in Pauline Theology," *NTS* 28 (1982) 400-423.

[114]Käsemann, p. 71.

[115]Cf. Paul's use of διὰ παντός in Rom 11:10 and in 1 Thess 2:16, both meaning "always."

[116]Cf. also 1 Cor 1:18-25; 2 Cor 2:15-16; 4:3-4; 11:24; Gal 2:13; 5:10-12; Phil 3:2; and E. P. Sanders, "Paul's Attitude Toward the Jewish People," *USQR* 33 (1978) 175-87. Perhaps a view like that of 2 Macc 6:12-16 may account for the apparent contradiction. God sends calamities upon his people; not to destroy but to discipline them. His early judgment of Israel is a sign of his mercy, not that he has forsaken them. Cf. 1 Cor 11:21: "But when we are judged by the Lord, we are chastened, so that we may not be condemned along with the world" (RSV); Rom 11:32: "For God has consigned all men to disobedience, that he may have mercy upon all"

means certain that Paul does not mean by "Israel," here, all the elect "sons of Abraham," whether Jews or Gentiles (see e.g., Rom 2:25-29; 4:9-15; 9:6-13; Gal 3:6-29; 4:21-31; 6:17; Phil 3:2-11).

4. The Thessalonians: Persevering Sufferers

The rationale for Paul's continued thanksgiving for the Thessalonians in 2:13-16 is their acceptance of his preaching of the word of God to them, "not as the word of men, but, as it truly is, the word of God" (v. 13). The first expression of thanksgiving in 1:2-4 emphasizes God's choice of them and the proofs of it (1:5-2:12); the second, 2:13-16, emphasizes their response to God (cf. 1:6, 9), his continuing work in them (cf. 1:4, 6, 10; and 2:12),[117] and their consequent suffering (cf. 1:6). 1 Thess 2:13b-14 serves as a succinct recapitulation of 1:2-2:12, maintaining the unity of the thanksgiving period.

The γάρ introducing 2:14 suggests that the Thessalonians' imitation demonstrates their faith-appropriation of the word of God and its supernatural activity within them (2:13) as it does in 1:6. Why Paul appeals this time to the example of the Judean churches as opposed to his own or that of others remains a matter of conjecture.[118] For although the explicit model changes, the virtue extolled remains unchanged—Christian perseverance in the midst of trial. The frequent use of historical examples (παράδειγμα) as a normal feature of ancient parenetic letters may provide a partial explanation.[119] Another explanation may be found in Plutarch's recommendation that praise of others whose behavior and motives are like

---

(RSV); 1 Cor 5:5: "Deliver this man to Satan for the destruction of the flesh, that his spirit may be saved in the day of the Lord Jesus" (RSV); cf. 1 Cor 5:3, 9.

[117]See Robert C. Tannehill, *Dying and Rising with Christ* (BZNW 32; Berlin: Töpelmann, 1967) p. 101; see 100-104.

[118]Best (p. 113) offers a number of possible explanations.

[119]Malherbe, "I Thessalonians," pp. 4, 14, and 20 n. 13. The appeal to the example of the Judean churches implies that Paul had either previously informed the Thessalonians of their experiences or that he intends only to indicate an existing similarity and not active imitation. See Patte's discussion of the "type/imitator" pattern (ch. 4). When moralists reminded their hearers of the qualities of virtuous men as models for imitation, actual association between the models and imitators was not required.

one's own should be mixed with self-praise as an antidote for its offensiveness.[120]

Whatever else may be involved, Paul's appeal to the experience of suffering and perseverance of the Judean Christians may be explained as due to its similarity to that of the Thessalonians: "You became imitators . . . in that you endured the same things . . . as they" (2:14). The extent of the similarity cannot be known. That it involved affliction experienced at the hands of their fellow countrymen is all that can be claimed with certainty. The reference to suffering (ἐπάθετε) in 2:14, as that to affliction (θλίψις) in 1:6, leaves the precise nature of such experiences ambiguous.[121] What the Jewish persecutors afflicted on the Judean churches is described in terms of the history of Jewish persecution of the righteous which has its precedent in the killing of the Lord Jesus and the prophets. Paul's use of ἀποκτεινάντων, "killing," to refer to the crucifixion of Jesus is unusual (2:15; but cf. Rom 11:3 quoting 1 Kgs 19:10), and perhaps may be explained by its application to the Thessalonian situation. At any rate, 4:13-18 addresses the problem presented by the deaths of some of the Christians there—whether by "natural" or extraordinary causes.

In addition to the similarity of the experiences of suffering of the two groups, Paul also seems implicitly to contrast the behavior of the persecutors with his behavior. Whereas he pleases God (2:4), and urges the Thessalonians to do the same (4:1), the persecutors do not please God (2:15); whereas he loves all men (2:5-8; 3:12) and urges the Thessalonians to do likewise (3:12; 4:9-10), the persecutors are hostile to all men (2:15). If Paul responds to opponents in Thessalonica, it is to attack them as persecutors of his converts, and, as such, enemies of God, who, like his Jewish opponents, are certain to be condemned (2:16; cf. 2 Thess 1:5-12). His denials serve to distinguish his ethos from that of such opponents. There is no reason to assume that he would find it necessary to refute their charges, had they made any.

C. AUTOBIOGRAPHICAL UPDATE: EVENTS SINCE PAUL'S DEPARTURE: 1 THESSALONIANS 2:17-3:13

In 1 Thessalonians 3:3b-4 Paul parenthetically reminds his readers of

---

[120]Plutarch *Moralia* 540 A-C and 542 C-D.

[121]See Arland J. Hultgren, "Paul's Pre-Christian Persecutions of the Church: Their Purpose, Locale, and Nature," *JBL* 95 (1976) 97-111; and the literature cited in Betz, pp. 67 nn. 103 and 110 and 81 n. 241.

his prediction, made while he was still with them, that they would experience suffering. Apart from these verses, 2:17-3:13 refers to the aftermath of his departure from Thessalonica. It refers to past events—the mission of Timothy necessitated by Paul's inability to visit his converts after their separation (2:17-3:5); more recent developments—Timothy's return and Paul's joyful thanksgiving at the news from Thessalonica (3:6-10; note ἄρτι in 3:6 and νῦν in 3:8, both "now"); and Paul's future plans—a personal visit (3:6, 10, 11). Closing the unit and the autobiographical section of the letter is a prayer for the continued moral development of the Thessalonians (3:11-13).

All of Paul's letters seem to have a discrete section concerned with the travel plans of Paul himself or his authorized representatives, or an explanation that the letter will have to do for the time being.[122] By means of his visit, emissary, or letter Paul intends to turn his ἀπουσία, "absence," into παρουσία, "presence."[123] Although these parallel passages have been analyzed as a recurring "form," the "apostolic parousia,"[124] it is probably more accurate to refer to a repeated "theme" of "visit talk."[125] The large place this theme plays in 1 Thess 2:17-3:13 is probably due to the close relationship between philophronesis and parenesis.[126]

1. Past Events

The emphatic ἡμεῖς δέ, "but we," which begins 2:17 may be explained in the same way as αὐτὸς δέ in the prayers in 3:11 and 5:23, as necessitated by a change in grammatical subjects[127] and/or by the implicit contrast between the persecutors[128] or the Thessalonians[129] in 2:13-16 and Paul. The explicit contrast is between the time when Paul was once

---

[122]See Rom 1:8-13; 15:14-33; 1 Cor 4:14-21; 16:1-12; 2 Cor 1:1-2:13; 7:5-16; 11:17-22; 13:1-13; Gal 4:12-20; Phil 1:1-2:18; 2:25-30; Phlm 21-22; cf. Eph 6:21-22; Col 4:7-10.
[123]This precise terminology appears in Phil 2:12; cf. 2 Cor 13:2 where the participles ἀπών and παρών appear.
[124]Proposed first by Robert W. Funk in 1966, see n. 38 above.
[125]Terrence Y. Mullins, "Visit Talk in New Testament Letters," CBQ 35 (1973) 350-58.
[126]Malherbe, "I Thessalonians," pp. 15-16.
[127]So e.g., Lightfoot, Notes, p. 48.
[128]So e.g., Rigaux, Thessaloniciens, p. 457.
[129]So e.g., Schmithals, Gnostics, pp. 180-81.

present with them, the circumstances since their separation, and their longed-for reunion (2:17).

Despite Paul's intense and sustained yearning[130] to visit his orphaned children in Thessalonica (see 3:6, 10 and 11) his plans were more than once[131] thwarted. His explanation for the failure is brief and cryptic,"— but Satan hindered us" (2:18)[132]—perhaps referring again to the activities of his Jewish opponents (2:15-16).

In 2:19-20 Paul offers a further explanation for his yearning to visit the Thessalonians—they are his "hope," "joy," and "crown of boasting" before the Lord. The authenticity of their divinely wrought conversions and continued faithfulness to the Lord is intimately tied to the satisfactory fulfillment of Paul's divine commission (see 1 Thess 1:4-10; 2:5, 12-13; 5:23-24; Phil 4:1). In this way his churches provide him with a legitimate ground for boasting (cf. Phil 2:16; 1 Cor 1:31; 15:10; 2 Cor 1:14; 10:17).[133] The theme runs throughout his letters that "the judgment of an apostle must be the standard of his commission or office."[134] Paul answers to God for his faithfulness in the execution of his sacred trust (cf. Rom 1:5; 1 Cor 3:10; 4:1-2; 2 Cor 2:17ff.; 1 Thess 2:4), and he expects to receive God's praise, if his work (viz., his communities) survives (1 Cor 3:14-15; 4:5). Thus all Paul's efforts are directed toward the end that his work in the Lord might not prove to be fruitless (1 Thess 3:5; 2 Cor 9:27; 1 Cor

---

[130]On the frequent yearning motif in Hellenistic letters, see: Heikki Koskenniemi, *Studien zur Idee und Phraseologie des griechischen Briefes bis 700 n Chr.* (trans. Margareta Horn; Annales Academie Scientiarum Fennicas, Ser. B, vol. 102.1; Helsinki: Suomalaisen Kirjallisuuden Kerjapaino, 1956) pp. 38-42 and 169-72; and the literature cited in Betz, p. 236 nn. 178, 180, and 181.

[131]See Leon Morris, "ΚΑΙ ΑΠΑΞ ΚΑΙ ΔΙΕ," *NovT* 1 (1965) 205-9.

[132]Suggestions as to the immediate causes are purely conjectural; see Gustav Stählin, "κοπετός, κτλ," *TDNT* 3:855-57; and the various commentaries. It would be interesting to know why Paul assigns ultimate responsibility for his failed visit in this instance to Satan, on another occasion to the Lord (1 Cor 16:7-9; cf. Acts 16:6-10), on another to unavoidable circumstances (Rom 15:22ff.), and on still another to his autonomous decision in the best interests of the community (2 Cor 1:23-2:5). To my knowledge, no study of the subject has been attempted.

[133]See Rudolf Bultmann, "καυχάομαι, κτλ," *TDNT* 3:645-54. Plutarch considers self-praise in which the major credit is assigned to God an "antidote" for its offensiveness (*Moralia* 543E-544A).

[134]Ibid., p. 651.

9:14-18).[135] In 1 Thess 3:5, one explicit purpose of Timothy's mission to Thessalonica as Paul's representative is "so that [Paul's] labor might not be in vain." Similar parenetic purposes motivate the letter, which also represents him in his absence, and determine the function of the autobiographical remarks within it.

When Paul faithfully executes his commission and his communities stand fast in the Lord, the credit goes to God (1 Thess 3:6-10). But if God gives the "occasion . . . to glory, this glorying is also thanksgiving."[136] To God alone goes the credit for the salvation of all believers, but in the judgment, what one has done with that salvation will be judged for better or worse.[137]

> Paul does not merely want to be saved personally, he wants a reward and praise for the results of his life because they prove to be enduring. The fact that they endure finds expression in the churches as his crown and joy and hope and glory on the day of the parousia.[138]

This calls for faithfulness and perseverance to the end, not only on his part, but on the part of his churches. The evidence of their faithfulness already occasions Paul's joy, thanksgiving, and boasting (see Phil 2:16-18; 4:1; 1 Thess 2:19-20; 3:8-13; 5:16-18). Establishing them in their faith (1 Thess 3:2, 5) and supplying what is lacking in their faith (3:10) is Paul's task as surely as evangelizing them was. To fulfill this task he needs to visit them. But when this is impossible, his delegate, Timothy, and the letter fulfill this parenetic function. Both Timothy and the letter offer the same encouragement Paul would have offered had he been in Thessalonica in person.

The similarities between 3:1-3a and 3:5 are so complete as to suggest that they are doublets. Apart from minor variations due to the use of synonymns and a somewhat fuller description in the first passage, the essential difference boils down to the use of the first person plural in the first narrative and the singular in the second. They both say the same

---

[135]See Ernst Käsemann, *New Testament Questions of Today* (trans. W. J. Montague; Philadelphia: Fortress, 1967) pp. 217-35 on 1 Cor 9:14-18, "A Pauline Version of the 'Amor Fati.'"

[136]Bultmann, p. 651.

[137]See Karl Paul Donfried, "Justification and Last Judgment in Paul," *ZNW* 67 (1976) 90-110.

[138]Walter Grundmann, "στέφανος, στεφανόω," *TDNT* 7:630.

thing: Because Paul had been hindered from going to Thessalonica himself, he sent Timothy in his place to encourage them so that their faith might not collapse under the pressure of persecution.[139] By assigning responsi-

---

[139]The specific similarities are as follows: (1) The inferential conjunction διό, "therefore," introduces 3:1; the synonymous phrase διὰ τοῦτο, "therefore," introduces 3:5. At least the first "therefore" definitely refers backward to 2:17-20, which gives the circumstances necessitating the mission of Timothy reported in 3:1-5. The information given in the parenthetical vv. 3b-4, which separate the two accounts is taken for granted in both. Thus it is reasonable to conclude that the second "therefore" resumes the reference of the first (Best, p. 136; for an opposing view, see Lightfoot, Notes, p. 43).

(2) "Therefore" is followed in both instances by the negative temporal adverb μηκέτι, "no longer," and an adverbial participle of στέγειν, "to bear/stand/endure." In 3:1 it is στέγοντες, agreeing with the implicit, plural grammatical subject ἡμεῖς; in 3:5 στέγων agrees with κἀγώ, "I also." The context implies that what Paul was unable to bear any longer was his enforced separation from his converts (2:17-20) and his consequent inability to offer them the encouragement they needed to endure the afflictions he was certain they were suffering (3:1-5). The emphatic κἀγώ has been variously explained. (See Best, [p. 137] for a summary of the many attempts. He assumes that here, as in 2:18, Paul "cannot avoid stressing himself" since "he was in fact the initiator of the action," the inclusive "we" in 3:1-3a being merely a matter of "courtesy.") Probably as in 2:13, the fixed expression διὰ τοῦτο καί has resulted in the separation of the καί, "also," from the following verb it emphasizes (BDF, § 442 [12]). The pronoun makes it clear that Paul is the one responsible for the mission described in 3:1-5.

(3) Both present participle phrases describe the temporal circumstances accompanying the action of the aorist main verbs, both from πέμπω. In 3:2 it is ἐπέμψαμεν, "we sent"; in 3:5 ἔπεμψα, "I sent." "Therefore, when we/I could bear it no longer, we/I sent . . . ." The implicit subject of 3:1, ἡμεῖς, has a compound predicate. Between the participle στέγοντες and the verb ἐπέμψαμεν appears an explanatory phrase, "we were willing to be left alone in Athens and . . ." (3:1b). The word μόνοι, "alone" has the connotation of isolation or forsakenness, which makes its plural number seem particularly inappropriate and suggestive of the literary plural. (This is granted to a limited extent by commentators who otherwise reject the possibility of a literary plural. See Lightfoot, Notes, pp. 40-41; and Best, p. 131.)

(4) In both accounts Timothy is the one sent on the mission to Thessalonica. He is explicitly mentioned in 3:2. The proximity of 3:5 to 3:6, which mentions Timothy's return, and to 3:2 accounts for the lack of

bility for the afflictions of the Thessalonians to "the Tempter," viz. Satan,

---

explicit mention of any personal object in the second version. That Timothy is elliptically assumed however, is virtually certain. It is unlikely, given the other similarities, that Paul refers to two sendings and two different emissaries. It is difficult to say why he describes Timothy as fully as he does in 3:2, "our brother and God's co-laborer." (Schmithals [Gnostics, p. 181] considers "the commendatory addition to Timotheus' name" a suggestion that he "was not present during Paul's founding visit in Thessalonica." But this will not work unless his fragmentary theory is taken for granted [see pp. 123-218]. The textual tradition is as problematic at this point as Schmithals' theory; see Metzger, p. 631.) Timothy has already returned at the time of the letter's dispatch so it does not appear to be a recommendation. It is probably to be explained as the inoffensive praise of one's *alter ego*—Timothy as Paul's authorized representative did what Paul would have done, had he been able to visit them.

Both versions offer both positive and negative purpose clauses involving εἰς τὸ and an infinitive to explain the object of the mission. Although these purposes are not identically expressed, their concerns are so similar as to make it doubtful that Paul distinguishes his personal objectives in 3:5 from those of his associates in 3:2b-3a.

In 3:2b-3 the positive purposes of Timothy's mission are: "to strengthen [στηρίξαι] and encourage [παρακαλέσαι] you in your faith." The two infinitives are essentially synonymous in meaning, both being especially at home in parenetic contexts. (See Günther Harder, "στηρίζω, κτλ," TDNT 7:653-57; Otto Schmitz and Gustav Stählin, "παρακαλέω," TDNT 5:773-99, esp. p. 796). Paul's prayer in 3:13, that he may be enabled at last to visit the Thessalonians, has the similar objective, that God may strengthen [εἰς τὸ στηρίξαι] their hearts in holiness (3:13). That both God and Timothy may strengthen them shows the sense in which Paul's emissary is not only God's fellow-worker but like Paul. Paul's concern for his converts is expressed well in 2 Cor 6:1: "Since we work together with [Συνεργοῦντες] him, we exhort you [παρακαλοῦμεν], 'Do not accept the grace of God in vain.' "

The negative purpose for Timothy's mission is "in order that no one might be drawn aside [σαίνεσθαι] by these afflictions" (3:3a). Whatever the precise meaning of σαίνεσθαι, a New Testament *hapax legomenon*, in this context it is clearly to be understood in contrast to στριξαι in 3:2 and 13 and στήκετε in 3:8, both of which refer to strength, stability, and perseverance. Its meaning may also appear to be inferred from the negative purpose in the second report of the mission (3:5).

In 3:5 the positive purpose of Timothy's trip to Thessalonica is "to find out about your faith." Obviously Timothy did not go as a curious inquirer considering the possibility of their accepting the Christian faith. His

Paul connects their experience and his own. Satan has thus far hindered him from coming to visit them (2:18) and would also try to destroy their faith (3:5). The apostolic visit, or its surrogate, is essential to the securing of their faith (3:2 and 13) and of Paul's crown (2:19), so that his labor in their behalf will not fail to reach its goal.

Between the two reports of Timothy's mission to Thessalonica, 3:3b-4 appears as an almost parenthetical reminder of a twice repeated prediction made by Paul during his founding visit.[140] Implicit in the prediction

---

mission was to learn whether they were persevering in their faith or not, with the implicit task of encouraging them to do so.

Paul's apprehensions about the "whether" of his converts' faith lead him to formulate the negative purpose of Timothy's mission in a μή πως clause (BDF, § 370 [2]). "In order that the Tempter might not succeed in tempting you so that our labor would be in vain" (5b). Here (as also in 5:5; Gal 4:14; and 6:1) "to be tempted/tried" (see Heinrich Seesemann, "πεῖρα, κτλ," TDNT 6:23-36) is to fall victim to the Tempter, not merely to be enticed or afflicted. What Paul fears might happen is precisely that to which Timothy's preventive measures in 3:2c-3a are directed, that they may be strengthened and encouraged so that no one will apostatize as a result of their afflictions.

[140]The formal parallels, Gal 1:9; 5:21; 2 Cor 13:2; 1 Thess 4:6; Did 7:1 (see Betz, Galatians, p. 284) suggest that Paul uses a quotation formula to indicate what he had predicted earlier. The double warning could be two different warnings or variations of the same warning. Both are introduced by ὅτι. Both employ the present tense of verbs referring to the divine destiny or necessity (see Bauer, s.vv. κεῖμαι 2a; and μέλλω 1c) of the suffering of afflictions. Both use the confessional first person plural. Both may be translated, "We Christians are destined to be afflicted. Enclosing the prediction are appeals for the readers to acknowledge its truth—that Paul indeed made the prediction, and that it has come to pass as predicted.

The apparent conceptual background of the warning is apocalyptic Judaism, in which the divine necessity of suffering refers to the tribulation that anticipates the dawning of the eschatological "day of the Lord" (see 1 Thess 5:2), sometimes referred to as "the birth pangs of the Messiah" (see 1 Thess 5:2), and Friedrich Lang, πῦρ, κτλ," TDNT 6:936-48; Heinrich Schlier, "θλίβω, κτλ," TDNT 3:139-48; Gerhard Delling, "ἡμέρα," TDNT 2:943-53; Ernst Bammel, "Judenverfolgung und Nahwartung. Zur Eschatologie des Ersten Thessalonicherbriefes," ZTK 56 (1959) 294-315; and Georg Braumann and Colin Brown, "ἡμέρα," NIDNTT 2:887-95, and the references on p. 931). "Paul offers a variation to the extent that in him it does not precede the coming of the Messiah but

is the encouraging reminder that their mutual afflictions are not a reason to abandon their faith. Far from it, these are a guarantee that as surely as Paul's prediction that they would suffer afflictions had come to pass, so too would soon come the parousia their suffering announces.

2. Recent Developments and Future Plans

With ἄρτι δέ, "but now," in 3:6, Paul turns from his rehearsal of past events, with which his readers were already familiar, to the first, and probably only, primary autobiographical information in the letter, 3:6-10. These verses report Paul's response to Timothy's return from his mission of encouragement to Thessalonica, which may be summarized in a word— παρεκλήθημεν, "we were encouraged" (v. 7a). The reciprocal nature of the philophronetic relationship between Paul and his converts is once again emphasized. 1 Thessalonians, the letter of thanksgiving and encouragement, was almost certainly occasioned by (causa) the receipt of Timothy's "good news" (v. 6), which gave Paul fresh hope that his never-abandoned desire to visit the Thessalonians himself would now shortly be granted in response to his earnest and unending prayer (vv. 10-13). The perseverance of the Thessalonians embodied the "good news" of the gospel. Paul's unstated assumption is that God's victory over Satan's designs in Thessalonica forecasts the soon removal of the hindrance preventing his visit (cf. Rom 1:8-15; 15:14-33; 16:20). We do not know whether Paul ever succeeded in returning to Thessalonica; the Corinthian correspondence (see 1 Cor 16:5; 2 Cor 1:16; 8:1-7) suggests that he did, although, remarkably, there is no hint of it in 2 Thessalonians.

The specific content of Timothy's good news concerns "the faith and love" of the Thessalonians (3:6). The lack of explicit reference to the third

---

characterizes the period between the first coming and the second" (Käsemann, *Romans,* p. 232, commenting on the concept in Rom 1:18-30).

It appears that the imminent expectation of the parousia provided the original basis for Christian parenesis (see Anton Grabner-Haider, *Paraklese und Eschatologie bei Paulus, Mensch und Welt im Anspruch der Zukunft Gottes* [NTAbh n.F. 4; Münster: Aschendorf, 1968] pp. 108ff.). This provides a reasonable explanation for the remarkable mixture of parenesis and eschatology (see 1:10; 2:12, 16, 19-20; 3:13; 4:13-5:11; 5:23) in 1 Thessalonians and its repeated emphasis on the experience of afflictions (cf. Rom 13:11-14; Käsemann, *Romans,* p. 362; and Hans Conzelmann, "φῶς, κτλ," *TDNT* 9:346).

member of the triad, "hope" (see 1:3 and 5:8) is without significance.[141] It is the afterglow of the news of their "endurance of hope" (1:3) which occasions the letter.[142] "Endurance of hope" is comprehended by the term "faith" here, which implies "faithfulness to God" (cf. 3:7 and 8). They have persevered in the faith despite their afflictions (3:3, 5). Paul's claim in 3:8, "We live so long as you stand firm in the Lord,"[143] emphasizes the reciprocal relationship between him and the Thessalonians. They encourage him as he encourages them and vice versa.[144]

As "faith" comprehends the Thessalonians' relationship to God in 3:6, so "love" comprehends their relationship to Paul. Their love for Paul causes them to remember him constantly in their prayers as he does them (cf. 1 Thess 3:6; 1:2; Rom 1:9; Eph 1:16; Phil 1:3; 1 Tim 1:3-4; Phlm 4).[145] They yearn to see him as he longs to see them (1 Thess 3:6; cf. 2:8, 17; 3:10-12). Again, the reciprocal and philophronetic relationship of imitators to their model is emphasized. They remember one another (1:3; 2:9); they mention one another in their prayers (1:2; 3:6); and they long to see one another again (2:17; 3:6, 10). Their friendship toward him as well as their faithfulness to God give him encouragement in the midst of his "distress" and "affliction" (3:7). Similarly, the intent of the reminders of his friendship toward them in 2:1-12 is to encourage them in their endurance of suffering, not to respond apologetically to charges that he was a false friend.

Even in Paul's more complete catalogs of sufferings,[146] terms like

---

[141]Best, p. 140.

[142]Nor is there any implication of a deficiency of hope in Paul's exhortation in 4:13, which is merely a reminder of what their hope entails, as are the repeated eschatological references in the autobiographical chapters (1:10; 2:12, 16, 19; 3:13); contra ibid., pp. 179-86.

[143]See Bauer, s.v. ἐάν I 2 b.

[144]See Walter Grundmann, "στήκω, ἵστημι, TDNT 7:637: "Standing in the Lord has sustaining power and also the power to create fellowship."

[145]Bauer, s.v. μνεία 2.

[146]The περιστάσεις, or circumstantial, catalogs compile long lists of difficult experiences, which paradoxically characterize his personal or apostolic existence (1 Cor 4:9-13; 2 Cor 4:7-12; 6:3-10; 11:23-29; 12:10) and/or Christian existence in general (Rom 8:35-39). On the peristasis-catalogs, see Anton Fridrichsen, "Zum Stil des Paulinischen Peristasenkatalogs, 2 Kor 11, 23ff." SO 7 (1928) 25-29; Hans Dieter Betz, Der Apostel Paulus und die sokratische Tradition: Exegetische Untersuchung zu seiner "Apologie": 2 Korinther 10-13 (BHT 45; Tübingen: Mohr [Siebeck], 1972) p. 98, and p. 98 nn. 379-80 for further references; and

ἀνάγκη, "distress," and θλίψις, "affliction," remain ambiguous as to their precise nature. When he is more specific, referring to beatings, stoning, lashes, imprisonments, shipwrecks, hunger, etc. (2 Cor 11:23-28; cf. 6:4-5), he invariably returns to generalization and emphasizes the dialectical character of such experiences. This is the case in 1 Thess 3:7-10—"During all our distress and affliction . . . we were encouraged. . . . Now we live. . . . We are able to return thanks to God. . . . We rejoice. . . ." Between the first and second comings of Christ, all those who are his experience the paradox of an "already-but-not-yet" existence.[147] Christ already reigns as cosmic Lord but all his enemies have not yet been destroyed (1 Cor 15:20-28; cf. 1 Thess 2:18; 3:5). Christians are already children of the dawning day, though the darkness of the old age has not yet been fully dispelled (1 Thess 5:4-7). Paul and his readers share in the "eschatological struggle," in the "trials of the eschaton."[148] And yet, paradoxically, suffering is for Paul a "sign that evil is being overthrown."[149]

In 1 Thess 3:8 Paul explains his encouragement about Timothy's good news metaphorically, "Now we live so long as you stand firm in the Lord." This suggests that as he is a bearer of life to others (see 1 Cor 4:7-12; 2 Cor 4:11-12),[150] so his converts by their perseverance in affliction com-

---

idem, "Eine Christus-Aretalogie bei Paulus," *ZTK* 66 (1969) 288-305, esp. 303. Rudolf Bultmann's (*Der Stil der paulinischen Predigt und die kynisch-stoische Diatribe* [FRLANT 13; Göttingen: Vandenhoeck & Ruprecht, 1910] esp. pp. 19-20, 71-72) proposal of the Cynic Stoic diatribe as the place of origin has been widely accepted. See Abraham Malherbe, "The Beasts at Ephesus," *JBL* 87 (1968) 71-80; Victor C. Pfitzner, *Paul and the Agon Motif: Traditional Athletic Imagery in the Pauline Literature* (NovTSup 16; Leiden: Brill, 1967); Wolfgang Schrage, "Leid, Kreuz und Eschaton: Die Peristasenkataloge als Merkmale paulinischer Theologia Crucis und Eschatologie," *EvT* 34 (1974) 141-75; and Michael L. Barré, "Paul as 'Eschatologic Person. A New Look at 2 Cor 11:29," *CBQ* 37 (1975) 500-526.

[147]Schrage, pp. 154-55.

[148]See Barré, pp. 512-13.

[149]William A. Beardslee, *Human Achievement and Divine Vocation in the Message of Paul* (SBT 31; Naperville, IL: Allenson, 1961) p. 114. Beardslee (pp. 114-15) correctly emphasizes (against Barré, pp. 512-13) that although the apostle experiences this most sharply, suffering is "a calling or gift he shares with all the church."

[150]Jean Héring, *The Second Epistle of Saint Paul to the Corinthians* (trans. A. W. Heathcote and P. J. Allcock; London: Epworth, 1967) pp. 32-33.

municate "life" to him. They, like him, are imitators of Christ (1 Thess 1:6; 2:13-16; cf. 2 Cor 7:2-16) and embody the gospel (cf. 3:6). Although the news of the perseverance of the Thessalonians renews Paul's optimism and gives him fresh hope that the hindrance blocking his return to Thessalonica will be removed, his gratitude is expressed neither to the Thessalonians nor to Titus but to God.

Yet it is concerning the steadfastness of his Thessalonian converts that he gives thanks to God in 3:9, as in his earlier references to thanksgiving in 1:2 and 2:13, although the form is different. "The fact that he frames it as a question shows his realization that any thanksgiving he can offer is inadequate."[151] The parallel expressions in 3:7 and 9—"in all our distress and affliction" and "in all our rejoicing because of you"—are reminiscent of his earlier reference to the Thessalonians' Spirit-inspired joy in their afflictions in 1:6. The reciprocity of imitation is such that Paul imitates them (1:6), even if he does not say so explicitly. They are so fully his imitators, his true friends, that they are his *alter ego*.[152]

Because true friends yearn to be together (see 2:8, 17-19; 3:6), Paul's thanksgiving becomes in 3:10-11 a petition that he may see his friends again. The object of his prayed-for visit is clearly parenentic—"to complete what is lacking in your faith" (v. 10). This prepares for the specifically parenetic section of the letter in 4:1ff., which begins by making this explicit—"Finally, brethren, we beseech and exhort you in the Lord Jesus, that as you learned from us how you ought to live and to please God, just as you are doing, you do so more and more" (4:1 RSV). But parenensis is already implicit in the repeated and clear connections between Paul's model and his ethical advice in 4:1-5:24.

CONCLUSION

Specific aspects of Paul's exemplary ethos which become explicit aspects of his parenesis include: (1) his encouragement or exhortation itself (cf. 2:3, 11-12; 4:1; and 4:18; 5:11); (2) his holy and blameless moral conduct (cf. 2:3, 9-12; and 4:1-7; 5:22-23); (3) his sense of responsibility to please God (cf. 2:4, 15; and 4:1); (4) his brotherly love and constant friendship while with the Thessalonians and while apart from them (cf. 2:5-8, 17-18; 3:6, 10, 12; and 4:9-12; 5:15); (5) his manual labor and self-support (cf. 2:8-9 and 4:9-12; 5:12-14); (6) his constant prayers of thanksgiving (cf.

[151]Best, p. 143.
[152]See the references in Betz, *Galatians*, pp. 222-23 and nn. 31-32.

1:2; 2:13; 3:10; cf. 5:17-18); (7) his rejoicing in affliction (1:6; 3:9-10; and 5:16-18); and (8) his eschatological hope (cf. 1:10; 2:19-20; 3:13; and 4:13-5:11). Certainly this is not to suggest that all these exhortations were directed toward specific deficiencies in the ethical conduct of the Thessalonians. It does suggest, however, that these concerns were of particular importance to Paul. The same principles underlying the selection of those aspects of his "autobiography" which he chooses to emphasize are at work in his selection of the ethical precepts he emphasizes. Perhaps compensating for our loss of certainty as to the historical situation in Thessalonica, is the possibility that we have in 1 Thessalonians an indication of what Paul actually considers ethically momentous, and not simply an illustration of how he responds to ethical failures on the part of his converts.

Paul's recommendations of his own example might easily be regarded as "boasting." But the elements of self-praise in Paul's autobiographical remarks in 1 Thessalonians are appropriately accompanied with the necessary "antidotes" against their potential offensiveness.[153] (1) By assigning God the credit for his exemplary ethos, Paul also is consistent with his own principle, "Let him who boasts, boast of the Lord" (1 Cor 1:31; 2 Cor 10:17; referring to Jer 9:23-24). (2) Paul emphasizes the hardships and persecution involved in maintaining his good character. He nowhere stoops to self-pity. (3) His repeated use of antitheses contrasts his behavior with the shameful behavior of others, showing both the virtue to be pursued and the vice to be avoided. (4) He mixes "self-praise" with praise of the Thessalonians, also crediting God for their exemplary behavior. (5) He also praises the churches of Judea, whose ethos is similar to his own. (6) Paul's autobiographical remarks are clearly directed toward achieving the ethical purpose of encouraging his suffering converts in Thessalonica and not toward selfish ends.[154] That these features are quite normal "antidotes" prescribed to alleviate the possible offensiveness of autobiographical encomia obviates the need to assume that they are apologetically motivated.

The question of the rhetorical genre of 1 Thessalonians may now be addressed. The forensic genre, and thus both defense and accusation, may be eliminated by the extent to which the autobiographical section is directed toward the parenentic section. Even if "apology" were an appropriate designation for the autobiographical section, it would not be for the

---

[153]See chapter 1 section F above.
[154]See Plutarch *Moralia* 544C-E, quoted in chapter 1 section F above.

letter as a whole. It is difficult to determine to which of the traditional rhetorical genres parenesis belongs, since the ancient handbooks devote very little attention to it.[155] It would appear to be connected with the positive variety of deliberative oratory, the protreptic or hortatory speech of persuasion (προτροπὴ λόγος, *exhortatio,* or παράκλησις) since it is used at times as the antonymn of dissuasion (ἀποτροπὴ λόγος).[156] The first-century B.C. *Rhetoric* of Dionysius of Halicarnassus, however, treats the parenetic speech (παραινετικὸς λόγος) as a sub-type of the epideictic genre, which has been united with the deliberative.[157] Parenesis was widely used by both philosophers and orators in antiquity and admits a great variety of forms.[158] Burgess suggests that "technically the προτρεπτικὸς λόγος is an exhortation to some general course—philosophy, rhetoric, virtue. It gives a comprehensive view, setting forth the advantages and removing the objections," whereas "the παραίνεσις presents a series of precepts which will serve as a guide of conduct under fixed conditions."[159] Among the rhetors parenesis has an almost technical meaning, "the moral or application" of a speech of either genre.[160] Whether parenesis is considered deliberative or epideictic depends on "the controlling motive of the oration," persuasion or praise.[161]

The fact that thanksgiving, which dominates the first three chapters of the letter, is a definitely epideictic form would seem to tip the scale in the latter direction. This is also supported by the lack of intensity in Paul's exhortations. The Thessalonians are already doing well; he encourages them only to do so more and more. Yet for such recent converts from pagan idolatry and its immoral ethos, ethical reminders and encouragement are hardly perfunctory. In 1 Thessalonians, however, the intellectual aspect of edification, instruction as to what is right and what is wrong, is emphasized rather than the volitional aspect, exhortation to do the right and shun the wrong. This helps account for the numerous refer-

---

[155]Hildegard Cancik, *Untersuchungen zu Senecas Epistulae morales* (Spudasmata 18; Hildesheim: Olms, 1967) p. 23.

[156]The ancient sources are cited in Burgess, p. 231 n. 2, see also p. 229. On the ancient genres and sub-species see chapter 1 section C 1 above.

[157]Cited in ibid., pp. 112-13. Dionysius writes, "With praise mingle advice" (cited in ibid., p. 232).

[158]Ibid.

[159]Ibid., p. 230 n. 2.

[160]Ibid., p. 231 n. 2.

[161]Ibid., p. 231.

ences to knowing and remembering throughout the letter (1:2, 3, 4, 5; 2:1, 2, 5, 9, 10, 11, 17; 3:3, 4, 6; 4:2, 4, 5; 5:2, 12). Education and increasing the intensity of adherence to communally shared values are the normal objects of the epideictic genre.[162]

The autobiographical remarks in 1 Thessalonians function parenetically to remind Paul's converts of the Christian ethical values they share, as embodied in the ethos of their *typos*. They are his imitators, but they, too, are examples. They are his "crown of boasting," his "glory," his "joy" (2:19-20). But their relationship is one of mutuality and reciprocity. By praising his own exemplary ethos, as over against paganism, he is at the same time praising them and educating them. But the praise is ultimately directed toward God, who enables both Paul and the Thessalonians to live lives that are pleasing to him (2:4; 4:1) and worthy of him (2:12). Paul's closing prayer in 5:23, that the God who called them to holiness (4:7) would make their sanctification complete, and that they may be kept sound and blameless for the parousia, is followed by the expression of confidence, "He who called you is faithful, and he will do it" (5:24 RSV), and the request, "Brothers, pray for me" (5:25). In calling upon the Thessalonians to pray that he, too, will persevere to the end, Paul once again emphasizes the equality and reciprocity characterizing his friendship with his converts.[163]

---

[162]Wilhelm Wuellner, "Paul's Rhetoric of Argumentation in Romans: An Alternative to the Donfried-Karris Debate over Romans," *CBQ* 38 (1976) 343.
[163]See n. 94 above.

Conclusion

The lengthy conclusions at the end of each of the four chapters make it unnecessary to rehearse in detail the results of this investigation. It is enough to summarize the more significant conclusions and their implications for the study of Paul and his letters. The present dissertation is an attempt to address the literary phenomenon and function of Paul's autobiographical remarks, an investigation made necessary by Pauline scholarship's preoccupation with historical questions to the general neglect of antecedent literary questions. This neglect alone should point up the incongruity that scholars are nearly of one voice in asserting the function of these remarks. This consensus depends on largely unexamined, but widely accepted, methodological and historical assumptions, not textual evidence.

Central to this investigation has been a rejection of the usual approach to Paul's autobiographical remarks and the widely held assumptions supporting it—that Paul writes in the autobiographical mode only reluctantly and almost always apologetically. It may appear somewhat presumptuous in a doctoral dissertation to defend a thesis that is so completely at odds with the consensus of Pauline scholarship. In fact, the investigation began as an attempt to demonstrate the correctness of the consensus, which had previously been postulated but never proved. In its course, it became clear that the prevailing view owed more to methodological and historical assumptions, which were themselves untested, than to the textual data of the Pauline letters.

Among the factors which have led modern scholarship to its basic misunderstanding of the functions of Paul's autobiographical remarks is its failure to appreciate adequately the differences between ancient and modern autobiography. Chapter 1 attempted to provide this necessary background against which the Apostle's autobiographical statements are to be understood. Paul's apparent reluctance to write autobiographically—

despite the frequency with which he does so—probably owes less to an essentially humble disposition than to his attempts to avoid offending the sensibilities of antiquity, which found autobiography patently boastful. Certainly it has a theological explanation as well in Paul's personal compliance with the Old Testament dictum to which he alludes on more than one occasion in his letters—"Let him who boasts, boast in the Lord" (Jer 9:23-24; cf. Rom 1:21-23; 1 Cor 1:31; 2 Cor 10:17; Gal 6:4, 13-16; Phil 3:3). In order to avoid the offensiveness of boasting, empty self-praise, Paul employs the conventional "antidotes" of ancient autobiographers (see chapter 1 F), prominent among them being the frequent uilization of antithetical constructions. This feature of Paul's autobiographical remarks has been partly responsible for modern scholarship's mistaken assumption that these remarks are almost uniformly apologetic in function. This assumption exists in a kind of symbiotic relationship with other equally debatable historical speculations.

Chapter 2 attempted to demonstrate the extent to which most existing treatments of Paul's autobiographical remarks build upon indefensible methodological assumptions and historical reconstructions derived in part from preconceived notions about the history of earliest Christianity. Such assumptions open the door to equally unprovable and unfalsifiable speculations, which are hardly the basis for scientific exegesis. Only because we know more about Paul than about his opponents has it been possible to assume that they are monotonously predictable while his position varies on certain issues from one letter to the next. Even the underlying assumption that Paul's autobiographical remarks characteristically arise out of a polemical context and thus function apologetically may be doubted.

The function one assigns Paul's autobiographical remarks affects not only the interpretation of these sections of the letters but profoundly influences the generic conception of, and thus the interpretation of the letters as a whole (see chapter 2). Accordingly, the question addressed in this dissertation is hardly peripheral, but central to an adequate interpretation of Paul. The consensus approach to Paul's autobiographical remarks, the hypotheses which sponsor it, and the generally accepted interpretive technique, "mirror reading," as applied to Galatians and 1 Thessalonians is clearly a failure. This may not prove conclusively that the approach is inapplicable elsewhere, but it is certainly suggestive of the potential for thorough misinterpretation such an approach to Paul's autobiographical remarks entails.

Since we have only Paul's autobiographical remarks and not his opponents' accusations, which the consensus assumes provoked them, it is necessary to exercise restraint in asserting too confidently that specific charges actually existed, much less what they may have been. Even the existence of "opponents" in the usual sense of the word is far from certain. In a religious atmosphere in which comparison and competition among various philosophies and philosophers made autobiographical remarks de rigueur, it is not surprising that a serious representative of the gospel, such as Paul, should attempt to dispel any possible misunderstanding of his true message and character. This makes unnecessary the presumption that his self-presentation responds to actual charges. What he says is determined by his rhetorical approach and not by his opponents' reproaches. On a purely methodological basis it would appear to be preferable to begin with the reasonable assumption that the antithetical formulations, which are prominent not only in the autobiographical sections but throughout Paul's letters, reflect his own argumentative style—a style that was hardly unique in antiquity—and are not merely his adaptations of opposing formulations.

The dissertation will have succeeded in part if it is recognized that the usual view of Paul's autobiographical remarks may no longer remain an unexamined assumption from which exegesis and historical reconstructions may safely proceed. Perhaps even those scholars who are not persuaded to abandon the consensus opinion completely will at least be compelled to re-examine it, and join the investigation of the functions of Paul's autobiographical remarks. Even if one remains unpersuaded that Paul writes Galatians and 1 Thessalonians with no "opponents" in mind, chapters 3 and 4 have demonstrated that the assumptions undergirding the consensus view are by no means necessary. Paul's autobiographical remarks are fully intelligible apart from such assumptions when properly set in the context of antiquity. One should resort to conjecture only if Paul's autobiographical remarks remain unintelligible on this basis. The only real loss in such an approach is the arrogated certainty scholars have claimed concerning the situations of Paul's readers and opponents.

As in the ancient philosophical lives, Paul's autobiographical remarks are closely bound to his profession, i.e., his vocation as an apostle of Jesus Christ, and his "philosophy," the gospel which he proclaims and under the authority of which he himself lives. Thus Paul moves quite naturally from an autobiographical narrative to a discussion of the gospel and vice versa. The consistency of his words and his ethical walk demonstrates the truth of his "philosophy," the practical argument of his ethos being more persuasive than abstract theories. Paul at once proclaims and embodies the gospel, but he does not assert his uniqueness or authority on this basis. The same correspondence between words and deeds is, or should be, the common experience of all Christians. The extent to which this is true of

his converts determines in large part the different functions of the autobiographical remarks in the various letters, as is graphically illustrated by
a comparison of Galatians and 1 Thessalonians. There are few substantive
similarities between Paul's autobiographical remarks in the two letters.
What he writes is selective and determined by ulterior motives, strongly
suggesting that his remarks are supportive of and subordinate to the
letter's rhetorical argument. Thus it appears that these remarks are
intended primarily to persuade and/or edify and only secondarily, if at all,
to inform.

Proper recognition of the rhetorical element in Paul's autobiographical
remarks provides a further challenge to existing approaches, which characteristically reach historical conclusions before the question of literary
function has been adequately addressed. Paul's rhetorical motives suggest
that ethical characterization and edification were of greater concern than
historical completeness and exactitude—a fact which should significantly
affect the way in which his autobiographical remarks are employed in any
historical reocnstruction of the events they report.

The fact that Paul's autobiographical narrative in Galatians 1 and 2 and
his scriptural expositions in chs. 3 and 4 serve essentially similar hortatory functions and that the autobiographical section in 1 Thessalonians 1-3
and the parenetic chs. 4-5 highlight the same concerns raises several
questions that are beyond the scope of the present dissertation to answer.
To what extent does Paul consider his personal experience an authority
complementary to and/or comparable with that of Old Testament scripture or the word of the Lord? In Galatians, as often in his letters, he
appeals to scriptural *exempla,* "examples," rather than to *praecepta,*
"precepts." In this way he places his experience alongside that of the
leading figures of Old Testament history—Abraham (in addition to Galatians, cf. see also Romans 4), Isaiah and Jeremiah (cf. Gal 1:15 and Isa
49:1; Jer 1:5), Elijah (cf. Rom 11:1-5 and 1 Kgs 19:4-18), and Moses (cf.
2 Cor 3:4-18 and Ex 34:29-35)—and even that of the Lord Jesus (see
1 Thess 1:6; 2:14-16; 1 Cor 11:1; cf. 1 Cor 8:1-11:1 and Rom 14:1-15:13;
Phil 2:1-11 and 3:2-4:1). But this does not really set him apart from his
readers, whom he calls upon to model their conduct after that of the Lord
as mediated by him and/or others (see e.g. 1 Thess 1:6 and 2:14-16).

Succinctly and simply put, Paul's autobiographical remarks function not
to distinguish him from his converts nor to defend his person or authority
but to establish his ethos as an "incarnation" of the gospel of Jesus Christ.
He highlights his "autobiography" in the interests of this gospel and his
readers. He is concerned that, by imitating him, they too should incarnate
the gospel. Their faithfulness or unfaithfulness to the gospel, as Paul

understands it, determines which aspects of his life he brings to the fore. His autobiographical remarks rarely supplement the major concern of a letter, but rather support it by means of a flesh-and-blood illustration. Paul does not present himself as a paradigm of virtue in general, although he often emphasizes his praiseworthy moral behavior. Whether only to avoid offense or as a sincere expression of his self-understanding, he presents himself in such a way as to assign the credit for his exemplary conduct to God and/or Christ. Furthermore, he writes not for self-aggrandizement, but for the edification of his converts. Thus Paul's own words provide a fitting conclusion: ". . . What we preach is not ourselves, but Jesus Christ as Lord, with ourselves as your servants for Jesus' sake" (2 Cor 4:5 RSV).

Bibliography

Aland, Kurt; Black, Matthew; Martini, Carlo M.; Metzger, Bruce M.; and Wikgren, Allen; eds. *The Greek New Testament*. 3rd ed. New York: United Bible Societies, 1975.

Alford, Henry. *The Greek Testament*. 4 vols. Revised by Everett F. Harrison. Chicago: Moody Press, 1958.

Amiot, François. *Saint Paul: Epître aux Galates. Epîtres aux Thessaloniciens*. VS 14. Paris: Beauchesne, 1946.

Audet, J. P. "Literary Forms and Contents of a Normal εὐχαριστία in the First Century." *SE* 1 (= Texte und Untersuchungen 73) (1959) 643-62.

Andrews, E. A., trans. and ed. *Harpers' Latin Dictionary*. Edited by Charlton T. Lewis and Charles Short. New York: American Book Co., 1879.

Aristophanes. *Clouds*. Translated by Benjamin Bickley Rogers. Loeb Classical Library.

Aristotle. *The Nicomachean Ethics*. Translated by H. Rackham. Loeb Classical Library.

_____. *Rhetoric*. Translated by John Henry Freese. Loeb Classical Library.

Askwith, E. W. " 'I' and 'We' in the Thessalonian Epistles." *The Expositor*. 8th Series. 1 (1911) 149-59.

Attridge, H. W. *The Interpretation of Biblical History in the Antiquities of Flavius Josephus*. HDR 7. Missoula, MT: Scholars Press, 1976.

Auberlen, Charles Augustus and Riggenbach, D. J. "The First Epistle of Paul to the Thessalonians." Translated by John Lillie. *Commentary on the Holy Scriptures*. 12 vols. Edited by John Peter Lange and Philip Schaff. Grand Rapids: Zondervan, 1960; reprint of 1860ff. edition.

Bachmann, H. and Slaby, W. A., eds. *Computer-Konkordanz zum Novum Testamentum Graece*. Berlin: de Gruyter, 1980.

Bacon, B. W. "Wrath 'unto the Uttermost.' " *The Expositor*. 8th Series. 24 (1922) 356-76.

Bahr, Gordon J. "Paul and Letter Writing in the First Century." *CBQ* 28 (1966) 465-77.

_____. "The Subscriptions in the Pauline Letters." *JBL* 87 (1968) 27-41.

Bailey, John W. "The First and Second Epistles to the Thessalonians." *The Interpreter's Bible*. 12 vols. Edited by George Arthur Buttrick et al. New York: Abingdon, 1951-57.

Baird, J. Arthur. "Genre Analysis as a Method of Historical Criticism." *Society of Biblical Literature Seminar Papers*. Vol. 2. Edited by Lane C. McGaughy. Missoula, MT: Scholars Press, 1972.

Baird, W. "What is the Kerygma? A Study of 1 Cor 15.3-8 and Gal 1.11-17." *JBL* 76 (1957) 181-91.

Bammel, Ernst. "Judenverfolgung und Naherwartung. Zur Eschatologie des Ersten Thessalonicherbriefes." *ZTK* 56 (1959) 294-315.

Barish, David A. "The Autobiography of Josephus and the Hypothesis of a Second Edition of his Antiquities." *HTR* 71 (1978) 61-75.

Barré, Michael L. "Paul as 'Eschatologic Person': A New Look at 2 Cor 11:29." *CBQ* 37 (1975) 500-526.

Barrett, C. K. "The Acts—of Paul." *New Testament Essays*. London: SPCK, 1972.

_____. "Galatians as an 'Apologetic Letter.' " *Int* 34 (1980) 414-17.

_____. "Paul and the 'Pillar' Apostles." *Studia Paulina in honorem Johannis de Zwaan*. Haarlem: Erven Bohn, 1953.

_____. "Pauline Controversies in the Post-Pauline Period." *NTS* 20 (1973-74) 229-45.

_____. "Paul's Opponents in II Corinthians." *NTS* 17 (1971) 233-54.

_____. *The Signs of an Apostle*. London: Epworth Press, 1970.

Bauer, Walter. *A Greek-English Lexicon of the New Testament and Other Early Christian Literature*. 2nd ed. Translated and edited by William F. Arndt, F. Wilbur Gingrich, and Frederick W. Danker. Chicago: University of Chicago Press, 1979.

Bauernfeind, Otto. "Die Begegnung zwischen Paulus und Kephas, Gal 1:18-20." *ZNW* 47 (1956) 268-76.

_____. "τρέχω." *TDNT* 8:225-35.

Baur, Ferdinand Christian. *Paul the Apostle of Jesus Christ. His Life and Work, His Epistles and His Doctrine.* 2 vols. Translated by A. Menzies from the 2nd ed. by Eduard Zeller. Theological Translation Fund Library. London: Williams & Norgate, 1873-75.

Beardslee, William A. *Human Achievement and Divine Vocation in the Message of Paul.* SBT 31. Naperville, IL: Allenson, 1961.

Becker, Jurgen; Conzelmann, H.; and Friedrich, G. *Die Briefe an die Galater, Epheser, Philipper, Kolosser, Thessalonicher und Philemon.* NTD 8. 14th ed. Göttingen: Vandenhoeck & Ruprecht, 1976.

Beker, J. Christiaan. *Paul the Apostle: The Triumph of God in Life and Thought.* Philadelphia: Fortress, 1980.

Bertram, Georg. "ἀναστρέφω, κτλ" *TDNT* 7:715-17.

Best, Ernest. *A Commentary on the First and Second Epistles to the Thessalonians.* HNTC. New York: Harper & Row, 1972.

Betz, Hans Dieter. *Der Apostel Paulus und die sokratische Tradition. Eine exegetische Untersuchung zu seiner "Apologie": 2 Korinther 10-13.* BHT 45. Tübingen: J. C. B. Mohr (Paul Siebeck), 1972.

_____. "Eine Christus-Aretalogie bei Paulus (2 Kor 12,7-10)." *ZTK* 66 (1969) 288-305.

_____. "The Delphic Maxim ΓΝΩΘΙ ΣΑΥΤΟΝ in Hermetic Interpretation." *HTR* 63 (1970) 465-84.

_____. "In Defense of the Spirit: Paul's Letter to the Galatians as a Document of Early Christian Apologetics." *Aspects of Religious Propaganda in Judaism and Early Christianity.* Edited by Elisabeth Schüssler-Fiorenza. Notre Dame, IN: University of Notre Dame Press, 1976.

_____. *Galatians: A Commentary on Paul's Letter to the Churches in Galatia.* Hermeneia. Philadelphia: Fortress, 1979.

_____. "The Literary Composition and Function of Paul's Letter to the Galatians." *NTS* 21 (1975) 353-79.

_____. *Nachfolge und Nachahmung Jesu Christi im Neuen Testament.* Tübingen: J. C. B. Mohr (Paul Siebeck), 1967.

_____. *Paul's Apology II Corinthians 10-13 and the Socratic Tradition.* Protocol of the 2nd Colloquy. Edited by Wilhelm Wuellner. Berkeley: Center for Hermeneutical Studies in Hellenistic and Modern Culture, 1975.

_____. "2 Cor 6:14-7:1: An Anti-Pauline Fragment?" *JBL* 92 (1973) 88-108.

_____. "Spirit, Freedom, and Law: Paul's Message to the Galatian Churches." *SEÅ* 39 (1974) 145-60.

Betz, Hans Dieter, ed. *Plutarch's Ethical Writings and Early Christian Literature.* SCHNT 4. Leiden: Brill, 1978.

Beyer, Hermann W. "διακονέω, κτλ" *TDNT* 2:81-93.

Beyer, Hermann Wolfgang and Althaus, Paul. "Der Brief an die Galater." *Die kleineren Briefe des Apostels Paulus.* NTD 8. 6th ed. Göttingen: Vandenhoeck & Ruprecht, 1953.

Bietenhard, Hans. "Please." *NIDNTT* 2:815.

Binder, Hermann. "Die angebliche Krankheit des Paulus." *TZ* 32 (1976) 1-13.

Bjerkelund, Carl J. *Parakalō: Form, Funktion und Sinn der parakalō-Sätze im den paulinischen Briefen.* Bibliotheca Theologica Norvegica 1. Oslo: Universitetsforlaget, 1967.

Black, Edwin. *Rhetorical Criticism: A Study in Method.* Madison, WI: University of Wisconsin Press, 1978.

Blass, F. and Debrunner, A. *A Greek Grammar of the New Testament and Other Early Christian Literature.* Translated and revised by Robert W. Funk. Chicago: University of Chicago Press, 1962.

Blevins, J. L. "The Problem in Galatia." *RevExp* 69 (1972) 449-58.

Bligh, John. *Galatians in Greek: A Structural Analysis of St. Paul's Epistle to the Galatians with Notes on the Greek.* Detroit: University of Detroit Press, 1966.

Blunt, A. W. F. *The Epistle of Paul to the Galatians.* Clarendon Bible. Oxford: Clarendon Press, 1925.

Boer, Martinus C. de. "Images of Paul in the Post-Apostolic Period." *CBQ* 42 (1980) 359-80.

Boer, Willis Peter de. *The Imitation of Paul: An Exegetical Study.* Kampen: J. H. Kok, 1962.

Boers, Hendrikus. "Apocalyptic Eschatology in I Corinthians 15." *Int* 21 (1967) 50-65.

_____. "The Form Critical Study of Paul's Letters. I Thessalonians as a Case Study." *NTS* 22 (1975) 140-58.

_____. "Gen. 15:6 and the Discourse Structure of Galatians." Seminar paper presented at the Society of Biblical Literature meeting, 1976.

_____. Review of *Der Apostel Paulus und die sokratische Tradition: Eine exegetische Untersuchung zu seiner "Apologie": 2 Korinther 10-13*, by Hans Dieter Betz. *Int* 27 (1973) 488-90.

_____. "The Structure and Meaning of Galatians." Paper, 1976.

_____. "The Structure and Purpose of Galatians." Paper, 1974.

_____. *What is New Testament Theology?* Guides to Biblical Scholarship, NT Series. Philadelphia: Fortress, 1979.

Bohren, Rudolf. *Das Problem der Kirchenzucht im Neuen Testament*. Zürich: Evangelischer Verlag A. G. Zollikon, 1952.

Bonnard, Pierre. *L'Epître de Saint Paul aux Galates;* and Masson, Charles. *L'Epître de Saint Paul aux Ephesiens*. Commentaire du Nouveau Testament 9. Neuchâtel: Delachaux & Niestlé, 1953.

Bornemann, W. *Die Thessalonicherbriefe*. Vol. 10. MeyerK. 6th ed. Göttingen: Vandenhoeck & Ruprecht, 1894.

Bornkamm, Günther. *Paul*. Translated by D. M. G. Stalker. New York: Harper & Row, 1971.

Borse, Udo. *Der Standort des Galaterbriefes*. BBB 41. Cologne: Peter Hanstein, 1972.

Bousset, Wilhelm. "Der Brief an die Galater." *Die Schriften des Neuen Testaments*. Vol. 2. Edited by Johannes Weiss. 3rd ed. Göttingen: Vandenhoeck & Ruprecht, 1917-18.

Bradley, David G. "The Topos as a Form in the Pauline Paraenesis." *JBL* 72 (1953) 238-46.

Brandt, W. J. *The Rhetoric of Argumentation*. New York: Bobbs-Merrill, 1970.

Braumann, Georg and Brown, Colin. "ἡμέρα." *NIDNTT* 2:887-95.

Braun, Herbert. "πλανάω." *TDNT* 6:230-51.

Bring, Ragnar. *Commentary on Galatians.* Translated by Eric Wahlstrom. Philadelphia: Muhlenberg Press, 1961.

Brinsmead, Bernard Hungerford. "Galatians as Dialogical Response to Opponents." Ph.D. dissertation, Andrews University, 1979.

_____. *Galatians—Dialogical Response to Opponents.* Chico, CA: Scholars Press, 1982.

Brown, Colin, gen. ed. *The New International Dictionary of New Testament Theology.* 3 vols. Translated, with additions and revisions, from *Theologisches Begriffslexikon zum Neuen Testament,* ed. by Lothar Coenen, Erich Beyreuther, and Hans Bietenhard, by a team of translators. Grand Rapids: Zondervan, 1971-78.

Bruce, Frederick Fyvie. "Further Thoughts on Paul's Autobiography (Galatians 1:11-2:14)." *Jesus und Paulus: Festschrift für Werner Georg Kümmel zum 70. Geburtstag.* Edited by E. Earle Ellis and Erich Grässer. Göttingen: Vandenhoeck & Ruprecht, 1975.

_____. "The New Testament and Classical Studies." *NTS* 22 (1976) 229-42.

_____. *Paul: Apostle of the Heart Set Free.* Grand Rapids: Wm. B. Eerdmans, 1977.

_____. "Galatian Problems: 1. Autobiographical Data." *BJRLM* 51 (1969) 292-309.

Bullinger, E. W. *Figures of Speech Used in the Bible.* London: Eyre & Spottiswoode, 1898.

Bultmann, Rudolf. "καυχάομαι, κτλ" *TDNT* 3:645-54.

_____. "πείθω, κτλ" *TDNT* 6:1-11.

_____. "Is Exegesis Without Presuppositions Possible?" *Existence and Faith.* Edited and translated by Schubert Ogden. London: SCM, 1964.

_____. *Der Stil der paulinischen Predigt und die kynisch-stoische Diatribe.* FRLANT 13. Göttingen: Vandenhoeck & Ruprecht, 1910.

_____. *Theology of the New Testament.* 2 vols. Translated by Kendrick Grobel. New York: Scribner's Sons, 1951-55.

Burgess, Theodore C. "Epideictic Literature." *University of Chicago Studies in Classical Philology* 3 (1900) 89-261.

Burton, Ernest de Witt. *A Critical and Exegetical Commentary on the Epistle to the Galatians.* ICC 35. New York: Scribner's Sons, 1920.

Buttrick, George Arthur et al., eds. *The Interpreter's Bible*. New York: Abingdon-Cokesbury Press, 1951ff.

Callaway, M. C. "The Mistress and the Maid: Midrashic Traditions Behind Galatians 4:21-31." *Radical Religion* 2 (1975) 94-101.

Calvin, John. *The Epistles of Paul the Apostle to the Romans and to the Thessalonians*. Translated by Ross MacKenzie. Edited by David W. Torrance and Thomas F. Torrance. Calvin's Commentaries 8. Grand Rapids: Eerdmans, 1960.

Campenhausen, Hans von. *Ecclesiastical Authority and Spiritual Power in the Church of the First Three Centuries*. Translated by J. A. Baker. Stanford: Stanford University Press, 1969; German ed., 1953.

Cancik, Hildegard. *Untersuchungen zu Senecas Epistulae morales*. Spudasmata 18. Hildesheim: Olms, 1967.

Case, Shirley Jackson. "Josephus' Anticipation of a Domitianic Persecution." *JBL* 44 (1925) 10-20.

Catchpole, David R. "Paul, James and the Apostolic Decree." *NTS* 23 (1977) 428-44.

Church, F. Forrester. "Rhetorical Structure and Design in Paul's Letter to Philemon." *HTR* 71 (1978) 17-33.

Cicero. *De inventione*. Translated by H. M. Hubbell. Loeb Classical Library.

_____. *Letters to Atticus*. Translated by E. O. Winstedt. Loeb Classical Library.

_____. *Letters to His Friends*. Translated by Glynn Williams. Loeb Classical Library.

_____. *De officiis*. Translated by Walter Miller. Loeb Classical Library.

_____. *De oratore*. Translated by Edward William Sutton and Harris Rackham. Loeb Classical Library.

Cobb, John B. *The Structure of Christian Existence*. Philadelphia: Westminster Press, 1967.

Cohen, Shaye J. D. *Josephus in Galilee and Rome: His Vita and Development as a Historian*. Columbia Studies in the Classical Tradition 8. Leiden: Brill, 1979.

Collins, R. F. "Apropos the Integrity of 1 Thes." *ETL* 55 (1979) 67-106.

_____. "The Theology of Paul's First Letter to the Thessalonians." *Louvain Studies* 6 (1977) 315-37.

Conzelmann, Hans. *History of Primitive Christianity.* Translated by John L. Steely. Nashville: Abingdon, 1973.

_____. "φῶς, κτλ" *TDNT* 9:310-58.

Coppens, J. "Miscéllanees bibliques. LXXX. Une diatribe antijuive dans I Thess., II, 13-16." *ETL* 51 (1975) 90-95.

Crouzel, Henri. "L'imitation et la 'suite' de Dieu et du Christ, dans les premiers siècles chrétiens, ainsi que leurs sources gréco-romaines et hébraiques." *JAC* 21 (1978) 7-41.

Dahl, Nils Alstrup. "The Pauline Letters: Proposal for a Study Project of a Society for Biblical Literature Seminar on Paul." Paper presented at Society of Biblical Literature annual convention, 1970.

_____. "Paul's Letter to the Galatians: Epistolary Genre, Content, and Structure." Paper circulated among members of the Society of Biblica Literature Paul Seminar, 1973.

Daniel, Jerry L. "Anti-Semitism in the Hellenistic-Roman Period." *JBL* 98 (1979) 45-65.

Daube, David. "Rabbinic Methods of Interpretation and Hellenistic Rhetoric." *HUCA* 22 (1949) 239-64.

Delling, Gerhard. "ἡμέρα." *TDNT* 2:943-53.

Demosthenes. *De corona.* Translated C. A. Vince and J. H. Vince. Loeb Classical Library.

Denis, Albert-Marie. "L'Apôtre Paul, prophete 'messianique' des Gentils, Etude Thématique de I Thess II, 1-6." *ETL* 33 (1957) 245-318.

_____. "L'Investiture de la Fonction Apostolique par apocalypse." Etude thématique de Gal. 1, 16." *RB* 16 (1957) 335-62, 492-515.

Denniston, J. D. *The Greek Particles.* 2nd ed. Oxford: Clarendon Press, 1959).

Dibelius, Martin. *An die Thessalonicher I II. An die Philipper.* HNT 11. 3rd ed. Tübingen: J. C. B. Mohr (Paul Siebeck), 1937.

_____. *From Tradition to Gospel.* Translated by Bertram Lee Woolf. New York: Scribner's Sons, 1935.

_____. *James: A Commentary on the Epistle of James.* Revised by Heinrich Greeven. Translated by Michael A. Williams. Hermeneia. Philadelphia: Fortress, 1976.

_____. "Zur Formgeschichte des Neuen Testaments (ausserhalb der Evangelien)." *TRu* n.F. 3 (1931) 207-42.

Dibelius, Martin and Conzelmann, Hans. *The Pastoral Epistles. A Commentary on the Pastoral Epistles.* Translated by Philip Buttolph and Adela Yarbro. Edited by Helmut Koester. Hermeneia. Philadelphia: Fortress Press, 1972.

Dick, Karl. *Der Schriftstellerische Plural Bei Paulus.* Halle: Max Niemeyer, 1900.

Dio Chrysostom. *Orations.* Translated by J. W. Cohoon. Loeb Classical Library.

Dobschütz, Ernst von. *Die Thessalonicher-Briefe.* MeyerK. 7th ed. Göttingen: Vandenhoeck & Ruprecht, 1909.

_____. *Christian Life in the Primitive Church.* Translated by George Bremner. Edited by W. D. Morrison. New York: Putnam's Sons, 1904.

_____. "Wir und Ich bei Paulus." *ZST* 10 (1932) 251-77.

Dodd, C. H. *The Epistle of Paul to the Romans.* MNTC. New York: Harper & Bros., 1932.

_____. "The Mind of Paul: A Psychological Approach." *BJRLM* 17 (1933) 91-105.

Doeve, J. W. "Paulus der Pharisäer und Galater i.13-15." *NovT* 6 (1963) 170-81.

Donfried, Karl Paul. "False Presuppositions in the Study of Romans." *CBQ* 36 (1974) 332-55.

_____. "Justification and Last Judgment in Paul." *ZNW* 67 (1976) 90-110.

_____. *The Setting of Second Clement in Early Christianity.* NovTSup 38. Leiden: Brill, 1974.

Doskocil, Walter. *Der Bann in der Urkirche.* Münchener Theologische Studien. München: Kommissionsverlag Karl Zink, 1958.

Doty, William G. "The Classification of Epistolary Literature." *CBQ* 31 (1969) 183-99.

_____. "The Concept of Genre in Literary Analysis." *Society of Biblical Literature Seminar Papers.* Vol. 2. Edited by Lane C. McGaughy. Missoula, MT: Scholars Press, 1972.

_____. *Letters in Primitive Christianity.* Guides to Biblical Scholarship, NT Series. Philadelphia: Fortress, 1973.

Duncan, George S. *The Epistle of Paul to the Galatians.* MNTC. London: Hodder & Stoughton, 1934.

Dungan, David L. *The Sayings of Jesus in the Churches of Paul: The Use of the Synoptic Tradition in the Regulation of Early Church Life.* Philadelphia: Fortress, 1971.

Dupont, Jacques. "Pierre et Paul à Antioche et à Jerusalem." *RSR* 45 (1957) 42-60.

Eadie, John. *Commentary on the Greek Text of the Epistle of Paul to the Philippians.* London: Richard Griffin, 1859.

Eckart, K. G. "Der zweite echte Brief des Apostels Paulus an die Thessalonichers." *ZTK* 58 (1961) 30-44.

Eckert, Jost. *Die urchristliche Verkündigung im Streit Zwischen Paulus und seinin Gegnern nach dem Galaterbrief.* Biblische Untersuchungen 6. München: Friedrich Pustet Regensburg, 1971.

Edwards, Elizabeth Gordon. *Christ, a Curse, and the Cross: An Interpretative Study of Galatians 3:13.* Th.D. dissertation, Princeton Theological Seminary, 1972. Ann Arbor: University Microfilms, 1972.

Eichholz, Goerg. *Tradition und Interpretation: Studien zum Neuen Testament und zur Hermeneutik.* TBü 29. Neues Testament. München: Kaiser, 1965.

Eidem, E. "Imitatio Pauli." *Teologiska Studier Tillagnade Erik Stave.* Uppsala: Almquist & Wiksells, 1922.

Eisman, M. M. "Dio and Josephus: Parallel Analyses." *Latomus* 36 (1977) 657-73.

Ellis, E. Earle. "Paul and his Co-Workers." *NTS* 17 (1971) 437-52.

_____. *Paul's Use of the Old Testament.* Grand Rapids: Wm. B. Eerdmans, 1957.

Esser, H.-H. "στοιχεῖα." *NIDNTT* 2:451-53.

Faw, Chalmer E. "On the Writing of First Thessalonians." *JBL* 71 (1952) 217-25.

Filson, Floyd V. *A New Testament History.* Philadelphia: Westminster, 1964.

Fischel, Henry. "Story and History: Observations on Graeco-Roman Rhetoric and Pharisaism." *American Oriental Society, Middle West Branch, Semi-Centennial Volume.* Edited by Denis Sinor. Asian Studies Research Institute, Oriental Series 3. Bloomington, IN: Indiana University Press, 1969.

_____. "Studies in Cynicism and the Ancient Near East: the Trans-formation of a Chria." *Religions in Antiquity.* Edited by Jacob A. Neusner. Leiden: Brill, 1968.

Foerster, Werner. "Die δοκοῦντες in Gal 2." *ZNW* 36 (1937) 286-92.

_____. "ἀρέσκω, κτλ" *TDNT* 1:455-57.

Forestell, J. Terence. "The Letters to the Thessalonians." *The Jerome Biblical Commentary.* Edited by Raymond E. Brown, Joseph A. Fitzmyer, and Roland E. Murphy. Englewood Cliffs, NJ: Prentice-Hall, 1968.

Forkman, Göran. *The Limits of the Religious Community: Expulsion from the Religious Community within the Qumran Sect, within Rabbinic Judaism, and within Primitive Christianity.* Translated by Pearl Sjölander. ConBNT 5. Lund: CWK Gleerup, 1972.

Frame, James Everett. *A Critical and Exegetical Commentary on the Epistles of St. Paul to the Thessalonians.* ICC. Edinburgh: T & T Clark, 1912.

Freyne, Sean. "The Galileans in the Light of Josephus' *Vita.*" *NTS* 26 (1980) 397-413.

Fridrichsen, Anton. "Die Apologie des Paulus Gal. 1." *Paulus und die Urgemeinde.* Edited by Lyder Brun & Anton Fridrichsen. Giessen: Töpelmann, 1921.

_____. *The Apostle and His Message.* Uppsala universitets arsskrift 3. Uppsala: A.-B. Lundequistska, 1947.

_____. "Zum Stil des paulinischen Peristasenkatalogs, 2 Cor. 11, 23ff." *Symbolae osloenses* 7 (1928) 25-29.

Friedrich, Gerhard. "εὐαγγελίζω, κτλ" *TDNT* 2:707-37.

Funk, Robert W. "The Apostolic Parousia: Form and Significance." *Christian History and Interpretation: Studies Presented to John Knox.* Edited by W. R. Farmer, C. F. D. Moule, and R. R. Niebuhr. Cambridge: Cambridge University Press, 1967.

_____. *Language, Hermeneutic, and Word of God.* New York: Harper & Row, 1966.

Furnish, Victor Paul. *Theology and Ethics in Paul.* Nashville: Abingdon, 1968.

Galen. *On the natural faculties.* Translated by Arthur John Brock. Loeb Classical Library.

240 Pauline Autobiography

Gaston, Lloyd. "Israel's Enemies in Pauline Theology." *NTS* 28 (1982) 400-423.

Georgi, Dieter. *Die Gegner des Paulus im 2. Korintherbrief Studien zur religiösen Propaganda in der Spätantike.* WMANT 11. Neukirchen-Vluyn: Neukirchener Verlag, 1964.

_____. *Die Geschichte der Kollekte des Paulus für Jerusalem.* Theologische Forschung Wissenschaftliche Beiträge zur kirchlich-evangelischen Lehre 38. Hamburg-Bergestedt: Herber Reich: Evangelischer Verlag, 1965.

Goodspeed, Edgar J. *Paul.* Nashville: Abingdon, 1947.

Grabner-Haider, Anton. *Paraklese und Eschatologie bei Paulus, Mensch und Welt im Anspruch der Zukunft Gottes.* NTAbh n.f. 4. Münster: Aschendorf, 1968.

Grant, Frederick C. "The Historical Paul." *Early Christian Origins. Studies in Honor of Harold R. Willoughby.* Edited by Allen Wikgren. Chicago: Quadrangle Books, 1961.

Greenwood, David. "Rhetorical Criticism and Formgeschichte: Some Methodological Considerations." *JBL* 89 (1970) 418-26.

Grundmann, Walter. "στέφανος, στεφανόω." *TDNT* 7:615-36.

_____. "στήκω, ἵστημι." *TDNT* 7:636-53.

Gunkel, Hermann & Zstharnack, Leopold, eds. *Die Religion in Geschichte und Gegenwart,* 5 vols. 2nd ed. Tübingen: J. C. B. Mohr (Paul Siebeck), 1927-31.

Gunther, John J. *Paul: Messenger and Exile. A Study in the Chronology of His Life and Letters.* Valley Forge: Judson Press, 1972.

_____. *St. Paul's Opponents and their Background. A Study of Apocalyptic and Jewish Sectarian Teachings.* NovTSup 35. Leiden: Brill, 1973.

Guthrie, Donald. *New Testament Introduction.* 3rd ed. Downers Grove: Intervarsity, 1971.

Güttgemanns, Erhard. *Der leidende Apostel und sein Herr: Studien zur Paulinischen Christologie.* FRLANT 90. Göttingen: Vandenhoeck & Ruprecht, 1966.

Haacker, Klaus. "Paulus und das Judentum." *Judaica* 33 (1977) 161-77.

Hadot, Ilsetraut. *Seneca und die griechisch-römische Tradition der Seelenleitung.* Berlin: de Gruyter, 1969.

Haenchen, Ernst. *The Acts of the Apostles*. Translated by R. McL. Wilson et al. Philadelphia: Westminster, 1971.

Hammond, N. G. L. and Sculland, H. H., eds. *Oxford Classical Dictionary*. Oxford: Clarendon Press, 1970.

Hanson, Anthony Tyrrell. *Studies in Paul's Technique and Theology*.Grand Rapids: Eerdmans, 1974.

Harder, Günther. "στηρίζω, κτλ" *TDNT* 7:653-57.

Hare, Douglas R. A. *The Theme of Jewish Persecution of Christians in the Gospel according to St Matthew*. SNTSMS 6. Cambridge: Cambridge University Press, 1967.

Hauck, Friedrich, "ἀκάθαρτος, ἀκαθαρσία." *TDNT* 3:427-29.

Hawkins, John Gale. *The Opponents of Paul in Galatia*. Ph.D. dissertation, Yale University, 1971. Ann Arbor: University Microfilms, 1971.

Hay, David M. "Paul's Indifference to Authority." *JBL* 88 (1969) 36-44.

Hendriksen, William. *Exposition of I and II Thessalonians*. New Testament Commentary. Grand Rapids: Baker, 1964.

Hennecke, Edgar and Schneemelcher, Wilhelm, eds. *New Testament Apocrypha*. 2 vols. Translated and edited by Robert McL. Wilson. Philadelphia: Westminster, 1963-65.

Henrichs, Albert. Review of *Der Apostel Paulus und die sokratische Tradition: Eine Exegetische Untersuchung zu seiner "Apologie": 2 Korinther 10-13*, by Hans Dieter Betz. *JBL* 94 (1975) 310-14.

Héring, Jean. *The Second Epistle of Saint Paul to the Corinthians*. Translated by A. W. Heathcote and P. J. Allcock. London: Epworth, 1967.

Hester, James D. "Epistolography in Antiquity and Early Christianity." Paper presented at the Pacific Coast Region Society of Biblical Literature meeting, 1975.

Hiebert, D. Edmond. *The Thessalonian Epistles: A Call to Readiness*. Chicago: Moody Press, 1971.

Hirsch, E. D. *Validity in Interpretation*. New Haven: Yale University Press, 1967.

Hobbs, Edward C. "Recognition of Conceptuality as a Hermeneutical Tool." *SE* 3 (= Texte und Untersuchungen 88) (1964) 464-77.

Hock, Ronald. "Paul's Tentmaking and the Problem of His Social Class." *JBL* 97 (1978) 555-64.

_____. "Simeon the Shoemaker as an Ideal Cynic." *GRBS* 17 (1976) 41-53.

_____. *The Social Context of Paul's Ministry: Tent-making and Apostleship.* Philadelphia: Fortress, 1980.

_____. *The Working Apostle: An Examination of Paul's Means of Livelihood.* Ph.D. dissertation, Yale University, 1974. Ann Arbor: University Microfilms, 1974.

_____. "The Workshop as a Social Setting for Paul's Missionary Preaching." *CBQ* 41 (1979) 438-50.

Holmberg, Bengt. *Paul and Power.* Philadelphia: Fortress, 1980.

Holtz, Traugott, "Die Bedeutung des Apostelkonzils für Paulus." *NovT* 16 (1974) 110-48.

_____. "Zum Selbstverständnis des Apostels Paulus." *TLZ* 91 (1966) 321-30.

Holzmeister, U. "De Plurali categoriae in Novo Testamento et a Patribus adhito." *Bib* 14 (1933) 68-95.

Horowitz, I. L. "Autobiography as the Presentation of Self for Social Immortality." *New Literary History* 9 (1977) 173-79.

Howard, George. *Paul: Crisis in Galatia. A Study in Early Christian Theology.* SNTSMS 35. Cambridge: Cambridge University Press, 1979.

Hultgren, Arland J. "Paul's Pre-Christian Persecutions of the Church: Their Purpose, Locale, and Nature." *JBL* 95 (1976) 97-111.

Hurd, John C. "Concerning the Structure of 1 Thessalonians." Paper presented at the Society of Biblical Literature Paul Seminar, 1972.

_____. *The Origin of 1 Corinthians.* London: SPCK, 1965.

Isocrates. *Antidosis.* Translated by George Norlin. Loeb Classical Library.

_____. *Helen.* Translated by George Norlin. Loeb Classical Library.

_____. *Panathenaicus.* Translated by George Norlin. Loeb Classical Library.

Jaeger, Werner. *Paideia: The Ideals of Greek Culture.* Vol. 3. Translated by Gilbert Highet. New York: Oxford University Press, 1944.

Jaspers, Karl. *The Origin and Goal of History.* Translated by Michael Bullock. London: Routledge & Paul, 1953.

Jeske, R. L. "Luke and Paul on the Apostle Paul." *CTM* 4 (January 1977) 28-38.

Jewett, Robert. "The Agitators and the Galatian Congregation." *NTS* 17 (1970) 198-212.

_____. *A Chronology of Paul's Life.* Philadelphia: Fortress, 1979.

_____. "Enthusiastic Radicalism and the Thessalonian Correspondence." Paper presented at the Society of Biblical Literature Paul Seminar, 1972.

_____. *Paul's Anthropological Terms. A Study of their Use in Conflict Settings.* AGJU 10. Leiden: Brill, 1971.

_____. "Romans as an Ambassadorial Letter." *Int* 36 (1982) 5-20.

Johnson, Alfred M., ed. and trans. *The New Testament and Structuralism.* PTMS 11. Pittsburgh: Pickwick Press, 1976.

Josephus. *Against Apion.* Translated by H. St. J. Thackeray. Loeb Classical Library.

_____. *Jewish Antiquities.* Translated by H. St. J. Thackeray, R. Marcus, A. Wikgren, and L. H. Feldman. Loeb Classical Library.

_____. *The Jewish War.* Translated by H. St. J. Thackeray. Loeb Classical Library.

_____. *The Life.* Translated by H. St. John Thackeray. Loeb Classical Library.

Judge, Edwin A. "The Conflict of Educational Aims in New Testament Thought." *Journal of Christian Education* 9 (1966) 32-45.

_____. "The Early Christians as a Scholastic Community." *JRH* 1 (1961) 127-31.

_____. "Paul's Boasting in Relation to Contemporary Professional Practice." *AusBR* 16 (1968) 37-50.

_____. *The Social Pattern of Christian Groups in the First Century.* London: Tyndale Press, 1960.

_____. "St. Paul and Classical Society." *JAC* 15 (1972) 19-36.

Käsemann, Ernst. *Commentary on Romans.* Translated and edited by Geoffrey W. Bromiley. Grand Rapids: Eerdmans, 1980.

_____. "Die Legitimität des Apostels. Eine Untersuchung zu II Korinther 10-13." *ZNW* 41 (1942) 33-71.

_____. *New Testament Questions of Today*. Translated by W. J. Montague. Philadelphia: Fortress, 1967.

_____. *Perspectives on Paul*. Translated by Margaret Kohl. Philadelphia: Fortress Press, 1971.

Keck, Leander E. "On the Ethos of Early Christians." *JAAR* 42 (1974) 435-52.

_____. *Paul and His Letters*. Proclamation Commentaries. Philadelphia: Fortress, 1979.

Kee, Howard Clark. "Aretalogy and Gospel." *JBL* 92 (1973).

Kennedy, George. *The Art of Persuasion in Greece*. Princeton, NJ: Princeton University Press, 1963.

_____. *The Art of Rhetoric in the Roman World 300 B.C.-A.D. 300*. Princeton: Princeton University Press, 1972.

_____. *Quintilian*. Twayne's World Authors Series 59: Latin Literature. New York: Twayne Publishers, 1969.

Kennedy, H. A. A. "St. Paul's Apostolic Consciousness and the Interpretation of the Epistles." *ExpTim* 17 (1915/16) 8-13.

Kirk, J. A. "Apostleship since Rengstorf: Toward a Synthesis." *NTS* 21 (1974/75) 249-64.

Kittel, Gerhard and Friedrich, Gerhard, eds. *Theological Dictionary of the New Testament*. 10 vols. Translated and edited by Geoffrey W. Bromiley. Grand Rapids: Wm. B. Eerdmans, 1964-76.

Klein, Günter. *Die zwölf Apostel. Ursprung und Gehalt einer Idee*. FRLANT 77. Göttingen: Vandenhoeck & Ruprecht, 1961.

Klostermann, Erich. "Zur Apologie des Paulus Galater 1, 10-2, 21." *Gottes ist der Orient. Festschrift für Otto Eissfeldt zu seinem 70. Geburtstag*. Berlin: Evangelische Verlagsanstalt, 1959.

Koskenniemi, Heikki. *Studien zur Idee und Phraseologie des griechischen Briefes bis 700 n. Chr.* Translated by Margareta Horn. Annales Academie Scientiarum Fennicas, Ser. B, vol. 102.2. Helsinki: Suomalaisen Kirjallisuuden Kerjapaino, 1956.

Kuhn, Karl Georg. "προσήλυτος." *TDNT* 6:730-36.

Kümmel, Werner Georg. *Introduction to the New Testament*. Revised ed. Translated by Howard Clark Kee. Nashville: Abingdon, 1975.

_____. "Das literarische und geschichtliche Problem des ersten Thessalonicherbriefes." *Neotestamentica et Patristica. Eine Freundsgabe. Herrn Professor Dr. Oscar Cullmann zu seinem 60. Geburtstag Überreicht.* NovTSup 6. Leiden: Brill, 1962.

_____. *Man in the New Testament.* Revised and enlarged edition. Translated by John J. Vincent. London: Epworth Press, 1963.

_____. *The New Testament. The History of the Investigation of Its Problems.* Translated by S. McLean Gilmour and Howard C. Kee. Nashville: Abingdon, 1972.

_____. *Römer 7 und die Bekehrung des Paulus.* Leipzig: J. G. Hinrichs'sche Buchhandlung, 1929. Republished in *Römer 7 und das Bild des Menschen im neuen Testament.* München: Kaiser, 1974.

_____. *The Theology of the New Testament.* Translated by John E. Steely. Nashville: Abingdon, 1973.

Kustas, Georg L. *Diatribe in Ancient Rhetorical Theory.* Edited by Wilhelm Wuellner. Protocol of the 22nd Colloquy. Berkeley: Center for Hermeneutical Studies in Hellenistic and Modern Culture, 1976.

Ladd, George Eldon. *A Theology of the New Testament.* Grand Rapids: Eerdmans, 1974.

Lagrange, M.-J. *Saint Paul. Epître aux Galates.* 2nd ed. Etudes Bibliques. Paris: Librairie Lecoffre, J. Gabalda et Cie, 1926.

Lang, Friedrich. "πῦρ, κτλ" *TDNT* 6:936-48.

Laqueur, R. *Der judische Historiker Flavius Josephus: Ein biographischer Versuch auf neuer quellenkritischer Grundlage.* Giessen: Munchow, 1920; reprint ed., Darmstadt: Wissenschaftliche Buchgesellschaft, 1972.

Laurent, J. C. W. "Den Pluralis maiestaticus in den Thessalonischerbriefen." *TSK* 41 (1868) 159-66.

Lausberg, Heinrich. *Elemente der literarischen Rhetorik.* 3rd ed. München: Max Hueber Verlag, 1967.

_____. *Handbuch der literarischen Rhetorik: Eine Grundlegung der Literaturwissenschaft.* 2 vols. München: Max Hueber Verlag, 1960.

Lejeune, P. "Autobiography in the Third Person." Translated by A. Tomarken and E. Tomarken. *New Literary History* 9 (1977) 27-50.

Lenski, R. C. H. *The Interpretation of St. Paul's Epistles to the Galatians, to the Ephesians, and to the Philippians.* Columbus, OH: Wartburg Press, 1946.

Leo, Friedrich. *Die griechisch-römische Biographie nach ihrere literarischen Form.* Hildesheim: Georg Olms Verlagsbuchhandlung, 1965; reprint of 1901 ed.

Liddell, Henry George; Scott, Robert; and Jones, Henry Stuart. *A Greek-English Lexicon.* New ed. Oxford: Clarendon Press, 1940.

Lietzmann, Hans. *An die Galater.* 3rd ed. HNT 10. Tübingen: J. C. B. Mohr (Paul Siebeck), 1932.

Lightfoot, J. B. *The Epistle of St. Paul to the Galatians.* Grand Rapids: Zondervan, 1972; reprint of 1865 ed.

_____. *Notes on Epistles of St. Paul.* Edited by J. R. Harmer. Grand Rapids: Baker, 1980; reprint of the 1895 ed.

_____. *Paul's Epistles to the Colossians and to Philemon.* Grand Rapids: Zondervan, 1959; reprint of the 1879 ed.

Lincoln, Andrew T. " 'Paul the Visionary': The Setting and Significance of the Rapture to Paradise in II Corinthians xii.1-10." *NTS* 25 (1979) 204-20.

_____. *Paradise Now and Not Yet.* SNTSMS 43. Cambridge: Cambridge University Press, 1981.

Lindars, Barnabas. *New Testament Apologetic: The Doctrinal Significance of the Old Testament Quotations.* Philadelphia: Westminster Press, 1961.

Lindemann, Andreas. *Paulus im ältesten Christentum: Das Bild des Apostels und die Rezeption der paulinischen Theologie in der fruhchristlichen Literatur bis Marcion.* BZHT 58. Tübingen: J. C. B. Mohr (Paul Siebeck), 1979.

Lindeskoy, G. "Jews and Judaism in the New Testament. Four Theses." *ASTI* 11 (1977-78) 63-67.

Lipsius, R. A. "Galaterbrief." *Hand-Kommentar zum neuen Testament.* Vol. 2. 2nd ed. revised. Freiburg: J. C. B. Mohr (Paul Siebeck), 1892.

Lofthouse, W. F. " 'I' and 'We' in the Pauline Letters." *ExpTim* 64 (1952-53) 241-45.

_____. "Singular and Plural in St. Paul's Letters." *ExpTim* 58 (1947) 179-82.

Loheit, Fritz. *Untersuchungen zur antiken Selbstapologie.* Rostock: Adlers Erben, 1928.

Loisy, Alfred. *L'Epître aux Galates.* Paris: Nourry, 1916.

Longenecker, Richard N. *Paul, Apostle of Liberty.* Grand Rapids: Baker, 1976; reprint of 1964 ed.

Louw, Johannes P. "Discourse Analysis and the Greek New Testament." *BT* 24 (1973) 101-18.

Lucian of Samosata. *The Dead Come to Life or the Fisherman.* Translated by A. M. Harmon. Loeb Classical Library.

_____. *How to Write History.* Translated by A. M. Harmon. Loeb Classical Library.

_____. *Parasite: Parasitic an Art.* Translated by A. M. Harmon. Loeb Classical Library.

_____. *Philosophies for Sale.* Translated by A. M. Harmon. Loeb Classical Library.

Lünemann, Gottlieb. "Critical and Exegetical Hand-book to the Epistles to the Thessalonians." Translated by Paton J. Gloag. Meyer's *Critical and Exegetical Hand-book.* Vol. 8. New York: Funk & Wagnalls, 1889.

Lütgert, Wilhelm. *Gesetz und Geist: Eine Untersuchung zur Vorgeschichte des Galaterbriefes.* Gütersloh: Bertelsmann, 1919.

Luz, Ulrich. *Das Geschichtsverstandnis des Paulus.* Beiträge zur evangelischen Theologie; theologische Abhandlungen 49. München: Kaiser, 1968.

McEleney, Neil J. "Conversion, Circumcision and the Law." *NTS* 20 (1974) 319-41.

Machen, J. Gresham. *The Origin of Paul's Religion.* New York: Macmillan, 1921.

M'Michael, W. F. "Be Ye Followers of Me." *ExpTim* 5 (1893-94) 287.

Malherbe, Abraham J. "The Beasts at Ephesus." *JBL* 87 (1968) 71-80.

_____. " 'Gentle as a Nurse.' The Cynic Background to I Thess ii." *NovT* 12 (1970) 203-17.

_____. *Social Aspects of Early Christianity.* Baton Rouge: Louisiana State University Press, 1977.

_____. "I Thessalonians as a Paraenetic Letter." Paper presented at the Society of Biblical Literature annual meeting, 1972.

Manson, T. W. "St. Paul in Ephesus: (2) The Problem of the Epistle to the Galatians." *BJRLM* 24 (1940) 59-80.

Marrow, Stanley B. "Parrhesia and the New Testament." *CBQ* 44 (1982) 435-36.

Martz, Louis L. and Williams, Aubrey, eds. *The Author in His Work: Essays on a Problem in Criticism.* New Haven: Yale University Press, 1978.

Marxsen, Willi. *Introduction to the New Testament.* Translated by G. Buswell. Philadelphia: Fortress, 1974.

Mason, A. J. "The First Epistle of Paul the Apostle to the Thessalonians." *The Epistles to the Colossians, Thessalonians, and Timothy.* Edited by Charles John Ellicott. London: Cassell, 1889.

Masson, Charles. *Les deux Epîtres de Saint Paul aux Thessaloniciens.* Commentaire du Nouveau Testament 11. Neuchâtel Delachaux & Niestlé, 1957.

Mearns, C. L. "Early Eschatological Development in Paul: The Evidence of I and II Thessalonians." *NTS* 27 (1981) 145.

Meeks, Wayne A. Review of *Galatians: A Commentary on Paul's Letter to the Churches in Galatia,* by Hans Dieter Betz. *JBL* 100 (1981) 304-7.

Merk, Otto. "Der Beginn der Paranese im Galaterbrief." *ZNW* 60 (1969) 83-104.

_____. *Handeln aus Glauben. Die Motivierungen der paulinischen Ethik.* Marburg: Elwert, 1968.

Metzger, Bruce M. *A Textual Commentary on the Greek New Testament.* London: United Bible Societies, 1971.

Meyer, Heinrich August Wilhelm. *Critical and Exegetical Hand-book.* 11 vols. Translated and edited by William P. Dickson et al. New York: Funk & Wagnalls, 1884-89.

_____. "Critical and Exegetical Hand-book to the Epistle to the Galatians." Translated by G. H. Venables. Edited by Henry E. Jacobs. Meyer's *Critical and Exegetical Hand-book.* New York: Funk & Wagnalls, 1884.

Michaelis, Wilhelm. "μιμέομαι, κτλ" *TDNT* 4:659-74.

Michel, Otto. *Der Brief an die Römer.* MeyerK 4/13. Göttingen: Vandenhoeck & Ruprecht, 1966.

Milligan, George. *St. Paul's Epistles to the Thessalonians.* London: Macmillan, 1980.

Misch, Georg. *A History of Autobiography in Antiquity.* 2 vols. Translated by the author and E. W. Dickes. Cambridge: Harvard University Press, 1951.

Mitton, C. Leslie. *The Formation of the Pauline Corpus of Letters.* London: Epworth Press, 1955.

Moffatt, James. "The First and Second Epistles to the Thessalonians." Vol. 4. *The Expositor's Greek Testament.* 5 vols. Edited by W. Robertson Nicoll. London: Hodder & Stoughton, 1897-1910.

_____. "The Responsibility of Self-Assertion: A Study in Two Characters." *ExpTim* 10 (1898-99) 445-49.

Momigliano, Arnaldo. *The Development of Greek Biography.* Cambridge, MA: Harvard University Press, 1971.

_____. "Second Thoughts on Greek Biography." *Mededelingen der koninklijke Nederlandse Akademie van Wetenschappen.* Afd. Letterkunde, nieuwe reeks 34, 7 (1971).

Moody, R. A. "The First Person Plural as used by St. Paul." *ExpTim* 43 (1931-32) 379.

Moore, A. L. *1 and 2 Thessalonians.* NCB. Greenwood, SC: Attic Press, 1969.

Morris, Leon. *The Epistles of Paul to the Thessalonians.* Tyndale New Testament Commentary. Grand Rapids: Eerdmans, 1957.

_____. *The First and Second Epistles to the Thessalonians.* NICNT. Edited by F. F. Bruce. Grand Rapids: Eerdmans, 1959.

_____. "ΚΑΙ ΑΠΑΞ ΚΑΙ ΔΙΕ." *NovT* 1 (1965) 205-9.

Morton, A. Q. and McLeman, James. *Paul, the Man and the Myth: A Study in the Authorship of Greek Prose.* London: Hodder & Stoughton, 1966.

Moule, C. F. D. *An Idiom Book of New Testament Greek.* 2nd ed. Cambridge: Cambridge University Press, 1959.

Moulton, James Hope. *Prolegomena.* Vol. 1. *A Grammar of New Testament Greek.* 3rd ed. Edinburgh: T & T Clark, 1930.

Moulton, James Hope and Milligan, George. *The Vocabulary of the Greek Testament: Illustrated from the Papyri and Other Non-Literary Sources.* Grand Rapids: Eerdmans, 1972; reprint of 1930 ed.

Moulton, W. F. and Geden, A. S. *A Concordance to the Greek Testament.* Edinburgh: T & T Clark, 1897.

Mullins, Terrence Y. "Disclosure, a Literary Form in the New Testament." *NovT* 7 (1964) 44-50.

_____. "Formulas in New Testament Epistles." *JBL* 91 (1972) 380-90.

_____. "Visit Talk in New Testament Letters." *CBQ* 35 (1973) 350-58.

Munck, Johannes. *Paul and the Salvation of Mankind.* Translated by Frank Clarke. Richmond, VA: John Knox, 1959.

Mussner, Franz. *Der Galaterbrief.* HTKNT 9, Freiburg: Herder, 1974.

Neil, William. *The Epistle of Paul to the Thessalonians.* MNTC. London: Hodder & Stoughton, 1950.

_____. *St. Paul's Epistles to the Thessalonians.* Torch Bible Commentary. London: SCM Press, 1957.

Neill, Stephen. *The Interpretation of the New Testament, 1861-1961.* London: Oxford University Press, 1964.

Nestle, Eberhard; Nestle, Erwin; and Aland, Kurt; eds. *Novum Testamentum Graece.* 25th ed. London: United Bible Societies, 1963.

Neugebauer, Fritz. *In Christus.* EN XPIΣTΩI. Eine Untersuchung zum paulinischen Glaubensverstandnis. Göttingen: Vandenhoeck & Ruprecht, 1961.

Nicoll, W. Robertson, ed. *The Expositor's Greek Testament.* 5 vols. London: Hodder & Stoughton, 1897-1910.

Nock, Arthur Darby. *St. Paul.* Swander Lectures, 1938. New York: Harper & Brothers, 1938.

Nutton, V. "Galen and Medical Autobiography." *Cambridge Philological Society, Cambridge, England, Proceedings* 198 (1972) 50-62.

O'Brien, Peter Thomas. *Introductory Thanksgivings in the Letters of Paul.* NovTSup 49. Leiden: Brill, 1977.

Oepke, Albrecht. "Die Briefe an die Thessaloniker." *Das Neue Testament Deutsch.* Vol. 8 9th ed. Göttingen: Vandenhoeck & Ruprecht, 1962.

_____. *Der Brief des Paulus an die Galater.* 3rd ed. Revised by J. Rohde. THKNT 9. Berlin: Evangelische Verlagsanstalt, 1973.

Okeke, G. E. "I Thess. ii.13-16: The Fate of the Unbelieving Jews." *NTS* 27 (1980) 127-36.

Olney, James. "Autos-Bios-Graphein: The Study of Autobiographical Literature." *South Atlantic Quarterly* 77 (1978) 113-23.

_____. *Metaphors of Self: The Meaning of Autobiography.* Princeton: Princeton University Press, 1972.

Olshausen, Hermann. "Exposition of the Epistles to the Thessalonians." *Biblical Commentary on the New Testament.* Revised by A. C. Kendrick. New York: Sheldon, 1862.

O'Neill, J. C. *The Recovery of Paul's Letter to the Galatians.* London: SPCK, 1972.

Overbeck, Franz. *Uber die Auffassung des Streits des Paulus mit Petrus in Antiochien (Gal. 2, 11ff.) bei den Kirchenvatern.* Darmstadt: Wissenschaftliche Buchgesellschaft, 1968; reprint of 1877 ed.

Pascal, Roy. *Design and Truth in Autobiography.* Cambridge: Harvard University Press, 1960.

Patte, Daniel. *Paul's Faith and the Power of the Gospel: A Structural Introduction to the Pauline Letters.* Philadelphia: Fortress, 1983.

Pearson, Birger A. "I Thessalonians 2:13-16: A Deutero-Pauline Interpolation." *HTR* 64 (1971) 79-94.

Perelman, Chaim and Olbrechts-Tyteca, L. *The New Rhetoric: A Treatise on Argumentation.* Translated by John Wilkinson and Purcell Weaver. Notre Dame, IN: University of Notre Dame Press, 1969.

Perrin, Norman. *The New Testament: An Introduction: Proclamation and Parenesis, Myth and History.* New York: Harcourt Brace Jovanovich, 1974.

Peterson, H. "Real and Alleged Literary Projects of Josephus." *American Journal of Philology* 79 (1958) 262.

Pfitzner, Victor C. *Paul and the Agon Motif: Traditional Athletic Imagery in the Pauline Literature.* NovTSup 16. Leiden: Brill, 1967.

Philo. *Legatione ad Gaium.* Translated by F. H. Colson. Loeb Classical Library.

Pilch, John J. *Paul's Usage and Understanding of Apokalypsis in Galatians 1-2: A Structural Investigation.* Ph.D. dissertation, Marquette University, 1972. Ann Arbor: University Microfilms, 1973.

Pindar. *The Odes of Pindar.* Translated by John Sandys. Loeb Classical Library.

Plato. *Apology of Socrates.* Translated by H. N. Fowler. Loeb Classical Library.

_____. *Gorgias.* Translated by M. R. W. Lamb. Loeb Classical Library.

_____. *Phaedrus.* Translated by H. N. Fowler. Loeb Classical Library.

Pliny. *Letters*. Translated by William Melmoth and W. M. L. Hutchinson. Loeb Classical Library.

Plummer, Alfred. *A Commentary on St. Paul's First Epistle to the Thessalonians*. London: Scott, 1918.

Plutarch. *Cicero*. Translated by Bernadote Perrin. Loeb Classical Library.

_____. *Demosthenes and Cicero*. Translated by Bernadote Perrin. Loeb Classical Library.

_____. *Moralia*. Translated by Frank Cole Babbit. Loeb Classical Library.

_____. *Solon and Publicola*. Translated by Bernadote Perrin. Loeb Classical Library.

Polybius. *The Histories*. Translated by W. R. Paton. Loeb Classical Library.

Price, James L. "'Example' and 'Imitation' in Paul's Parenesis." Paper read at the Society of Biblical Literature Southeastern Region Annual Meeting, 1976.

Quintilian. *Institutio oratoria*. Translated by H. E. Butler. Loeb Classical Library.

Rahlfs, Alfred, ed. *Septuaginta*. 7th ed. Stuttgart: Württembergische Bibelanstalt, 1962.

Reitzenstein, Richard. *Hellenistic Mystery-Religions: Their Basic Ideas and Significance*. Translated by John E. Steely. PTMS 15. Pittsburgh: Pickwick Press, 1978; German ed. 1926.

Rendall, Frederic. "The Epistle to the Galatians." Vol. 4. *The Expositor's Greek Testament*. 5 vols. Edited by W. Robertson Nicoll. London: Hodder & Stoughton, 1897-1910.

Rengstorf, Karl Heinrich. "ἀποστέλλω, κτλ" *TDNT* 1:398-447.

_____. "δοῦλος, κτλ" *TDNT* 2:261-80.

Rhetorica ad Herennium. Translated by Harry Caplan. Loeb Classical Library.

Rhoads, David M. *Israel in Revolution: 6-74 C.E.: A Political History Based on the Writings of Josephus*. Philadelphia: Fortress, 1976.

Richardson, Peter. "Pauline Inconsistency: I Corinthians 9:19-23 and Galatians 2:11-14." *NTS* 26 (1980) 347-62.

_____. *Paul's Ethic of Freedom*. Philadelphia: Westminster, 1979.

Ridderbos, Herman Nicholaas. *The Epistle of Paul to the Churches of Galatia*. Translated by Henry Zylstra. NICNT. Grand Rapids: Eerdmans, 1953.

_____. *Paul: An Outline of His Theology*. Translated by John Richard DeWitt. Grand Rapids: Eerdmans, 1975.

Rigaux, Béde. *The Letters of St. Paul: Modern Studies*. Translated and edited by Stephen Yonick. Chicago: Franciscan Herald Press, 1968.

_____. *Saint Paul: Les Epîtres aux Thessaloniciens*. Etudes bibliques. Paris: Librairie Lecoffre: J. Duculot, 1956.

Robertson, A. T. *A Grammar of the Greek New Testament in the Light of Historical Research*. 3rd ed. New York: George H. Doran, 1919.

Robinson, James M. "Die Hodajot-Formal in Gebet und Hymnus des Frühchristentums." *Apophoreta. Festschrift für Ernst Haenchen*. Edited by W. Eltester and F. H. Kettler. Berlin: Alfred Töpelmann, 1964.

_____. "Kerygma and History in the New Testament." *Trajectories through Early Christianity*. Edited by James M. Robinson and Helmut Koester. Philadelphia: Fortress, 1971.

Roetzel, Calvin. "I Thess. 5:12-28: A Case Study." *Society of Biblical Literature Seminar Papers*. Vol. 2. Edited by Lane C. McGaughy. Missoula, MT: Scholars Press, 1972.

Roller, Otto. *Das Formular der paulinischen Briefe: Ein Beiträge zur Lehre vom antiken Briefe*. BWANT 4. Stuttgart: W. Kohlhammer, 1933.

Ropes, James Hardy, *The Singular Problem of the Epistle to the Galatians*. HTS 14. Cambridge: Harvard University Press, 1929.

Russell, D. A. *Plutarch*. London: Duckworth, 1973.

Sampley, J. Paul. " 'Before God, I do not lie' (Gal. 1.20): Paul's Self-Defence in the Light of Roman Legal Praxis." *NTS* 23 (1977) 477-82.

_____. *Pauline Partnership in Christ*. Philadelphia: Fortress, 1980.

Sanders, E. P. *Paul and Palestinian Judaism: A Comparison of Patterns of Religion*. Philadelphia: Fortress, 1977.

_____. "Paul's Attitude Toward the Jewish People." *USQR* 33 (1978) 175-87.

Sanders, Jack T. "Paul's 'Autobiographical' Statements in Galatians 1-2."
    JBL 85 (1966) 335-43.

_____. "The Transition from Opening Epistolary Thanksgiving to
    Body in the laetters of the Pauline Corpus." *JBL* 81 (1962) 348-62.

Sandmel, Samuel. "Parallelomania." *JBL* 81 (1962) 1-13.

Schlier, Heinrich. *Der Brief an die Galater*. 4th ed. MeyerK 7, 13.
    Göttingen: Vandenhoeck & Ruprecht, 1965.

_____. "θλίβω, κτλ" *TDNT* 3:139-48.

Schmithals, Walter. *Gnosticism in Corinth*. Translated by John E. Steely.
    Nashville: Abingdon, 1971.

_____. *The Office of Apostle in the Early Church*. Translated by
    John E. Steely. New York: Abingdon, 1969.

_____. *Paul and James*. Translated by Dorthea M. Barton. SBT 46.
    Naperville: Allenson, 1965.

_____. *Paul and the Gnostics*. Translated by John E. Steely. Nash-
    ville: Abingdon, 1972.

_____. *Der Römerbrief als historisches Problem*. SNT 9. Gütersloh:
    Gütersloher Verlagshaus Gerd Mohn, 1975.

_____. "Die Thessalonicher als Briefkomposition." *Zeit und
    Geschichte: Dankesgabe an Rudolf Bultmann zum 80. Geburtstag*.
    Edited by Erich Dinkler. Tübingen: J. C. B. Mohr (Paul Siebeck),
    1964.

Schmitz, Otto and Stählin, Gustav. "παρακαλέω, παράκλησις." *TDNT*
    5:773-99.

Schneider, Johannes. "κολακεύω." *TDNT* 3:817-18.

Schneider, Norbert. *Die Eigenart der paulinischen Antithese*. Hermeneu-
    tische Untersuchungen zur Theologie 11. Tübingen: J. C. B. Mohr
    (Paul Siebeck), 1970.

Schoeps, H. J. *Paul: The Theology of the Apostle in the Light of Jewish
    Religious History*. Translated by Harold Knight. Philadelphia: West-
    minster, 1961.

Schrage, Wolfgang. "Leid, Kreuz und Eschaton: die Peristasenkataloge als
    Merkmale paulinischer Theologia Crucis und Eschatologei." *EvT* 34
    (1974) 141-75.

Schubert, Paul. *Form and Function of the Pauline Thanksgiving.* BZNW 20. Berlin: Alfred Töpelmann, 1939.

Schulz, Anselm. *Nachfolgen und Nachahmen: Studien über das Verhältnis der neutestamentlichen Jüngerschaft zur urchristlichen Vorbildethik.* SANT 6. München: Kosel-Verlag, 1962.

Schütz, John Howard. *Paul and the Anatomy of Apostolic Authority.* SNTSMS 26. Cambridge: Cambridge University Press, 1975.

Schweitzer, Albert. *The Mysticism of Paul the Apostle.* Translated by William Montgomery. New York: Seabury, 1968; German original 1931.

Scott, Robert. *The Pauline Epistles: A Critical Study.* Edinburgh: T & T Clark, 1909.

Seesemann, Heinrich. "πεῖρα, κτλ" *TDNT* 6:23-36.

Selby, D. J. *Toward the Understanding of St. Paul.* Englewood Cliffs, NJ: Prentice-Hall, 1962.

Seneca. *Ad Lucilium epistulae morales.* Translated by Richard M. Gummere. Loeb Classical Library.

Sieffert, Friedrich. *Handbuch über den Brief an die Galater.* MeyerK. 7th ed. Göttingen: Vandenhoeck & Ruprecht, 1886.

Smalley, William A. "Some Interactional and Textual Interrelations in the Structure of Galatians." Paper, 1976.

Smith, M. "Pauline Problems: Apropos of J. Munck, 'Paulus und die Heilsgeschichte.' " *HTR* 50 (1957) 107-32.

Smyth, Herbert Weir. *Greek Grammar.* Revised by Gordon M. Messing. Cambridge: Harvard University Press, 1959.

Stählin, Gustav. "κοπετός, κτλ" *TDNT* 3:830-60.

Stamm, Raymond T. "The Epistle to the Galatians," (Introduction and Exegesis). *Interpreter's Bible.* Vol. 10. Nashville: Abingdon, 1953.

Stanley, D. M. " 'Become Imitators of Me': The Pauline Conception of Apostolic Tradition." *Bib* 40 (1959) 859-77.

Stauffer, Ethelbert. "ἐγώ." *TDNT* 2:343-62.

Stendahl, Krister. "The Apostle Paul and the Introspective Conscience of the West." *HTR* 56 (1963) 199-215.

_____. *Paul Among Jews and Gentiles and Other Essays*. Philadelphia: Fortress Press, 1976.

Stirewalt, M. Luther, Jr. "Form Criticism and the Letters of Paul: Suggestions to the Paul Seminar." Paper presented at the Society of Biblical Literature Meeting, 1971.

Strelen, John G. "Burden-bearing and the Law of Christ: A Reexamination of Galatians 6:2." *JBL* 94 (1975) 266-76.

Stuart, Duane Reed. *Epochs in Greek and Roman Biography*. Sather Classical Lectures 4. Berkeley: University of California Press, 1928.

Stuhlmacher, Peter. *Das paulinische Evangelium I. Vorgeschichte*. FRLANT 95. Göttingen: Vandenhoeck & Ruprecht, 1968.

The Supplement to the Oxford English Dictionary. Edited by R. W. Burchfield. Oxford: Clarendon Press, 1972.

Suhl, Alfred. *Paulus und seine Briefe: Ein Beiträg zur paulinischen Chronologie*. SNT 11. Gütersloh: Gütersloher Verlagshaus Gerd Mohn, 1975.

Tacitus. *Agricola*. Translated by William Peterson. Loeb Classical Library.

_____. *Dialogus*. Translated by William Peterson. Loeb Classical Library.

_____. *Germania*. Translated by William Peterson. Loeb Classical Library.

Talbert, Charles H. *What is a Gospel? The Genre of the Canonical Gospels*. Philadelphia: Fortress, 1977.

Tannehill, Robert C. *Dying and Rising with Christ*. BZNW 32. Berlin: Alfred Töpelmann, 1967.

Theime, K. "Die Struktur des ernst Thessalonicherbriefes." *Abraham Unser Vater. Juden und Christen im Gesprach über die Bibel. Festschrift für Otto Michel zum 60. Geburtstag*. Edited by O. Betz, M. Hengel, and P. Schmidt. Leiden: Brill, 1963.

Theissen, G. "Legitimation und Lebensunterhals: Ein Beitrag zur Soziologie urchristlicher Missionare." *NTS* 21 (1975) 192-221.

_____. "Soziale Schichtung in der korinthischen Gemeinde: Ein Beitrag zur Soziologie des hellenistischen Urchristentums." *ZNW* 65 (1974) 232-72.

Thiselton, Anthony C. *The Two Horizons: New Testament Hermeneutics and Philosophical Description*. Grand Rapids: Eerdmans, 1980.

Thompson, William M. *Christ and Consciousness: Exploring Christ's Contribution to Human Consciousness: The Origins and Development of Christian Consciousness.* New York: Paulist Press, 1977.

Thraede, Klaus. *Grundzüge griechisch-römischer Brieftopik.* München: C. H. Beck, 1970.

Thyen, Hartwig. *Der Stil der Jüdisch-Hellenistischen Homilie.* Göttingen: Vandenhoeck & Ruprecht, 1955.

Tinsley, E. J. *The Imitation of God in Christ.* The Library of History and Doctrine. Philadelphia: Westminster Press, 1960.

Tucker, Gene M. *Form Criticism of the Old Testament.* Guides to Biblical Scholarship, OT Series. Philadelphia: Fortress Press, 1971.

Turner, Geoffrey. "Pre-understanding and New Testament Interpretation." *SJT* 28 (1975) 227-42.

Turner, Nigel. *Syntax.* Vol. 3. *A Grammar of New Testament Greek,* by James Hope Moulton. Edinburgh: T. & T. Clark, 1963.

_____. *Style.* Vol. 4. *A Grammar of New Testament Greek,* by James Hope Moulton. Edinburgh: T & T Clark, 1976.

Tyson, Joseph B. "Paul's Opponents in Galatia." *NovT* 10 (1968) 241-54.

Unnik, W. C. van. "Luke's Second Book and the Rules of Hellenistic Historiography." *Les Actes des Apôtres.* Edited by J. Kremer. BETL 48. Gembloux: Duculot, 1979.

Veltman, Frederick. *The Defense Speeches of Paul in Acts: Gattungsforschung and its Limitations.* Th.D. dissertation, Graduate Theological Union, 1975. Ann Arbor: University Microfilms, 1975.

Vielhauer, Philipp. *Geschichte der urchristlichen Literatur.* Berlin: de Gruyter, 1975.

Voegelin, Eric. *Order and History.* Vol. 2: *The World of the Polis.* Vol. 4: *The Ecumenic Age.* Baton Rouge: Louisiana State University Press, 1956-74.

Wallach, Barbara P. *A History of the Diatribe from the Origin up to the First Century B.C. and a Study of the Influence of the Genre upon Lucretius III, 830-1094.* Ph.D. dissertation, University of Illinois, 1974. Ann Arbor: University Microfilms, 1974.

Ward, Ronald A. *Commentary on 1 and 2 Thessalonians.* Waco, TX: Word Books, 1973.

Wegenast, Klaus. *Das Verständnis der Tradition bei Paulus und in den Deuteropaulinen.* WMANT 8. Neukirchen: Neukirchener Verlag, 1962.

Weil, Eric. "What is a Breakthrough in History?" *Daedalus* 104 (1975) 21-36.

Weizsäcker, Karl von. *The Apostolic Age of the Christian Church.* 2 vols. Translated by James Millar. Theological Translation Library. Edited by T. K. Cheyne and A. B. Bruce. London: Williams & Norgate, 1907, 1912.

Wendland, Paul. *Die hellenistisch-römische Kultur in ihrer Beziehung zu Judentum und Christentum.* Die urchristlichen Literaturformen. HNT. Tübingen: J. C. B. Mohr (Paul Siebeck), 1912.

Wengst, Klaus. "Der Apostel und die Tradition." *ZTK* 69 (1972) 155-56.

White, John Lee. *The Form and Function of the Body of the Greek Letter: A Study of the Letter-Body in the Non-literary Papyri and in Paul the Apostle.* SBLDS 2. Missoula, MT: Society of Biblical Literature, 1972.

_____. *The Form and Structure of the Official Petition: A Study in Greek Epistolography.* M.A. Thesis, Vanderbilt University, 1968. Missoula, MT: Society of Biblical Dissertation Series, 1972.

Whiteley, D. E. H. *The Theology of St. Paul.* Philadelphia: Fortress, 1972.

_____. *Thessalonians in the Revised Standard Version.* The New Clarendon Bible. London: Oxford University Press, 1969.

Wikenhauser, Alfred. *New Testament Introduction.* Translated by Joseph Cunningham. New york: Herder & Herder, 1963.

Wilamowitz-Moellendorf, Ulrich von. "Asianismus und Atticismus." *Hermes* 35 (1900) 1-52.

_____. "Die Autobiographie im Altertum." *Internationale Wochenschrift für Wissenschaft, Kunst und Technik* 1 (1907) 1105-14.

Wilckens, Ulrich. "Die Bekehrung des Paulus als religionsgeschichtliches Problem." *ZTK* 56 (1959) 273-93.

Wilder, Amos. *Early Christian Rhetoric.* 2nd ed. Cambridge: Harvard University Press, 1971.

Wiles, Gordon P. *Paul's Intercessory Prayers: The Significance of the Intercessory Prayer Passages in the Letters of St. Paul.* SNTSMS 24. Cambridge: Cambridge University Press, 1974.

Wiles, Maurice F. *The Divine Apostle: The Interpretation of St. Paul's Epistles in the Early Church.* Cambridge: Cambridge University Press, 1967.

Williams, A. Lukyn. *The Epistle of Paul the Apostle to the Galatians.* Cambridge Bible. Cambridge: Cambridge University Press, 1921.

Williamson, Clarke M. *Has God Forsaken His People: Anti-Judaism in the Christian Church.* Nashville: Abingdon, 1982.

Wilson, R. A. "'We' and 'You' in the Epistle to the Ephesians." *SE* 2 (= Texte und Untersuchungen 87) (1964) 676-80.

Wilson, Robert McL. "Gnostics—in Galatia?" *SE* 4. Berlin: Akademie-Verlag, 1968.

_____. *Gnosis and the New Testament.* Oxford: Blackwell, 1968.

Wilson, Stephen G. *The Gentiles and the Gentile Mission in Luke-Acts.* SNTSMS 23. Cambridge: Cambridge University Press, 1973.

Winer, George Benedict. *A Grammar of the Idiom of the New Testament.* 7th ed. by Gottlieb Lünemann. Revised and translated by J. Henry Thayer. Andover: Draper, 1874.

Wrede, William. *Paul.* Translated by Edward Lummis. Boston: American Unitarian Association, 1908.

Wuellner, Wilhelm. "Digressions in I Corinthians: The Rhetoric of Argumentation in Paul." Paper presented at the Society of Biblical Literature Paul Seminar, 1974.

_____. "Paul's Rhetoric of Argumentation in Romans: An Alternative to the Donfried-Karris Debate over Romans." *CBQ* 38 (1976) 330-51.

Wuest, Kenneth S. *Galatians in the Greek New Testament for the English Reader.* Grand Rapids: Eerdmans, 1944.

Xenophon. *Anabasis.* Translated by E. C. Marchant. Loeb Classical Library.

_____. *Apology of Socrates.* Translated by O. J. Todd. Loeb Classical Library.

_____. *Memorabilia.* Translated by E. C. Marchant. Loeb Classical Library.

Zahn, Theodor von. *Introduction to the New Testament.* 3 vols. Translated by Melancthon Williams Jacobus et al. Edinburgh: T & T Clark, 1909.

Index

*Numbers in parentheses following page citations refer to footnotes.